WORKBOOK

Houghton
Mifflin
Harcourt

STECK-VAUGHN

SOCIAL STUDIES

TEST PREPARATION FOR THE 2014 GED® TEST

- Civics and Government
- United States History
- Economics
- Geography and the World
- Social Studies Practices

POWERED BY
PAXEN

Houghton
Mifflin
Harcourt

POWERED BY
PAXEN

Acknowledgments

For each of the selections and images listed below, grateful acknowledgment is made for permission to excerpt and/or reprint original or copyrighted material, as follows:

Text

79 From *The New York Times*, June 14, 1987. © *The New York Times*. All rights reserved. Used by permission and protected by the Copyright Laws of the United States. The printing, copying, redistribution, or retransmission of the Material without express written permission is prohibited. **82** From *The Washington Post*, April 7, 2013. © *The Washington Post*. **84** From *The Washington Post*, October 25, 2012. © *The Washington Post*. **85** (Fisher): Used with the permission of © Carolina Academic Press. **85** (Post and Siegel): Used with the permission of Yale Law School, Faculty Scholarship Series, Yale Law School Legal Scholarship Repository. **88** Used with the permission of The Cato Institute. **88** From *The Washington Post*, October 23, 2010. © *The Washington Post*. **94** From *The Washington Post*, August 28, 2012. © *The Washington Post*. **103** From *The New York Times*, August 29, 2004. © *The New York Times*. All rights reserved. Used by permission and protected by the Copyright Laws of the United States. The printing, copying, redistribution, or retransmission of the Material without express written permission is prohibited. **105** From © mikebloomberg.com. **111** From *The New York Times*, April 17, 1985. © *The New York Times*. All rights reserved. Used by permission and protected by the Copyright Laws of the United States. The printing, copying, redistribution, or retransmission of the Material without express written permission is prohibited. **115** © The Estate of Dr. Martin Luther King, Jr.; used with permission. **121** From *The New York Times*, April 15, 2012. © *The New York Times*. All rights reserved. Used by permission and protected by the Copyright Laws of the United States. The printing, copying, redistribution, or retransmission of the Material without express written permission is prohibited.

Images

Cover (bg) © Vito Palmisano/Photographer's Choice/Getty Images; **cover** (inset) © Ellen Rooney/Robert Harding World Imagery/Getty Images. **61** From history.state.gov. **74** Used with the permission of the Herb Block Foundation. **75** New Deal Political Cartoon, 1934. Library of Congress. **75** From Pittsburgh Talboit/Franklin Delano Roosevelt Library. **76** Illinois WPA Art Project poster, 1941. Library of Congress. **76** Division of Political History, National Museum of American History, Smithsonian Institution. **77** From Greaves/Princeton.edu. **77** Cages cost money!, published by *PM Magazine* on December 15, 1941, Dr. Seuss Collection, MSS 230. Mandeville Special Collections Library, UC San Diego. **84** Used with the permission of the Herb Block Foundation. **87** Redrawn with the permission of Worth Publishers. **96** Used with the permission of Pat Oliphant/Universal Press Syndicate. **101** Redrawn with the permission of the Lyme Disease Association, Inc. **107** Used with the permission of the Herb Block Foundation. **108** From California State University, Long Beach, American Indian Studies. **109** Copyright by Bill Mauldin (1962). Courtesy of the Bill Mauldin Estate LLC.

Social Studies

Workbook

Table of Contents

About the GED® Test

Welcome to the first day of the rest of your life. Now that you've committed to study for your GED® credential, an array of possibilities and options—academic, career, and otherwise—await you. Each year, hundreds of thousands of people just like you decide to pursue a GED® credential. Like you, they left traditional school for one reason or another. Now, just like them, you've decided to continue your education by studying for and taking the GED® Test.

Today's GED® Test is very different from the one your grandparents may have taken. Today's GED® Test is new, improved, and more rigorous, with content aligned to the Common Core State Standards. For the first time, the GED® Test serves both as a high-school equivalency degree and as a predictor of college and career readiness. The new GED® Test features four subject areas: Reasoning Through Language Arts (RLA), Mathematical Reasoning, Science, and Social Studies. Each subject area is delivered via a computer-based format and includes an array of technology-enhanced item types.

The four subject-area exams together comprise a testing time of seven hours. Preparation can take considerably longer. The payoff, however, is significant: more and better career options, higher earnings, and the sense of achievement that comes with a GED® credential. Both employers and colleges and universities alike accept the GED® credential as they would a high school diploma. On average, GED® graduates earn at least $8,400 more per year than those with an incomplete high school education.

The GED® Testing Service has constructed the GED® Test to mirror a high school experience. As such, you must answer a variety of questions within and across specific subject areas. For example, you may encounter a Social Studies passage on the Reasoning Through Language Arts Test, and vice versa. The following table details the content areas, quantity of items, score points, Depth of Knowledge (DOK) levels—the cognitive effort required to answer a given item—and total testing time.

Subject Area Test	Content Areas	Items	Raw Score Points	DOK Level	Time
Reasoning Through Language Arts	**Informational texts**—75% **Literary texts**—25%	*51	65	80% of items at Level 2 or 3	150 minutes
Mathematical Reasoning	**Algebraic Problem Solving**—55% **Quantitative Problem Solving**—45%	*46	49	50% of items at Level 2	115 minutes
Science	**Life Science**—40% **Physical Science**—40% **Earth/Space Science**—20%	*34	40	80% of items at Level 2 or 3	90 minutes
Social Studies	**Civics/Government**—50% **U.S. History**—20% **Economics**—15% **Geography and the World**—15%	*35	44	80% of items at Level 2 or 3	90 minutes

* Number of items may vary slightly by test.

Because the demands of today's high school education and its relationship to workforce needs differ from those of a decade ago, the GED® Testing Service has moved to a computer-based format. Although multiple-choice questions remain the dominant type of item on the new, computer-based GED® Test series, they've been joined by a variety of new, technology-enhanced item types: drop-down, fill-in-the-blank, drag-and-drop, hot spot, short answer, and extended response items.

The table to the right illustrates the various item types and their distribution on the new subject-area exams. As you can see, all four tests include multiple-choice, drop-down, fill-in-the-blank, and drag-and-drop items. Some variation occurs with hot spot, short answer, and extended response items.

2014 ITEM TYPES

	RLA	Math	Science	Social Studies
Multiple-choice	✓	✓	✓	✓
Drop-down	✓	✓	✓	✓
Fill-in-the-blank	✓	✓	✓	✓
Drag-and-drop	✓	✓	✓	✓
Hot spot		✓	✓	✓
Short answer			✓	
Extended response	✓			✓

Items on each subject-area exam connect to three factors:

- **Content Topics/Assessment Targets:** These topics and targets describe and detail the content on the GED® Test. They tie to the Common Core State Standards, as well as state standards for Texas and Virginia.
- **Content Practices:** These practices describe the types of reasoning and modes of thinking required to answer specific items on the GED® Test.
- **Depth of Knowledge (DOK):** The Depth of Knowledge model details the level of cognitive complexity and steps required to arrive at a correct answer on the test. For the new GED® Test, there are three levels of DOK complexity:
  - **Level 1:** Test takers must recall, observe, question, or represent facts or simple skills. Typically, they must exhibit only a surface understanding of text.
  - **Level 2:** Test takers must process information beyond simple recall and observation to include summarizing, ordering, classifying, identifying patterns and relationships, and connecting ideas. Test takers must scrutinize text.
  - **Level 3:** Test takers must explain, generalize, and connect ideas by inferring, elaborating, and predicting. Test takers must summarize from multiple sources, and use that information to develop compositions with multiple paragraphs. Those paragraphs should feature a critical analysis of sources, include supporting positions from the test takers' own experiences, and reflect editing to ensure coherent, correct writing.

Approximately 80 percent of items across all four content areas will be written to DOK Levels 2 and 3, with the remainder at Level 1. Writing portions, such as the extended response item in Social Studies (25 minutes) and Reasoning Through Language Arts (45 minutes), are considered DOK Level 3 items.

Now that you understand the basic structure of the GED® Test and the benefits of earning a GED® credential, you must prepare for the GED® Test. In the pages that follow, you will find a recipe of sorts that, if followed, will guide you toward successful completion of your GED® credential. So turn the page. The next chapter of your life begins right now.

GED® Test on Computer

Along with fresh item types, the 2014 GED® Test also unveils a new, computer-based testing experience. The GED® Test will be available on computer and only at approved Pearson VUE Testing Centers. Along with content knowledge and the ability to read, think, and write critically, you must perform basic computer functions—clicking, scrolling, and typing—to succeed on the test. The screen below closely resembles a screen that you will experience on the GED® Test.

The **INFORMATION** button contains material vital to the successful completion of the item. Here, by clicking the Information button, a test taker enables a map about the American Revolution. On the Mathematical Reasoning exam, similar buttons for **FORMULA SHEET** and **CALCULATOR REFERENCE** provide information that will help learners like you answer items that require use of formulas or the TI-30XS calculator. You may move a passage or graphic by clicking and dragging to a different part of the test screen.

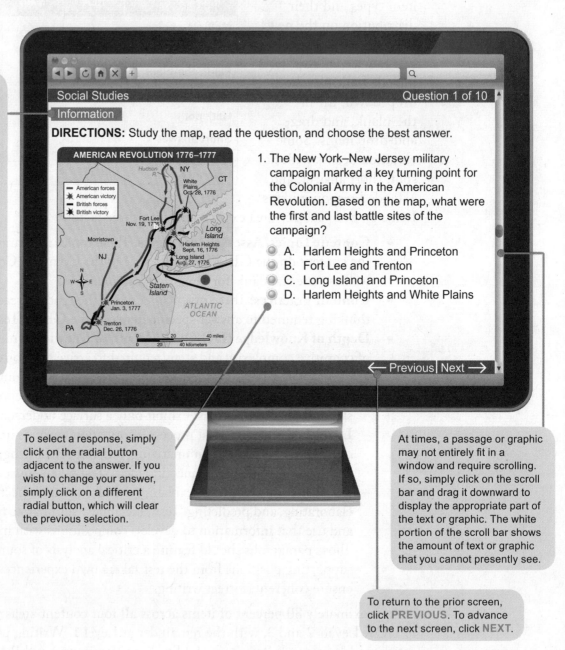

To select a response, simply click on the radial button adjacent to the answer. If you wish to change your answer, simply click on a different radial button, which will clear the previous selection.

At times, a passage or graphic may not entirely fit in a window and require scrolling. If so, simply click on the scroll bar and drag it downward to display the appropriate part of the text or graphic. The white portion of the scroll bar shows the amount of text or graphic that you cannot presently see.

To return to the prior screen, click **PREVIOUS**. To advance to the next screen, click **NEXT**.

Some items on the new GED® Test, such as fill-in-the-blank, short answer, and extended response questions, will require you to type answers into an entry box. In some cases, the directions may specify the range of typing the system may accept. For example, a fill-in-the-blank item may allow you to type a number from 0 to 9, along with a decimal point or a slash, but nothing else. The system also will tell you keys to avoid pressing in certain situations. The annotated computer and keyboard below provide strategies for entering text and data for fill-in-the-blank, short answer, and extended response items.

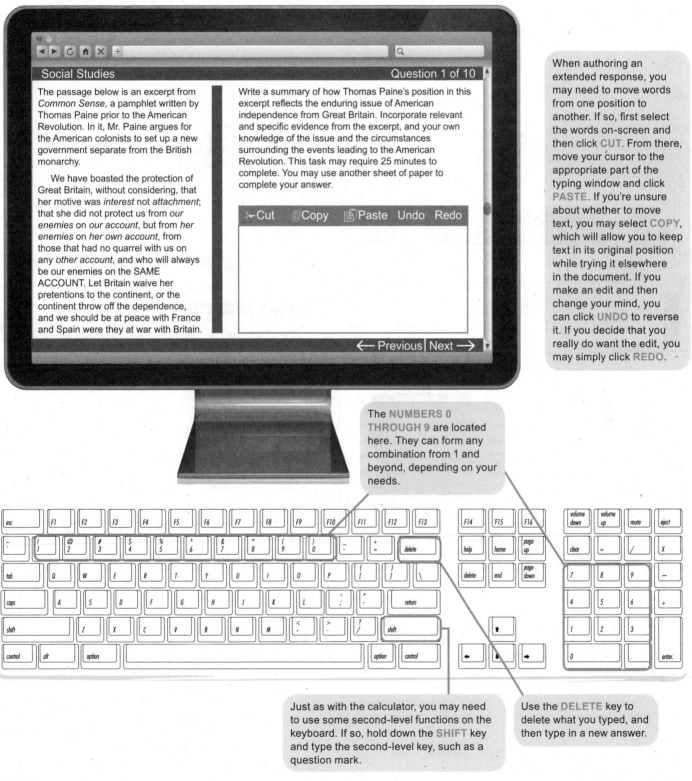

Social Studies   Question 1 of 10

The passage below is an excerpt from *Common Sense*, a pamphlet written by Thomas Paine prior to the American Revolution. In it, Mr. Paine argues for the American colonists to set up a new government separate from the British monarchy.

We have boasted the protection of Great Britain, without considering, that her motive was *interest* not *attachment*; that she did not protect us from *our enemies* on *our account*, but from *her enemies* on *her own account*, from those that had no quarrel with us on any *other account*, and who will always be our enemies on the SAME ACCOUNT. Let Britain waive her pretentions to the continent, or the continent throw off the dependence, and we should be at peace with France and Spain were they at war with Britain.

Write a summary of how Thomas Paine's position in this excerpt reflects the enduring issue of American independence from Great Britain. Incorporate relevant and specific evidence from the excerpt, and your own knowledge of the issue and the circumstances surrounding the events leading to the American Revolution. This task may require 25 minutes to complete. You may use another sheet of paper to complete your answer.

✂Cut   📋Copy   📋Paste   Undo   Redo

← Previous | Next →

When authoring an extended response, you may need to move words from one position to another. If so, first select the words on-screen and then click CUT. From there, move your cursor to the appropriate part of the typing window and click PASTE. If you're unsure about whether to move text, you may select COPY, which will allow you to keep text in its original position while trying it elsewhere in the document. If you make an edit and then change your mind, you can click UNDO to reverse it. If you decide that you really do want the edit, you may simply click REDO.

The NUMBERS 0 THROUGH 9 are located here. They can form any combination from 1 and beyond, depending on your needs.

Just as with the calculator, you may need to use some second-level functions on the keyboard. If so, hold down the SHIFT key and type the second-level key, such as a question mark.

Use the DELETE key to delete what you typed, and then type in a new answer.

About *Steck-Vaughn*
Test Preparation for the 2014 GED® Test

Along with choosing to pursue your GED® credential, you've made another smart decision by selecting *Steck-Vaughn's Test Preparation for the 2014 GED® Test* as your main study and preparation tool. Our emphasis on the acquisition of key reading and thinking concepts equips learners like you with the skills and strategies to succeed on the GED® Test.

Two-page micro-lessons in each student book provide focused and efficient instruction. For those who require additional support, we offer companion workbooks, which provide *twice* the support and practice exercises. Each lesson in the series includes a *Spotlighted Item* feature that corresponds to one of the technology-enhanced item types that appear on the GED® Test.

The **LEARN THE SKILL** section provides information about the skill to be studied.

Each lesson includes correlations to subject-area **CONTENT TOPICS** and **PRACTICES** that will help focus your studies.

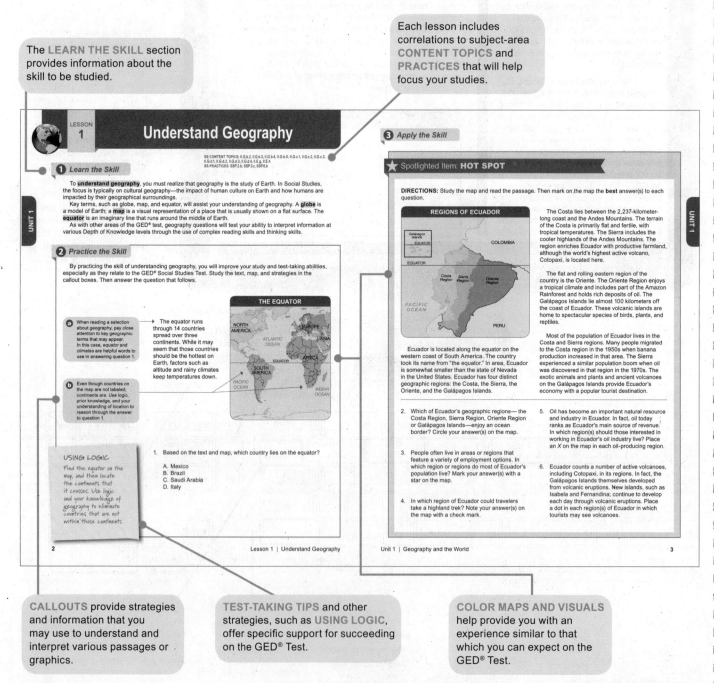

CALLOUTS provide strategies and information that you may use to understand and interpret various passages or graphics.

TEST-TAKING TIPS and other strategies, such as **USING LOGIC**, offer specific support for succeeding on the GED® Test.

COLOR MAPS AND VISUALS help provide you with an experience similar to that which you can expect on the GED® Test.

About *Steck-Vaughn Test Preparation for the 2014 GED® Test*

Unit Reviews and Answer Keys

Every unit opens with the feature GED® Journeys, a series of profiles of people who earned and used their GED® credential as a springboard to future success. From there, you receive in-depth instruction and practice through a series of linked lessons, all of which tie to Content Topics/Assessment Targets, Content Practices, and Depth of Knowledge levels.

Each unit closes with an eight-page review that includes a representative sampling of items, including technology-enhanced item types, from the lessons that comprise the unit. You may use each unit review as a posttest to gauge your mastery of content and skills and readiness for that aspect of the GED® Test.

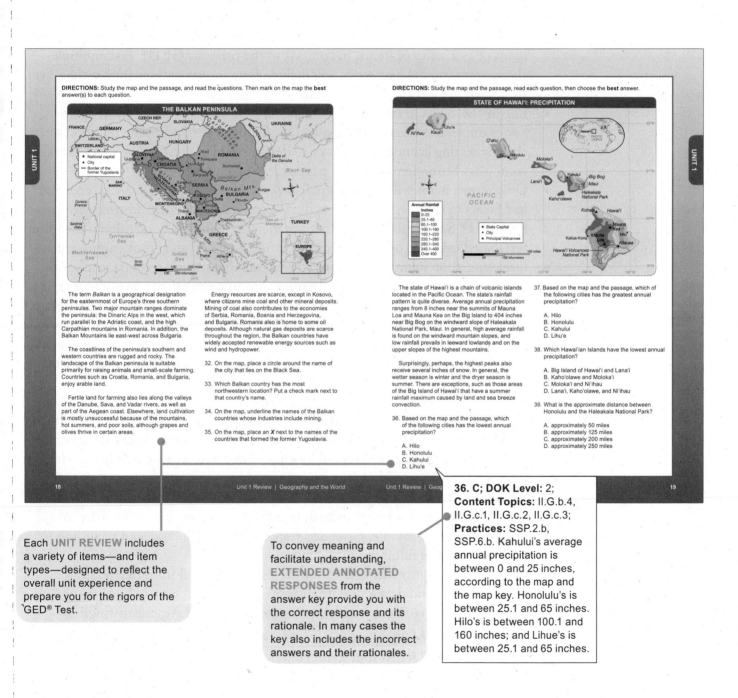

DIRECTIONS: Study the map and the passage, and read the questions. Then mark on the map the **best** answer(s) to each question.

THE BALKAN PENINSULA

The term *Balkan* is a geographical designation for the easternmost of Europe's three southern peninsulas. Two major mountain ranges dominate the peninsula: the Dinaric Alps in the west, which run parallel to the Adriatic coast, and the high Carpathian mountains in Romania. In addition, the Balkan Mountains lie east-west across Bulgaria.

The coastlines of the peninsula's southern and western countries are rugged and rocky. The landscape of the Balkan peninsula is suitable primarily for raising animals and small-scale farming. Countries such as Croatia, Romania, and Bulgaria, enjoy arable land.

Fertile land for farming also lies along the valleys of the Danube, Sava, and Vadar rivers, as well as part of the Aegean coast. Elsewhere, land cultivation is mostly unsuccessful because of the mountains, hot summers, and poor soils, although grapes and olives thrive in certain areas.

Energy resources are scarce, except in Kosovo, where citizens mine coal and other mineral deposits. Mining of coal also contributes to the economies of Serbia, Romania, Bosnia and Herzegovina, and Bulgaria. Romania also is home to some oil deposits. Although natural gas deposits are scarce throughout the region, the Balkan countries have widely accepted renewable energy sources such as wind and hydropower.

32. On the map, place a circle around the name of the city that lies on the Black Sea.

33. Which Balkan country has the most northwestern location? Put a check mark next to that country's name.

34. On the map, underline the names of the Balkan countries whose industries include mining.

35. On the map, place an **X** next to the names of the countries that formed the former Yugoslavia.

DIRECTIONS: Study the map and the passage, read each question, then choose the **best** answer.

STATE OF HAWAI'I: PRECIPITATION

The state of Hawai'i is a chain of volcanic islands located in the Pacific Ocean. The state's rainfall pattern is quite diverse. Average annual precipitation ranges from 8 inches near the summits of Mauna Loa and Mauna Kea on the Big Island to 404 inches near Big Bog on the windward slope of Haleakala National Park, Maui. In general, high average rainfall is found on the windward mountain slopes, and low rainfall prevails in leeward lowlands and on the upper slopes of the highest mountains.

Surprisingly, perhaps, the highest peaks also receive several inches of snow. In general, the wetter season is winter and the dryer season is summer. There are exceptions, such as those areas of the Big Island of Hawai'i that have a summer rainfall maximum caused by land and sea breeze convection.

36. Based on the map and the passage, which of the following cities has the lowest annual precipitation?

A. Hilo
B. Honolulu
C. Kahului
D. Lihu'e

37. Based on the map and the passage, which of the following cities has the greatest annual precipitation?

A. Hilo
B. Honolulu
C. Kahului
D. Lihu'e

38. Which Hawai'ian Islands have the lowest annual precipitation?

A. Big Island of Hawai'i and Lana'i
B. Kaho'olawe and Moloka'i
C. Moloka'i and Ni'ihau
D. Lana'i, Kaho'olawe, and Ni'ihau'

39. What is the approximate distance between Honolulu and the Haleakala National Park?

A. approximately 50 miles
B. approximately 125 miles
C. approximately 200 miles
D. approximately 250 miles

Each **UNIT REVIEW** includes a variety of items—and item types—designed to reflect the overall unit experience and prepare you for the rigors of the GED® Test.

To convey meaning and facilitate understanding, **EXTENDED ANNOTATED RESPONSES** from the answer key provide you with the correct response and its rationale. In many cases the key also includes the incorrect answers and their rationales.

36. C; DOK Level: 2; **Content Topics:** II.G.b.4, II.G.c.1, II.G.c.2, II.G.c.3; **Practices:** SSP.2.b, SSP.6.b. Kahului's average annual precipitation is between 0 and 25 inches, according to the map and the map key. Honolulu's is between 25.1 and 65 inches. Hilo's is between 100.1 and 160 inches; and Lihue's is between 25.1 and 65 inches.

About the GED® Social Studies Test

The new GED® Social Studies Test is more than just a set of dates and events. In fact, it reflects an attempt to increase the rigor of the GED® Test to better meet the demands of a 21st-century economy. To that end, the GED® Social Studies Test features an array of technology-aided item types. All of the items are delivered via computer-based testing. The items reflect the knowledge, skills, and abilities that a student would master in an equivalent high school experience.

Multiple-choice questions remain the majority of items on the GED® Social Studies Test. However, a number of technology-enhanced items, including fill-in-the-blank, drop-down, drag-and-drop, hot spot, and extended response questions—will challenge learners like you to master and convey knowledge in deeper, fuller ways. For example:

- Multiple-choice items will assess virtually every content standard as either discrete items or as a series of items. In contrast to the previous GED® Test, multiple-choice items on the new series will include four answer options (rather than five), structured in an A./B./C./D. format.

- Fill-in-the-blank items allow test takers to type in one-word or short answers. For example, test takers may be asked to identify a particular data point on a chart reflecting economic trends or to demonstrate understanding of an idea or vocabulary term mentioned in a passage.

- Drop-down items will include a pull-down menu of response choices, enabling test takers to complete statements. Test takers may encounter drop-down items on the GED® Social Studies Test that ask them to identify a conclusion drawn from text-based evidence or make a generalization based on an author's argument.

- Drag-and-drop items involve interactive tasks that require test takers to move small images, words, or numerical expressions into designated drop zones on a computer screen. They may assess how well test takers make comparisons between concepts or data or how well they classify or order information. For example, test takers may be asked to place labels on a map to indicate commodities produced in various regions. Other items may ask test takers to place data points or labels drawn from a brief passage onto a graph or chart.

- Hot spot items consist of a graphic with virtual sensors placed strategically within it. They allow you to demonstrate understanding of geographic concepts with regard to mapping. Other uses of hot spot items may involve selecting data or points in a table, chart, or graph that support or refute a given conclusion stated in the text.

- An extended response item on the GED® Social Studies Test will be a 25-minute task that requires test takers to analyze one or more source texts in order to produce a writing sample. Extended response items will be scored according to how well learners fulfill three key traits:
  - analyzing arguments and gathering evidence found in source texts
  - organizing and developing their writing
  - demonstrating fluency with conventions of Edited American English

You will have a total of 90 minutes in which to answer about 35 items. The social studies test is organized across four main content areas: civics and government (50 percent of all items), United States history (20 percent), economics (15 percent), and geography and the world (15 percent). All told, 80 percent of the items on the GED® Social Studies Test will be written at Depth of Knowledge Levels 2 or 3.

About *Steck-Vaughn Test Preparation for the 2014 GED® Test: Social Studies*

Steck-Vaughn's student book and workbook help unlock the learning and deconstruct the different elements of the test by helping learners like you build and develop core reading and thinking skills. The content of our books aligns to the new GED® social studies content standards and item distribution to provide you with a superior test preparation experience.

Our *Spotlighted Item* feature provides a deeper, richer treatment for each technology-enhanced item type. On initial introduction, a unique item type—such as drag-and-drop—receives a full page of example items in the student book lesson and three pages in the companion workbook. The length of subsequent features may be shorter depending on the skill, lesson, and requirements.

A combination of targeted strategies, informational call-outs and sample questions, assorted tips and hints, and ample assessment help to clearly focus study efforts in needed areas.

In addition to the book features, a highly detailed answer key provides the correct answer and the rationale for it so that you know exactly why an answer is correct. The *Social Studies* student book and workbook are designed with an eye toward the end goal: Success on the GED® Social Studies Test.

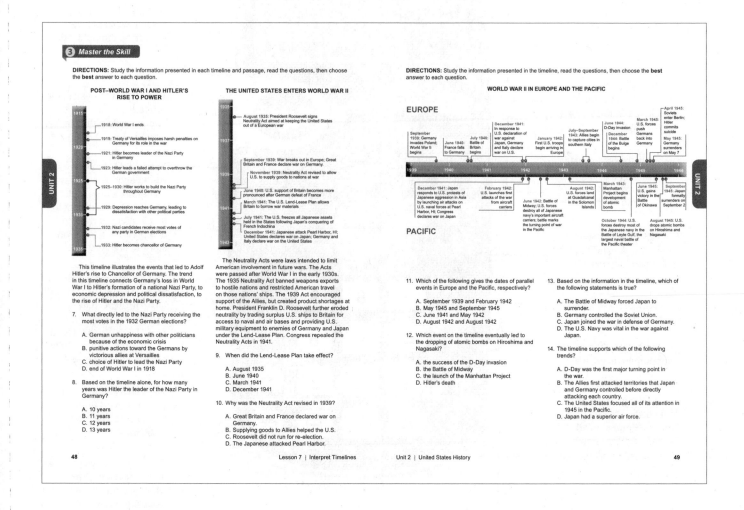

Calculator Directions

Certain items on the GED® Mathematical Reasoning Test allow for the use of a calculator to aid in answering questions. That calculator, the TI-30XS, is embedded within the testing interface. The TI-30XS calculator will be available for most items on the GED® Mathematical Reasoning Test and for some items on the GED® Science Test and GED® Social Studies Test. The TI-30XS calculator is shown below, along with callouts of some of its most important keys. A button that will enable the calculator reference sheet will appear in the upper right corner of the testing screen.

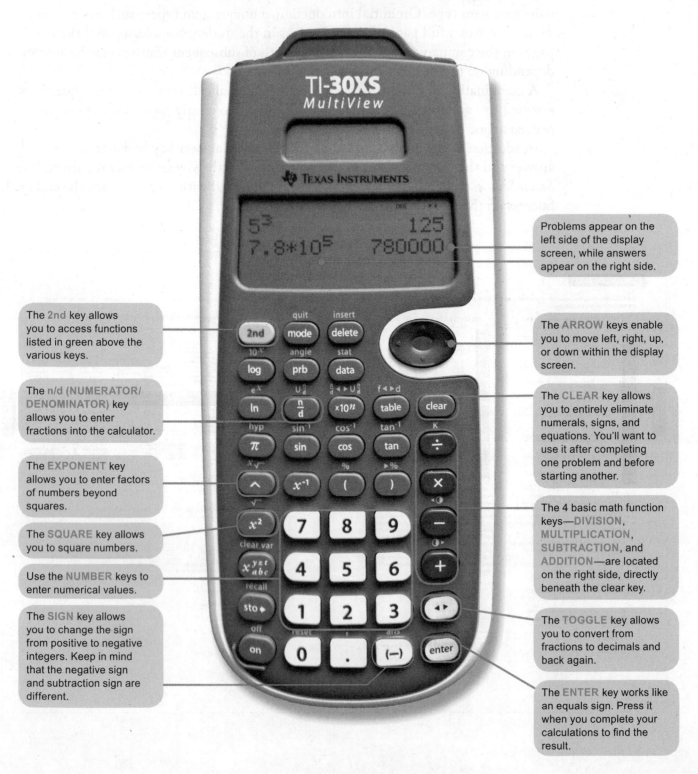

The 2nd key allows you to access functions listed in green above the various keys.

The n/d (NUMERATOR/ DENOMINATOR) key allows you to enter fractions into the calculator.

The EXPONENT key allows you to enter factors of numbers beyond squares.

The SQUARE key allows you to square numbers.

Use the NUMBER keys to enter numerical values.

The SIGN key allows you to change the sign from positive to negative integers. Keep in mind that the negative sign and subtraction sign are different.

Problems appear on the left side of the display screen, while answers appear on the right side.

The ARROW keys enable you to move left, right, up, or down within the display screen.

The CLEAR key allows you to entirely eliminate numerals, signs, and equations. You'll want to use it after completing one problem and before starting another.

The 4 basic math function keys—DIVISION, MULTIPLICATION, SUBTRACTION, and ADDITION—are located on the right side, directly beneath the clear key.

The TOGGLE key allows you to convert from fractions to decimals and back again.

The ENTER key works like an equals sign. Press it when you complete your calculations to find the result.

Getting Started

To enable the calculator on a question that allows it, click on the upper left-hand portion of the testing screen. If the calculator displays over top of a problem, you may move it by clicking and dragging it to another part of the screen. Once enabled, the calculator will be ready for use (no need to push the **on** key).

- Use the **clear** key to clear all numbers and operations from the screen.
- Use the **enter** key to complete all calculations.

2nd key

The green **2nd** key is located in the upper left corner of the TI-30XS. The **2nd** key enables a second series of function keys, which are located above other function keys and noted in green type. To use the 2nd-level function, first click the numeral, next click the **2nd** key, and then click the 2nd-level function key you need. For example, to enter **25%**, first enter the number [**25**]. Then click the **2nd** key, and finally click the 2nd-level **%** key (1st-level *beginning parenthesis* sign).

Fractions and Mixed Numbers

To enter fractions, such as $\frac{3}{4}$, click the **n/d** (**numerator/denominator**) key, followed by the numerator quantity [**3**]. Next, click the **down arrow** button (upper right corner of the calculator), followed by the denominator quantity [**4**]. To calculate with fractions, click the **right arrow** button and then the appropriate function key and other numerals in the equation.

To enter mixed numbers, such as $1\frac{3}{8}$, first enter the whole number quantity [**1**]. Next, click the **2nd** key and the **mixed number** key (1st level **n/d**). Then enter the fraction numerator [**3**], followed by the **down arrow** button, and the denominator [**8**]. If you click **enter**, the mixed number will convert to an improper fraction. To calculate with mixed numbers, click the **right arrow** button and then the appropriate function key and other numerals in the equation.

Negative Numbers

To enter a negative number, click the **negative sign** key (located directly below the number **3** on the calculator). Please note that the negative sign key differs from the subtraction key, which is found in the far right column of keys, directly above the plus (+) key.

Squares, Square Roots, and Exponents

- **Squares:** The x^2 key squares numbers. The **exponent** key (^) raises numbers to powers higher than squares, such as cubes. To find the answer to 5^3 on the calculator, first enter the base number [**5**], then click the exponent key (^), and follow by clicking the exponent number [**3**], and the **enter** key.
- **Square Roots:** To find the square root of a number, such as 36, first click the **2nd** key, then click the **square root** key (1st-level x^2), then the number [**36**], and finally **enter**.
- **Cube Roots:** To find the cube root of a number, such as 125, first enter the cube as a number [**3**], followed by the **2nd** key and **square root** key. Finally, enter the number for which you want to find the cube [**125**], followed by **enter**.
- **Exponents:** To perform calculations with numbers expressed in scientific notation, such as 7.8×10^9, first enter the base number [**7.8**]. Next, click the **scientific notation** key (located directly beneath the **data** key), followed by the exponent level [**9**]. You then have 7.8×10^9.

Test-Taking Tips

The new GED® Test includes more than 160 items across the four subject-area exams of Reasoning Through Language Arts, Mathematical Reasoning, Science, and Social Studies. The four subject-area exams represent a total test time of seven hours. Most items are multiple-choice questions, but a number are technology-enhanced items. These include drop-down, fill-in-the-blank, drag-and-drop, hot spot, short answer, and extended response items.

Throughout this book and others in the series, we help learners like you build, develop, and apply core reading and thinking skills critical to success on the GED® Test. As part of an overall strategy, we suggest that you use the test-taking tips below and throughout the book to improve your performance on the GED® Test.

- **Always thoroughly read directions so that you know exactly what to do.** As we've noted, the 2014 GED® Test has an entirely new computer-based format that includes a variety of technology-aided items. If you are unclear of what to do or how to proceed, ask the test provider whether directions can be explained.

- **Read each question carefully so that you fully understand what it is asking.** Some items, for example, may present information beyond what is necessary to correctly answer them. Other questions may use boldfaced words for emphasis (for example, "Which statement represents the **most** appropriate revision for this hypothesis?").

- **Manage your time with each question.** Because the GED® Test is a series of timed exams, you want to spend enough time with each question, but not *too* much time. For example, on the GED® Mathematical Reasoning Test, you have 115 minutes in which to answer approximately 46 questions. That works out to an average of about 2 minutes per item. Obviously, some items will require more time than that and others will require less, but you should remain aware of the overall number of items and amount of testing time. The new GED® Test interface may help you manage time. It includes an on-screen clock in the upper right corner that provides the remaining time in which to complete a test.

You may also monitor your progress by viewing the **Question** line, which will give you the current question number, followed by the total number of questions on that subject-area exam.

- **Answer all questions, regardless of whether you know the answer or are guessing.** There is no benefit in leaving questions unanswered on the GED® Test. Keep in mind the time that you have for each test and manage it accordingly. If you wish to review a specific item at the end of a test, you may click **Flag for Review** to mark the question. When you do, the flag will display in yellow. At the end of a test, you may have time to review questions you've marked.

- **Skim and scan.** You may save time by first reading each question and its answer options before reading an accompanying passage or graphic. Once you understand what the question is asking, review the passage or visual for the appropriate information.

- **Note any unfamiliar words in questions.** First attempt to re-read the question by omitting any unfamiliar word(s). Next, try to substitute another word in its place.

- **Narrow answer options by re-reading each question and re-examining the text or graphic that goes with it.** Although four answers are *possible* on multiple-choice items, keep in mind that only one of them is *correct*. You may be able to eliminate one answer immediately; you may need to take more time or use logic or assumptions to eliminate others. In some cases, you may need to make your best guess between two options.

- **Go with your instinct when answering questions.** If your first instinct is to choose **A** in response to a question, it's best to stick with that answer unless you know that answer is incorrect. Usually, the first answer someone chooses is the correct one.

Study Skills

You've already made two very smart decisions in studying for your GED® credential and in purchasing *Steck-Vaughn Test Preparation for the 2014 GED® Test: Social Studies* to help you to do so. Following are additional strategies to help you optimize success on the GED® Test.

4 weeks out ...

> **Set a study schedule for the GED® Test.** Choose times in which you are most alert and places, such as a library, that provide the best study environment.

> **Thoroughly review all material in *Steck-Vaughn Test Preparation for the 2014 GED® Test: Social Studies*, using the *Social Studies Workbook* to extend understanding of concepts in the *Social Studies Student Book*.**

> **Keep notebooks for each of the subject areas that you are studying.** Folders with pockets are useful for storing loose papers.

> **When taking notes, restate thoughts or ideas in your own words rather than copying them directly from a book.** You can phrase these notes as complete sentences, as questions (with answers), or as fragments, provided you understand them.

2 weeks out ...

> **Take the pretests, noting any troublesome subject areas.** Focus your remaining study around those subject areas.

The day before ...

> **Map out the route to the test center, and visit it a day or two before your scheduled exam.** If you drive, find a place to park at the center.

> **Get a good night's sleep the night before the GED® Test.** Studies have shown that students with sufficient rest perform better in testing situations.

The day of ...

> **Eat a hearty breakfast high in protein.** As with the rest of your body, your brain needs ample energy to perform well.

> **Arrive 30 minutes early to the testing center.** This will allow sufficient time in the event of change to a different testing classroom.

> **Pack a sizeable lunch,** especially if you plan to be at the testing center most of the day.

> **Remember to relax.** You've come this far and have spent weeks preparing and studying for the GED® Test. Now, it's your time to shine!

Understand Geography

Use with *Student Book* pp. 2–3

SS CONTENT TOPICS: II.G.b.1, II.G.b.2, II.G.b.4, II.G.b.5, II.G.c.1, II.G.c.2, II.G.c.3, II.G.d.1, II.G.d.2, II.G.d.3, II.G.d.4, II.E.d.1, II.E.g, II.USH.e
SS PRACTICES: SSP.2.b, SSP.3.c, SSP.4.a, SSP.6.b

UNIT 1

① Review the Skill

The study of Earth is known as geography. The importance of learning how to accurately read a map is critical to **understanding geography** and the world. Becoming familiar with key terms, such as **map**, **globe**, and **equator**, will increase your understanding of geography. A map is a visual representation of a place, usually shown on a flat surface. The three primary types of maps are physical maps, political maps, and special-purpose maps. A globe is a model of Earth, usually spherical in shape. The equator is an imaginary line that runs around the middle of Earth, separating the world into the Northern and Southern Hemispheres.

② Refine the Skill

By refining the skill of understanding geography, you will improve your study and test-taking abilities, especially as they relate to the GED® Social Studies Test. Remember that geography is more than just features on a map. It illustrates the way people affect and are affected by Earth. Study the map and information contained in the callout boxes. Then answer the questions that follow.

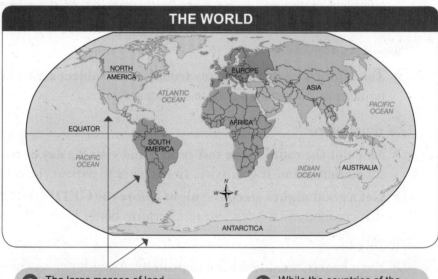

THE WORLD

a The large masses of land labeled on this map are Earth's seven continents.

b While the countries of the world are not labeled on this map, their borders are outlined. Locate the United States on the map.

TEST-TAKING TIPS

Because Earth is spherical, it is difficult to show on a flat map, so different map projections are used. Some projections distort the shapes of continents, as well as distance and scale, to retain the spherical properties of Earth.

1. Which two continents lie entirely in the Southern Hemisphere?

   A. Africa and North America
   B. Europe and Australia
   C. Antarctica and Asia
   D. Australia and Antarctica

2. How many continents lie in both the Northern and Southern Hemispheres?

   A. two
   B. three
   C. four
   D. five

★ Spotlighted Item: **HOT SPOT**

DIRECTIONS: Study the map and read the passage. Then mark on the map the **best** answer(s) to each question.

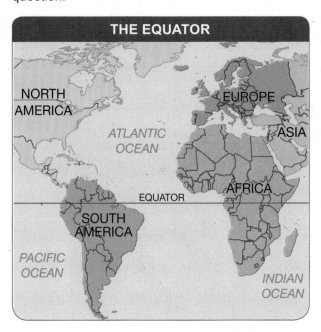

THE EQUATOR

The equator runs through fourteen different countries. It is located, geographically, the same distance from the North Pole and the South Pole. The equator divides Earth into the Northern and Southern Hemispheres.

3. Which continent has the most land mass located in the Southern Hemisphere? Circle it on the map.

4. Which country is located north of the equator: Chile, Egypt, Madagascar, or South Africa? Underline on the map the name of the continent that is home to that country.

5. Of Argentina, China, Switzerland, and the United States, which country is located in the Southern Hemisphere? Place an **X** on the map next to the name of the continent that is home to that country.

DIRECTIONS: Study the map and read the passage. Then select the best answer(s) to each question that follows. NOTE that there might be more than one correct answer per question.

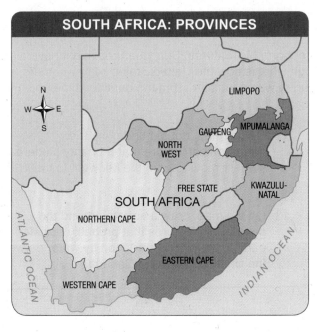

SOUTH AFRICA: PROVINCES

South Africa has a population of approximately 49 million people. The country is home to several national parks, including Kruger National Park in the Limpopo and Mpumalanga provinces.

Mining in the interior plateau, which yields gold, diamonds, and coal, has sustained the economy of South Africa for decades. In the 1800s, South Africa was a destination for British, Dutch, and German imperialist expansion.

6. Circle the province(s) on the map to indicate where Kruger National Park is located.

7. Which of South Africa's provinces border the Indian Ocean? Underline the names of the province(s) on the map.

8. Which of South Africa's provinces borders Free State? Put an **X** next to those the province(s) on the map.

UNIT 1

⭐ Spotlighted Item: **HOT SPOT**

DIRECTIONS: Study the map and read the passage. Then mark on the map the **best** answer(s) to each question.

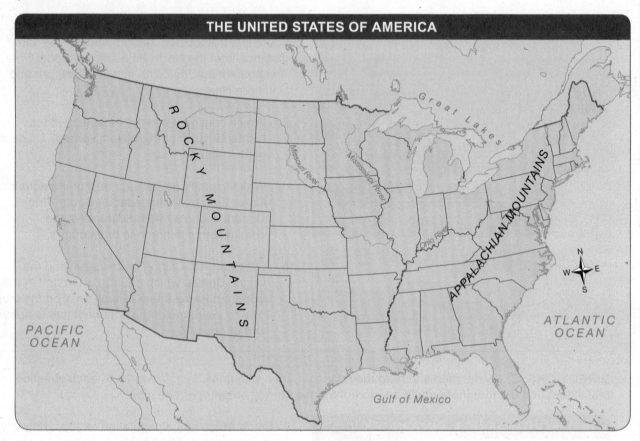

THE UNITED STATES OF AMERICA

   Oceans, rivers, and mountain ranges are natural geographic features. Such features might have aided or hindered the settlement of or transportation through what is now the United States by newcomers wishing to make their homes in this country. The country was populated from the outside in, meaning that the coastal areas were settled before the interior areas.

9. Underline the natural feature(s) that are located south and west of the United States.

10. Put an **X** next to the mountain range that separates the East Coast from the Midwest.

11. Which geographic features probably aided settlement in the Midwest? Circle those features on the map.

12. On the map, double underline the geographical feature that probably hindered settlers moving from the Midwest to the West Coast.

13. On the map, draw a square around the geographic features that probably assisted early settlers' transportation by water between the United States and Canada.

DIRECTIONS: Study the map and read the passage. Then mark on the map the **best** answer(s) to each question.

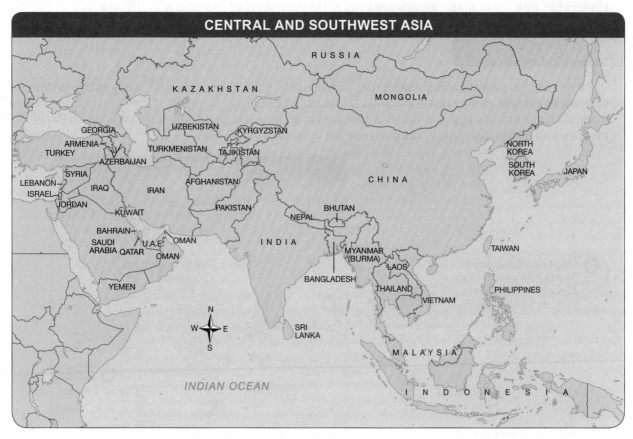

CENTRAL AND SOUTHWEST ASIA

Asia is the largest continent on Earth. It stretches from Russia in the north, to India in the south, and to the islands of Japan and Indonesia in the east. The Middle East region is located in central and southwest Asia. The term "Middle East" is a term that originated with early European exploration, which divided Asia into the Near East, the Middle East, and the Far East.

14. On the map, draw a box around the smallest country that lies on the Indian Ocean.

15. On the basis of the map and the passage above, which country or countries probably can be considered to be located in the Far East? Circle your answer(s) on the map.

16. Which countries on the map are landlocked? Underline those countries on the map.

17. Which country shown fully on the map is largest? Double underline that country.

18. Which country lies between Russia and China? Place a check mark next to that country's name on the map.

19. Which countries border the country of Thailand? Place an **X** on those countries on the map.

Understand Map Components

Use with **Student Book** pp. 4–5

1 Review the Skill

SS CONTENT TOPICS: II.G.b.1, II.G.b.4, II.G.b.5, II.G.c.1, II.G.c.2, II.G.c.3, II.G.d.1, II.G.d.2, II.G.d.3, II.G.d.4, I.USH.b.1
SS PRACTICES: SSP.2.b, SSP.3.c, SSP.4.a, SSP.6.a, SSP.6.b, SSP.10.c

Map symbols, such as dots, stars, and triangles, show specific geographic information. Other elements that can help you understand information on a map include the map title, a compass rose, scales, the map key, and labels. Latitude (east-west) and longitude (north-south) lines can help you pinpoint absolute location. **Understanding** these **map components** will aid in your study of geography.

2 Refine the Skill

By refining the skill of understanding map components, you will improve your study and test-taking abilities, especially as they relate to the GED® Social Studies Test. Remember that the various features on maps can help provide you with valuable geographic information about a specific location on Earth. Study the map and information below. Then answer the questions that follow.

a Use the compass rose on the map to help you determine directions such as north, east, south, and west.

b Use the map key to determine what the map symbols and shading represent. The map's key is the guide to understanding the map.

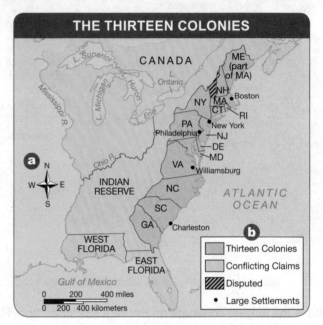

THE THIRTEEN COLONIES

Thirteen Colonies
Conflicting Claims
Disputed
• Large Settlements

TEST-TAKING TIPS

You might need to understand more than one map component or the meaning of more than one map symbol to answer a question. Take time to understand all of the map components before answering each question.

1. Which of the following statements best describes the area of the Indian Reserve?

   A. It is concentrated in the north.
   B. It is between the thirteen colonies and the Mississippi River.
   C. It includes the areas of West Florida and East Florida.
   D. It is near several large settlements.

2. Which of the following statements is accurate?

   A. Large settlements stretched from the northern to the southern colonies.
   B. North Carolina had just one large settlement.
   C. Large settlements were located in colonies with disputed land.
   D. There were no large settlements in the south.

DIRECTIONS: Study the map and read each question, then choose the **best** answer.

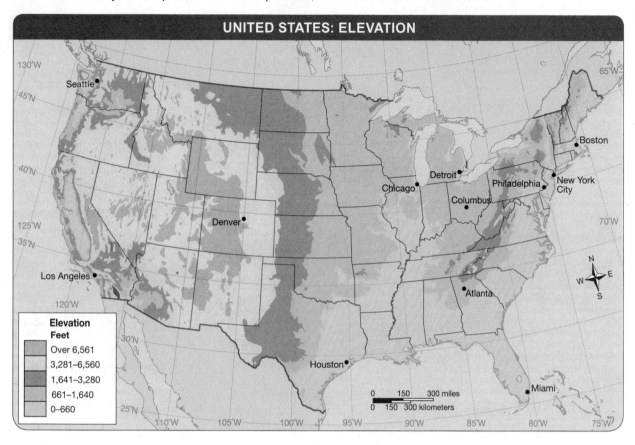

UNIT 1

3. What is the distance between Houston and Atlanta?

    A. The distance is approximately 1,850 miles.
    B. The distance is approximately 1,500 miles.
    C. The distance is approximately 900 miles.
    D. The distance is approximately 625 miles.

4. Based on the map, which state would most likely have one of the highest points in the nation?

    A. Minnesota
    B. Colorado
    C. Maine
    D. Arkansas

5. Which city is located near 35°N and 85°W?

    A. Philadelphia
    B. Columbus
    C. Atlanta
    D. Houston

6. Based on the map, what is the relative location of Detroit?

    A. north of Columbus
    B. west of Denver
    C. 45°N, 80°W
    D. 40°N, 90°W

7. In which area of the United States would you find land with the lowest elevation?

    A. in the Midwest
    B. in the Southeast
    C. in the Northwest
    D. in the Southwest

8. Approximately how many miles would you travel if you left Columbus, Ohio, to visit Denver, Colorado?

    A. approximately 950 miles
    B. approximately 1,000 miles
    C. approximately 1,200 miles
    D. approximately 2,250 miles

DIRECTIONS: Study the map and read each question, then choose the **best** answer.

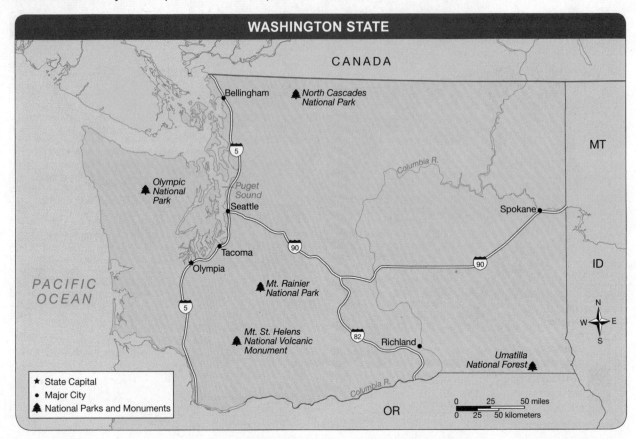

WASHINGTON STATE

9. Which national park is closest to the capital?

   A. Olympic National Park
   B. Mt. Rainier National Park
   C. Mt. St. Helens National Volcanic Monument
   D. North Cascades National Park

10. Which of the following statements is accurate?

    A. I-90 connects Spokane and Richland.
    B. I-90 runs north to south.
    C. I-5 connects four major cities.
    D. I-82 merges with I-5.

11. Based on the information in the map, which of the following best describes Washington?

    A. Washington is east of Idaho.
    B. Washington is landlocked.
    C. Washington borders Canada and California.
    D. Washington has several national parks and monuments.

12. Why might Puget Sound be an important waterway?

    A. Puget Sound is close to all of the national parks in Washington.
    B. Puget Sound is the source of the Columbia River.
    C. Puget Sound extends into Oregon.
    D. Puget Sound connects major cities to the Pacific Ocean.

13. Approximately how many miles apart are the cities of Bellingham and Olympia?

    A. approximately 25 miles
    B. approximately 150 miles
    C. approximately 210 miles
    D. approximately 240 miles

14. Which national park or monument is closest to Oregon?

    A. North Cascades National Park
    B. Mt. St. Helens National Volcanic Monument
    C. Mt. Rainier National Park
    D. Umatilla National Forest

DIRECTIONS: Study the map, read the passage, then choose the **best** answer to each question.

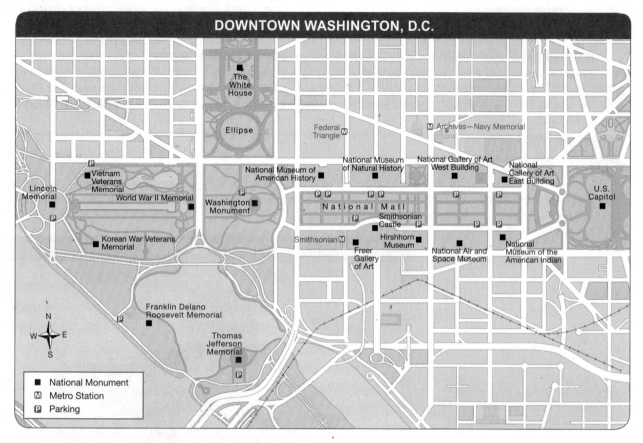

DOWNTOWN WASHINGTON, D.C.

Each year close to 20 million people visit Washington, D.C., the capital of the United States. Most of the main government buildings and national monuments are located in one area of the city. Visitors can walk, ride on a tour bus, or take the metro, the city's subway system, to visit these sites. Although some attractions, such as the White House tour, require advance tickets, all government buildings, including the White House and the National Archives, as well as all monuments, memorials, and Smithsonian museums, have free admission. They are supported by and belong to the American taxpayers.

15. Where is most of the parking located?

A. by the Vietnam Veterans Memorial
B. by the U.S. Capitol
C. by the National Mall
D. by the Thomas Jefferson Memorial

16. Which metro station is closest to the White House?

A. Smithsonian
B. Federal Triangle
C. Ellipse
D. Archives-Navy Memorial

17. Which is the most logical route for a walking tour?

A. U.S. Capitol to National Gallery, to Washington Monument, to F.D.R. Memorial, to Jefferson Memorial
B. Lincoln Memorial to Jefferson Memorial, to Korean War Veterans Memorial, to White House, to Washington Monument
C. Vietnam Veterans Memorial to Lincoln Memorial, to White House, to U.S. Capitol, to Washington Monument
D. Washington Monument to Lincoln Memorial, to White House, to National Gallery, to Vietnam Veterans Memorial

18. Which site is located farthest away from the World War II Memorial?

A. the Freer Gallery of Art
B. the White House
C. the Ellipse
D. the U.S. Capitol

Physical Maps

Use with *Student Book* pp. 6–7

SS CONTENT TOPICS: II.G.b.1, II.G.b.2, II.G.b.4, II.G.b.5, II.G.c.1, II.G.c.3, II.G.d.1, II.G.d.2, II.G.d.3, II.G.d.4
SS PRACTICES: SSP.2.b, SSP.3.a, SSP.3.b, SSP.3.c, SSP.6.b, SSP.6.c

UNIT 1

① Review the Skill

A **physical map** uses different colors, shading, and/or symbols to illustrate land and water features. A map key is a useful tool when examining and analyzing a physical map. It tells you what the different colors, shading, and symbols represent. The title of a physical map is also an important tool. The map title might include words such as *physical*, *natural features*, *climate*, *elevation*, *temperature*, *precipitation*, or even *land use* or *water use*.

② Refine the Skill

By refining your knowledge and understanding of physical maps, you will improve your study and test-taking abilities, especially as they relate to the GED® Social Studies Test. Study the map and information below. Then answer the questions that follow.

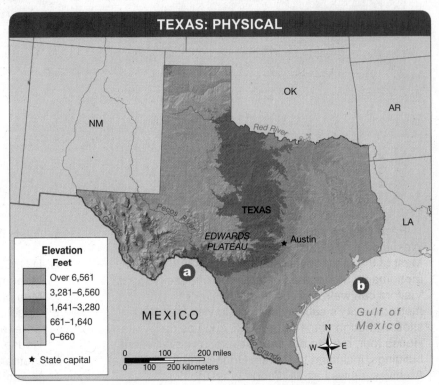

a People use rivers and other water sources for drinking water and transportation.

b Fishing and shipping are often important economic activities in coastal areas.

USING LOGIC

Physical features affect where people settle as well as how they live. Physical features can affect the work that people do, the clothing they wear, and the recreational activities in which they participate.

1. How would early settlers most likely have traveled from Austin into New Mexico?

   A. via the Red River
   B. via the Edwards Plateau
   C. via the Gulf of Mexico
   D. via the Pecos River

2. The Red River flows along the border of which state?

   A. Oklahoma
   B. Louisiana
   C. Arkansas
   D. New Mexico

DIRECTIONS: Study the maps and read each question. Then choose the **best** answer.

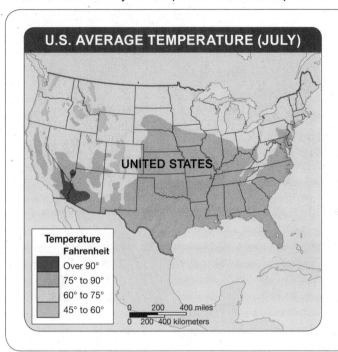

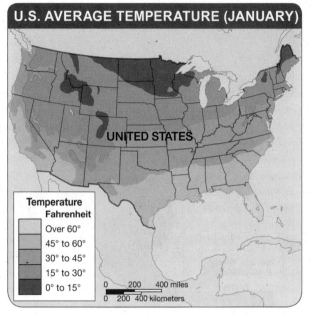

3. Based on the maps, which of the following are possible temperatures for Virginia?

   A. 20 degrees in January; 75 degrees in July
   B. 30 degrees in January; 80 degrees in July
   C. 50 degrees in January; 70 degrees in July
   D. 60 degrees in January; 80 degrees in July

4. Which of the following states is the coldest in January?

   A. Washington
   B. Pennsylvania
   C. Ohio
   D. Maine

5. Which of the following statements best summarizes the content of the maps?

   A. The United States is a cold country.
   B. The United States is a warm country.
   C. The United States has a wide range of temperatures.
   D. The United States has uniform temperatures.

6. Which of the following factors affects the climate of the southeastern part of the United States?

   A. its proximity to the equator
   B. its longitude
   C. its vegetation
   D. its proximity to islands

7. Based on the maps, which of the following are possible temperatures for New Mexico?

   A. 10 degrees in January; 90 degrees in July
   B. 30 degrees in January; 90 degrees in July
   C. 30 degrees in January; over 90 degrees in July
   D. 50 degrees in January; over 90 degrees in July

8. Which of the following states has the highest average temperature in July?

   A. Nevada
   B. New Mexico
   C. Florida
   D. California

9. In which of the following states would there be the highest probability of snow during January?

   A. Mississippi
   B. South Carolina
   C. Tennessee
   D. Louisiana

10. Which state experiences the warmest average temperatures in January?

    A. Florida
    B. New Mexico
    C. California
    D. Arizona

DIRECTIONS: Study the map and the information in the passage, read each question, then choose the **best** answer.

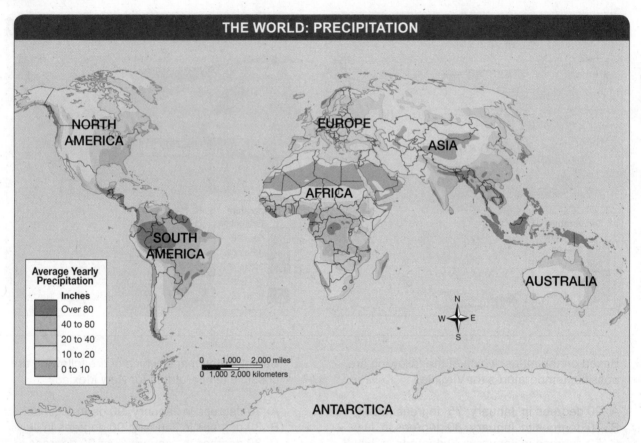

One of the wettest areas of the world is in South Asia. Here, the people of the region experience a monsoon, or rainy, season that lasts from June through October. During this season, the region receives much of its rain for the year. The farmers depend on these rains to water their crops, knowing that there will be little rain the rest of the year. Rainforests, such as those located in South America, are also very wet. However, the rainfall is steadier and spread throughout the year.

There are two types of rainforests: tropical and temperate. Tropical rainforests are found closer to the equator, where it is warm. Tropical rainforests are known for their dense vegetation that prevents whatever sunlight there might be from reaching the ground. Temperate rainforests are found near the cooler coastal areas farther north or south of the equator. In the United States, for example, the state of Washington is home to an unspoiled temperate rainforest, which is located in the northern reaches of the Olympic National Park.

11. Why is farming in South Asia problematic?

   A. There is never enough rain.
   B. It is constantly raining in the region.
   C. The region has three rainy seasons per year.
   D. The region receives most of its yearly rain from June to October.

12. According to the map, which continent uniformly experiences a yearly average rainfall of 10 to 20 inches?

   A. North America
   B. South America
   C. Antarctica
   D. Asia

UNIT 1

DIRECTIONS: Study the map and the information in the passage, read each question, then mark on the map the **best** answer(s) to each question.

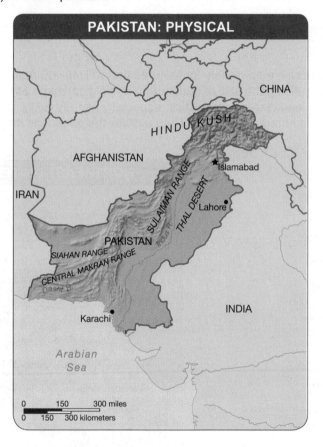

PAKISTAN: PHYSICAL

CHINA

HINDU KUSH

AFGHANISTAN

★ Islamabad

SULAIMAN RANGE

THAL DESERT

IRAN

Indus R.

Lahore

PAKISTAN

SIAHAN RANGE

CENTRAL MAKRAN RANGE

Dasht R.

INDIA

Karachi

Arabian
Sea

0   150   300 miles
0   150   300 kilometers

   Pakistan is located in South Asia and extends from the Himalayas to the Arabian Sea. The four geographic regions of Pakistan include mountains and plateaus in western Pakistan, mountains in the north, plains in the valley of the Indus River, and hills in the northwest.

   Pakistan's terrain is as diverse as its people. Because of the country's vast, rugged land, agriculture is not an economic mainstay of many of the country's regions. However, the use of irrigation has helped in the growing of crops such as wheat, rice, and cotton. About 40 percent of the population lives in urban areas. Karachi is a port city located along the coast in the south. The capital city, Islamabad, and the city of Lahore are located in the east-central part of the country. These three cities are Pakistan's most populated urban areas.

13. Place an **X** on the map next to Pakistan's major port city.

14. Locate the most mountainous area of Pakistan. Place a check mark on this area.

15. Locate all of the waterways of Pakistan, and then circle them on the map.

16. Locate the country with the longest natural border with Pakistan. Underline that country's name on the map.

Political Maps

Use with **Student Book** pp. 8–9

SS CONTENT TOPICS: II.G.b.1, II.G.b.2, II.G.b.3, II.G.b.4, II.G.b.5, II.G.c.1, II.G.c.2, II.G.c.3, II.G.d.1, II.G.d.2, II.G.d.3, II.E.g
SS PRACTICES: SSP.2.b, SSP.3.c, SSP.6.b, SSP.6.c, SSP.10.c

UNIT 1

1 Review the Skill

Unlike physical maps, **political maps** generally do not show physical features such as landforms, waterways, or elevations. However, political maps have some of the same map elements as physical maps. Both types of maps often include a map title, symbols, a compass rose, a scale, and lines of latitude and longitude.

2 Refine the Skill

It is important that you read a map closely for features that will tell you more about the information presented on the map. By refining the skill of understanding political maps and the information they provide, you will improve your study and test-taking abilities, especially as they relate to the GED® Social Studies Test. Study the map and the information below. Then answer the questions that follow.

a Political maps often use stars for capital cities and dots for large cities. Use the map key to help you understand what the symbols represent.

b Maps often use shading to show unofficial borders, such as regions. In this case, the region encompasses all of the states shaded on the map. Sometimes shaded areas will not include all of a given state or country. For example, if a map were used to illustrate how people voted in the most recent election, the shaded areas would not necessarily correspond to state borders.

NORTHEAST UNITED STATES

0   100   200 miles
0   100   200 kilometers

MAINE
Augusta ★
VERMONT
Montpelier ★
Concord
NEW HAMPSHIRE
Albany ★
NEW YORK
Boston ★
MASSACHUSETTS
★ Providence
Hartford ★
RHODE ISLAND
CONNECTICUT
PENNSYLVANIA
ATLANTIC OCEAN
Harrisburg ★   ★ Trenton
NEW JERSEY

a ★ State capital

MAKING ASSUMPTIONS

Political maps usually include state and country borders, but might not include regional borders. Knowing a region's borders can help you make assumptions about its population, economics, and culture.

1. What does the symbol designating Concord, New Hampshire, represent?

   A. large city
   B. state capital
   C. state capital and county seat
   D. large city and state capital

2. Which of the following statements best describes how this map could be used?

   A. to determine the climate of the Northeast
   B. to find the population density of cities in the Northeast
   C. to find the location of the states along the East Coast of the United States
   D. to identify the states that comprise the Northeast region

DIRECTIONS: Study the map and the information in the passage, and read the questions, then choose the **best** answer.

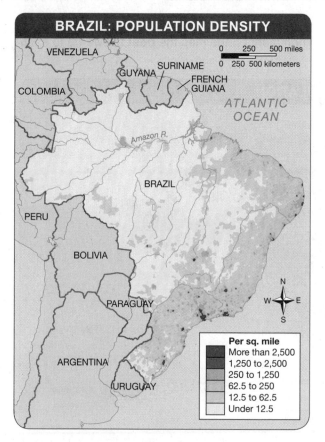

BRAZIL: POPULATION DENSITY

Per sq. mile
More than 2,500
1,250 to 2,500
250 to 1,250
62.5 to 250
12.5 to 62.5
Under 12.5

Almost 200 million people live in Brazil. The fifth-largest country in the world, Brazil is home to the Amazon River Delta. In the north and the west, Brazil has thousands of acres of rainforest in the Amazon basin. During the early period of colonization, few colonists ventured into the rainforests of the Amazon.

Unlike the other countries of South America, in which the official language is Spanish, the official language of Brazil is Portuguese. Brazil's indigenous population traded with the colonizers from Portugal who arrived in the 1500s. Because the majority of the indigenous population perished due to wars and disease, enslaved Africans were brought into Brazil to work the fields. Of the 9.5 million people captured in Africa and brought to the Americas between the sixteenth and the nineteenth centuries, nearly 4 million landed in Brazil—ten times more than those sent to the United States.

Brazil won its independence from the Portuguese in 1822 after more than 300 years as a colony. Brazil became the last American nation to abolish slavery, on May 13, 1888. At that time Rio de Janeiro, Brazil's second-largest city, had the largest urban

concentration of enslaved people—more than 40% of its population—since the end of the Roman Empire.

3. Based on the map, where can you assume that Brazil's major cities are located?

   A. along the Bolivian border
   B. along the east coast
   C. in the Amazon basin
   D. in the center of the country

4. Which geographic features most likely impact Brazil's population centers?

   A. the equator and the Pacific Ocean
   B. the Amazon delta and the Peruvian border
   C. the Amazon rainforest and the Atlantic Ocean
   D. the Amazon rainforest and the mountains

5. According to the passage, how is the population of modern Brazil similar to the population during the early period of colonization?

   A. It is low in the Amazon area.
   B. It is low in the coastal area.
   C. It is high in the Amazon area.
   D. It is high near the Bolivian border.

6. Based on the passage, how many years elapsed between Brazil's independence and its abolishment of slavery?

   A. 45 years
   B. 46 years
   C. 56 years
   D. 66 years

7. Based on the information, which of the following statements about Brazil is correct?

   A. Brazil's population is a mixture of people of different ethnicities.
   B. Brazil's population is primarily Portuguese.
   C. Brazil's population is distributed evenly throughout the country.
   D. Brazil's only peaceful neighbor is Uruguay.

⭐ Spotlighted Item: **HOT SPOT**

DIRECTIONS: Study the map and read the questions. Then mark on the map the **best** answer(s) to each question.

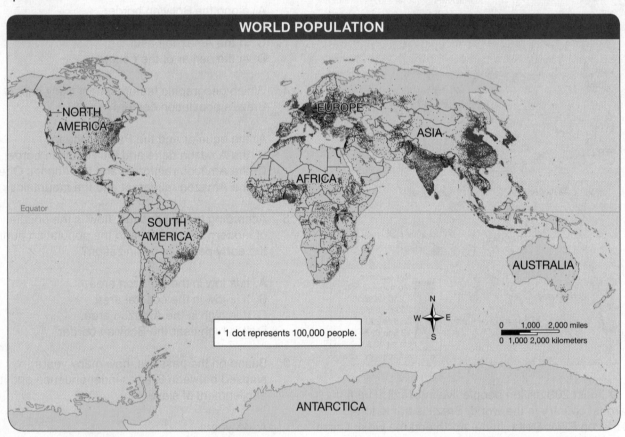

WORLD POPULATION

- 1 dot represents 100,000 people.

8. On the map, circle the name of the continent that has the smallest population.

9. Which continent is most densely populated? Underline the name of that continent.

10. Which continent located solely in the Southern Hemisphere has a population of at least 200,000? Circle the name of the continent.

11. Which continent partially located in the Southern Hemisphere shows very sparsely populated central region(s)? Place a double-**X** next to the name of the continents.

12. Which continent, located solely in the Northern Hemisphere, has most of its population on the eastern coast? Place a triple-**X** next to its name on the map.

DIRECTIONS: Study the map and read the questions, then choose the **best** answer.

IRELAND: COUNTIES AND COUNTY SEATS

DIRECTIONS: Study the map, read the passage and the questions, then choose the **best** answer.

UNITED STATES: MIDWEST REGION

13. Which of the following counties in Ireland is not landlocked?

A. Tipperary
B. Roscommon
C. Dublin
D. Monaghan

14. Based on the map, which of the following statements about Ireland is accurate?

A. All of the counties in Ireland are about the same size.
B. Several county capitals in Ireland share the same name as the county.
C. The complete area north of Dublin belongs to the United Kingdom.
D. The Celtic Sea is east of County Wicklow.

15. Which of the following cities is the seat of County Tipperary?

A. Kilkenny
B. Tipperary
C. Clonmel
D. Limerick

The Midwest region of the United States includes the Great Lakes states, as well as Missouri, Iowa, Kansas, Nebraska, and North and South Dakota. In 2010, almost 70 million people made the Midwest region their home. The state with the largest population is Illinois. North Dakota has the smallest population in the Midwest.

16. Based on the map and the passage, which of the following statements is accurate?

A. The Midwest region features the largest state in the United States.
B. Illinois has the largest population among all 50 states.
C. The Midwest is the largest region in the United States.
D. Ohio is in the Midwest region.

17. Which of the following cities is located in the Midwest?

A. Albany
B. St. Louis
C. Nashville
D. Pittsburgh

Movement on Maps

Use with *Student Book* pp. 10–11

1 Review the Skill

SS CONTENT TOPICS: I.G.a, II.G.b.1, II.G.c.1, II.G.c.3, II.G.d.1, II.G.d.2, II.G.d.3, I.USH.b.1, I.E.g
SS PRACTICES: SSP.2.b, SSP.3.c, SSP.6.b, SSP.6.c

Maps use a variety of techniques—colors, shading, symbols, and even lines and arrows—to show **movement**. When examining a map, read all of the information on it, especially the map key, so that you understand movement. Often, a map key provides information about movement, such as what was moved, who moved it, and when. In addition, lines, arrows, and a compass rose can help you determine the direction of the movement.

2 Refine the Skill

By refining the skill of understanding movement on maps, you will improve your study and test-taking abilities, especially as they relate to the GED® Social Studies Test. Study the map and information below. Then answer the questions that follow.

a Use the map key to help you identify symbols specific to the map.

b Information about movement on a map is not always presented in the key. Lines and arrows can provide more details.

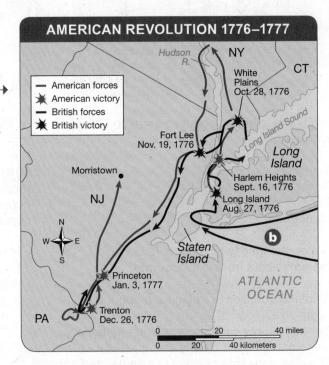

AMERICAN REVOLUTION 1776–1777

Key:
— American forces
✳ American victory
— British forces
✳ British victory

Labels on map: Hudson R., NY, CT, White Plains Oct. 28, 1776, Long Island Sound, Fort Lee Nov. 19, 1776, Long Island, Morristown, Harlem Heights Sept. 16, 1776, Long Island Aug. 27, 1776, NJ, Staten Island, Princeton Jan. 3, 1777, ATLANTIC OCEAN, Trenton Dec. 26, 1776, PA

Scale: 0 20 40 miles / 0 20 40 kilometers

USING LOGIC

Movement on maps often can be shown as a chronology or sequence. Tracing a line or an arrow from event to event will help you better understand the order in which such movement occurs.

1. The New York-New Jersey military campaign marked a key turning point for the Colonial Army in the American Revolution. Based on the map, what were the first and last battle sites of the campaign?

   A. Harlem Heights and Princeton
   B. Fort Lee and Trenton
   C. Long Island and Princeton
   D. Harlem Heights and White Plains

2. Where did the British forces go after the Battle of White Plains?

   A. southwest into New Jersey
   B. north across the Hudson River
   C. south across the Long Island Sound
   D. southeast to Staten Island

DIRECTIONS: Study the map, read each question, and choose the **best** answer.

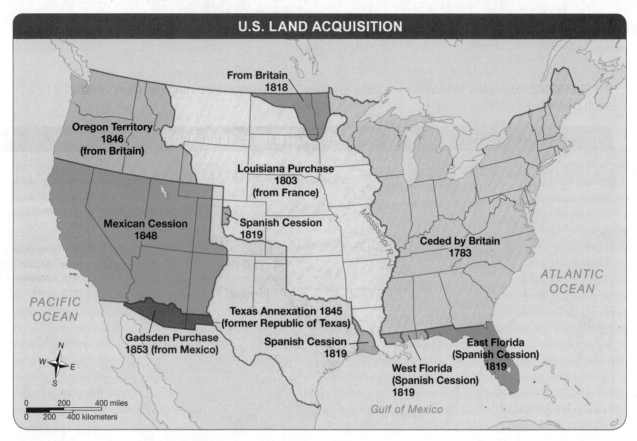

U.S. LAND ACQUISITION

3. Which statement best describes the map?

A. The map shows western expansion between 1803 to 1853.
B. The map illustrates the acquisition of territories between 1783 to 1853.
C. The map shows the battles fought for western expansion.
D. The map shows the sequence of events that led to eastern expansion.

4. Based on information on the map, when was much of the land west of the Mississippi River first opened for settlement?

A. in 1783, with the British cession
B. in 1803, with the Louisiana Purchase
C. in 1819, with the Spanish cession
D. in 1853, with the Gadsden Purchase

5. Which nation ceded the least amount of land to the United States?

A. Britain
B. France
C. Mexico
D. Spain

6. Which of the following states was included in the Mexican Cession of 1848?

A. Florida
B. Illinois
C. Oklahoma
D. California

7. How many years elapsed between the first and the last cessions of British land?

A. 35 years
B. 33 years
C. 53 years
D. 63 years

8. Which of the following nations ceded the most land along the Gulf of Mexico?

A. Britain
B. Spain
C. Mexico
D. France

★ Spotlighted Item: **HOT SPOT**

DIRECTIONS: Study the map and read the passage. Then mark on the map the **best** answer(s) to each question.

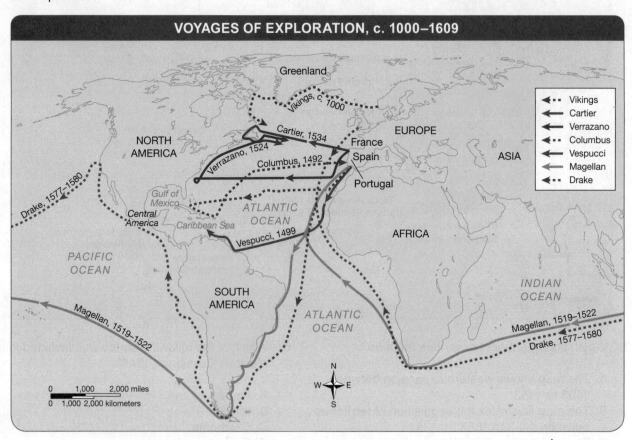

VOYAGES OF EXPLORATION, c. 1000–1609

In the 1400s, Henry the Navigator of Portugal helped start the Age of Discovery in Europe by funding numerous expeditions abroad. One of his goals was to find a sea route to Asia. He also wanted to gain geographic knowledge. Before the 1400s, exploration did exist, but on a smaller scale. However, sea and ocean expeditions did not venture very far away from their home bases. It was not until the Viking explorations of the Atlantic that expeditions penetrated distant waters.

9. From which two European countries did the majority of explorers begin their journeys? Circle the country names on the map.

10. On the map, place an **X** on the first expedition to reach North America.

11. On the map, locate and underline the name of the explorer who first circumnavigated the world.

12. On the map, draw a box around the name of the explorer who explored the Caribbean Islands.

DIRECTIONS: Study the map, read each question, and choose the **best** answer.

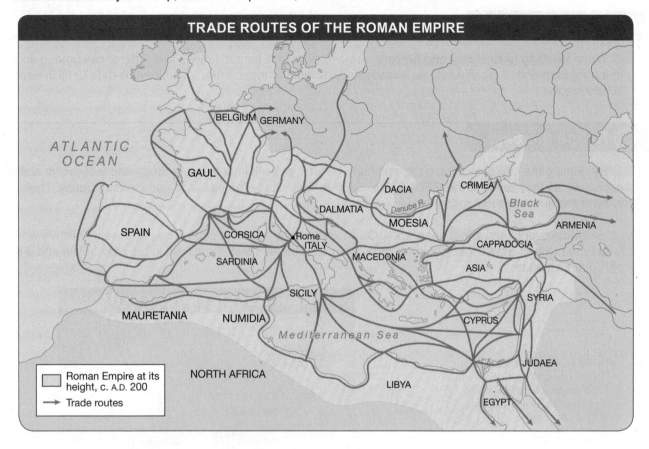

TRADE ROUTES OF THE ROMAN EMPIRE

13. Based on the map, which of the following best describes the trade activity of the Roman Empire?

    A. The Roman Empire was so large that only trade within the empire was required.
    B. The Romans preferred not to trade with people to the north and south of Rome.
    C. The Romans only traded within their empire.
    D. The Romans traded extensively, including outside their empire.

14. Into which continents did the trade routes of the Roman Empire stretch?

    A. Europe, Asia, Africa, and South America
    B. Europe, Asia, and Africa
    C. Europe and Africa
    D. Europe and Asia

15. Which is true about the Roman trade routes?

    A. Germany was not a trade destination.
    B. Most trade occurred via the Atlantic Ocean.
    C. Rivers were the primary form of waterway transport.
    D. Most trade occured via the Mediterranean Sea.

16. Based on the map, which of the following statements is accurate?

    A. Rome itself saw very little trade activity.
    B. The Black Sea was the busiest waterway.
    C. The Romans extended their trade routes into Spain.
    D. The Roman Empire included all of present-day Europe.

17. Which of the following was most likely a consequence of the Roman trade routes?

    A. The trade routes caused the Romans to become increasingly isolated.
    B. The trade routes allowed Rome to enforce its laws throughout the world.
    C. The trade routes were the main cause of the Roman economic collapse.
    D. The trade routes allowed for an exchange of cultural knowledge.

Relate Geography and History

Use with **Student Book** pp. 22–23

1 Review the Skill

SS CONTENT TOPICS: II.G.b.1, II.G.c.1, II.G.c.2, II.G.c.3, II.G.d.1, II.G.d.2, II.G.d.3, II.G.d.4, I.USH.b.1, II.USH.b.2, I.USH.b.3, II.USH.b.6, II.USH.g.3
SS PRACTICES: SSP.1.a, SSP.1.b, SSP.2.a, SSP.2.b, SSP.3.a, SSP.3.b, SSP.3.c, SSP.4.a, SSP.6.a, SSP.6.b, SSP.7.b, SSP.8.a

When **relating geography and history**, remember to look for similarities and differences among sources of information and to recall what you already know about the topic. Then, combine this data to fill in gaps in information.

2 Refine the Skill

By refining the skill of relating geography and history, you will improve your study and test-taking abilities, especially as they relate to the GED® Social Studies Test. Study the passage and the map below. Then answer the questions that follow.

Historical events can affect geography. Often, geography affects history. The Northwest Territory added land to the United States that would eventually become the five states outlined in the map below and a small part of a sixth state.

a Geographical features such as lakes and rivers form many of the borders of the states created from the Northwest Territory.

b The Ohio River may have been part of a shifting political boundary, but as a physical characteristic, it never changes.

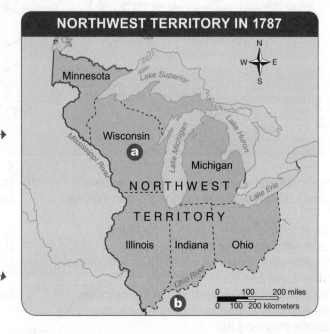

NORTHWEST TERRITORY IN 1787

1. Based on the map, which of the following most completely lists the geographical features that form part of Michigan's borders?

   A. Lake Michigan, Lake Huron
   B. Lake Superior, Lake Huron, Lake Erie, Lake Michigan
   C. Lake Superior, Lake Huron, Lake Erie, the Ohio River
   D. Lake Michigan, Lake Huron, the Ohio River

2. Based on the map and the passage, which of the following states of the Northwest Territory shares a border with both the Ohio and Mississippi Rivers?

   A. Ohio
   B. Wisconsin
   C. Indiana
   D. Illinois

TEST-TAKING TIPS

Use dates and other facts presented on maps to place geography into a historical context. For example, think about why the writers of The Northwest Ordinance used bodies of water as political boundaries for states.

DIRECTIONS: Study the map and read the passage. Then fill in your answers in the boxes below.

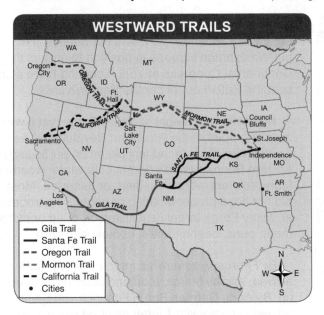

WESTWARD TRAILS

Legend:
— Gila Trail
— Santa Fe Trail
- - - Oregon Trail
- - - Mormon Trail
- - - California Trail
• Cities

In the mid-1800s, William Henry Hart traveled the California Trail. He kept a diary of his adventures:

June 22d Rolled out early. Road very bad being all hills, steep and rocky, up mountains and down vales, over or around the rocky ridges, with many a sudden creek or steep pitch. I was driver and on one of the steepest rocky descents my lock chain became loosened and the wagon instantly commenced going down much faster than [was] proper and threatened to crowd the team off the side [of] the road into a deep ravine. In trying to catch the wheel with my hands I put my foot too near it and immediately my right great toe underwent a flattening process that was decidedly disagreeable. I was still striving to stop the wagon however when I was reinforced by Streeter + Reed who had not been far off and by the driver of the succeeding team. By each catching a wheel we stopped the wagon and relocked it.

3. Based on the map and passage, Nevada and California have these three land formations:

[ ] ,

[ ] , and

[ ] .

4. Based on the map, the California Trail intersects with the

[ ] Trail

and the

[ ] Trail.

5. Based on the passage, Hart faces two situations that are dangerous for settlers on the Westward Trails: loss of a

[ ] and

[ ] .

UNIT 2

★ Spotlighted Item: **FILL-IN-THE-BLANK**

DIRECTIONS: Study the map and read the passage. Then fill in your answers in the boxes below.

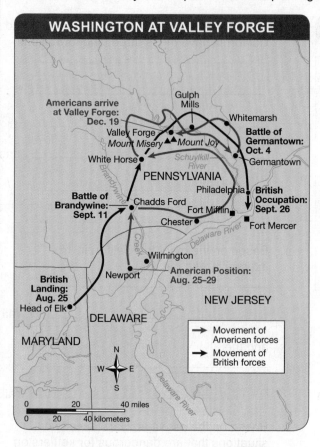

WASHINGTON AT VALLEY FORGE

Americans arrive at Valley Forge: Dec. 19
Gulph Mills
Whitemarsh
Valley Forge
Mount Misery
Mount Joy
Battle of Germantown: Oct. 4
White Horse
Schuylkill River
Germantown
PENNSYLVANIA
Philadelphia
British Occupation: Sept. 26
Battle of Brandywine: Sept. 11
Chadds Ford
Fort Mifflin
Chester
Fort Mercer
Delaware River
Wilmington
Creek
American Position: Aug. 25–29
Newport
British Landing: Aug. 25
Head of Elk
NEW JERSEY
DELAWARE
MARYLAND
Delaware River

→ Movement of American forces
→ Movement of British forces

N W E S

0   20   40 miles
0   20   40 kilometers

The events leading to General George Washington's Continental Army spending the winter at Valley Forge in Pennsylvania began in August 1777, when British forces landed at the top of Chesapeake Bay with the objective of taking Philadelphia, which was then the American capital. The Americans were defeated at the Battle of Brandywine on September 11. Philadelphia was left undefended, as members of the Continental Congress fled to York above Lake Ontario, where the capital was reestablished. The British then took Philadelphia on September 26, 1777.

The Continental Army suffered another British defeat at the Battle of Germantown, just north of Philadelphia on October 4. General Washington led his disheartened army to Valley Forge to winter over and prepare for battle in the spring. Washington chose Valley Forge, located 18 miles northwest of Philadelphia, because it was easily

defensible. The geographic barriers formed by Mount Joy, Mount Misery, and the Schuylkill River put Washington's troops in position to protect the Continental Congress at York. Locating there also kept the British out of central Pennsylvania.

No battle was fought at Valley Forge, yet it was a turning point of the American Revolution. The Continental Army faced terrible odds, particularly eastern Pennsylvania's harsh, cold winter weather. Many soldiers were sick, died, or deserted. Most did not have proper clothing or boots. The troops at Valley Forge largely subsisted on dried or salted meat, peas, beans, pears, apples, and corn.

By February, somewhat more **clement** weather arrived, and by March, food and supplies showed up. By April, German Baron Friedrich von Steuben arrived in camp with a letter of introduction from Benjamin Franklin, whom he had met in Paris. Von Steuben tirelessly helped General Washington in drilling the troops and in their strategies for training, reestablishing their confidence. On June 19, 1778, six months later, a renewed army pulled out of Valley Forge toward New Jersey to fight the British.

6. General George Washington selected Valley Forge as his encampment for the winter of 1777–1778 because of these three geographical features:

   [   ].

7. Based on the map and the passage, the

   Continental Army [   ]

   in keeping the British out of central Pennsylvania.

8. Based on the context of the passage, the word *clement* probably means

   [   ].

DIRECTIONS: Study the map and read the passage. Then fill in your answers in the boxes below.

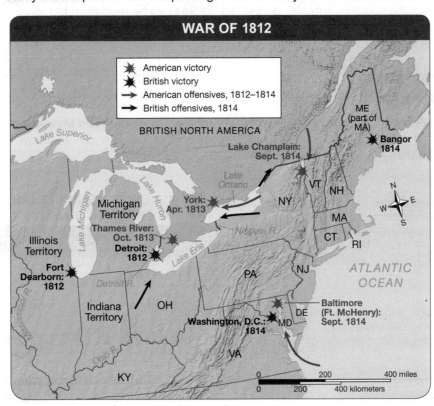

WAR OF 1812

American victory
British victory
American offensives, 1812–1814
British offensives, 1814

BRITISH NORTH AMERICA

Lake Superior

Lake Michigan

Lake Huron

Lake Ontario

Lake Erie

Lake Champlain: Sept. 1814

ME (part of MA)

Bangor 1814

VT   NH

NY

MA

CT   RI

York: Apr. 1813

Michigan Territory

Thames River: Oct. 1813

Detroit: 1812

Illinois Territory

Fort Dearborn: 1812

Detroit R.

Indiana Territory

OH

PA

NJ

DE

ATLANTIC OCEAN

Mississippi R.

Ohio R.

Niagara R.

St. Lawrence R.

Washington, D.C.: 1814

MD

VA

Baltimore (Ft. McHenry): Sept. 1814

KY

0   200   400 miles
0   200   400 kilometers

By 1812 Britain and France were at war again. The British stopped U.S. ships from supplying Europe. They captured American sailors and forced them to serve on British ships. France began to show an equal disregard for the rights of the Americans at sea, but Americans knew that France had come to the aid of the Continental Army in the American Revolution against Britain.

Thus, the United States sided with France and went to war against Britain to protect its own shipping rights. The War of 1812 lasted just eighteen months. Neither side won much in the treaty that ended the war, but the United States established its sea rights and gained the respect of foreign nations.

9. Based on the passage, the primary reason the United States entered the War of 1812 against Britain was

.

10. The two earliest American victories in the war were at

.

11. During the War of 1812, American and British conflicts took place near Lakes

,

, and

because the lakes formed borders between British North America and the United States.

Interpret Tables

Use with **Student Book** pp. 24–25

1 Review the Skill

SS CONTENT TOPICS: II.E.f, II.E.g, I.USH.b.7, I.USH.c.1, II.USH.e.1, II.G.b.1, II.G.b.2, II.G.b.4, II.G.c.1, II.G.c.2, II.G.d.1, II.G.d.3, II.G.d.4
SS PRACTICES: SSP.1.a, SSP.2.b, SSP.4.a, SSP.6.b, SSP.6.c

A **table** presents important facts or details in a visual format, using **rows** and **columns**. This visual presentation can make the information easier to read and understand. By **interpreting tables**, you can draw conclusions about the subjects or topics presented. Tables can be read from top to bottom and from side to side. Be sure to determine what the headings for each column or row of the table mean. Carefully study the facts and details in a table.

2 Refine the Skill

By refining the skill of interpreting tables, you will improve your study and test-taking abilities, especially as they relate to the GED® Social Studies Test. Study the table and information below. Then answer the questions that follow.

UNIT 2

a Based on the title of the table, you can determine that the table will detail regional differences among colonial agricultural products.

a COLONIAL AGRICULTURE BY REGION, *circa* 1700

REGION	**b** MAIN CROPS
New England	corn
Middle Colonies	wheat
Southern Colonies	tobacco, rice, indigo

b Tables are particularly useful for comparing information. In this case, the headings indicate that the table compares main crops grown in different regions of the colonies.

Land and climate played an important role in determining the types of crops that could be grown in each colonial region. Crops did not thrive in New England's cool climate and rocky soil. However, colonists did grow corn in the region. The milder climate and more fertile soil of the Middle Colonies allowed colonists there to produce many grains, such as wheat. The Southern Colonies also had fertile soil, as well as a lengthy growing season. As a result, many planters built large plantations on which they raised cash crops such as tobacco, rice, and indigo.

USING LOGIC

For some questions, you need to access prior knowledge. For example, which colonies were located in each region? This information is not presented on the page. You have to use what you already know about American history.

1. What was the main crop grown in the Middle Colonies?

   A. corn
   B. rice
   C. indigo
   D. wheat

2. In which of the following colonies would crops have been the least likely to thrive?

   A. Rhode Island
   B. Georgia
   C. Pennsylvania
   D. Virginia

DIRECTIONS: Study the table, read each question, then choose the **best** answer.

COLONIAL POPULATIONS OF ENSLAVED PEOPLE

COLONY	1720	1750	1770
Connecticut	1,093	3,010	5,689
New York	5,740	11,014	19,062
Maryland	12,499	43,450	63,818
Virginia	26,550	107,100	187,600
South Carolina	11,828	39,000	75,178

3. Based on information in the table, which statement is accurate?

   A. South Carolina's population of enslaved people doubled between 1720 and 1750.
   B. New England Colonies typically had larger populations of enslaved people than the Middle Colonies.
   C. Virginia's population of enslaved people increased by more than 150,000 between 1720 and 1770.
   D. Connecticut's population of enslaved people began to decrease after 1750.

4. Which colony's population of enslaved people increased the least from 1720 to 1750?

   A. South Carolina
   B. New York
   C. Maryland
   D. Connecticut

5. Which colony's population of enslaved people increased by the greatest number from 1720 to 1750?

   A. New York
   B. Virginia
   C. Maryland
   D. South Carolina

DIRECTIONS: Study the table and the passage, read each question, then choose the **best** answer.

ESTIMATED REGIONAL POPULATION OF COLONIES, 1770

REGION	POPULATION
New England	539,800
Middle Colonies	555,900
Southern Colonies	994,400

As the late 1700s approached, the British colonies began to grow at an extremely fast rate. In fact, by 1775, the colonial population would reach nearly ten times the size it had been in 1700. Some of this growth resulted from continued immigration to the colonies. However, the bulk of this population growth was caused by very high birth rates and low death rates.

6. Based on information in the table, which statement accurately describes the Middle Colonies?

   A. The Middle Colonies had the smallest population of any colonial region.
   B. Massachusetts represented more than half of the Middle Colonies' population.
   C. About 400,000 fewer people lived in the Middle Colonies than in the Southern Colonies.
   D. The Middle Colonies had a smaller average population per colony than New England.

7. Which of the following best accounts for the population growth in the colonies?

   A. The colonies experienced natural increases due to birth and death rates.
   B. German and Scots-Irish settlers began moving to the colonies.
   C. The health of colonists declined over time.
   D. Many people moved to the colonies to find manufacturing jobs.

UNIT 2

⭐ Spotlighted Item: **FILL-IN-THE-BLANK**

DIRECTIONS: Study the table, read each question, then write your answers in each box.

NATIVE AMERICAN CONFLICTS IN COLONIAL AMERICA

CONFLICT	REGION	EVENTS/OUTCOME
Pequot Revolt (1636–1637)	New England	Conflict grows as colonists move west into Massachusetts and Connecticut; colonists accuse a Pequot Indian of killing a settler, and they burn a village in retaliation; Pequot attack Connecticut town; settlers and Narragansett Indians then burn and destroy Pequot's primary village; many Pequot lose their lives
King Philip's War (1675–1676)	New England	Wampanoag and other groups respond to encroachment on lands in southeastern Massachusetts with armed conflict; many losses for colonists and Native Americans; Native American forces eventually weaken; many Native Americans forced to leave their homes
Yamassee War (1715)	Southern Colonies	Conflict grows between colonists and Creek Indians seeking new lands; colonists enlist help from Cherokee and Yamassee to defeat Creek
Raid on Kittanning (1756)	Middle Colonies	Pennsylvania colonists raid Delaware village of Kittanning; part of a series of violent conflicts between Native Americans and colonists over rights to land

8. Based on information in the table, the earliest conflict between Native Americans and Colonial Americans occurred in the region of

   [   ] .

9. During the Yamassee War, colonists fought the Creek Indians and defeated them with the help of the

   [   ] .

10. According to information in the table, Pennsylvania colonists were involved in a battle in which Native American village?

    [   ]

11. Based on information in the table, conflicts between Native Americans and inhabitants of Colonial America usually began over disputes about

    [   ] .

12. According to information in the table, which event occurred first: settlers and Narragansett Indians destroy the Pequot's village, or the Pequot attack a town in Connecticut?

    [   ]

13. To what does the term *Delaware* refer in the phrase "Delaware village of Kittanning"?

    [   ]

DIRECTIONS: Study the table and the passage, read each question, then choose the **best** answer.

REGIONAL DIFFERENCES

REGION	ECONOMY	SETTLEMENT PATTERNS
New England	Agriculture, fishing, shipping, lumber, trade	Towns
Middle Colonies	Agriculture, trade, small industries	Small farms and some large cities
Southern Colonies	Agriculture	Large plantations and small farms

While the original thirteen colonies were united under British rule, each colonial region developed a different way of life. In New England, most colonists lived in towns. Many colonists in the region farmed, but others worked in industries such as fishing, shipping, lumber, and trade.

In the Middle Colonies, most people lived and worked on small farms. However, some large cities, such as Philadelphia and New York, grew in the region. Trade and some small industries were also important.

The Southern Colonies featured many large plantations. Agriculture was the dominant economic activity in this region.

14. Based on the table and the passage, which economic activity occurred in each region?

    A. agriculture
    B. commerce
    C. fishing
    D. small industries

15. The second column of the table contains information about which topic?

    A. New England Colonies
    B. Middle Colonies
    C. economic activities of each region
    D. settlement patterns of each region

16. In which colony might people be more quickly informed about news and events?

    A. Maryland
    B. South Carolina
    C. Massachusetts
    D. Georgia

17. What information could you learn from the passage that you could not find in the table?

    A. the number of people living in each colonial region
    B. specific examples of large cities in the Middle Colonies
    C. the types of plantations found in the Southern Colonies
    D. the industries in which New England colonists worked

18. The economic patterns established in the colonial era relate directly to which future historical event?

    A. the French and Indian War
    B. the American Revolution
    C. the Great Depression
    D. the Civil War

19. Which of the following assumptions can you logically make about the reason for the differences among the colonies?

    A. Geography and climate played a large part in the differences among the colonies.
    B. The temperate New England climate fostered the growth of large plantations.
    C. Because the Southern Colonies were farthest south, their climate and geography encouraged industries.
    D. The large forests and rocky lands of the Middle Colonies encouraged fur trapping and the lumber industry.

Main Idea and Details

Use with **Student Book** pp. 26–27

SS CONTENT TOPICS: I.USH.a, I.USH.b.1, I.USH.b.5, I.CG.a, I.CG.b.2, I.CG.b.3, I.CG.b.4, I.CG.b.5, I.CG.b.6, I.CG.c.1, I.CG.c.3, II.CG.d.1, II.CG.d.2, I.E.f, , II.G.c.1, II.G.c.3
SS PRACTICES: SSP.1.a, SSP.1.b, SSP.2.a, SSP.2.b, SSP.4.a, SSP.6.a, SSP.6.b, SSP.6.c

1 Review the Skill

The **main idea** is the most important point of a passage or paragraph. **Supporting details** provide additional information about the main idea. Such details may include facts, statistics, explanations, descriptions, and graphics. A main idea may be clearly stated, such as in a title or topic sentence, or it may be implied. If the main idea is implied, you must use logic and make assumptions to determine it. The main idea is an all-encompassing concept, not a small detail.

2 Refine the Skill

By refining the skill of understanding the main idea and identifying details in a passage, you will improve your study and test-taking abilities, especially as they relate to the GED® Social Studies Test. Study the passage and map below. Then answer the questions that follow.

The original territory of the United States, as defined by the treaties of November 30, 1782, and September 3, 1783, with Great Britain, was bounded on the north by Canada, on the south by the Spanish Colonies of East and West Florida, on the east by the Atlantic Ocean, and on the west by the Mississippi River. It included the Thirteen Original Colonies and the areas claimed by them. One of the difficult problems of the new nation was the existence of extensive unoccupied territory between the Thirteen Original Colonies and the Mississippi River. Seven of the Colonies claimed large parts of this territory and some of the claims were conflicting.

From nationalatlas.gov, accessed 2013

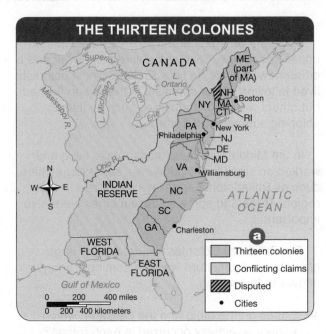

THE THIRTEEN COLONIES

a On this map, the key provides details about the boundary divisions of different lands.

USING LOGIC

A writer may support a main idea with a graphic, such as a map. To understand the relationships among ideas, look for connections between the passage and the graphic.

1. What is the main idea of the passage?

   A. The colonies were in conflict with Great Britain over parts of Canada.
   B. There were disputed land claims among the colonies.
   C. The colonies were arguing with Spain over ownership of West and East Florida.
   D. There were conflicting claims among the colonies over land west of the Mississippi River.

2. How does the map provide a supporting detail for the main idea in the passage?

   A. It shows the thirteen colonies.
   B. It shows West and East Florida.
   C. It shows the large size of the unoccupied territory.
   D. It shows that the Great Lakes border Canada.

★ Spotlighted Item: **HOT SPOT**

DIRECTIONS: Study the passage and map. Then mark on the map the **best** answer to the question.

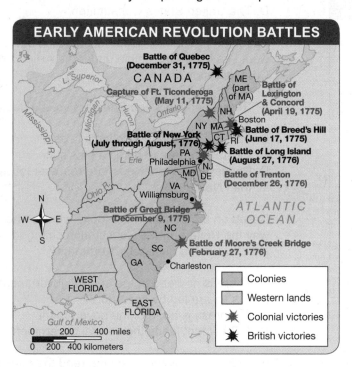

EARLY AMERICAN REVOLUTION BATTLES

From William S. Styker's "An Eyewitness Account of the Battle of Trenton":

Dec. 27, 1776—Here we are back in our camp with the prisoners and trophies. ...

It is a glorious victory. It will rejoice the hearts of our friends everywhere and give new life to our hitherto waning fortunes. Washington has baffled the enemy in his retreat from New York. ... If he does nothing more he will live in history as a great military commander.

3. The colonists' first victory after declaring independence was significant. Circle on the map the state in which that victory occurred.

4. Place an **X** on the map next to the battle to which Styker most likely refers when he references Washington's retreat.

DIRECTIONS: Study the passage and read the questions, then choose the **best** answer to each question.

From the Declaration of Independence:

We, therefore, the representatives of the United States of America, in General Congress, assembled ... do, in the name, and by the authority of the good people of these colonies, solemnly publish and declare, that these united colonies are, and of right ought to be free and independent states; that they are absolved from all allegiance to the British Crown, and that all political connection between them and the state of Great Britain, is and ought to be totally dissolved; and that as free and independent states, they have full power to levy war, conclude peace, contract alliances, establish commerce, and to do all other acts and things which independent states may of right do.

5. What is the main idea of the Declaration of Independence?

A. overthrow Britain's government
B. end political loyalty to Britain
C. declare war on Britain
D. end oppressive governments everywhere

6. Which detail supports the main idea that the colonists will govern themselves?

A. "We, ... in the name, and by the authority of the good people of these colonies"
B. "these united colonies are ... free and independent"
C. "all political connection between them and the state of Great Britain, is ... dissolved"
D. "as free and independent states, they have full power to levy war"

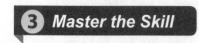

DIRECTIONS: Study the information presented in the table and the passage, read the questions, then choose the **best** answers to each question.

COMPARING GOVERNMENT PLANS

	ARTICLES OF CONFEDERATION	U.S. CONSTITUTION
Government	Weak central government, with no executive	Strong central government, with President
Legislature	One house; one vote per state	Two houses; one vote per senator or representative
Taxes	Collected by states	Collected by national government
New states	Admitted through agreement of nine states	Admitted through agreement by Congress
Amendments	Agreed upon by all states	Agreed upon by three-fourths of states

After declaring independence from Britain, the American colonies set forth to govern themselves. First, however, they needed a plan of government. In 1776 and 1777, colonial leaders wrote the Articles of Confederation. American leaders purposefully designed the Articles to limit the national government's power to make and enforce laws. The Articles were adopted by Congress on November 15, 1777, and fully ratified by all states on March 1, 1781.

Some important achievements occurred under the Articles, including a plan for new states in the Northwest Ordinance of 1787. However, the weak central government made it difficult for the states to function as one nation. In particular, under the Articles of Confederation, the national government was unable to tax or regulate trade among states. In 1787, American leaders proposed the United States Constitution, which established a strong national government.

7. Which of the following titles best expresses the main idea of the passage?

   A. Birth of the Northwest Ordinance
   B. End of the American Revolution
   C. The First Plan of Government
   D. The United States Constitution

8. Based on the details of the table, which act would have been possible under the Articles of Confederation?

   A. Representatives and Senators vote to declare war.
   B. The state of Virginia collects taxes.
   C. All states agree to admit a new state.
   D. Pennsylvania receives more representatives than New Jersey.

9. Based on the details of the table, what is one way the United States Constitution changed the structure of the national government?

   A. There is no head of the central government.
   B. States are led by governors.
   C. Congress is head of the government.
   D. A President leads the central government.

DIRECTIONS: Study the passage, read the question, then choose the **best** answer.

After the American Revolution ended in 1783, the United States had a large amount of debt. The situation was so bad that the government could not pay many soldiers for their services during the war. Also, they did not have money to pay government officials. The United States had a national debt of around $40 million and owed $12 million to foreign countries. The individual states carried a combined debt of $25 million.

10. Based on the details of the table, why would the structure of the Articles of Confederation make it difficult for the national government to solve this debt problem?

    A. Only the states had the power to levy taxes.
    B. There was no President to submit a national budget.
    C. The states had no economic plan.
    D. Congress had to negotiate for loans with foreign governments.

DIRECTIONS: Study the information presented in the passage and the table, read the questions, then choose the **best** answer to each question.

In the summer of 1787, a total of 55 delegates attended the Constitutional Convention in Philadelphia. The United States Constitution that they submitted for ratification in September was vastly different from the Articles of Confederation. The Constitution established a strong national government, with a President, a bicameral (two houses) legislature, and a Supreme Court. The legislature was a mixture of equal and proportional representation.

All three branches of the national government were powerful, but checked one another in a system popularly known as "checks and balances." At the time it was submitted for ratification, the Constitution had no provision for protecting personal freedoms. Many states remembered how the oppression of those freedoms caused the colonies to break from Britain and were concerned about having a strong national government that did not secure freedoms in the new United States. Nevertheless, the Constitution would become law after ratification by nine states. The Bill of Rights was added to the Constitution in 1791.

RATIFICATION OF U.S. CONSTITUTION

DATE	STATE	VOTE
Dec. 7, 1787	Delaware	30–0
Dec. 12, 1787	Pennsylvania	46–23
Dec. 18, 1787	New Jersey	38–0
Jan. 9, 1788	Connecticut	128–40
Feb. 2, 1788	Georgia	26–0
Feb. 6, 1788	Massachusetts	187–168
April 28, 1788	Maryland	63–11
May 23, 1788	South Carolina	149–73
June 21, 1788	New Hampshire	57–47
June 25, 1788	Virginia	89–79
July 26, 1788	New York	30–27
Nov. 21, 1789	North Carolina	194–77
May 29, 1790	Rhode Island	34–32

11. Based on the details in the passage, which small state may have been most concerned about proportional representation in Congress?

    A. Rhode Island
    B. Pennsylvania
    C. New York
    D. South Carolina

12. Based on the details in the passage, why might the vote for ratification have been marginal in a state such as Massachusetts, for example?

    A. John Adams was not elected as the first President.
    B. The state wanted to be its own country.
    C. Leaders were concerned that personal liberties were not protected.
    D. Massachusetts had few delegates.

13. Which of the following titles best expresses the main idea of the passage?

    A. Checks and Balances
    B. The Constitutional Convention
    C. Protecting Personal Freedoms
    D. From Convention to Ratification

14. Which of the following best expresses the main idea of the passage as supported by the table?

    A. New York and Virginia preferred the Articles of Confederation over the Constitution.
    B. States had various concerns about and timetables for ratifying the Constitution.
    C. Most states ratified the Constitution unanimously.
    D. New Hampshire's ratification of the Constitution led New York and Virginia to do the same.

Categorize

Use with *Student Book* pp. 28–29

SS CONTENT TOPICS: I.USH.b.3, I.USH.b.4, I.USH.b.6, II.USH.e, II.G.b.1, II.G.c.1, II.G.c.3, II.G.d.1, II.G.d.2, II.G.d.3, II.G.d.4, II.CG.e.1, I.E.a, II.E.g
SS PRACTICES: SSP.1.a, SSP.1.b, SSP.2.b, SSP.6.b

1 Review the Skill

To **categorize** means to place pieces of information into groups or categories of similar or related items. In social studies, you may categorize people, ideas, or events. You may also categorize types of history, such as social, military, political, or gender histories. Categorizing allows you to gain a fuller understanding of the information presented.

When you categorize information, look for parallel terms that you can identify as categories. For instance, when learning about the history of a place, you might formulate categories based on population, ethnicity, and gender distribution.

2 Refine the Skill

By refining the skill of categorizing information, you will improve your study and test-taking abilities, especially as they relate to the GED® Social Studies Test. Study the table and the information presented below. Then answer the questions that follow.

a Statistics often lend themselves to being categorized in different ways. For instance, these percentages may be categorized by high numbers, low numbers, or gender.

b The title of this table refers to gender, so look for the percentages to be organized into two categories: male and female. In addition, they are further categorized into years.

b IMMIGRATION TO THE UNITED STATES BY GENDER, 1820–1830

Year	Percentage **a**	
	Male	Female
1820	69.8	30.2
1821	74.2	25.8
1822	77.5	22.5
1823	79.0	21.0
1824	80.1	19.9
1825	74.2	25.8
1826	70.9	29.1
1827	71.7	28.3
1828	65.4	34.6
1829	65.2	34.8
1830	72.5	27.5

TEST-TAKING TIPS

Look closely at the title of the table and the column headings. The title and headings describe the contents of the table, allowing you to understand how the information has been categorized.

1. Which statement best describes the category 1824?

   A. the year with equal percentages of male and female immigrants
   B. the year with the lowest percentage of male immigrants
   C. the year with the lowest percentage of female immigrants
   D. the year with the highest percentage of female immigrants

2. In what other categories might these immigration statistics best be organized?

   A. countries of origin
   B. military events
   C. Federalists and Anti-Federalists
   D. political and economic histories

★ Spotlighted Item: **FILL-IN-THE-BLANK**

DIRECTIONS: Study the map. Then fill in your answers in the boxes below.

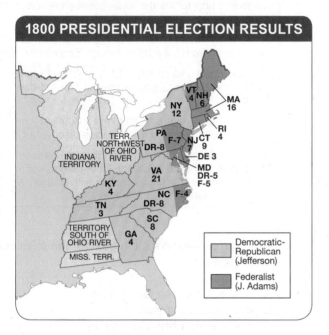

1800 PRESIDENTIAL ELECTION RESULTS

3. Which state categorized as voting Democratic-Republican had the most electoral votes?

4. Which states were categorized as casting both Democratic-Republican and Federalist electoral votes?

5. In which category is the state of Vermont?

DIRECTIONS: Study the passage, read the questions, then choose the **best** answer to each question.

George Washington believed that political parties would prove harmful to the new United States. In his 1796 farewell address as President, he discussed his views of these parties and his concerns for their impact on the country:

"the common and continual mischiefs of the spirit of party are sufficient to make it the interest and duty of a wise people to discourage and restrain it.

It serves always to distract the public councils and enfeeble public administration. It agitates the community with ill-founded jealousies and false alarms, kindles the animosity of one against another, foments occasionally riot and insurrection. It opens the door to foreign influence and corruption, which finds a facilitated access to the government itself through the channels of party passions."

6. In the passage, Washington describes several types of potentially harmful effects of political parties. The bribery of an elected official by another government can be categorized under which of the following harmful effects?

A. distracted public councils
B. animosity between groups
C. riot and insurrection
D. foreign influence and corruption

7. Today, into what two major political parties are Americans categorized?

A. Council and Administration
B. Democrat and Republican
C. Federalist and Anti-Federalist
D. Libertarian and Independent

UNIT 2

DIRECTIONS: Study the passage, read the questions, then choose the **best** answer to each question.

In 1803, French Emperor Napoleon Bonaparte, faced with an imminent war with Britain, finally agreed to sell the Louisiana Territory to the United States. Napoleon feared that Britain might try to occupy the territory. The Louisiana Purchase, as it became known, included more than 800,000 square miles of land west of the Mississippi River. The United States paid $15 million for the land. President Thomas Jefferson wanted to acquire the land to continue westward expansion of the United States and to gain full control of the Mississippi River.

8. How is Bonaparte's decision to sell the Louisiana Territory best categorized?

   A. economic
   B. religious
   C. political
   D. social

9. How is President Jefferson's decision to make the Louisiana Purchase based on the acquirement of land best categorized?

   A. geographic
   B. political
   C. safety
   D. military

10. How is President Jefferson's decision to make the Louisiana Purchase based on control of the Mississippi River best categorized?

    A. military
    B. economic
    C. political
    D. social

11. Under which U.S. history category would the Louisiana Purchase best be categorized?

    A. Articles of Confederation
    B. Manifest Destiny
    C. Indian policy
    D. slavery

DIRECTIONS: Study the table, read each question, then choose the **best** answer to each question.

THE LEWIS AND CLARK EXPEDITION

Commissioned by President Thomas Jefferson; officially called the Corps of Discovery; main goal was to find northern water route between Atlantic and Pacific oceans
Led by army officers Meriwether Lewis and William Clark; lasted from May 1804 through September 1806
Journey began and ended in St. Louis; the Corps reached the Pacific Ocean bordering present-day Oregon
Clark served as naturalist and kept a detailed journal of the new plants and animal species discovered
Failed in main mission to find Northwest Passage; information gathered about the land, plants, and animals and successful interaction with Native American groups proved valuable

12. How can Jefferson's main goal for the mission be categorized?

    A. Native American interaction
    B. westward expansion
    C. national security and military
    D. commerce and trade

13. Under which categories might the results of the Lewis and Clark expedition be placed?

    A. trade and commerce
    B. science and culture
    C. arts and volunteerism
    D. military and defense

14. The justification for the Louisiana Purchase and the Lewis and Clark expedition could both be placed under what category?

    A. religion
    B. politics
    C. economics
    D. civil rights

DIRECTIONS: Study the table and the passage, read the questions, then choose the **best** answer to each question.

NORTHWEST TERRITORY STATES

State	Year of Statehood	State Number
Ohio	1803	17th
Indiana	1816	19th
Illinois	1818	21st
Michigan	1837	26th
Wisconsin	1848	30th

When Congress passed the Northwest Ordinance in July of 1787, the Northwest Territory was created. The new territory was a sizeable area of federal land east of the Mississippi River between the Great Lakes and the Ohio River. At the same time, Congress established a form of government for the Northwest Territory and declared how various areas of the land might eventually become states.

The Northwest Ordinance required the creation of at least three but not more than five states from the Northwest Territory, and the boundaries of each new state were defined. The Ordinance prohibited slavery and required each new state to number at least 60,000 inhabitants to qualify for statehood.

15. Which state could be placed in a category of states formed after 1840?

   A. Ohio
   B. Indiana
   C. Michigan
   D. Wisconsin

16. The information presented in the table and the passage categorizes states created from the Northwest Territory. How else could this group of states be categorized?

   A. free states
   B. states west of the Mississippi River
   C. states south of the Ohio River
   D. slave states

DIRECTIONS: Study the passage, read the questions, then choose the **best** answer to each question.

In October of 1803, President Thomas Jefferson addressed Congress and encouraged the lawmakers to approve the Louisiana Purchase.

From Thomas Jefferson's Third Annual Message to Congress, 1803:

While the prosperity and sovereignty of the Mississippi and its waters secure an independent outlet for the produce of the western States, and an uncontrolled navigation through their whole course, free from collision with other powers and the dangers to our peace from that source, the fertility of the country, its climate and extent, promise in due season important aids to our treasury, an ample provision for our prosperity, and a wide-spread field for the blessings of freedom and equal laws.

17. What two categories of benefits does Jefferson say the United States will receive from the Louisiana Purchase?

   A. alliances with Spain and control of the Gulf of Mexico
   B. opportunities for building factories and the use of military facilities in the region
   C. safe passage through the area and financial gain from the area's resources
   D. support from French colonists and the acquisition of a well-settled territory

18. Which category of the nation's economy does Jefferson mention twice?

   A. industry
   B. agriculture
   C. shipping
   D. tourism

Sequence

Use with *Student Book* pp. 30–31

① Review the Skill

SS CONTENT TOPICS: II.CG.e.3, I.USH.a, I.USH.b.2, I.USH.b.6, I.USH.b.7, II.G.b.1, II.G.c.1, II.G.d.1, II.G.d.2, II.G.d.3, II.G.d.4
SS PRACTICES: SSP.1.a, SSp.1.b, SSP.2.a, SSP.2.b, SSP.3.a, SSP.3.b, SSP.6.b, SSP.10.c

To **sequence** events is to arrange them in the order in which they occur. Understanding the sequence in which events take place is vital to the study of social studies. Sequencing is especially important when studying history. The sequence in which historical events take place can help to explain how a single event might be the outcome of an earlier event and also how it might affect a later event.

Watch closely for words or phrases that indicate a sequence of events. Authors usually write about historical events chronologically, or in the order in which they occur. At times, however, authors may move back and forth in time to write about a particular subject.

② Refine the Skill

By refining the skill of sequencing, you will improve your study and test-taking abilities, especially as they relate to the GED® Social Studies Test. Study the graphic organizer and information below. Then answer the questions that follow.

| A lengthy era of peace started in Europe in 1815. | → | Political leaders in the United States began to focus on domestic issues. | → | Americans began to push Native Americans off their lands east of the Mississippi River. | → | Many Americans established farms on lands once controlled by Native Americans. |

a Sequential graphic organizers show the order of events from left to right or top to bottom. The arrows indicate movement from one event to the next.

b Look for key words in passages that indicate sequence. Here the author uses the word *after* to indicate when Monroe went to New England.

What became known as the Era of Good Feelings began around the time that James Monroe took office for his first term as President of the United States. The Democratic-Republican Party, which Monroe represented, had become much stronger than the Federalist Party. Monroe proved to be a very popular President with the American people. After his victory in the 1816 election, President Monroe embarked on a tour of New England. During this celebratory tour, a Massachusetts newspaper coined the term "Era of Good Feelings."

TEST-TAKING TIPS

When you are asked to sequence historical events in a test passage, use the margin or scrap paper to make a chronological list of key events.

1. Which of the following events preceded James Monroe's tour of New England?

   A. use of the term "Era of Good Feelings"
   B. fall of the Democratic-Republican Party
   C. Monroe's reelection as President
   D. election of 1816

2. Why did many Native Americans lose their lands?

   A. A war began in Europe.
   B. They wanted to move west of the Mississippi.
   C. Settlers wanted to farm the land.
   D. President Monroe ordered them off their lands.

Spotlighted Item: HOT SPOT

DIRECTIONS: Study the graphic organizer and the questions. Then mark on the graphic organizer the **best** answer to each question.

BATTLE OF NEW ORLEANS

British hope to gain access to Mississippi Valley by capturing New Orleans.

↓

British and American forces arrive near New Orleans in late 1814.

↓

On December 24, 1814, British and American diplomats in Belgium make peace and agree to Treaty of Ghent.

↓

Many small conflicts occur near New Orleans in late 1814 and early 1815. News of the signing of the treaty has not yet reached the United States.

↓

The main battle of New Orleans occurs on January 8, 1815.

↓

The Americans win a decisive victory.

↓

The British give up plans and leave for Britain.

3. Circle the information on the graphic organizer that describes what happened after the Americans won a decisive victory in the Battle of New Orleans.

4. Place a check mark on the graphic organizer next to the box that explains where the British and the American forces were located when the Treaty of Ghent was signed.

DIRECTIONS: Study the information presented in the passage, read the questions, then choose the **best** answer to each question.

From James Monroe's "First Inaugural Address":

Such, then, being the highly favored condition of our country, it is in the interest of every citizen to maintain it. What are the dangers which menace us? If any exist they ought to be ascertained and guarded against.

In explaining my sentiments on this subject it may be asked, What raised us to the present happy state? How did we accomplish the Revolution? How remedy the defects of the first instrument of our Union … ? How sustain and pass with glory through the late war? The Government has been in the hands of the people.

5. Which of the following events occurred first?

A. Monroe's inauguration
B. the election of 1816
C. the American Revolution
D. the writing of the Articles of Confederation

6. The last challenge Monroe describes, maintaining "glory through the late war," refers to which of the following events?

A. the Civil War
B. the War of 1812
C. the American Revolution
D. the French and Indian War

7. To which most recent document is President Monroe likely referring when he states, "The Government has been in the hands of the people"?

A. the Articles of Confederation
B. the Treaty of Ghent
C. the Declaration of Independence
D. a Massachusetts news article

UNIT 2

DIRECTIONS: Study the information presented in the passage, read the questions, then choose the **best** answer to each question.

From Andrew Jackson's "Message to Congress on Indian Removal," 1830:

It gives me pleasure to announce to Congress that the benevolent policy of the Government, steadily pursued for nearly thirty years, in relation to the removal of the Indians beyond the white settlements is approaching to a happy consummation. Two important tribes have accepted the provision made for their removal at the last session of Congress, and it is believed that their example will induce the remaining tribes also to seek the same obvious advantages. …

The present policy of the Government is but a continuation of the same progressive change by a milder process. The tribes which occupied the countries now constituting the Eastern States were annihilated or have melted away to make room for the whites. The waves of population and civilization are rolling to the westward, and we now propose to acquire the countries occupied by the red men of the South and West by a fair exchange, and, at the expense of the United States, to send them to land where their existence may be prolonged and perhaps made perpetual.

8. According to Jackson's speech, which of the following events has already taken place?

    A. Most Native American groups are gone from the eastern United States.
    B. The final two Native American groups in the eastern United States refused to leave their lands.
    C. Migration of white settlers to the western portions of the United States has slowed.
    D. The policy the government has used for the past thirty years to relocate Native Americans has failed.

9. What does Jackson suggest about the evolution of the policies of the United States toward Native Americans?

    A. The policies have been only moderately successful over time.
    B. The policies have become less harsh and confrontational toward Native Americans.
    C. The policies have led to a consensus agreement among Native American groups facing relocation.
    D. The policies have been inconsistent between presidencies.

DIRECTIONS: Study the information presented in the passage, read the questions, then choose the **best** answer to each question.

After serving as Secretary of State, James Monroe received the Democratic-Republican nomination for President in 1816 and handily won the general election. Monroe faced many foreign policy challenges. In 1817, an agreement led to the reduction of both British and American forces on the Great Lakes. Another agreement made official the United States' control of Florida.

Monroe won reelection in 1820. The most notable event of Monroe's second term proved to be his endorsement of Manifest Destiny and the proposal of the Monroe Doctrine in 1823. The Monroe Doctrine became one of the foundations of foreign policy for the young nation. The United States government has upheld this doctrine ever since. The Monroe Doctrine states that European nations must not interfere with any nations in the Western Hemisphere or try to acquire new territory there.

10. How many years passed between the time Monroe was first elected President and his proposal of the Monroe Doctrine?

    A. two years
    B. four years
    C. five years
    D. seven years

11. Why might voters have reelected Monroe in 1820?

    A. He settled many disputes with foreign countries.
    B. He had been Secretary of State.
    C. He saved the Federalist Party.
    D. He proposed the Monroe Doctrine.

12. Which of the following events occurred after 1820?

    A. President Monroe won reelection.
    B. President Monroe endorsed Manifest Destiny and proposed the Monroe Doctrine.
    C. President Monroe helped form an agreement between the British and the Americans regarding the Great Lakes.
    D. President Monroe secured the state of Florida for the United States.

DIRECTIONS: Study the graphic organizer, read the questions, then fill in your answer in each box.

U.S. EXPANSION IN THE EARLY 1800s

1804: Lewis and Clark expedition begins the exploration of the Louisiana Purchase.

↓

1812: Louisiana becomes the first U.S. state located west of the Mississippi River.

↓

1821: Missouri joins the United States.

↓

1830s: United States designates some western areas as Indian Territory.

↓

1835: American settlers in Texas lead the Texas Revolution against Mexican forces.

↓

1836: Arkansas joins the United States.

13. Which state gained statehood before Missouri?

14. Based on the graphic organizer, what event occurred first that led to the exploration of western territories and expansion of the United States?

DIRECTIONS: Study the information presented in the passages, read the questions, then choose the **best** answer to each question.

After the War of 1812, many political leaders in the United States believed that the nation should look to expand its boundaries. One such leader was James Monroe's Secretary of State, John Quincy Adams. Adams helped develop the policy that became known as the Monroe Doctrine. This policy stated that European colonization in the Americas would be viewed as an act of aggression toward the United States. In addition, the Monroe Doctrine allowed for the possibility of future U.S. expansion within the Americas.

From James Monroe's "Seventh Annual Message to Congress," December 2, 1823:

With the existing colonies or dependencies of any European power we have not interfered and shall not interfere. But with the Governments who have declared their independence and maintain it, and whose independence we have … acknowledged, we could not view any interposition for the purpose of oppressing them, or controlling in any other manner

their destiny, by any European power in any other light than as the manifestation of an unfriendly disposition toward the United States.

15. The Monroe Doctrine was likely issued after which event?

   A. The United States annexed Texas.
   B. John Quincy Adams became President.
   C. Britain agreed to stop continued expansion into western North America.
   D. Spain asked other European countries to stop revolts in Spanish-American colonies.

16. Which later event reflected the Monroe Doctrine's importance to the United States?

   A. the Vietnam War
   B. the Korean War
   C. the Mexican War
   D. the Civil War

UNIT 2

Cause and Effect

Use with **Student Book** pp. 32-33

1 Review the Skill

SS CONTENT TOPICS: I. USH.a.1, I.USH.c.1, I.USH.c.2, I.USH.c.3, I.USH.c.4, I.CG.d.2, II.CG.e.1, II.CG.e.3, II.G.b.1, II.G.c.2, II.G.d.2, II.G.d.3, I.E.a
SS PRACTICES: SSP.1.a, SSP.1.b, SSP.2.a, SSP.2.b, SSP.3.b, SSP.3.c, SSP.4.a, SSP.6.b, SSP.11.b

By understanding **causes** and **effects**, you can examine how historical events relate to one another. For instance, the effect of one event may be the cause of another event or many events. In this way, you can link a series of events together like a chain to understand how they all relate to one another and produce an ultimate outcome.

A single cause will most likely have more than one effect, and a single effect often has multiple causes. This is particularly true when studying historical events.

2 Refine the Skill

By refining the skill of understanding causes and effects, you will improve your study and test-taking abilities, especially as they relate to the GED® Social Studies Test. Study the map and the passage below. Then answer the questions that follow.

[O]n December 20, South Carolina seceded from the Union and called on other southern states to do likewise. … Though Lincoln was not yet in office, his actions and opinions were influential. He received numerous letters about the secession crisis, asking for his position and offering advice. … Within forty days, Mississippi, Florida, Alabama, Georgia, Louisiana, and Texas followed South Carolina's lead. They established the Confederate States of America and inaugurated Jefferson Davis of Mississippi as their president, all before Lincoln took office. On March 4, 1861, Lincoln delivered his inaugural address to a divided Union.

From loc.gov, accessed 2013

a A visual such as a map may help to clarify causes and effects.

b Notice where the people who voted for Lincoln lived. Where did many of his opponents live?

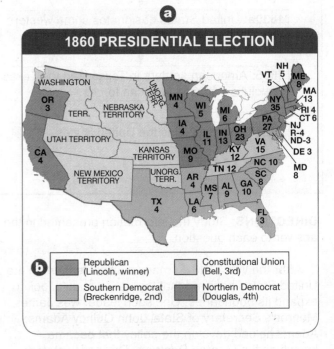

a

1860 PRESIDENTIAL ELECTION

b
- Republican (Lincoln, winner)
- Southern Democrat (Breckenridge, 2nd)
- Constitutional Union (Bell, 3rd)
- Northern Democrat (Douglas, 4th)

USING LOGIC

Sometimes a sequence of events suggests a cause. You can ask yourself these questions: What happened first? What happened next? How are these two events related?

1. What caused the Southern states to secede from the Union?

   A. Davis's election
   B. Lincoln's election
   C. votes from the territories
   D. establishment of the Confederacy

2. What was one effect of the South's secession?

   A. a divided nation with two presidents
   B. Lincoln resigned from office
   C. territories were made states
   D. Oregon joined the Confederacy

DIRECTIONS: Study the table, read the passage, and read the questions. Then choose the **best** answer to each question.

SLAVES AS PERCENT OF TOTAL POPULATION

State	1750 African American/ total population	1790 Slave/ total population	1810 Slave/ total population	1860 Slave/ total population
Alabama				45.12
Arkansas				25.52
Delaware	5.21	15.04	5.75	1.60
Florida				43.97
Georgia	19.23	35.45	41.68	43.72
Kentucky		16.87	19.82	19.51
Louisiana				46.85
Maryland	30.80	32.23	29.30	12.69
Mississippi				55.18
Missouri				9.72
North Carolina	27.13	25.51	30.39	33.35
South Carolina	60.94	43.00	47.30	57.18
Tennessee			17.02	24.84
Texas				30.22
Virginia	43.91	39.14	40.27	30.75
Overall	**37.97**	**33.95**	**33.25**	**32.27**

Sources: Historical Statistics of the United States (1970), Franklin (1988).

Throughout Colonial and pre–Civil War history, people who were enslaved in the United States lived primarily in the South. They comprised less than a tenth of the total Southern population in 1680, but grew to a third of the South's population by 1790. By that time, 293,000 enslaved workers lived in the state of Virginia alone, amounting to more than 40 percent of all enslaved people in the country.

The states of Maryland, North Carolina, and South Carolina each had more than 100,000 slaves. By 1810, the Southern enslaved population reached about 1.1 million; in 1860, that number grew to more than 3.9 million.

Surprisingly, then, in spite of their ever-expanding numbers, enslaved workers typically comprised a minority of local populations. Only in South Carolina and Mississippi prior to the Civil War did enslaved

people outnumber free persons. The majority of Southerners, however, owned no enslaved people. Less than a fourth of white Southerners kept enslaved workers, with half of these holding fewer than five, and fewer than 1% holding more than 100.

Rather than living on large plantations, most enslaved workers lived in small groups. By 1860, the average number of enslaved people residing together was about 10.

3. What was the primary cause for the continuing increase in the number of enslaved people held in Southern states prior to the Civil War?

   A. The U.S. Constitution did not forbid slavery.
   B. Northern states did not require as many workers for their plantations.
   C. Southern states required more workers as their plantations grew in size and number.
   D. The total ratio of enslaved people to the general population grew at the natural rate.

4. Why would you assume that the ratio of the number of enslaved people to the general population declined over time in Delaware?

   A. Plantation agriculture declined over time so enslaved workers became a smaller percentage of the population.
   B. Delaware was not considered a true Southern state.
   C. The population ratio changed because more enslaved people moved to states such as South Carolina and Mississippi, where they made up a larger ratio.
   D. Plantation owners in Delaware decided not to have as many enslaved people.

5. Which statement is true regarding the effect of a population trend?

   A. The percentage of enslaved people in the state of South Carolina in 1860 was less than half of the state's population.
   B. The percentage of enslaved people in the state of Mississippi in 1860 was more than half of the state's population.
   C. The percentage of enslaved people in the state of South Carolina in 1810 was more than half of the state's population.
   D. The percentage of enslaved people in the state of Mississippi in 1810 was more than half of the state's population.

UNIT 2

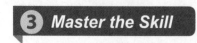

DIRECTIONS: Study the information presented in the table and the passage, read each question, then choose the **best** answer.

CIVIL WAR AMENDMENTS

Thirteenth Amendment	Fourteenth Amendment	Fifteenth Amendment
The Thirteenth Amendment was ratified on December 6, 1865. It abolished slavery "within the United States, or any place subject to their jurisdiction."	Congress ratified the Fourteenth Amendment, sometimes called the "Great Amendment," on July 28, 1868.	The Fifteenth Amendment was ratified March 30, 1870, to protect freed African Americans' voting rights.
Although Congress abolished slavery in the District of Columbia in 1862, and President Abraham Lincoln's Emancipation Proclamation ended the practice of slavery in Confederate states in 1863, at the end of the Civil War, in 1865, the issue had not been resolved at a national level.	The amendment granted citizenship to all persons "born or naturalized in the United States," including former enslaved people, and provided all citizens with "equal protection under the laws," extending the provisions of the Bill of Rights to the states.	It prohibited the national and state governments from disenfranchising voters "on account of race, color, or previous condition of servitude."
Many states passed laws to protect the rights of African Americans, but white people who were against racial equality, mostly from the South, fought against similar laws when Congress tried to pass them.	It also prohibited any state from making or enforcing any laws that took away or hurt an individual's civil rights.	After the Fifteenth Amendment was passed, a large number of freedmen voted during the late 1860s through the 1880s. Freed African Americans used their voting rights to gain political power and to protect their rights.

Prior to the Civil War's Union victory in 1865, Congress had planned for the challenges America would face, especially the integration of four million newly freed African Americans and the readmission to federal representation of former states in rebellion.

Congressional Reconstruction included the Thirteenth, Fourteenth, and Fifteenth Amendments to the Constitution, which provided legal and civil protection to former enslaved people.

Some Southern plantation owners wanted the government to pay for their former enslaved workers. Many people in the North wanted the newly freed African Americans to remain in the South, for fear of losing their jobs to them for less pay and poorer working conditions. Many freedmen were not able to obtain good jobs because of their lack of education and rampant discrimination. The right to vote was an important issue for the newly freed African Americans.

Although many people in the South and the North were against the amendments, the Thirteenth, Fourteenth, and Fifteenth Amendments played an important part in the Civil Rights Movement to come within the next 100 years.

6. What was the primary cause of the ratification of the Thirteenth, Fourteenth, and Fifteenth Amendments?

   A. The Southern states no longer had the need for enslaved workers.
   B. The Northern states decided that they should be entitled to have enslaved workers, too.
   C. The Civil War ended and the North lost.
   D. The Civil War ended and the South lost.

7. Which of the following was a direct effect of the ratification of the Fourteenth Amendment?

   A. Slavery was abolished at the federal level.
   B. Former enslaved people became U.S. citizens.
   C. President Lincoln issued the Emancipation Proclamation.
   D. President Lincoln gave free African Americans the right to vote.

DIRECTIONS: Study the passage and read the questions, then choose the **best** answer to each question.

Congressional Reconstruction, which lasted from 1866 to 1877, was intended to reorganize the Southern states following the Civil War. Reconstruction's goal also was to provide the means for readmitting the former Confederate states back into the Union and to define the means by which whites and freed African Americans would live together in a society where slavery had been abolished. The South, however, did not especially welcome Reconstruction.

During the years after the Civil War, white and African American churches, missionary organizations, and schools began the process of giving the newly emancipated population the opportunity to learn. Former enslaved people of all ages welcomed the opportunity to learn to read and write.

With the protection of the Thirteenth, Fourteenth, and Fifteenth Amendments and the Civil Rights Act of 1866, African Americans enjoyed such freedoms as being allowed to vote, actively participate in political processes, buy land, sometimes even from their former owners, gain meaningful employment, and use public services. Opponents of this progress, however, soon rallied against the newly freed African Americans, trying to erode the gains provided by the amendments.

Many emancipated workers fled from their owners; others became wage earners for them. Most importantly, African Americans could make choices for themselves about where they labored and the type of work they performed.

Although many Southerners disliked Reconstruction, by the 1870s, all of the Southern states were part of the Union again. The South was rebuilding and its cities were growing. Farms also were replanted, with crops such as tobacco and sugar that were not food cash crops, which meant that farmers were growing less food to feed people who lived nearby. Therefore, much of the food had to be shipped in from other parts of the country.

8. What effect of Reconstruction might have hurt the South's economy?

A. Slavery cost more money during Reconstruction.
B. Slavery had been abolished under the Emancipation Proclamation.
C. There were no laborers to employ after the Civil War ended.
D. Slavery had been abolished and workers had to be paid for their labor.

9. Which of the following describes the primary cause for Reconstruction?

A. Northern states wanted to punish the Southern states for damages during the Civil War.
B. Southern states wanted to provide education and jobs to the newly freed African Americans.
C. Congress needed a plan for government of the Southern states and treatment of former enslaved workers following the Civil War.
D. Congress needed a plan for governing the Southern states during the latter years of the Civil War.

10. Which of the following describes one of the ways in which agricultural practices changed in the South as a result of Reconstruction?

A. Northern states planted more cash crops in order to feed the newly freed African Americans.
B. Southern states replanted their plantations with crops that were not food cash crops.
C. Southern farmers had to grow more food to feed the people who lived near their former plantations.
D. Southern farmers shipped most of their food to other parts of the country for others to eat.

Interpret Timelines

Use with *Student Book* pp. 34–35

① Review the Skill

SS CONTENT TOPICS: II.G.b.1, I.USH.d.2, II.USH.f.1, II.USH.f.2, I.USH.f.4, II.USH.f.5, II.USH.f.6, II.USH.f.8, II.USH.f.9
SS PRACTICES: SSP.1.a, SSP.1.b, SSP.2.a, SSP.2.b, SSP.3.a, SSP.4.a, SSP.6.b

Timelines are visual representations of sequences of events. A timeline features equivalent intervals to divide a time period into smaller segments. The dots or buttons placed along the timeline indicate the actual dates during which the events shown on the timeline occur.

Specific details can aid in discovering historical trends that link the events in a timeline. Remember that a trend is not always the culmination of all events on a timeline. A general trend may occur over time, but trends can occur during shorter terms, as well. For example, the last few months before an election can show a small trend, whereas evaluating which political party has controlled the White House or Congress over the past several decades can reveal a large trend.

② Refine the Skill

By refining the skill of interpreting timelines, you will improve your study and test-taking abilities, especially as they relate to the GED® Social Studies Test. Study the information and timeline below. Then answer the questions that follow.

When the National Woman Suffrage Association published *The Blue Book*, the group intended to dispute objections to women having the right to vote. For example, one objection was that it would double the number of people voting who were ignorant. *The Blue Book* cited statistics proving that more girls than boys were graduating from high school, ensuring equal suffrage would increase the number of educated voters.

Another objection was that voting would stop women from caring for their families. *The Blue Book* argued that the act of voting took little time and that most women could find time to read newspapers and educate themselves on issues before voting. Some people believed that women were too emotional and sentimental and could not be trusted with the ballot. The authors of *The Blue Book* pointed out several instances of men in government who had made emotional or sentimental decisions about war and economic policy instead of relying on logic.

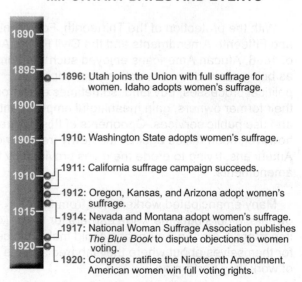

WOMEN'S SUFFRAGE: IMPORTANT DATES AND EVENTS

1896: Utah joins the Union with full suffrage for women. Idaho adopts women's suffrage.

1910: Washington State adopts women's suffrage.

1911: California suffrage campaign succeeds.

1912: Oregon, Kansas, and Arizona adopt women's suffrage.

1914: Nevada and Montana adopt women's suffrage.

1917: National Woman Suffrage Association publishes *The Blue Book* to dispute objections to women voting.

1920: Congress ratifies the Nineteenth Amendment. American women win full voting rights.

MAKING ASSUMPTIONS

You can assume that all events on a timeline relate to a trend of some type. If the relationship of the events is not clear at first, review the events, then draw conclusions.

1. What can you infer about the authors of *The Blue Book*?

   A. They were relatively uninformed about the issues.
   B. They were amused by the objections to women's suffrage.
   C. Even if an objection was true, they denied it.
   D. They used a logical, methodical approach to win an argument.

2. How many states adopted women's suffrage before publication of *The Blue Book*?

   A. eight
   B. nine
   C. seven
   D. ten

DIRECTIONS: Study the information presented on the timeline and in the passage, read the questions, then choose the **best** answer to each question.

MAJOR EVENTS OF WORLD WAR I

World War I, also known as WWI, the First World War, the Great War, or the War to End All Wars, was a world conflict lasting from 1914 to 1919, with fighting lasting until 1918. A Serbian nationalist assassinated Archduke Franz Ferdinand of Austria-Hungary in Sarajevo on June 28, 1914, setting in motion a war that included, among other atrocities, the century's first aerial large-scale bombing and the first large-scale civilian massacres.

Europe's powers aligned themselves after the assassination, a move which escalated the conflicts into war. The allies—chiefly Britain, Russia, and France—fought against the Central Powers—primarily Germany, Turkey, and Austria-Hungary. The war spread, with Europe turning to its friends and colonies for aid. Britain was determined to keep its colonial territories and feared that unless it entered the war, its rival Germany would control Western Europe. The United States joined the war in 1917, when President Woodrow Wilson called on Americans to "make the world safe for democracy." The Treaty of Versailles, signed on June 28, 1919, forced Germany to accept responsibility for the war and ordered it to pay costly reparations. The war thus brought to an end the Austro-Hungarian and German empires.

UNIT 2

1914
June 28: Franz Ferdinand assassinated at Sarajevo
July 28: Austria declares war on Serbia
August 1: Germany declares war on Russia
August 3: Germany declares war on France; invades Belgium
August 4: Britain declares war on Germany
September 6: Battle of Marne begins
October 29: Turkey enters war on Germany's side

1915
January 19: First Zeppelin raid on Britain
April 25: Allied troops land in Gallipoli
May 7: The *Lusitania* passenger liner is sunk by a German U-boat
May 23: Italy declares war on Germany and Austria
August 5: Germany captures Warsaw
December 19: The Allies evacuate Gallipoli

1916
February 21: Start of the Battle of Verdun
April 29: British forces surrender to Turkish forces at Kut
June 4: Start of the Brusilov Offensive
July 1: Start of the Battle of the Somme
August 10: End of the Brusilov Offensive
September 15: First use of tanks en masse at the Somme

1917
February 1: Germany begins submarine warfare campaign
April 6: United States declares war on Germany
October 24: Battle of Caporetto; Italian Army is defeated
November 6: Britain launches major offensive on Western Front
November 20: British tanks win at Cambrai
December 5: Armistice is signed between Germany and Russia

1918
March 3: Russia and Germany sign Treaty of Brest-Litovsk
March 21: Germany breaks through on the Somme
July 15: Second Battle of the Marne
September 19: Turkish forces collapse at Megiddo
October 4: Germany asks Allies for armistice
October 30: Turkey makes peace
November 3: Austria makes peace
November 11: Armistice is signed, ending the war at 11:00 AM

Postwar 1919
January 4: Peace Conference meets at Paris
June 28: Treaty of Versailles is signed by the Germans

3. Which of the following was most responsible for turning the conflicts that started World War I into a world war?

   A. nationalism in Austria-Hungary
   B. extensive alliances formed among nations
   C. territorial disputes in Asia
   D. arms race among European nations

4. How many months elapsed from the assassination of Archduke Ferdinand until the signing of the Treaty of Versailles?

   A. 45 months
   B. 50 months
   C. 60 months
   D. 65 months

5. The rivalry between which two nations became an important cause of World War I?

   A. Britain and Germany
   B. Serbia and Germany
   C. Russia and Austria-Hungary
   D. the United States and France

6. Which event listed below preceded all of the others?

   A. Turkish forces collapse at Megiddo
   B. Battle of Marne begins
   C. British tanks win at Cambrai
   D. end of the Brusilov Offensive

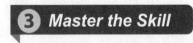

3 *Master the Skill*

DIRECTIONS: Study the information presented in each timeline and passage, read the questions, then choose the **best** answer to each question.

POST–WORLD WAR I AND HITLER'S RISE TO POWER

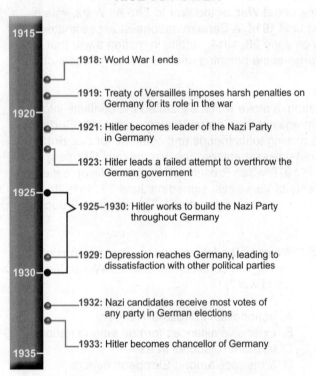

1918: World War I ends

1919: Treaty of Versailles imposes harsh penalties on Germany for its role in the war

1921: Hitler becomes leader of the Nazi Party in Germany

1923: Hitler leads a failed attempt to overthrow the German government

1925–1930: Hitler works to build the Nazi Party throughout Germany

1929: Depression reaches Germany, leading to dissatisfaction with other political parties

1932: Nazi candidates receive most votes of any party in German elections

1933: Hitler becomes chancellor of Germany

THE UNITED STATES ENTERS WORLD WAR II

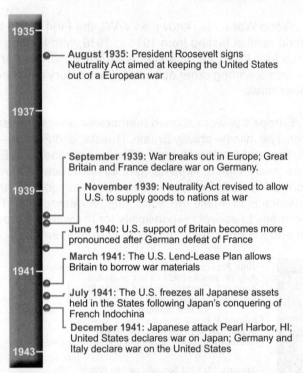

August 1935: President Roosevelt signs Neutrality Act aimed at keeping the United States out of a European war

September 1939: War breaks out in Europe; Great Britain and France declare war on Germany.

November 1939: Neutrality Act revised to allow U.S. to supply goods to nations at war

June 1940: U.S. support of Britain becomes more pronounced after German defeat of France

March 1941: The U.S. Lend-Lease Plan allows Britain to borrow war materials

July 1941: The U.S. freezes all Japanese assets held in the States following Japan's conquering of French Indochina

December 1941: Japanese attack Pearl Harbor, HI; United States declares war on Japan; Germany and Italy declare war on the United States

This timeline illustrates the events that led to Adolf Hitler's rise to Chancellor of Germany. The trend in this timeline connects Germany's loss in World War I to Hitler's formation of a national Nazi Party, to economic depression and political dissatisfaction, to the rise of Hitler and the Nazi Party.

7. What directly led to the Nazi Party receiving the most votes in the 1932 German elections?

   A. German unhappiness with other politicians because of the economic crisis
   B. punitive actions toward the Germans by victorious allies at Versailles
   C. choice of Hitler to lead the Nazi Party
   D. end of World War I in 1918

8. Based on the timeline alone, for how many years was Hitler the leader of the Nazi Party in Germany?

   A. 10 years
   B. 11 years
   C. 12 years
   D. 13 years

The Neutrality Acts were laws intended to limit American involvement in future wars. The Acts were passed after World War I in the early 1930s. The 1935 Neutrality Act banned weapons exports to hostile nations and restricted American travel on those nations' ships. The 1939 Act encouraged support of the Allies, but created product shortages at home. President Franklin D. Roosevelt further eroded neutrality by trading surplus U.S. ships to Britain for access to naval and air bases and providing U.S. military equipment to enemies of Germany and Japan under the Lend-Lease Plan. Congress repealed the Neutrality Acts in 1941.

9. When did the Lend-Lease Plan take effect?

   A. August 1935
   B. June 1940
   C. March 1941
   D. December 1941

10. Why was the Neutrality Act revised in 1939?

   A. Great Britain and France declared war on Germany.
   B. Supplying goods to Allies helped the U.S.
   C. Roosevelt did not run for re-election.
   D. The Japanese attacked Pearl Harbor.

DIRECTIONS: Study the information presented in the timeline, read the questions, then choose the **best** answer to each question.

WORLD WAR II IN EUROPE AND THE PACIFIC

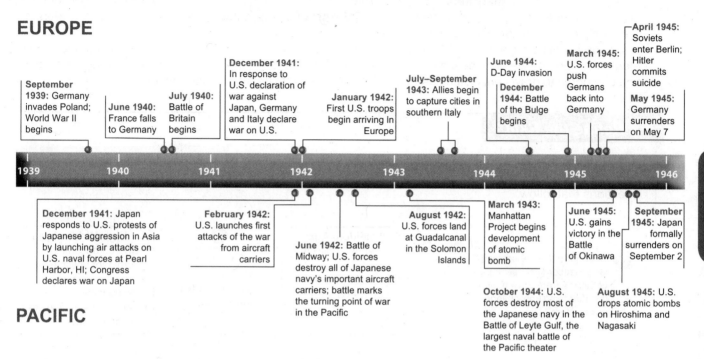

EUROPE

September 1939: Germany invades Poland; World War II begins

June 1940: France falls to Germany

July 1940: Battle of Britain begins

December 1941: In response to U.S. declaration of war against Japan, Germany and Italy declare war on U.S.

January 1942: First U.S. troops begin arriving In Europe

July–September 1943: Allies begin to capture cities in southern Italy

June 1944: D-Day invasion

December 1944: Battle of the Bulge begins

March 1945: U.S. forces push Germans back into Germany

April 1945: Soviets enter Berlin; Hitler commits suicide

May 1945: Germany surrenders on May 7

1939 · 1940 · 1941 · 1942 · 1943 · 1944 · 1945 · 1946

December 1941: Japan responds to U.S. protests of Japanese aggression in Asia by launching air attacks on U.S. naval forces at Pearl Harbor, HI; Congress declares war on Japan

February 1942: U.S. launches first attacks of the war from aircraft carriers

June 1942: Battle of Midway; U.S. forces destroy all of Japanese navy's important aircraft carriers; battle marks the turning point of war in the Pacific

August 1942: U.S. forces land at Guadalcanal in the Solomon Islands

March 1943: Manhattan Project begins development of atomic bomb

October 1944: U.S. forces destroy most of the Japanese navy in the Battle of Leyte Gulf, the largest naval battle of the Pacific theater

June 1945: U.S. gains victory in the Battle of Okinawa

August 1945: U.S. drops atomic bombs on Hiroshima and Nagasaki

September 1945: Japan formally surrenders on September 2

PACIFIC

11. Which of the following gives the dates of parallel events in Europe and the Pacific, respectively?

   A. September 1939 and February 1942
   B. May 1945 and September 1945
   C. June 1941 and May 1942
   D. August 1942 and August 1942

12. Which event on the timeline eventually led to the dropping of atomic bombs on Hiroshima and Nagasaki?

   A. the success of the D-Day invasion
   B. the Battle of Midway
   C. the launch of the Manhattan Project
   D. Hitler's death

13. Based on the information in the timeline, which of the following statements is true?

   A. The Battle of Midway forced Japan to surrender.
   B. Germany controlled the Soviet Union.
   C. Japan joined the war in defense of Germany.
   D. The U.S. Navy was vital in the war against Japan.

14. The timeline supports which of the following trends?

   A. D-Day was the first major turning point in the war.
   B. The Allies first attacked territories that Japan and Germany controlled before directly attacking each country.
   C. The United States focused all of its attention in 1945 in the Pacific.
   D. Japan had a superior air force.

Interpret Diagrams

Use with *Student Book* pp. 46–47

1 Review the Skill

SS CONTENT TOPICS: I.CG.a.1, I.CG.b.5, I.CG.b.6, I.CG.b.7, I.CG.b.9, I.CG.c.1, I.CG.c.2, I.CG.c.3, I.CG.c.4, I.CG.c.6, II.G.b.3, II.G.b.5,
SS PRACTICES: SSP.1.a, SSP.1.b, SSP.3.c, SSP.6.b

Authors often utilize **diagrams** to help illustrate how information is related. Diagrams can show sequences of events or make comparisons or contrasts. By **interpreting diagrams** correctly, you can quickly learn a great deal of information about the diagram's subject.

As you examine a diagram, read the title and headings to identify the diagram's main subject and individual elements. Then notice how the elements are related. By understanding how the items relate to one another, you can begin to draw conclusions about the information contained in the diagram.

2 Refine the Skill

By refining the skill of interpreting diagrams, you will improve your study and test-taking abilities, especially as they relate to the GED® Social Studies Test. Study the information below. Then answer the questions that follow.

a *Government* is the common idea that connects each part of this diagram. How does this diagram show changes in government?

Early Middle Ages
- Small, varied political bodies
- No central authority
- Feudal system provides main European political system

a
European Government Systems in the Middle Ages

High Middle Ages
- Church becomes dominant political force
- Provides some centralization
- Feudal system weakens in some towns

Into Modern Times
- Church's power diminishes through internal and external disputes
- Feudal system diminishes in importance
- Stronger, more centralized national governments emerge

b The arrows in this diagram suggest a progression or sequence of information. Events in a sequence diagram usually are linked.

During 10th–12th centuries, invasions cease and European population growth occurs. **b** → Lords want to clear forests and swamps to create new farm lands. → Peasants help clear land and receive more generous terms from lords. → Advances in agricultural technology improve production and efficiency for peasants.

USING LOGIC

When studying a diagram, examine its format, and think about the clues it gives. Does it suggest a sequence or flow of information? Does it invite a comparison between two or more things?

1. Based on the first diagram, which of the following can be determined about the High Middle Ages?

   A. The Church became the dominant political force in Europe.
   B. No central government authority existed in Europe.
   C. Feudal systems grew in strength in many towns.
   D. Many small, varied political parties first came to power.

2. Which idea can you link to step 4 in the sequence diagram?

   A. Lands cleared for farming were called assarts.
   B. The use of metal tools made cultivating crops easier.
   C. Male and female peasants performed different tasks.
   D. Lords often controlled the mills used to grind flour.

⭐ Spotlighted Item: **DROP-DOWN**

DIRECTIONS: The passage below is incomplete. Use information from the diagram to complete the passage. For each drop-down item, choose the option that correctly completes the sentence.

Rights and Powers	Articles of Confederation	U.S. Constitution
Type of Government	Confederation, with states holding most of the power	Federal system, with power divided between states and central government
Structure of Central Government	Congress with 2 to 7 delegates from each state	Government with 3 branches: executive, legislative and judicial
Executive Branch	No executive at national level; state governors	President and cabinet
Legislative Branch	Congress with 1 house; states have 2 to 7 delegates but each state has 1 vote	Congress with 2 houses: Senate and House of Representatives
Judicial Branch	None at national level; only state courts	System of federal courts and state courts
Trade	Regulates trade with other nations, but not between states	Regulates trade with other nations and between states
Foreign Relations	Conducts relations with other nations	Conducts relations with other nations
Waging War	Carried out by national government	Carried out by national government
Postal Service	Run by national government	Run by national government
Money	Each state coins its own money; no national currency	Federal government coins all money for the nation
Taxation	State governments have power to tax; no taxation power at national level	Both federal and state governments have power to tax
Other Rights Not Mentioned	Powers not listed are retained by the states	Powers not listed are retained by the states

▢ Powers that are the same in Articles and Constitution

Drop-Down Answer Options

3. The Articles of Confederation was the first plan of government for the United States. It lasted only a few years before the U.S. Constitution replaced it. The diagram shows that the central government of the United States under the Articles was much [3. Drop-down 1] than it became under the Constitution. Still, some powers were the same under both documents. For example, the central government controlled the waging of war, foreign relations, foreign trade, and [3. Drop-down 2] under both the Articles and the Constitution.

However, the structure of government under the Constitution is much different than under the Articles. The Articles did not have a national [3. Drop-down 3] or [3. Drop-down 4] branch of government.

3.1 A. stronger
B. larger
C. weaker
D. stricter

3.2 A. taxation
B. money
C. courts
D. mail

3.3 A. executive
B. legislative
C. postal
D. war

3.4 A. postal
B. judicial
C. legislative
D. regulation

UNIT 3

DIRECTIONS: The passage below is incomplete. Use information from the diagram to complete the passage. For each drop-down item, choose the option that correctly completes the sentence.

CHECKS AND BALANCES

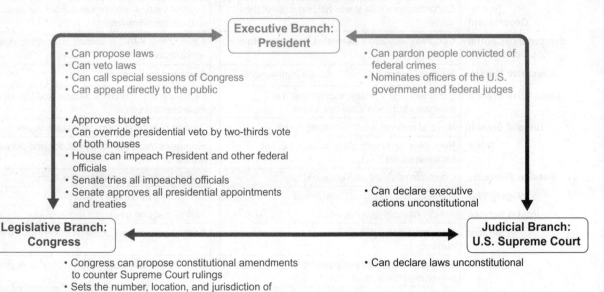

Executive Branch: President

- Can propose laws
- Can veto laws
- Can call special sessions of Congress
- Can appeal directly to the public

- Can pardon people convicted of federal crimes
- Nominates officers of the U.S. government and federal judges

- Approves budget
- Can override presidential veto by two-thirds vote of both houses
- House can impeach President and other federal officials
- Senate tries all impeached officials
- Senate approves all presidential appointments and treaties

- Can declare executive actions unconstitutional

Legislative Branch: Congress

- Congress can propose constitutional amendments to counter Supreme Court rulings
- Sets the number, location, and jurisdiction of federal courts

Judicial Branch: U.S. Supreme Court

- Can declare laws unconstitutional

4. The federal system of government in the United States divides responsibility among three equal branches. Each branch has powers that can check or balance the powers of the others. For example, the President can reject, or [4. Drop-down 1] , laws that Congress passes. But Congress can still pass a vetoed law with a two-thirds vote that [4. Drop-down 2] the President's action. The people who created the United States' plan of government included checks and balances because they feared [4. Drop-down 3] .

The use of checks and balances occurs primarily in constitutional governments. They are fundamentally important in tripartite governments, such as that of the United States, which separate powers among legislative, executive, and [4. Drop-down 4] branches.

Drop-Down Answer Options

4.1 A. rewrite
B. veto
C. restate
D. postpone

4.2 A. upholds
B. carries out
C. overrides
D. confirms

4.3 A. centralized power
B. local government
C. judicial power
D. foreign powers

4.4 A. political
B. administrative
C. congressional
D. judicial

DIRECTIONS: The passage below is incomplete. Use information from the diagram to complete the passage. For each drop-down item, choose the option that correctly completes the sentence.

PRESIDENTIAL SUCCESSION

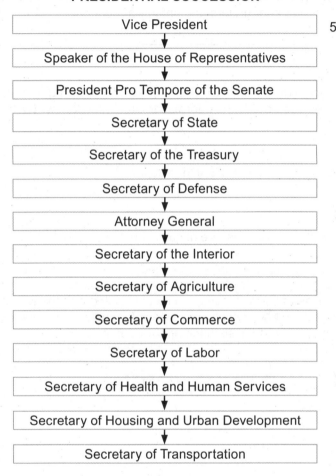

5. If for some reason the President of the United States is unable to carry out his or her duties, the | 5. Drop-down 1 | takes over as President. According to law, there is a line of presidential succession—a specific sequence of those who would become President in case the President or others in the succession could not serve. For example, the next person in line is the | 5. Drop-down 2 | . From within the President's appointed Cabinet, the person who would be first in the line of succession is the | 5. Drop-down 3 | . The Cabinet Secretaries who are highest in the line of succession are responsible for foreign affairs, finance, and | 5. Drop-down 4 | . The line of succession ensures that the U.S. government can continue to perform its functions without disruption if there is a national crisis.

Drop-Down Answer Options

| 5.1 A. Speaker of the House
B. Secretary of Homeland Security
C. Vice President
D. Chief Justice of the U.S. Supreme Court | 5.2 A. Vice President
B. President Pro Tempore of the Senate
C. Secretary of State
D. Speaker of the House of Representatives | 5.3 A. Attorney General
B. Vice President
C. Secretary of State
D. President Pro Tempore of the Senate | 5.4 A. the military
B. agriculture
C. trade
D. labor |

SS CONTENT TOPICS: I.CG.b3, I.CG.b5, I.CG.b6, I.CG.b7, I.CG.b9, I.CG.b8,
I.CG.c1, I.CG.c2, I.CG.c3, I.CG.c5, I.CG.d1, I.CG.d2, I.USH.a
SS PRACTICES: SSP.1.a, SSP.1.b, SSP.3.b, SSP.4.a

➊ Review the Skill

To **interpret the United States Constitution**, you must take a close look at the language of the document. Find familiar words that will help you determine the document's meaning. Look for key words that may help you identify the main topics. By clarifying the main ideas, you can gain a more complete understanding of the plan of government laid out in the Constitution.

For most readers, the language of the Constitution features a combination of familiar and unfamiliar ideas. Restating these ideas in your own words may help you better understand unfamiliar concepts.

➋ Refine the Skill

By refining the skill of interpreting the Constitution, you will improve your study and test-taking abilities, especially as they relate to the GED® Social Studies Test. Study the information presented below. Then answer the questions that follow.

From the Bill of Rights of the U.S. Constitution:

Amendment VI

a Some of the words used in the writing of the Constitution are synonyms for words that are more commonly used today. *Ascertained* is a synonym for *determined* or *made certain*.

In all criminal prosecutions, the accused shall enjoy the right to a speedy and public trial, by an impartial jury of the state and district wherein the crime shall have been committed, which district shall have been previously **a** <u>ascertained</u> by law; and to be informed of the nature and cause of the accusation; to be confronted with the witnesses against him; to have **b** <u>compulsory</u> process for obtaining witnesses in his favor, and to have the assistance of **counsel** for his defense.

b *Compulsory* is a synonym for *required* or *mandatory*.

CONTENT TOPICS

The Constitution's first 10 amendments are called the Bill of Rights. These amendments protect individual rights from government interference.

1. Which of the following provides the **best** title for the content of Amendment VI?

   A. freedom of expression
   B. powers of the courts
   C. rights of the accused
   D. procedures for jury trials

2. What does the word *counsel* mean in this excerpt?

   A. a plan of action
   B. a type of behavior
   C. a goal or purpose
   D. a legal advisor

DIRECTIONS: Study the excerpt, read each question, then choose the **best** answer.

From Article II of the U.S. Constitution:

Section 2. The President shall be commander in chief of the Army and Navy of the United States, and of the militia of the several states, when called into the actual service of the United States; he may require the opinion, in writing, of the principal officer in each of the executive departments, upon any subject relating to the duties of their respective offices, and he shall have power to grant reprieves and pardons for offenses against the United States, except in cases of impeachment.

He shall have power, by and with the advice and consent of the Senate, to make treaties, provided two thirds of the Senators present **concur;** …

3. Which of the following powers does the U.S. Constitution grant the President?

   A. the power to request the advice of executive officers
   B. the power to reject treaties approved by the Senate
   C. the power to grant pardons in impeachment cases
   D. the power to command state militias during times of peace

4. Which of the following can be substituted for the term *concur* in order to provide the most accurate interpretation of the text?

   A. admit
   B. agree
   C. investigate
   D. refuse

5. Which of the following **best** explains why it is stated that the President shall be commander in chief of the U.S. Army and Navy, but the U.S. Air Force is not mentioned?

   A. The authors of the U.S. Constitution did not wish to make the President commander in chief of the U.S. Air Force.
   B. The Vice President is commander in chief of the U.S. Air Force.
   C. The U.S. Air Force, originally part of the U.S. Navy, was not formally established until 1865.
   D. The U.S. Air Force, originally part of the U.S. Army, was not formally established until 1947.

DIRECTIONS: Study the excerpt, read each question, then choose the **best** answer.

From Article V of the U.S. Constitution:

The Congress, whenever two thirds of both houses shall deem it necessary, shall propose amendments to this Constitution, or, on the application of the legislatures of two thirds of the several states, shall call a convention for proposing amendments, which, in either case, shall be valid to all intents and purposes, as part of this Constitution, when ratified by the legislatures of three fourths of the several states, or by conventions in three fourths thereof, as the one or the other mode of ratification may be proposed by the Congress; provided that no amendment which may be made prior to the year one thousand eight hundred and eight shall in any manner affect the first and fourth clauses in the ninth section of the first article; and that no state, without its consent, shall be deprived of its equal **suffrage** in the Senate.

6. Who has the authority to propose amendments to the United States Constitution?

   A. the Supreme Court
   B. federal judges
   C. Congress and state legislatures
   D. the President and state legislatures

7. How do proposed amendments become part of the United States Constitution?

   A. when three fourths of state legislatures or conventions ratify them
   B. when the President endorses them
   C. when two thirds of state legislatures or conventions ratify them
   D. when three fourths of the Senate ratifies them

8. Which of the following can be substituted for the term *suffrage* in order to provide the most accurate interpretation of the text?

   A. power of taxation
   B. right to vote
   C. ability to investigate
   D. freedom to assemble

UNIT 3

DIRECTIONS: Study the information, read each question, then choose the **best** answer.

The first ten amendments to the U.S. Constitution are known as the Bill of Rights. The excerpt below begins with the Preamble, or the introductory statement, of the Bill of Rights. This excerpt includes the first four amendments that follow the Preamble.

The Preamble to the Bill of Rights

Congress of the United States begun and held at the city of New York, on Wednesday the fourth of March, one thousand seven hundred and eighty nine.

THE conventions of a number of the states, having at the time of their adopting the Constitution, expressed a desire, in order to prevent misconstruction or abuse of its powers, that further declaratory and restrictive clauses should be added: and as extending the ground of public confidence in the government, will best ensure the **beneficent** ends of its institution.

RESOLVED by the Senate and House of Representatives of the United States of America, in Congress assembled, two thirds of both houses concurring, that the following articles be proposed to the legislatures of the several states, as amendments to the Constitution of the United States, all, or any of which articles, when ratified by three fourths of the said legislatures, to be valid to all intents and purposes, as part of the said Constitution; viz.

ARTICLES in addition to, and Amendment of the Constitution of the United States of America, proposed by Congress, and ratified by the legislatures of the several states, pursuant to the fifth article of the original Constitution.

Amendment I

Congress shall make no law respecting an establishment of religion, or prohibiting the free exercise thereof; or abridging the freedom of speech, or of the press; or the right of the people peaceably to assemble, and to petition the government for a redress of grievances.

Amendment II

A well regulated militia, being necessary to the security of a free state, the right of the people to keep and bear arms, shall not be infringed.

Amendment III

No soldier shall, in time of peace be quartered in any house, without the consent of the owner, nor in time of war, but in a manner to be prescribed by law.

Amendment IV

The right of the people to be secure in their persons, houses, papers, and effects, against unreasonable searches and seizures, shall not be violated, and no warrants shall issue, but upon probable cause, supported by oath or affirmation, and particularly describing the place to be searched, and the persons or things to be seized.

---

9. Which of the following is protected by the First Amendment?

   A. the refusal to house federal troops
   B. the right to publish criticism about the government
   C. the right of a militia to possess weapons
   D. the right to participate in local military units

10. Which of the following is protected by the Second Amendment?

   A. the refusal to house federal troops
   B. the right of a militia to possess weapons
   C. protection against unreasonable searches
   D. the right to infringe on a well-regulated militia

11. Which of the following can be substituted for the term *beneficent* in order to provide the most accurate interpretation of the text?

   A. resulting in a truce with another country
   B. resulting in forgiveness of others
   C. resulting in a final conclusion
   D. resulting in goodness

DIRECTIONS: Study the information, read each question, then choose the **best** answers.

As you learned on the previous page, the Bill of Rights consists of the first ten amendments to the U.S. Constitution. The final six of these amendments are presented below.

Amendment V

No person shall be held to answer for a capital, or otherwise infamous crime, unless on a presentment or indictment of a grand jury, except in cases arising in the land or naval forces, or in the militia, when in actual service in time of war or public danger; nor shall any person be subject for the same offence to be twice put in jeopardy of life or limb; nor shall be compelled in any criminal case to be a witness against himself, nor be deprived of life, liberty, or property, without due process of law; nor shall private property be taken for public use, without just compensation.

Amendment VI

In all criminal prosecutions, the accused shall enjoy the right to a speedy and public trial, by an impartial jury of the state and district wherein the crime shall have been committed, which district shall have been previously ascertained by law, and to be informed of the nature and cause of the accusation; to be confronted with the witnesses against him; to have compulsory process for obtaining witnesses in his favor, and to have the assistance of counsel for his defense.

Amendment VII

In suits at common law, where the value in controversy shall exceed twenty dollars, the right of trial by jury shall be preserved, and no fact tried by a jury, shall be otherwise re-examined in any court of the United States, than according to the rules of the common law.

Amendment VIII

Excessive bail shall not be required, nor excessive fines imposed, nor cruel and unusual punishments inflicted.

Amendment IX

The enumeration in the Constitution, of certain rights, shall not be construed to deny or disparage others retained by the people.

Amendment X

The powers not delegated to the United States by the Constitution, nor prohibited by it to the states, are reserved to the states respectively, or to the people.

---

12. Which of the following amendments to the U.S. Constitution prohibits excessive bail or fines?

    A. the Tenth Amendment
    B. the Ninth Amendment
    C. the Sixth Amendment
    D. the Eighth Amendment

13. Which of the following amendments to the U.S. Constitution prohibits what is popularly known as "double jeopardy"?

    A. the Fifth Amendment
    B. the Sixth Amendment
    C. the Ninth Amendment
    D. the Tenth Amendment

14. If the U.S. Constitution does not specifically give or prohibit the U.S. government a particular right, and it is not prohibited by the states, who then is granted that right?

    A. the states alone
    B. individual people, then the states
    C. individual people
    D. the states, or the people

15. Which of the following amendments to the U.S. Constitution guarantees a right to trial by jury?

    A. the Fifth Amendment
    B. the Sixth Amendment
    C. the Seventh Amendment
    D. the Eighth Amendment

Summarize

Use with *Student Book* pp. 50–51

SS CONTENT TOPICS: I.CG.b.2, I.CG.b.3, I.CG.b.4, I.CG.b.7, I.CG.b.8, I.CG.b.9, I.CG.d.1, I.USH.a.1, I.USH.b.1
SS PRACTICES: SSP.1.a, SSP.1.b, SSP.2.a, SSP.2.b, SSP.3.c, SSP.5.a, SSP.6.b, SSP.9.a, SSP.9.b, SSP.9.c

1 Review the Skill

To **summarize** information, try to identify the main ideas or themes expressed in the information. Then, think of a way to restate those ideas in your own words. The ability to summarize information will help you clarify the most important information in a paragraph or visual element.

Be certain that you read or study a passage or visual carefully before trying to summarize it. Important ideas can appear in many places.

2 Refine the Skill

By refining the skill of summarizing, you will improve your study and test-taking abilities, especially as they relate to the GED® Social Studies Test. Study the information below. Then answer the questions that follow.

a Restating the main idea is essential in an effective summary. Titles of tables often convey the main idea. From this table's title you understand that the Bill of Rights is the main idea.

b When summarizing a table, notice any subtitles. They describe the main details the table contains.

THE BILL OF RIGHTS a

AMENDMENT	RIGHTS GUARANTEED b
I	Freedom of speech, the press, religion, assembly; right to protest against government actions
II	Right to bear arms, for duty in a militia
III	Government cannot force citizens to keep soldiers in their homes during peacetime
IV	Prevents government from improper searches of someone's person, property, or home
V	Right of accused to grand jury for serious crimes; person cannot be tried twice for same crime or forced to give evidence against himself; government cannot take property without just compensation
VI	Guarantees a speedy and impartial public trial by jury; right to an attorney; right to face accusers
VII	Right to jury trial in most civil cases
VIII	Prohibits unreasonably high bail or fines for those accused of crimes; outlaws cruel and unusual punishment
IX	States that the rights of the people are not limited by what is written in the Constitution
X	States that any rights not expressly given to the federal government are reserved to the states, or to the people

TEST-TAKING TIPS

Tables present information organized into one or more categories. Knowing what type of information is shown can help you summarize the table's content.

1. Which of the following statements is the most accurate summary of the table?

   A. The table lists the rights guaranteed by the Bill of Rights.
   B. The table shows the exact text of the Bill of Rights.
   C. The table explains rights guaranteed in the U.S. Constitution.
   D. The table shows several Articles of the U.S. Constitution.

2. Which of these could be included in a summary of this table?

   A. the complete text of each amendment
   B. the number of amendments in the Bill of Rights
   C. the date when the Bill of Rights was ratified
   D. examples of each of the rights as applied in everyday life

UNIT 3

Spotlighted Item: **EXTENDED RESPONSE**

DIRECTIONS: Read the excerpt and the question, then write your answer on the lines below. Please refer to Unit 3 and Unit 4 in the Reasoning Through Language Arts Student Edition and Workbook for detailed information about reading, writing, and editing Extended Response answers.

The passage below is an excerpt from *Common Sense*, a pamphlet written by Thomas Paine prior to the American Revolution. In it, Mr. Paine argues for the American colonists to set up a new government separate from the British monarchy.

We have boasted the protection of Great Britain, without considering, that her motive was *interest* not *attachment*; that she did not protect us from *our enemies* on *our account*, but from *her enemies* on *her own account*, from those that had no quarrel with us on any *other account*, and who will always be our enemies on the SAME ACCOUNT. Let Britain waive her pretentions to the continent, or the continent throw off the dependence, and we should be at peace with France and Spain were they at war with Britain.

3. Write a summary of how Thomas Paine's position in this excerpt reflects the enduring issue of American independence from Great Britain. Incorporate relevant and specific evidence from the excerpt, and your own knowledge of the issue and the circumstances surrounding the events leading to the American Revolution. This task may require 25 minutes to complete. You may use another sheet of paper to complete your answer.

UNIT 3

Spotlighted Item: **EXTENDED RESPONSE**

DIRECTIONS: Read the passage and the question, then write your answer on the lines below. Please refer to Unit 3 and Unit 4 in the Reasoning Through Language Arts Student Edition and Workbook for detailed information about reading, writing, and editing Extended Response answers.

   After the Constitution was sent to the states for ratification, James Madison was one of three prominent Americans who wrote essays to help people understand the new form of government and to encourage support for the Constitution. These 85 essays were known as The Federalist Papers. They described the structure and function of the legislative, executive, and judicial branches of government. They also explained how the new government would conduct trade, provide defense, and earn revenue. Many newspapers published the essays to make them available to the people, who had different opinions about the Constitution.

   In "Federalist No. 37," Madison described the difficulties faced by the delegates in their efforts to draft the Constitution. First, there were no precedents for them to follow; they only knew that the existing Confederation was weak and that they must try to avoid the past errors of other nations. In addition, delegates had to design a stable government that provided security and enforced laws while ensuring personal liberty. Finally, the appropriate balance of power between the national and state governments had to be found. Madison concluded the essay with his opinion on the reasons for the Convention's success: there was little divisiveness along political party lines, and the delegates knew the importance of sacrificing personal interests for the greater good.

4. This passage provides information about the essays known as the Federalist Papers. Write a summary of this passage, including just the key information. Give one example of information that should not be included in the summary. Incorporate relevant and specific evidence from the excerpt, and your own knowledge of the issue and the circumstances surrounding the events leading to the establishment of the U.S. system of government. This task may require 25 minutes to complete. You may use another sheet of paper to complete your answer.

_____

_____

_____

_____

_____

_____

_____

_____

_____

_____

UNIT 3

DIRECTIONS: Study the political cartoon, read the information and the question, then write your answer on the lines below. Please refer to Unit 3 and Unit 4 in the Reasoning Through Language Arts Student Edition and Workbook for detailed information about reading, writing, and editing Extended Response answers.

This political cartoon first appeared in Benjamin Franklin's *Pennsylvania Gazette* in 1754 and was widely reprinted. The pieces of the snake represent several colonies and the region of New England. At first, the cartoon referred to an early plan for uniting the British colonies in North America. Franklin thought that unified colonies could help Britain win the conflict with France over land west of the British colonies. Like the snake cut into pieces, the colonies risked "death" by remaining separate. At the same time, many people believed a popular superstition that putting the pieces of a snake back together before sunset would bring the snake back to life. Later, after passage of the Stamp Act and other events leading to the American Revolution, patriots revived the cartoon to support the cause of independence.

5. Write a summary of the messages this cartoon gave to the colonies in their relationship with Britain. Incorporate relevant and specific evidence from the cartoon, the information, and your own knowledge of the issue and the circumstances surrounding the events leading to the American Revolution. This task may require 25 minutes to complete. You may use another sheet of paper to complete your answer.

_____

_____

_____

_____

_____

_____

_____

SS CONTENT TOPICS: I.CG.b.7, I.CG.b.8, I.CG.c.3, I.CG.d.2, USH.c.1, I.USH.c.3, I.USH.c.4, I.USH.d.1
SS PRACTICES: SSP.1.a, SSP.1.b, SSP.2.a, SSP.2.b, SSP.3.c, SSP.6.b, SSP.6.c

1 Review the Skill

To **compare and contrast** is to examine the ways in which two or more things are alike and how they are different. At times, these comparisons may be clearly stated in a text or graphic. At other times, you must study descriptions, use logic, and make assumptions to determine the similarities and differences between items.

In the excerpts in this lesson, the text does not explicitly **compare and contrast** the pieces of information. You must look closely at them to recognize the ways in which they are alike and ways in which they are different. Study their subjects, writing styles, and main arguments.

2 Refine the Skill

By refining the skill of comparing and contrasting, you will improve your study and test-taking abilities, especially as they relate to the GED® Social Studies Test. Study the information below. Then answer the questions that follow.

a The titles of passages like these tell you what information will be covered. These titles can provide hints to similarities and differences that you may find within the passages.

b Consider the purpose that the author or authors had for writing these passages. How are their goals for writing similar, and how are they different?

a

From South Carolina's Ordinance of Secession:

We, the people of the State of South Carolina, in convention assembled, do declare and ordain … That the ordinance adopted by us in convention … whereby the Constitution of the United States of America was ratified, and also all acts and parts of acts of the General Assembly of this State ratifying amendments of the said Constitution, are hereby repealed; and that the union now subsisting between South Carolina and other States, under the name of the "United States of America," is hereby dissolved. **b**

a

From South Carolina's Declaration of Immediate Causes:

… the State of South Carolina having resumed her separate and equal place among nations, deems it due to herself, to the remaining United States of America, and to the nations of the world, that she should declare the immediate causes which have **b** led to this act.

1. Which of the following do **both** of these passages address?

   A. South Carolina's secession from the United States
   B. disputes between Northern and Southern states
   C. slavery in the United States
   D. South Carolina's place among world nations

2. Which of the following features of these excerpts is most different?

   A. writing style
   B. purpose
   C. time period
   D. subject matter

TEST-TAKING TIPS

When answering a compare-and-contrast question on a test, look closely at the main ideas of each passage or graphic. Ask yourself how those main ideas are similar or different.

UNIT 3

DIRECTIONS: Read the passage and the questions, then choose the **best** answers.

An agricultural system known as sharecropping emerged in the South at the end of the Civil War. Planters hired many formerly enslaved people to work specific areas of plantations, cultivating crops such as cotton. These workers came to Southern farms with their families and provided the labor planters required to continue producing crops. The planters provided nearly all of the equipment and supplies the workers used. In addition, planters often extended credit to the workers for their living expenses.

At the end of the growing season, workers typically received half of the proceeds from the sale of the crops. However, planters usually deducted expenses, money workers owed, and interest from the workers' portion of the profits. These factors, as well as other dishonest practices by many planters, prevented workers from making a living at sharecropping. Federal reforms intended to help formerly enslaved people did not have a lasting effect in the South. Both local and state governments reasserted themselves to maintain economic and social control over newly freed African Americans.

3. In which of the following ways did the system of sharecropping differ from slavery in the South?

   A. Workers on plantations were often mistreated.
   B. Workers could receive payment for their work on a plantation.
   C. Workers used the materials provided by the planters.
   D. Workers helped cultivate cash crops such as cotton.

4. In which of the following ways were the experiences of sharecroppers similar to those of enslaved people?

   A. Both received credit to cover the cost of their living expenses.
   B. Both traveled together with their families.
   C. Both had some control over the cultivation process.
   D. Both worked primarily at agricultural tasks.

DIRECTIONS: Read the passages and the questions, then choose the **best** answer.

From the Thirteenth Amendment to the U.S. Constitution:

Section 1. Neither slavery nor involuntary servitude, except as punishment for crime whereof the party shall have been duly convicted, shall exist within the United States, or any place subject to their jurisdiction.

Section 2. Congress shall have the power to enforce this article by appropriate legislation.

From the Fifteenth Amendment to the U.S. Constitution:

Section 1. The right of citizens of the United States to vote shall not be denied or abridged by the United States or by any State on account of race, color, or previous condition of servitude.

Section 2. The Congress shall have power to enforce this article by appropriate legislation.

5. In which of the following ways are these amendments similar?

   A. Both deal with the voting rights of United States citizens.
   B. Both describe qualifications needed to hold federal or state offices.
   C. Both grant Congress the authority to enforce their provisions.
   D. Both prohibit slavery within the territory of the United States.

6. Which of the following is illegal under the Fifteenth Amendment but is not addressed in the Thirteenth Amendment?

   A. poll taxes for certain ethnic groups
   B. the imprisonment of convicted criminals
   C. voter registration drives
   D. involuntary servitude in United States territories

UNIT 3

DIRECTIONS: Study the information, read the questions, then choose the **best** answers.

After Reconstruction, 22 African Americans from the South represented their states in Congress. By the end of the 19th century, however, Jim Crow laws began to influence the results of elections in the South. No African Americans from any state served in the Senate between 1881 and 1967. Similarly, the House of Representatives had no African American members between 1901 and 1929. Since then, however, Congress has continually had African American members. As of 2013, the House has had 139 African-American members, while the Senate has had eight.

EARLY AFRICAN AMERICAN LEGISLATORS FROM FORMER CONFEDERATE STATES

Name	State	Accomplishment
Hiram Revels	Mississippi	First African American member of U.S. Senate; elected by Mississippi state legislature on February 23, 1870
Blanche K. Bruce	Mississippi	First African American to serve a full term in U.S. Senate, from 1875 to 1881; elected by Mississippi state legislature; last African American Senator until 1967
Joseph Hayne Rainey	South Carolina	First African American popularly elected to Congress; a formerly enslaved person, he joined Congress in 1870 and served four more terms in the House
George Henry White	North Carolina	The last formerly enslaved person to serve in Congress and last African American in the House until 1929; served from 1897 to 1901

7. Which of the following describes a way in which the Senate and the House of Representatives were similar?

   A. Both experienced lengthy periods in the 1900s with no African American members.
   B. Hiram Revels served in both houses of Congress.
   C. Both houses of Congress have had at least one African American member since 1929.
   D. African Americans were popularly elected to both houses of Congress in 1870.

8. Based on the table and the information, which of the following describes a way in which the Senate and the House of Representatives have been different?

   A. The House of Representatives has had far more African American members than the Senate.
   B. The Senate has had far more African American members than the House of Representatives.
   C. African Americans have served in the House of Representatives throughout the entire 20th century.
   D. African Americans have served in the Senate throughout the entire 20th century.

9. In which of the following ways were Hiram Revels and Joseph Hayne Rainey different?

   A. Hiram Revels was elected years later than Joseph Hayne Rainey.
   B. Joseph Hayne Rainey served in the Senate, and Hiram Revels joined the House of Representatives.
   C. Hiram Revels was formerly enslaved, but Joseph Hayne Rainey was not.
   D. Joseph Hayne Rainey was popularly elected, but Hiram Revels was not.

10. Which of the following statements accurately compares or contrasts Jim Crow laws and the Fugitive Slave Acts?

    A. Jim Crow laws, unlike the Fugitive Slave Acts, were not actual legislation.
    B. Both were established to prevent African Americans from serving in government.
    C. The Fugitive Slave Acts were federal laws, but Jim Crow laws were state or local acts.
    D. Both were enacted to preserve slavery in the South.

11. In which of the following ways were the careers of Blanche K. Bruce and George Henry White the same?

    A. Both served only one term.
    B. They were the last African Americans to serve in their respective branch of Congress for many years.
    C. Both were popularly elected to office.
    D. They both represented the same state in Congress.

DIRECTIONS: Study the information, read the questions, then choose the **best** answers.

1863: President Lincoln proposes plan for Reconstruction

1864: Congress passes Wade-Davis Bill requiring 50 percent of states' male voters to take a loyalty oath. President Lincoln vetoes the bill

1865: President Lincoln is assassinated

1865: President Andrew Johnson issues amnesty proclamation designed to take control of Reconstruction from Southern aristocracy

1865: Most states ratify the Thirteenth Amendment, abolishing slavery, and set up civil governments

1865: Congress denies seats to former Confederates; President Johnson criticizes Republicans and vetoes their Reconstruction legislation

1866: Congress passes Civil Rights Act

1866: The Fourteenth Amendment, which guarantees citizenship to all people born in the United States, including formerly enslaved people, is rejected by most Southern states

1867: Reconstruction Acts pass Congress and establish military districts to govern the South

1868: Congress impeaches President Johnson but falls short of removing him from office

1868: Six Confederate states rejoin the Union

1870: The remaining Confederate states rejoin the Union

1870: The Fifteenth Amendment is ratified, guaranteeing all citizens the right to vote, regardless of race, color, or previous condition of servitude

1876: Reconstruction ends, with the election of Rutherford B. Hayes as President

---

12. Andrew Johnson's Reconstruction policies were most similar to which of the following?

   A. the policies of the Radical Republicans
   B. the policies of Rutherford B. Hayes
   C. the policies of Abraham Lincoln
   D. the policies of the former Confederates

13. In which of the following ways did the Thirteenth and Fourteenth Amendments differ?

   A. One dealt with Reconstruction, while the other dealt with foreign policy.
   B. One was adopted quickly, while the other was initially rejected by most Southern states.
   C. Abraham Lincoln authored one amendment, while Congressional leaders wrote the other.
   D. Radical Republicans supported one amendment but not the other.

14. With which of the following actions did Andrew Johnson demonstrate a Reconstruction strategy similar to that of the Radical Republicans?

   A. vetoing the Reconstruction acts
   B. criticizing the decision to not seat former Confederates in Congress
   C. arguing against the establishment of military districts in the South
   D. taking control of Reconstruction away from the Southern aristocracy

15. In which of the following ways were the Fourteenth and Fifteenth Amendments similar?

   A. Both guaranteed rights that African Americans had not previously had.
   B. Both were rejected by the Southern states.
   C. Both established civil governments in the South.
   D. Both were supported by President Rutherford B. Hayes.

1 Review the Skill

SS CONTENT TOPICS: II.CG.e.2, II.CG.e.3, II.G.c.3, II.G.d.1, II.G.d.3, II.G.d.4, II.USH.g.3
SS PRACTICES: SSP.1.a, SSP.1.b, SSP.2.a, SSP.2.b, SSP.3.a, SSP.3.c, SSP.6.b, SSP.6.c, SSP.10.a

Charts, graphs, and flowcharts present various types of information in a visual format. Line graphs and bar graphs are especially useful for showing change over time. Circle graphs show the relationship of the parts to a whole. Flowcharts are useful for presenting information shown in sequence. Each step is usually explained by words within a figure, with the order of the sequence most often designated by arrows. A flowchart may describe a simple sequence, a complex and interconnected sequence, or a cycle.

Be sure to determine exactly what information is presented on a chart, graph, or flowchart. The titles of these visuals can help you do so. Also, carefully read all of the labels included on a chart, graph, or flowchart. Labels help you understand what each part of the visual represents.

2 Refine the Skill

By refining the skill of interpreting charts, graphs, and flowcharts, you will improve your study and test-taking abilities, especially as they relate to the GED® Social Studies Test. Study the information presented in the graphs below. Then answer the questions that follow.

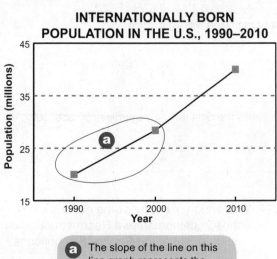

INTERNATIONALLY BORN POPULATION IN THE U.S., 1990–2010

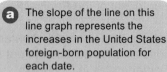

a The slope of the line on this line graph represents the increases in the United States foreign-born population for each date.

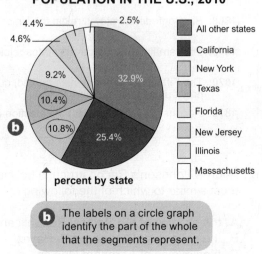

INTERNATIONALLY BORN POPULATION IN THE U.S., 2010

percent by state

All other states
California
New York
Texas
Florida
New Jersey
Illinois
Massachusetts

b The labels on a circle graph identify the part of the whole that the segments represent.

CONTENT TOPICS

A decrease on a graph or chart is not always bad, and an increase is not always good. If a chart shows a change in infant mortality rate, a decrease would be positive, and an increase would cause concern.

1. Which of the following states is third highest in the total number of internationally born residents?

A. New York
B. Texas
C. Florida
D. New Jersey

2. By about how much did the internationally born population of the United States increase between 1990 and 2010?

A. about 500,000
B. about 6,000,000
C. about 10,000,000
D. about 20,000,000

DIRECTIONS: Study the information and the flowchart, read the questions, then choose the **best** answers.

The Spanish-American War was a brief conflict that lasted less than one year, but when it ended, the United States was a changed nation. As a result of winning the war, the United States suddenly was in control of former Spanish territories reaching from Cuba to the Philippines.

EVENTS LEADING TO START OF SPANISH-AMERICAN WAR

> Rebels in Cuba start a war of independence against Spain.

↓

> Spain uses harsh measures to put down the rebellion.

↓

> Newspapers print exaggerated tales of Spanish brutality, causing Americans to turn against Spain.

↓

> President McKinley sends the battleship *Maine* to Cuba.

↓

> On February 15, 1898, an unexplained explosion destroys the *Maine* and kills 267 crewmembers.

↓

> Although the source of the explosion is unknown, several U.S. newspapers fan the flames of public anger against Spain.

↓

> President McKinley declares war; the U.S. victory takes only eight months.

3. Why were Spain and Cuba fighting against each other prior to the Spanish-American War?

   A. Spain wanted independence from Cuba.
   B. Spain was attempting to put down a Cuban rebellion.
   C. Spain was an ally of the United States, which was fighting against Cuba.
   D. A Spanish ship had blown up in Havana harbor.

4. How did newspapers influence the actions of the U.S. government before the Spanish-American War?

   A. Newspapers refused to print stories about Spain's actions in Cuba.
   B. Members of Congress controlled what newspapers printed about Spain.
   C. Newspapers turned American public opinion against Spain with sensationalized stories.
   D. Newspaper editors funded Cuba's rebellion against Spain.

5. In which of the following ways did the Spanish-American War change the United States?

   A. It no longer considered Cuba an enemy.
   B. It decided to get involved in additional conflicts to gain new territories.
   C. It became a world power and had to act with that in mind.
   D. It began to curtail individual rights at home.

DIRECTIONS: Study the information presented in the circle graphs, read the question, then choose the **best** answer.

PRESIDENTIAL ELECTION OF 1908

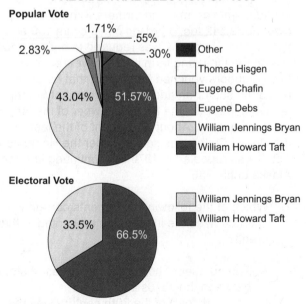

6. Which of the following statements is accurate?

   A. Three candidates received no electoral votes.
   B. Taft won a larger percentage of the popular vote than of the electoral vote.
   C. Bryan finished first in the popular vote.
   D. The two top candidates together received less than 75 percent of the popular and the electoral votes.

DIRECTIONS: Study the bar graph and the information, read the questions, then choose the **best** answers.

HOMESTEADS, 1871–1960

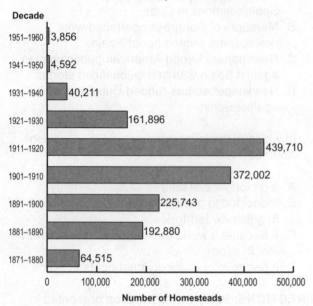

Decade

1951–1960	3,856
1941–1950	4,592
1931–1940	40,211
1921–1930	161,896
1911–1920	439,710
1901–1910	372,002
1891–1900	225,743
1881–1890	192,880
1871–1880	64,515

0   100,000   200,000   300,000   400,000   500,000

Number of Homesteads

The Homestead Act of 1862 opened the possibility of landownership to millions of people from all walks of life, including single women, former enslaved workers, immigrants, and farmers without land of their own. For a $12 fee, a person could claim 160 acres of public land. He or she was required to build a house, live on the land, and farm it for five years. Then, after two neighbors vouched for the fact that he or she had done so, for an additional payment of $6, the homesteader became the legal owner of the land and received a deed. About 10 percent of the land area of the United States was settled under the Homestead Act. It was repealed in 1976 but continued in effect in Alaska until 1986.

7. Which of the following statements correctly characterizes the information presented in the graph?

   A. The number of homesteads increased steadily between the 1870s and 1960s.
   B. The early part of the 20th century was the busiest period for homesteading.
   C. There was no homesteading after 1950.
   D. There were more homesteaders between 1911 and 1920 than in all previous decades combined.

8. Which of the following was most likely a result of the Homestead Act?

   A. There were fewer landowners throughout the United States.
   B. Slavery continued many years beyond what it would have without the Act.
   C. Many people felt a stronger tie to the federal government.
   D. Cities were abandoned as people set out to own homesteads.

DIRECTIONS: Study the bar graph, read the questions, then choose the **best** answers.

ALABAMA RURAL AND URBAN POPULATION, 1900 AND 1910

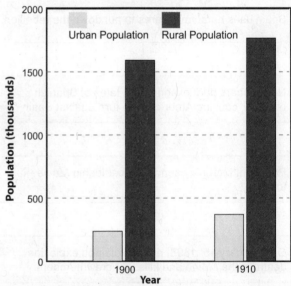

9. In which of the following ways could Alabama's population in both 1900 and 1910 best be described?

   A. Alabama's population was divided almost evenly between urban and rural areas.
   B. The state's population was heavily urbanized.
   C. Most people in Alabama lived in rural areas.
   D. The state had more than 2,000,000 people.

10. By 1910, how had Alabama's population changed?

   A. The population increased by fewer than 1,000.
   B. The population was slightly more urbanized.
   C. The population was more than 90 percent urban.
   D. The population had decreased in both rural and urban areas.

UNIT 3

DIRECTIONS: The passage below is incomplete. Use information from the graph to complete the passage. From each drop-down item, choose the option that correctly completes the sentence.

CAMPAIGN EXPENDITURES: HOUSE OF REPRESENTATIVES, 2000–2010, NET DOLLARS

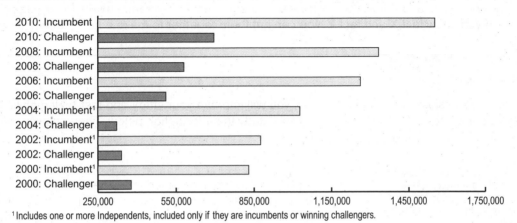

[1] Includes one or more Independents, included only if they are incumbents or winning challengers.

HOUSE OF REPRESENTATIVES CAMPAIGN SPENDING

11. The increasing cost of campaigning for the House of Representatives, especially the cost of

| 11. Drop-down 1 | in the media, has made many representatives virtual part-time legislators and full-time | 11. Drop-down 2 |. Although the quest for campaign financing places a heavy burden on members of Congress, they continue to hold a significant advantage over | 11. Drop-down 3 | running against them.

| 11. Drop-down 4 | also have the advantage of being more familiar to voters due to their visibility in the news media, and the salaried staff that assists them. The escalating imbalance in fund-raising between challengers and incumbents has contributed to the high rate of | 11. Drop-down 5 | to Congress, leading to demands for campaign fund-raising reform and even for term limits.

Drop-Down Answer Options

11.1
A. get-out-the-vote campaigns
B. debates on college campuses
C. political advertisements
D. door-to-door campaigning

11.2
A. fund-raisers
B. congresspeople
C. Presidential candidates
D. television actors

11.3
A. media reporters
B. professional fund-raisers
C. Presidential candidates
D. challenger candidates

11.4
A. Challenger candidates
B. Incumbents
C. News media
D. Presidential candidates

11.5
A. falsified election results
B. losing at the polls
C. reelections
D. too few people running for election

UNIT 3

Make Inferences

Use with **Student Book** pp. 56–57

① Review the Skill

SS CONTENT TOPICS: I.CG.b.6, I.CG.b.8, I.CG.c.1, I.CG.c.3, I.CG.c.4, I.CG.c.5, I.CG.c.6, I.CG.d.2, II.CG.e.2, II.CG.e.3, I.USH.d.2, II.USH.f.4, II.USH.f.5, II.USH.g.3
SS PRACTICES: SSP.1.a, SSP.1.b, SSP.2.a, SSP.2.b, SSP.3.a, SSP.3.c, SSP.5.a, SSP.6.b, SSP.9.a, SSP.9.b, SSP.9.c

An **inference** is a logical assumption made by considering two or more pieces of information and your previous knowledge. As you continue reading a text, new information may confirm or contradict your inference. It may be necessary to revise the inference. By **making inferences**, you can use the information you have to develop new ideas about a particular subject. When reading historical information, making inferences enables you to connect people, events, and ideas in ways that may not be explicitly stated in the text.

As you read, think about how the information fits together. An inference works like a puzzle or an addition problem. If you know fact X and fact Y, you can put them together to make a new piece of information.

② Refine the Skill

By refining the skill of making inferences, you will improve your study and test-taking abilities, especially as they relate to the GED® Social Studies Test. Study the information below. Then answer the questions that follow.

ⓐ This paragraph provides information about the start of President Wilson's second term as President. Pay close attention to the facts, and keep them in mind as you read his speech.

World War I was being waged in Europe during President Woodrow Wilson's second term. In 1916, Germany announced that its submarines would no longer refrain from attacking U.S. ships, even though the United States was officially neutral. On April 2, 1917, President Wilson went before Congress to address the rising conflict with Germany.

From Wilson's message to Congress:

ⓑ Identify details in this speech that you can put together with the information in the paragraph above, as well as your previous knowledge. Use the information to make an inference about President Wilson and his message.

ⓑ It is a distressing and oppressive duty, gentlemen of Congress, which I have performed in thus addressing you. There are, it may be, many months of fiery trial and sacrifice ahead of us. It is a fearful thing to lead this great peaceful people into war, into the most terrible and disastrous of all wars, civilization itself seeming to be in the balance. But the right is more precious than peace, and we shall fight for the things which we have always carried nearest our hearts.

TEST-TAKING TIPS

You sometimes will make inferences based on information presented in a passage or a visual. At other times, you must combine new information with your previous knowledge to make an educated guess.

1. Which of the following situations led President Wilson to address Congress?

   A. the status of the war in Europe
   B. the beginning of President Wilson's second term as President
   C. the increasing military power of Germany
   D. the announcement that Germany would attack U.S. ships

2. What can you infer about President Wilson's view about the United States entering World War I?

   A. He believed it soon would be necessary.
   B. He became more determined to remain neutral.
   C. He believed the United States could win the war quickly.
   D. He believed the war was being fought for economic reasons.

DIRECTIONS: Study the information, read the questions, then choose the **best** answers.

In 1872, Susan B. Anthony voted in the presidential election and was arrested and fined. She refused to pay her fine and used her arrest to highlight her beliefs about women's rights, especially the right to vote. The campaign to gain national voting rights for women in the United States continued well into the 20th century and did not meet success until after the end of World War I.

From an 1873 speech by Susan B. Anthony:

Friends and fellow citizens: I stand before you tonight under indictment for the alleged crime of having voted at the last presidential election, without having a lawful right to vote. It shall be my work this evening to prove to you that in thus voting, I not only committed no crime, but, instead, simply exercised my citizen's rights, guaranteed to me and all United States citizens by the national Constitution, beyond the power of any state to deny.

It was we, the people; not we, the white male citizens; nor yet we, the male citizens; but we, the whole people, who formed the Union … . And it is a downright mockery to talk to women of their enjoyment of the blessings of liberty while they are denied the use of the only means of securing them provided by this democratic-republican government— the ballot.

3. To what text is Ms. Anthony referring in the second paragraph of her speech?

   A. the Preamble to the U.S. Constitution
   B. the Declaration of Independence
   C. the Twentieth Amendment
   D. the Emancipation Proclamation

4. Which of the following can you infer based on the information?

   A. Susan B. Anthony is mocking the Constitution.
   B. Susan B. Anthony believes that the Constitution already guarantees women the right to vote.
   C. Susan B. Anthony believes that women enjoy liberty.
   D. Susan B. Anthony is opposed to amending the Constitution for any reason.

DIRECTIONS: Study the information, read the questions, then choose the **best** answers.

Spain ceded Puerto Rico to the United States following the Spanish-American War. It was placed under military rule until 1900, when the United States established an administrative government there. The 1917 Jones Act officially made Puerto Rico a territory of the United States, granting Puerto Ricans U.S. citizenship. The Jones Act separated the three branches of Puerto Rican government, provided civil rights to individuals, and created a locally elected bicameral legislature. However, Puerto Rico's governor and the U.S. President had the power to veto any law that the legislature passed. Also, the U.S. Congress had the power to stop any action taken by the legislature in Puerto Rico. The United States maintained control over fiscal and economic matters and exercised authority over mail services, immigration, defense, and other basic governmental matters.

Source: loc.gov, accessed 2013

From the Eighteenth Amendment:

Section 1. After one year from the ratification of this article the manufacture, sale, or transportation of intoxicating liquors within, the importation thereof into, or the exportation thereof from the United States and all territory subject to the jurisdiction thereof, for beverage purposes, is hereby prohibited.

Section 2. The Congress and the several States shall have concurrent power to enforce this article by appropriate legislation.

5. Which of the following can be inferred about Puerto Rico?

   A. Puerto Rico objected to Spanish rule.
   B. Puerto Ricans were subject to the same rules as U.S. citizens under the Eighteenth Amendment.
   C. Puerto Rico was allowed to continue some production of alcoholic beverages.
   D. Puerto Rico had to ratify the Eighteenth Amendment before it could become law.

6. The Eighteenth Amendment was ratified in 1919. In which year can you infer that the amendment's measures took effect?

   A. 1918
   B. 1919
   C. 1920
   D. 1921

DIRECTIONS: Study the information, read the questions, then choose the **best** answers.

Prohibition refers to a period during which the making, transporting, and selling of alcoholic beverages was prohibited, or illegal. In the United States, a movement to outlaw alcohol began in the mid-1800s and quickly rose to national attention. During World War I, the need to conserve resources reduced alcohol consumption in the nation. Afterward, the Eighteenth Amendment to the U.S. Constitution instituted Prohibition as a national law. However, this law proved very difficult to enforce. Many Americans participated in the illegal production of alcohol, known as bootlegging. Underground drinking establishments and organized criminal activity flourished. By 1933, the Twenty-First Amendment had repealed Prohibition. As of 1966, no state Prohibition laws remained in effect.

7. What can be inferred based on the repeal of Prohibition by the Twenty-First Amendment?

   A. Congress no longer supported Prohibition by 1933.
   B. The Great Depression led people to reduce alcohol consumption.
   C. Bootlegging proved to be unprofitable.
   D. Prohibition was more difficult to enforce at the local level.

8. What can you infer from the passage above about state Prohibition laws?

   A. These laws were superseded by the Twenty-First Amendment.
   B. State laws sought to control underground drinking establishments.
   C. These laws proved easier to enforce than national Prohibition measures.
   D. Some state legislatures believed that consumption of alcohol was dangerous and immoral.

9. What can you infer based on the fact that many Americans took part in the illegal production and consumption of alcohol?

   A. Most Americans were not law-abiding people.
   B. Americans believed Prohibition restricted their individual rights as citizens.
   C. The police did not try to enforce the law.
   D. The jobs of most Americans depended on the production of alcohol.

DIRECTIONS: Study the information presented in the table, read the questions, then choose the **best** answers.

MILESTONES OF THE 1920s

World's Firsts	1920: First commercial radio broadcast by radio station KDKA
	1920: Automobile with combustion engine invented by Henry Ford, leading to creation of thousands of new jobs
	1920: Traffic light invented by police officer William Potts
	1927: First transatlantic airplane flight made by Charles Lindbergh
	1927: First "talking" movie, *The Jazz Singer*, released
Arts / Culture	1921: Louis Armstrong joins "King" Oliver's Creole Jazz Band
	1921: Edith Wharton wins Pulitzer Prize for her novel *The Age of Innocence*
Society	1925: Women cut their hair and shed their corsets to embrace "flapper" fashion
	1929: Chicago organized-crime members killed in "St. Valentine's Day Massacre"
Labor / Law	1920: League of Nations is dissolved, although the United States never became a member
	1923: U.S. Steel institutes an eight-hour workday
	1929: Ford Motor Company increases minimum wage from $6.00 to $7.00 per day

10. Based on the milestones reported in the table, which of the following can be inferred about the 1920s?

    A. Life in the 1920s was dangerous.
    B. Life for working people was more difficult in the 1920s than in the decades prior.
    C. Artists and musicians gained international fame in the 1920s.
    D. The 1920s was a time of exciting innovation.

11. Of the following experiences, which can be inferred to have empowered women in the 1920s?

    A. working in factories during World War II
    B. going to plays and movies
    C. gaining the right to vote
    D. being able to drive cars

UNIT 3

Spotlighted Item: **EXTENDED RESPONSE**

DIRECTIONS: Study the table and the information, read the question, then write your answer on the lines below. Please refer to Unit 3 and Unit 4 in the Reasoning Through Language Arts Student Edition and Workbook for detailed information about reading, writing, and editing Extended Response answers.

HOOVER AND ROOSEVELT ADMINISTRATIONS

Hoover Administration	Roosevelt Administration
Agricultural Marketing Act: Government purchase of farm surplus to boost farm prices	**Emergency Banking Act:** Stabilizes banking system and reopens banks
Hawley-Smoot Tariff: High tariffs set to protect American farm goods	**Glass-Steagall Banking Act:** Government insures bank deposits to reestablish confidence in banks
Reconstruction Finance Corporation: Government loans to banks and corporations in danger of closing	**Civil Works Administration:** Provides government funds to employ people to build roads, bridges, schools
Voluntary deals between government and businesses to keep businesses open and workers employed	**Civilian Conservation Corps:** Puts young men to work planting trees, doing soil conservation projects, working on facilities in national parks
Red Cross asked to distribute government surplus food to those in need	**Works Projects Administration:** Employs the jobless on public works projects such as roads, airports, parks; includes employing thousands of artists who paint murals on public buildings, authors who write travel guides, actors and musicians who give free performances
Federal government makes loans to states to help with state and local relief programs	**Farm Credit Bureau:** Government provides loans to heavily indebted farmers to prevent farm foreclosures
	Rural Electrification Administration: Loans funds to local utilities to bring electricity to most of rural America
	Agricultural Adjustment Act: Provides funds to farmers to stop growing surplus crops with the goal of raising crop prices
	Tennessee Valley Authority: Provides jobs for building a system of dams to provide electricity and flood control to rural areas in six states

After the stock market crash of 1929, the United States sank into a deep economic crisis called the Great Depression. Banks all over the country failed, taking the savings of millions of Americans with them. Jobs became increasingly hard to find. Within a few years, about one-fourth of American workers were unemployed. Increasing numbers of people were hungry, homeless, and had little hope. President Hoover attempted several measures to bring the nation out of its economic crisis, but the situation worsened. With the presidential election of 1932, Americans wanted a change of direction, and with the election of Franklin D. Roosevelt, they got a "New Deal" in contrast to the policies of President Hoover.

12. Using inferences you have made based on the table and the passage, describe the ways in which Presidents Herbert Hoover and Franklin D. Roosevelt viewed the responsibilities and powers of the federal government. Support your inferences by incorporating relevant and specific examples from the table and the passage, as well as your own knowledge of the enduring issue and the circumstances surrounding the two administrations. This task may require 25 minutes to complete. You may use additional sheets of paper to complete your answer.

_____

_____

UNIT 3

Interpret Political Cartoons

Use with *Student Book* pp. 58–59

SS CONTENT TOPICS: I.CG.c.1, I.CG.c.3, I.CG.c.6, II.CG.e.1, II.E.d.7, II.E.d.10, II.USH.f.8, II.USH.f.9
SS PRACTICES: SSP.1.a, SSP.1.b, SSP.2.a, SSP.2.b, SSP.5.a, SSP.5.b, SSP.6.b, SSP.7.a

1 Review the Skill

Interpreting a political cartoon calls for close study of the various elements in order to determine how cartoonist creates a message through images and text. The artist will **editorialize**, or express his or her opinion on a newsworthy or controversial issue.

One way in which political cartoonists convey their ideas to readers is through the use of caricature. A caricature exaggerates or distorts the characteristics of someone or something in order to make a comment, or editorialize, upon it. Political cartoonists also use symbols and visual details to convey meaning.

2 Refine the Skill

By refining the skill of interpreting political cartoons, you will improve your study and test-taking abilities, especially as they relate to the GED® Social Studies Test. Study the information below. Then answer the questions that follow.

a THE PHILANTHROPIST

a The titles and text of cartoons often provide valuable clues for interpreting their meaning.

b Political cartoonists do not typically depict situations in a realistic fashion. Look for the ways in which the images in a cartoon are distorted or exaggerated. Consider what purpose the cartoonist might have for using these exaggerations and distortions.

"The Philanthropist," A 1930 Herblock Cartoon © Copyright The Herb Block Foundation

USING LOGIC

In this cartoon, the man eating apples has a top hat and a cane. The other man wears an old hat and coat. Based on clothing, you can infer that the man eating apples is rich, and the other man is poor.

1. Which of the following elements in this cartoon could be considered a caricature?

   A. the sign
   B. the man standing beside the light pole
   C. the man eating the apples
   D. the city pictured in the background

2. What statement is the cartoonist making about the Depression?

   A. It caused unemployment to increase.
   B. It caused the price of food in the nation to increase.
   C. It affected people in urban areas more than in rural areas.
   D. It affected the wealthy as well as the poor.

UNIT 3

★ Spotlighted Item: **DROP-DOWN**

DIRECTIONS: The passage below is incomplete. Use the information from the political cartoon to complete the passage. For each drop-down item, choose the option that correctly completes the sentence.

NEW DEAL TO THE RESCUE

This political cartoon presents one cartoonist's viewpoint on President Franklin Roosevelt's New Deal programs. President Roosevelt (FDR) is shown as a [3. Drop-down 1] trying to cure the sick man sitting in the chair. The sick man is [3. Drop-down 2]. There are several medicine bottles arrayed on the table. The initials on the medicine bottles represent [3. Drop-down 3] that are meant to cure the sick man. You can infer that the artist's attitude about the New Deal is generally [3. Drop-down 4].

Drop-Down Answer Options

3.1 A. member of Congress
   B. nurse
   C. businessman
   D. doctor

3.2 A. the New Deal
   B. the Constitution
   C. the United States
   D. the Congress

3.3 A. New Deal programs
   B. members of Congress
   C. popular medicines
   D. failed U.S. banks

3.4 A. extremely negative
   B. indifferent
   C. cautiously positive
   D. suspicious

UNIT 3

DIRECTIONS: Study the cartoon, read the questions, then choose the **best** answers.

4. In this cartoon, which of the following is represented by the figure holding the cards?

   A. Herbert Hoover
   B. Woodrow Wilson
   C. the United Nations
   D. the United States

5. The cartoonist uses the images and text together to convey which of the following feelings?

   A. optimism
   B. skepticism
   C. confusion
   D. calmness

DIRECTIONS: Study the information and the poster, read the questions, then choose the **best** answers.

Similar to political cartoons, political posters are created by artists to editorialize or express messages or beliefs. These posters may sometimes be used as propaganda, which is something designed to promote a particular idea or doctrine. This poster promotes one of the New Deal's most popular programs, the Civilian Conservation Corps. Known as the "CCC," it provided labor-intensive work for unskilled men who lived away from home in campsites where the work was located.

6. Which of the following best describes the way the artist depicts the young Civilian Conservation Corps worker on this poster?

   A. angry
   B. proud
   C. courteous
   D. exhausted

7. What was the program featured in this poster most likely designed to confront?

   A. bank failures
   B. political corruption
   C. outbreaks of disease
   D. unemployment

8. What was most likely the reason the poster had a positive propagandist message?

   A. There were too many applicants.
   B. The jobs were highly desirable.
   C. The jobs were very difficult.
   D. The wages were very good.

DIRECTIONS: Study the poster, read the questions, then choose the **best** answers.

9. Based on the information presented in the poster, what is a "Victory Home"?

   A. It is a home that flies the American flag.
   B. It is a home in which several residents own war bonds.
   C. It is a home that displays a victory sticker in the window.
   D. It is a home that finds ways to support the war effort.

10. Which of the measures listed on the poster is aimed directly at preventing shortages of gasoline?

   A. finding time to work for the war
   B. raising and sharing food
   C. walking and carrying packages
   D. conserving everything you have

11. From the information on the poster, what might one conclude about the impact of the war on society?

   A. Most people were eagerly working to support the war.
   B. The war was consuming many critical resources and causing shortages.
   C. The war provided a good way to invest money.
   D. The war effort was limited to the military and their families.

DIRECTIONS: Study the information and the cartoon, read the questions, then choose the **best** answers.

The U.S. Constitution does not specify the number of terms a President can serve. In 1940, President Roosevelt decided to run for a third term, and he won. Republicans were able to push an amendment through Congress in 1947, limiting a President to only two terms. It was ratified as the Twenty-Second Amendment in 1951.

12. Why does the cartoonist portray President Roosevelt dressed as a king?

    A. He believes Presidents should wear robes to command more respect for the office.
    B. He believes President Roosevelt is acting like a king because of his desire for a third term.
    C. He wants the United States to become a monarchy.
    D. He is mocking the monarchy of America's British allies.

13. Which of the following can be inferred as the reason a Republican-controlled Congress supported the Twenty-Second Amendment?

    A. They wanted to make sure that all future Presidents had at least two terms.
    B. They were eager to satisfy a public that wanted to place term limits on the President.
    C. They were following President Roosevelt's wish to be the only four-term President.
    D. They wanted to ensure that no other Democrat could win election more than two times.

DIRECTIONS: Study the information and the cartoon, read the questions, then choose the **best** answers.

After the Japanese bombed Pearl Harbor in late 1941, the United States was propelled into World War II. For almost four years, Americans fought in Europe against Nazi Germany and its allies and against Japan in the Pacific.

Retrieved from the Mandeville Special Collections Library, USCD

14. Which of the following does the animal in the cage represent?

    A. the United States
    B. Nazi Germany and its allies
    C. people who resisted serving in the military during World War II
    D. the lands Japan controlled in the Pacific

15. According to the cartoon, which of the following will occur as a result of buying savings bonds and stamps?

    A. allow the building of more zoos
    B. make millions of dollars for people who buy bonds and stamps
    C. help American soldiers win the war
    D. help the United States and Germany become friendly toward each other

16. According to the cartoon, in which of the following roles is the United States **best** represented?

    A. as Uncle Sam the zookeeper, keeping the dangerous Nazi animal from doing harm
    B. as a smiling duck-like bird carrying a rifle
    C. as a zookeeper trying to raise money for more cages
    D. as a large, dinosaur-like animal being carted about in a cage

Draw Conclusions

Use with *Student Book* pp. 60–61

SS CONTENT TOPICS: I.CG.b.3, I.CG.b.9, I.CG.c.1, I.CG.c.2, I.CG.c.3, I.CG.c.4, I.CG.c.6, E.a
SS PRACTICES: SSP.1.a, SSP.1.b, SSP.2.a, SSP.3.c, SSP.4.a, SSP.6.b

① Review the Skill

Recall that an inference is a logical guess based on facts or evidence. To **draw conclusions**, read the entire selection and put together the inferences you make as you read. Think about those inferences using your prior knowledge and all of the facts in the selection. Then make a judgment.

An effective conclusion should express a new idea or realization about a piece of information that is not expressed directly in the piece itself. Verify that your conclusions take the information presented further than that which has already been expressed.

② Refine the Skill

By refining the skill of drawing conclusions, you will improve your study and test-taking abilities, especially as they relate to the GED® Social Studies Test. Study the passage below. Then answer the questions that follow.

ⓐ President Franklin D. Roosevelt served during World War II. Think about the additional responsibilities laid upon a President's shoulders during wartime to help you draw conclusions.

ⓑ Use prior knowledge to help you draw conclusions. You know that the President travels often and security around the President is always tight. Use this information to answer the second question.

The Executive Office of the President, or EOP, was created in 1939 by President Franklin D. Roosevelt. The current EOP employs more than 1,800 people. **ⓐ**

The EOP is overseen by the White House Chief of Staff and is the organization in which many of the President's closest advisors work. Some advisors must be approved by Congress, but most are simply appointed by the President. These advisors oversee individual departments and offices that vary in size and number depending on the needs of the current President. Some of these offices were formed by Congress and others were created as the President needed them.

In addition to the visible parts of the EOP, such as the White House Communications Office, there are several offices responsible for maintaining the White House and providing logistic support for the President. **ⓑ** The White House Military Office is responsible for Air Force One while the Office of Presidential Advance prepares remote sites for the President's arrival when traveling.

TEST-TAKING TIP

In a test-taking situation, first make inferences. Look at the answer choices to find the conclusion that can be drawn based on those inferences.

1. Why was the Executive Office of the President created?

   A. to keep up with the increasing responsibilities of being President
   B. to create more jobs in the federal government
   C. to allow the President to press his or her agenda more clearly
   D. to increase the number of advisors to the President

2. Which of the following is the primary reason the Office of Presidential Advance prepares remote sites for a President's arrival?

   A. They need to set up meetings.
   B. They must create the President's itinerary.
   C. They are gathering information to give to the President.
   D. They are responsible for the President's safety.

UNIT 3

DIRECTIONS: Study the information, read each question, then choose the **best** answer.

The Twenty-First Amendment of the U.S. Constitution, which officially repealed Prohibition, grants individual states the right to regulate alcohol distribution and sale. The National Minimum Drinking Age Act of 1984, however, specifically requires all states to raise their minimum age for purchase and public possession of alcoholic beverages to people over age 21. States not complying face a reduction in highway funds under the Federal Highway Aid Act.

The U.S. Department of Transportation determined that all states now **comply** with the 1984 Act. The phrase "public possession" is strictly defined and does not apply to possession for the following: an established religious purpose, when accompanied by a parent, spouse, or legal guardian age 21 or older; medical purposes when prescribed or administered by a licensed physician, pharmacist, dentist, nurse, hospital, or medical institution; in private clubs or establishments; and in the course of lawful employment by a duly licensed manufacturer, wholesaler, or retailer.

3. What conclusion can you draw for the reason the federal government needed to impose a reduction in highway funds on states that did not comply with the minimum drinking age?

   A. States are routinely rewarded financially for agreeing to national guidelines.
   B. States may set their own minimum drinking age, and the only leverage the federal government had was financial.
   C. The federal government could save money by reducing highway funds.
   D. The federal government regularly fines states for not following its guidelines.

4. Based on the information in the passage, what can you conclude the meaning of *comply* to be?

   A. to admonish
   B. to oppose
   C. to compare
   D. to adhere

DIRECTIONS: Study the information, read each question, then choose the **best** answer.

The idea of "levels of government"—with the Federal Government supreme, as it was for half a century—is fading, according to the Advisory Commission on Intergovernmental Relations, a nonpartisan research agency. What has emerged, said John Shannon, executive director of the federally financed agency, is a "fend-for-yourself" system.

… According to scholars on the subject, the shift of authority is due to a broad range of forces in play over the last few years: not only the deep budget cuts in Federal domestic programs, but also the shift from a national economy based largely on manufacturing to an international economy based more on services and new technology; a new assertiveness on the part of state governments that once were dormant and **parochial**; and the mounting national debt that has robbed the Federal Government of its role in initiating new social and economic programs.

In the past, said John Kincaid, director of research for the commission, the national economy was such a dominant force that state and local governments felt powerless to act on their own, so they turned to the Federal Government for relief from economic distress. "But now the U.S. economy is no longer able, even if willing, to bail out states and localities in every instance," Mr. Kincaid wrote in *State Legislatures* magazine. "The U.S. economy and its state and local economies must all compete against powerful foreign economic forces."

From *The New York Times*' article LOOKING AT THE REAGAN RECORD ON FEDERALISM by John Herbers, ©1987

5. What was the overriding factor in the shift of authority among levels of government that was happening in the late 1980s?

   A. checks and balances
   B. separation of powers
   C. economics
   D. politics

6. With which of the following words can you replace the word *parochial* and still maintain the meaning of the passage?

   A. unsophisticated
   B. worldly
   C. broad-minded
   D. religious

DIRECTIONS: Study the information, read the question, then choose the **best** answer.

From "A Brief History of NASA":

An Act to provide for research into the problems of flight within and outside the Earth's atmosphere, and for other purposes." With this simple preamble, the Congress and the President of the United States created the National Aeronautics and Space Administration (NASA) on October 1, 1958. NASA's birth was directly related to the pressures of national defense. After World War II, the United States and the Soviet Union were engaged in the Cold War, a broad contest over the ideologies and allegiances of the nonaligned nations. During this period, space exploration emerged as a major area of contest and became known as the space race.

During the late 1940s, the Department of Defense pursued research and rocketry and upper atmospheric sciences as a means of assuring American leadership in technology. A major step forward came when President Dwight D. Eisenhower approved a plan to orbit a scientific satellite as part of the International Geophysical Year (IGY) for the period, July 1, 1957 to December 31, 1958, a cooperative effort to gather scientific data about the Earth. The Soviet Union quickly followed suit, announcing plans to orbit its own satellite.

The Naval Research Laboratory's Project Vanguard was chosen on 9 September 1955 to support the IGY effort, largely because it did not interfere with high-priority ballistic missile development programs. It used the non-military Viking rocket as its basis while an Army proposal to use the Redstone ballistic missile as the launch vehicle waited in the wings. Project Vanguard enjoyed exceptional publicity throughout the second half of 1955, and all of 1956, but the technological demands upon the program were too great and the funding levels too small to ensure success.

A full-scale crisis resulted on October 4, 1957, when the Soviets launched Sputnik 1, the world's first artificial satellite as its IGY entry. This had a "Pearl Harbor" effect on American public opinion, creating an illusion of a technological gap, and provided the impetus for increased spending for aerospace endeavors, technical and scientific educational programs, and the chartering of new federal agencies to manage air and space research and development.

Source: nasa.gov, accessed 2013

7. Which of the following conclusions can you draw based on the information?

   A. NASA was created for the primary purpose of defending the nation's borders.
   B. Sputnik gathered scientific data about Earth to be shared with the international community.
   C. NASA is the world's premier agency in space exploration.
   D. The general public plays a major role in deciding which government agencies receive the most funding and support.

DIRECTIONS: Study the information, read the question, then choose the **best** answer.

From the website of the United States Supreme Court:

EQUAL JUSTICE UNDER LAW—These words, written above the main entrance to the Supreme Court Building, express the ultimate responsibility of the Supreme Court of the United States. The Court is the highest tribunal in the Nation for all cases and controversies arising under the Constitution or the laws of the United States. As the final arbiter of the law, the Court is charged with ensuring the American people the promise of equal justice under law and, thereby, also functions as guardian and interpreter of the Constitution.

The unique position of the Supreme Court stems, in large part, from the deep commitment of the American people to the Rule of Law and to constitutional government. The United States has demonstrated an unprecedented determination to preserve and protect its written Constitution, thereby providing the American "experiment in democracy" with the oldest written Constitution still in force.

Source: supremecourt.gov, accessed 2013

8. By whom is the Supreme Court granted its power?

   A. the people of the United States
   B. the President
   C. the Congress
   D. the President's Cabinet

UNIT 3

DIRECTIONS: Study the information and the chart, read each question, then choose the **best** answer.

Prior to signing the Constitution, the thirteen original colonies had a system of government based primarily on state government. Although the colonies had formed a league of friendship under the Articles of Confederation, each state essentially governed itself. The people feared that living under a strong central government would be too similar to the way they had lived under Britain's rule. They soon discovered, however, that this system did not work, so the Constitution was drafted. The Constitution explicitly defines the powers and limits of the federal (or national) government and clarifies the relationship between the national government and the state governments. This system in which power is shared between the national and state governments is known as federalism.

Exclusive Powers of the Federal Government	Exclusive Powers of State Governments	Shared Powers	Services Typically Provided by Local Government
Print money	Establish local governments	Establish courts	Education
Declare war	Issue licenses	Create and collect taxes	Police
Establish an army and navy	Regulate intrastate commerce	Build highways	Fire
Enter into treaties with foreign governments	Conduct elections	Borrow money	Human services
Regulate commerce between states and international trade	Ratify amendments to the U.S. Constitution	Make and enforce laws	Public works
Establish post offices and issue postage	Exercise powers neither delegated to the national government nor denied to the states by the U.S. Constitution	Spend money for the betterment of the general welfare of residents	Economic development
	Establish a state Constitution	Transportation	Parks and recreation

9. Which level of government is responsible for setting aside green spaces within communities?

    A. federal government
    B. state government
    C. local government
    D. all government levels

10. Why are some powers shared between the state and federal governments?

    A. to ensure that one level of government does not become more powerful than another level of government
    B. because both levels of government need to have those powers to run their governments
    C. so that the two levels do not interfere with each other
    D. to be certain that all the responsibilities of government to its citizens are being met by all levels of government

11. Why do the exclusive powers of state governments include "Exercise powers neither delegated to the national government nor denied to the states by the U.S. Constitution"?

    A. The states were worried about a federal government that was too powerful, so they made sure that they would be able to exercise rights not explicitly delegated or prohibited.
    B. The states gave up their right to enter into treaties with foreign governments in exchange for all other rights not explicitly delegated or prohibited.
    C. The states wanted to be certain they would ultimately have power over the federal government.
    D. The states believed the federal government should only acquire new powers with the approval of two-thirds of the states.

Determine Point of View

Use with *Student Book* pp. 62–63

① Review the Skill

SS CONTENT TOPICS: I.CG.a.1, I.CG.b.2, I.CG.b.3, I.CG.b.4, I.CG.b.5, I.CG.b.6, I.CG.b.7, I.CG.b.8, I.CG.c.1, I.CG.c.3, I.CG.d.2
SS PRACTICES: SSP.1.a, SSP.1.b, SSP.2.a, SSP.2.b, SSP.5.a, SSP.5.c, SSP.5.d, SSP.6.b

It is crucial to **determine point of view** in order to gain a complete understanding of a writer's work. A writer's purpose, such as to inform or to persuade, can help clarify his or her point of view. Historians try to present facts impartially, without a clear point of view, but when examining historical documents, a point of view usually is evident.

In addition to written texts, other works such as political cartoons, paintings, and sculptures can also express the points of view of their creators. As in a written work, the point of view is the perspective that the artist expresses through the work.

② Refine the Skill

By refining the skill of determining point of view, you will improve your study and test-taking abilities, especially as they relate to the GED® Social Studies Test. Study the information below. Then answer the questions that follow.

a Look for the data or reasons used to support the author's point of view. In this passage, the author cites statistics to support his or her point.

b To determine the author's purpose for writing think about the topic, the intended audience, and the effect on the reader. Does the author just want to convey information, or does the author want to effect change?

The National Rifle Association is facing attacks from Gun Owners of America for being too soft on gun control. This is like a double cheeseburger coming under severe criticism for lacking enough cholesterol.

Universal background checks are supported by **a** 91 percent of Americans. Yet there is enormous resistance in Congress to passing a strong bill to keep arms out of the wrong hands. **b** What does "rule of the people" mean if a 9-to-1 issue is having so much trouble gaining traction?

Or consider the *Morning Joe/Marist* poll last week showing 64 percent of Americans saying that job creation should be the top priority for elected officials. Only 33 percent said their focus should be on reducing the deficit. In light of Friday's disappointing jobs report, the public's instinct is sound. Yet politicians in our nation's capital are so obsessed with the deficit you'd imagine they still haven't heard how many Americans are unemployed or underemployed.

From *The Washington Post's* article THE END OF MAJORITY RULE? by E. J. Dionne Jr., © 2013

MAKING ASSUMPTIONS

Assume that authors have beliefs that they express in their writings, although they may not explicitly state them. Look for opinions, and determine the point of view they convey.

1. Which of the following **best** describes the author's point of view?

   A. Legislators are not following the will of the people.
   B. The National Rifle Association is too soft on gun control.
   C. Congress should pass a strong gun bill.
   D. Elected officials should be focusing on reducing the deficit.

2. Which of the following **best** describes the author's purpose for writing?

   A. to commend Congress for its strong position on gun control
   B. to reprimand Congress for its action on gun control
   C. to explain Congress's reasons for resisting gun control
   D. to praise Congress on its commitment to deficit reduction

UNIT 3

DIRECTIONS: Study the information and the excerpt, read each question, then choose the **best** answer.

King Henry VIII of England closed Catholic monasteries and other religious houses when he declared himself head of the Church of England in 1536. The poor, along with older people and people with disabilities, who had previously relied on those religious organizations for relief, had to instead rely on the government.

From an English "Poor Law" written by William Marshall in 1536:

Therefore his highness, of his most blessed and godly disposition, like a virtuous prince and gracious head regarding as well the maintenance of the commonwealth of his realm, the body, as the relief of the poor, wretched and miserable people whereof be a great multitude in his realm, and the redress and avoiding of all valiant beggars and idle persons within the same ... has by the advice of the lords spiritual and temporary and the commons in this present Parliament assembled ... provided certain remedies as well for the help and relief of such idle, valiant beggars as has been before remembered, as of such poor and miserable people as be before rehearsed, in manner and form following ...

3. What can be determined about the king's point of view of the poor in England?

   A. He views them with love.
   B. He regards them with suspicion.
   C. He feels guilty about their situation.
   D. He believes that they have many advantages.

4. Based on the tone of this law, which of the following was most likely a provision of the law?

   A. Anyone expressing need for aid would receive it.
   B. Jobs were found for all poor people.
   C. Begging would be legal.
   D. Poor children would be provided with apprenticeships.

DIRECTIONS: Study the information, read each question, then choose the **best** answer.

From Chinese emperor K'ang His's *The Sacred Edicts* (1670):

1. Highly esteem familial piety and the proper relations among brothers in order to give due importance to social relations.

2. Give due weight to kinship in order to promote harmony and peace.

3. Maintain good relations with the neighborhood in order to prevent quarrels and lawsuits.

4. Give due importance to farming and the cultivation of mulberry trees in order to ensure sufficient clothing and food.

5. Be moderate and economical in order to avoid wasting your livelihood.

6. Make the most of schools and academies in order to honor the ways of scholars.

7. Denounce strange beliefs in order to elevate the true doctrine.

8. Explain laws and regulations in order to warn the ignorant and obstinate.

9. Show propriety and courtesy to improve customs and manners.

10. Work hard in your professions in order to quiet your ambitions.

5. In which of the following ways can the second part of each of the edicts be characterized?

   A. threatening
   B. explanatory
   C. persuasive
   D. cryptic

6. Think about the author's purpose for writing these edicts. To which of the following are these edicts most similar?

   A. instructions for assembling an appliance
   B. a series of e-mail messages about a project
   C. a list of civic responsibilities
   D. a timeline showing important historical events

UNIT 3

DIRECTIONS: Study the political cartoon and the information, read the question, then choose the **best** answer.

"IT'S ALL RIGHT TO SEAT THEM. THEY'RE NOT AMERICANS," a 1961 Herblock Cartoon, © The Herb Block Foundation

Many foreign diplomats visit the United States or live and work in the Washington, D.C., area at consulates and embassies. In the early 1960s, segregation and discrimination against African Americans in Southern states was common. Jim Crow laws were widespread. President John F. Kennedy urged governors from the South to assure "a friendly and dignified reception" for foreign diplomats. The governor of Virginia—a state that borders the capital—promised President Kennedy that he would provide courtesy, yet he strongly suggested that diplomats should identify themselves as such. This political cartoon by Herb Block was published in *The Washington Post* on April 27, 1961, and is based on an actual occurrence.

7. Which would you interpret as the cartoonist's viewpoint on the situation depicted in his cartoon?

   A. He believes it makes sense for diplomats to identify themselves.
   B. He finds it absurd that foreigners are treated with more respect than Americans.
   C. He believes that the restaurant owners and employees are capable of making distinctions between Americans and foreigners.
   D. He believes it would be best if foreign diplomats did not dine in restaurants in Southern states.

DIRECTIONS: Study the information, read each question, then choose the **best** answer.

The following is a response to an article that was published in *The Washington Post* on October 24, 2012, entitled "U.S. Set to Keep Kill Lists for Years." The response was written by Bruce Fein, of Washington, D.C., who was Associate Deputy Attorney General of the United States from 1981 to 1983:

Endowing the president with the authority to play prosecutor, judge, jury and executioner of any person on the planet (including U.S. citizens) that he secretly and unilaterally decrees to be dangerous to the United States epitomizes the executive tyranny that provoked the American Revolution.

Neither in the text nor subtext of the Constitution is there a syllable hinting at such harrowing power. The U.S. government has crossed into lawlessness, inviting every man to become a law unto himself. To borrow from words by Thomas Jefferson about slavery, "I tremble for my country when I reflect that God is just, and that his justice cannot sleep forever."

From washingtonpost.com, accessed 2013

8. Which of the following best characterizes the point of view of the writer?

   A. He believes the President should be a law unto himself.
   B. He believes that the decisions mentioned in the article should be made by consent of the people.
   C. He believes the rule of law is not being followed.
   D. He is concerned that the separation of powers is too limiting.

9. Based on the tone of this response, which of the following was most likely discussed in the original article?

   A. the winding down of counterterrorism efforts
   B. the intention of the U.S. government to continue adding names to "kill lists"
   C. the government's decision to phase out drone strikes
   D. the intent to declassify government information on terrorists

DIRECTIONS: Study the information, read the question, then choose the **best** answer.

From the introduction to *The Politics of Executive Privilege* by Louis Fisher:

Presidents and their advisers cite various legal principles when they withhold documents from Congress and refuse to allow executive officials to testify before congressional committees. Congress can marshal its own impressive list of legal citations to defend legislative access to information, even when Presidents assert executive privilege. These legal and constitutional principles, finely honed as they might be, are often overridden by the politics of the moment and practical considerations. Efforts to discover enduring and enforceable norms in this area invariably fall short …

… It is tempting to see executive-legislative clashes only as a confrontation between two branches, yielding a winner and a loser. It is more than that. Congressional access represents part of the framers' belief in representative government. When lawmakers are unable (or unwilling) to obtain executive branch information needed for congressional deliberations, the loss extends to the public, democracy, and constitutional government. Ever since World War II, there has been a steady flow of political power to the President. Some are comfortable with that trend because they believe that power is exercised more efficiently and effectively by the executive branch. The cost is great, however, to the checks and balances and separation of powers that the framers knew were essential to protect individual rights and liberties.

From THE POLITICS OF EXECUTIVE PRIVILEGE by Louis Fisher © 2004

10. Which of the following best expresses the author's point of view?

   A. Increasing the political power of the President is a mistake.
   B. Congress has no legal authority to demand documents from the executive branch.
   C. Executive privilege extends to all areas of government.
   D. Power is exercised most effectively by the executive branch.

DIRECTIONS: Study the information, read the question, then choose the **best** answer.

The following excerpt from Yale Law School Faculty Scholarship Series, Paper 178, is in response to Larry Kramer's 2002 Jorde Lecture in which Kramer argues for "popular constitutionalism," meaning a system in which the people assume control over interpretation and enforcement of constitutional law:

In contrast to Kramer, we do not understand judicial supremacy and popular constitutionalism to be mutually exclusive systems of constitutional ordering. Kramer defines judicial supremacy as resting on the concept of judicial finality. Yet some forms of judicial finality are essential to the rule of law, which is necessary for a functioning democracy. For this reason both judicial supremacy and popular constitutionalism each contribute indispensable benefits to the American constitutional polity. They are in fact dialectically interconnected and have long coexisted.

As Kramer models the problem, judicial supremacy and popular constitutionalism are distinct and competing forms of constitutional ordering; the nation must choose whether to institutionalize one or the other. Either the people or the Court must have the last word, and Kramer chooses the people. Although we agree with Kramer that there can be deep tension between judicial supremacy and popular constitutionalism, there are also vital interdependencies between judicial supremacy and popular constitutionalism that Kramer fails to appreciate. The question we pursue, therefore, is how the nation can strike a viable balance between the rule of law and the people's authority to speak to issues of constitutional meaning.

From POPULAR CONSTITUTIONALISM, DEPARTMENTALISM, AND JUDICIAL SUPREMACY by Robert C. Post and Reva B. Siegel, © 2004

11. Which of the following statements best summarizes the point of view of the two authors?

   A. For a democracy to function, popular constitutionalism must be followed.
   B. Judicial supremacy must be maintained at the cost of popular constitutionalism.
   C. The Court has the final say in all matters.
   D. Both rule of law and popular constitutionalism are necessary.

LESSON 10

Analyze Information Sources

Use with *Student Book* pp. 64–65

SS CONTENT TOPICS: I.CG.b.9, I.CG.c.3, I.CG.c.4, I.CG.c.5, I.CG.c.6
SS PRACTICES: SSP.1.a, SSP.1.b, SSP.2.a, SSP.3.d, SSP.5.a, SSP.5.b, SSP.6.b, SSP.8.a

UNIT 3

1 Review the Skill

By **analyzing information sources**, you can gain a better understanding of what you can expect to learn from these sources. You can also determine the reliability of the information found in each source. All sources have a degree of **bias**, so evaluate each source critically.

The ability to analyze information sources becomes particularly important when using online information. It is crucial to verify that online information comes from a trusted source. Typically, websites that end with *.edu*, *.gov*, or *.org* feature more reliable information than those that end with *.com*. A *.gov* is a government website; a *.edu* is a website from an educational institution (such as a university); and a *.org* is generally a website from a non-profit organization. Websites that end in *.com* are commercial websites that have the goal of selling or marketing.

2 Refine the Skill

By refining the skill of analyzing information sources, you will improve your study and test-taking abilities, especially as they relate to the GED® Social Studies Test. Study the information below. Then answer the questions that follow.

a This information comes from a *.gov* website. As a result, it should generally be considered trustworthy.

a From a *.gov* website:

The Department of Homeland Security was established in 2002, in response to the terrorist attacks on the United States on September 11, 2001. The goal of this organization was to provide a unified anti-terrorism agency focused on raising awareness of terrorist threats in the nation, as well as preventing future terrorist attacks from occurring.

b Information from a *.com* website such as this generally tends to be less trustworthy than information from a *.gov* website. Be sure to support information from *.com* sources with identical information found in a more reliable source.

b From a *.com* website:

The Department of Homeland Security was formed on September 11, 2001, after the terrorist attacks that happened on that day. The Department of Homeland Security was set up by George W. Bush. It is now involved in tracking down terrorists around the world. This agency has been very successful.

MAKING ASSUMPTIONS

Always use your best judgment when evaluating information. If the source appears to be unfairly biased, you should verify it with information from a more reputable source.

1. Which of the following is directly disputed between the two excerpts?

   A. the date on which the Department of Homeland Security was created
   B. the reason for the creation of the Department of Homeland Security
   C. the responsibilities of the Department of Homeland Security
   D. the creator of the Department of Homeland Security

2. In comparison to that of the second excerpt, in which of the following ways could the tone of the first excerpt be described?

   A. scholarly
   B. biased
   C. informal
   D. emotional

Spotlighted Item: **DROP-DOWN**

DIRECTIONS: The passage below is incomplete. Use information from the table to complete the passage. For each drop-down item, choose the option that correctly completes the sentence.

Type of Federalism	Time Period	Characteristics
Dual federalism	1789–1930	States and federal government are separate, sovereign, equal Federal government powers are limited to those listed in Constitution
Cooperative federalism	1930–1960	Federal powers increase in order to deal with effects of the Great Depression Federal and state governments share powers and cooperate
Creative federalism	1960–1980	Federal government bypasses states and gives special-purpose grants directly to local governments Grants can be used only for the designated purpose Local governments and states bear costs of implementing grants
New federalism	1981–	Federal government gives more open-ended "block" grants Local and state governments have more choice about how grants are used Power shifts to states for some programs

Federalism has shaped the United States from its beginning as a nation. The face of federalism itself has changed over the years. The table, whose source was most likely a

    3. Drop-down 1   , traces the history of the different

forms of federalism and their characteristics. It illustrates how the relationship between the states and the federal government has ebbed and flowed over the years in an attempt to find a balance between state and federal governments.

The information in the table is   3. Drop-down 2
based on its source. The table is most useful for

    3. Drop-down 3   . Although the table contains factual information about federalism and its history in the United States, one can interpret the information in different ways. For example, a statement such as "dual federalism was the most effective as evidenced by its longevity" is   3. Drop-down 4
interpretation of the table.

Drop-Down Answer Options

3.1 A. journal entry
    B. newspaper editorial
    C. political speech
    D. college history textbook

3.2 A. unreliable
    B. impartial
    C. biased
    D. propaganda

3.3 A. discovering how the types of federalism were named
    B. learning the characteristics of the different types of federalism
    C. determining the President's views on federalism
    D. categorizing government rights

3.4 A. a biased
    B. an impartial
    C. a bitter
    D. an angry

UNIT 3

DIRECTIONS: Study the passage, read each question, then choose the **best** answer.

From "Fiscal Federalism," by Chris Edwards of the CATO Institute, February 2009:

Under the Constitution, the federal government was assigned specific limited powers and most government functions were left to the states. To ensure that people understood the limits on federal power, the Framers added the Constitution's Tenth Amendment: "The powers not delegated to the United States by the Constitution, nor prohibited by it to the States, are reserved to the States respectively, or to the people."

The Tenth Amendment embodies federalism, the idea that federal and state governments have separate areas of activity and that federal responsibilities were "few and defined," as James Madison noted. Historically, federalism acted as a safeguard of American freedoms. Indeed, President Ronald Reagan noted in a 1987 executive order, "Federalism is rooted in the knowledge that our political liberties are best assured by limiting the size and scope of the national government."

Unfortunately, policymakers and courts have mainly discarded federalism in recent decades. Congress has undertaken many activities that were traditionally reserved to the states and the private sector. Grants-in-aid are a primary mechanism that the federal government has used to extend its power into state and local affairs. Grants are subsidy programs that are combined with federal regulatory controls to micromanage state and local activities.

The federal government spends about $500 billion annually on aid to the states, making it the third largest item in the budget after Social Security and national defense. The number of different aid programs has soared from 463 in 1990 to 814 by 2006.

With this large and complex array of aid activities, federal and state policymakers are mainly interested in the spending levels of programs and regulatory compliance, not on delivering quality services. And by involving all levels of government in just about every policy activity, the aid system creates a lack of accountability. Congress should reconsider aid programs, and begin terminating activities that could be better performed by the states or the private sector.

From downsizinggovernment.org, accessed 2013

4. Which of the following **best** describes the way this source is biased?

A. This source is biased against accountability.
B. This source is biased toward federal aid programs.
C. This source is biased against states' rights.
D. This source is biased toward federalism.

5. Which of the following **best** characterizes the tone of the article?

A. dissatisfied
B. elusive
C. indifferent
D. furious

DIRECTIONS: Study the passage, read the question, then choose the **best** answer.

From "My Endorsement: Checks and Balances," by Mike Henry, Adjunct Professor of History Prince George's Community College, for washingtonpost.com, October 23, 2010:

I endorse Robert Ehrlich for governor of Maryland.

I am a registered Democrat, and I do not support all of Mr. Ehrlich's positions. But I back him because I am a disciple of James Madison and believe in checks and balances. Our Founding Fathers were right: The people are safer and more secure in their liberty when power is divided.

Both houses of Maryland's General Assembly are firmly in Democratic hands, and with the governorship the party is in complete control. This single vision concerning taxes, services and social problems is unhealthy, as decisions are often made without serious debate or input from those with another point of view. We have witnessed the dangers of one-party control at the national level as both Republicans (2002–06) and Democrats (2009–10) ran roughshod over the opposition and failed to seek bipartisan cooperation. This situation is clearly not good for the people of Maryland.

From washingtonpost.com, accessed 2013

6. In which of the following ways does the author of this editorial support his opinion?

A. He describes the reliability of his argument.
B. He gives details about Mr. Ehrlich's positions.
C. He points out flaws in opposing arguments.
D. He refers to opinions similar to his own.

DIRECTIONS: Study the passage, read each question, then choose the **best** answer.

From The Center for Legislative Archives, a part of the National Archives and Records Administration:

Martha Griffiths (D-MI) was a member of the United States House of Representatives from 1955–1974. She was the first woman to serve on the powerful House Committee on Ways and Means and was instrumental in getting the prohibition of sex discrimination added to the landmark Civil Rights Act of 1964. Griffiths is also known for resurrecting the Equal Rights Amendment (ERA). The ERA was a proposed amendment to the U.S. Constitution that guaranteed equal rights under the law for Americans regardless of their sex. The ERA was first drafted in 1923 by suffragist Alice Paul. Following the enactment of the Nineteenth Amendment granting women the right to vote, Paul believed the ERA to be the next step in guaranteeing equal justice to all citizens.

From 1923 to 1970, some form of the ERA was introduced in every session of Congress. But, nearly every time that the ERA was introduced, it was held up in committee. In 1970, Griffiths filed a discharge petition to demand that the ERA be heard by the full House. A discharge petition, which requires the signatures of a majority of House members, forces proposed legislation out of committee so that it may be considered by the whole House of Representatives. Following the success of Griffiths's discharge petition, the ERA was passed by the House. However, the Senate attempted to add provisions exempting women from the draft, which effectively killed the chances of the ERA passing that session.

After some changes to the wording of the amendment, Griffiths re-introduced the ERA in the 92nd Congress as HJ Res. 208. After months of debate, hearings and House Judiciary Committee proposed changes, the ERA, as introduced by Griffiths, was approved by the House on October 12, 1971. The Senate approved an identical version on March 22, 1972, sending the ERA to the states with a seven-year deadline for ratification. In 1978, with the seven-year deadline fast approaching, and the ERA lacking the required number of state ratifications, Congress extended the time limit to June 30, 1982. However, by the time the extended deadline arrived, the ERA had only been ratified by 35 states— three states short of the three-fourths required for ratification of constitutional amendments.

Controversy surrounding the Equal Rights Amendment persists today. Despite failing to garner enough support from the states by the deadline, some proponents argue that the existing 35 ratifications are still valid, and that only an additional three state ratifications are needed to pass the ERA. As recently as 2005, resolutions attempting to revive the ERA have been introduced to Congress, but none of these resolutions have made it to a floor vote in either the House or the Senate.

From archives.gov, accessed 2013

7. Which of the following **best** describes this information source?

   A. unreliable
   B. balanced
   C. incorrect
   D. impassioned

8. Which of the following interpretations may be considered biased against the Equal Rights Amendment?

   A. The Equal Rights Amendment would guarantee equal justice to all citizens regardless of sex.
   B. The Equal Rights Amendment was a result of the suffragist movement.
   C. The Equal Rights Amendment should not have been heard by the whole House of Representatives.
   D. The Equal Rights Amendment needed to be ratified by three more states.

9. Which of the following can you determine using this information source?

   A. the representative who introduced the Equal Rights Amendment to Congress
   B. the fraction of states that must ratify an amendment for it to become part of the Constitution
   C. the number of Senators that approved the Equal Rights Amendment in 1972, sending it to the states to be ratified
   D. the House members that voted in favor of forcing the Equal Rights Amendment out of committee

Generalize

Use with *Student Book* pp. 66–67

SS CONTENT TOPICS: I.CG.c.1, I.CG.c.3, I.CG.c.5, I.CG.c.6
SS PRACTICES: SSP.1.a, SSP.1.b, SSP.2.a

1 Review the Skill

A **generalization** is a broad statement that applies to an entire group of items. You can **generalize** about people, places, things, events, and so on. In order to make a valid generalization, you must be able to support your generalization with factual evidence or examples. A faulty generalization, such as *all frogs are green*, does not correspond to the fact that frogs have many different skin colors.

Historians may generalize about a topic when most of the factual evidence points to one conclusion, even though exceptions may exist.

2 Refine the Skill

By refining the skill of generalizing, you will improve your study and test-taking abilities, especially as they relate to the GED® Social Studies Test. Study the information below. Then answer the questions that follow.

a You can use facts and information in a passage to make your own generalizations.

b Look for words that provide clues to indicate that the author is making a generalization. These clues may not always be obvious.

The Executive Branch conducts diplomacy with other nations, and the President has the power to negotiate and sign treaties, which also must be ratified by two-thirds of the Senate. The President can issue executive orders, which direct executive officers or clarify and further existing laws. The President also has unlimited power to extend pardons and clemencies for federal crimes, except in cases of impeachment. **a**

With these powers come several responsibilities, among them a constitutional requirement to "from time to time give to the Congress Information of the State of the Union, and recommend to their Consideration such Measures as he shall judge necessary and expedient." **b** Although the President may fulfill this requirement in any way he or she chooses, Presidents have traditionally given a State of the Union address to a joint session of Congress each January (except in inaugural years), outlining their agenda for the coming year.

From whitehouse.gov, accessed 2013

MAKING ASSUMPTIONS

A government website is a reliable source. You can assume that in an informative article on that website, generalizations are valid and the information may be used to support other generalizations.

1. "Presidents have traditionally given a State of the Union address to a joint session of Congress each January (except in inaugural years), outlining their agenda for the coming year." Which of the following words provides a clue that the author is making a generalization in this statement?

   A. traditionally
   B. joint
   C. each
   D. outlining

2. With which of the following do Presidents generally share many similar responsibilities?

   A. Representatives
   B. Senators
   C. governors
   D. Cabinet Secretaries

DIRECTIONS: Study the information, read the question, then choose the **best** answer.

From "What is the Sequester? Why Now?," February 2013:

In the last few years, President Obama and both parties in Congress have worked together to reduce our deficit by more than $2.5 trillion through a combination of spending cuts and increased tax rates.

In 2011, Congress passed a law saying that if they couldn't agree on a plan to reduce our deficit by $4 trillion—including the $2.5 trillion in deficit reduction lawmakers in both parties have already accomplished over the last few years—about $1 trillion in automatic, arbitrary and across-the-board budget cuts would start to take effect in 2013.

Unfortunately, Congress hasn't compromised, and as a consequence, harmful cuts—known as the sequester—begin March 1.

These cuts will jeopardize our military readiness and eviscerate job-creating investments in education and energy and medical research, and don't take into account whether they eliminate some bloated program that has outlived its usefulness, or cut a vital service that Americans depend on every single day.

"The whole design of these arbitrary cuts was to make them so unattractive and unappealing that Democrats and Republicans would actually get together and find a good compromise of sensible cuts as well as closing tax loopholes and so forth. And so this was all designed to say we can't do these bad cuts; let's do something smarter. That was the whole point of this so-called sequestration."

—President Obama

From whitehouse.gov, accessed 2013

3. Which of the following generalizations can be made based on the information in the passage?

   A. Many government programs cost too much money and have outlived their usefulness.
   B. Only government services that Americans depend on every day should not be cut.
   C. Democrats and Republicans are often forced to compromise.
   D. The plan for sequestration was agreed on by everyone in Congress.

DIRECTIONS: Study the information, read the question, then choose the **best** answer.

As stated in Article II, Section 4 of the Constitution of the United States, "The President, Vice President and all civil officers of the United States, shall be removed from office on impeachment for, and conviction of, treason, bribery, or other high crimes and misdemeanors."

The sole power of impeachment lies with the House of Representatives. The Constitution does not set forth exactly how this is done, but historically, the House issues a resolution authorizing the Judiciary Committee to investigate charges. If this Committee supports the charges, it issues an impeachment resolution, which includes Articles of Impeachment. The House of Representatives then discusses and votes on the Articles of Impeachment. A majority vote on any of the Articles is considered impeachment by the House.

The Senate has the sole power to try all impeachments, according to Article 1, Section 3 of the U.S. Constitution. During the trial, members of the House act as prosecutors, and the full Senate acts as a jury. The Senators meet in a closed session to discuss a verdict. A vote is taken in open session on each Article of Impeachment. If two-thirds of the Senate votes in favor of conviction, the official is impeached. The official is acquitted if no Article of Impeachment is approved by two-thirds of the Senate. To date, no President or Vice President of the United States has ever been impeached by the Senate.

4. What evidence from the passage supports the following generalization?

   All of the officers who have been impeached by the House of Representatives have been acquitted by the Senate.

   A. To date, no President or Vice President has been impeached by the Senate.
   B. A vote is taken in open session on each Article of Impeachment.
   C. The sole power of impeachment lies with the House of Representatives.
   D. The Senate discusses and votes on impeachment at the same time as the House of Representatives does.

Spotlighted Item: **EXTENDED RESPONSE**

DIRECTIONS: Read the information and the question, then write your answer on the lines below. Please refer to Unit 3 and Unit 4 in the Reasoning Through Language Arts Student Edition and Workbook for detailed information about reading, writing, and editing Extended Response answers. You may use another sheet of paper to complete your answer.

From "Digital Government: Building a 21st-Century Platform to Better Serve the American People":

   Today's amazing mix of cloud computing, ever-smarter mobile devices, and collaboration tools is changing the consumer landscape and bleeding into government as both an opportunity and a challenge. New expectations require the federal government to be ready to deliver and receive digital information and services anytime, anywhere and on any device. It must do so safely, securely, and with fewer resources. To build for the future, the federal government needs a Digital Strategy that embraces the opportunity to innovate more with less, and enables entrepreneurs to better leverage government data to improve the quality of services to the American people.

   … Building for the future requires us to think beyond programmatic lines. To keep up with the pace of change in technology, we need to securely architect our systems for interoperability and openness from conception. We need to have common standards and more rapidly share the lessons learned by early adopters. We need to produce better content and data, and present it through multiple channels in a program and device-agnostic way. We need to adopt a coordinated approach to ensure privacy and security in a digital age.

   These imperatives are not new, but many of the solutions are. We can use modern tools and technologies to seize the digital opportunity and fundamentally change how the federal government serves both its internal and external customers—building a 21st-century platform to better serve the American People.

From whitehouse.gov, accessed 2013

5. Identify a generalization made in the passage about the federal government's current use of technology. In your response develop an argument to support the generalization with evidence from the passage that reflects the enduring issue about "digital government." Incorporate relevant and specific evidence from the passage, and from your own knowledge of the issue and the circumstances surrounding the issue. This task may require 25 minutes to complete.

_____

_____

_____

_____

_____

_____

_____

DIRECTIONS: Study the information, read the question, then choose the **best** answer.

From "The Constitutional Amendment Process," National Archives and Records Administration:

The Constitution provides that an amendment may be proposed either by the Congress with a two-thirds majority vote in both the House of Representatives and the Senate or by a constitutional convention called for by two-thirds of the State legislatures. None of the 27 amendments to the Constitution have been proposed by constitutional convention. The Congress proposes an amendment in the form of a joint resolution. Since the President does not have a constitutional role in the amendment process, the joint resolution does not go to the White House for signature or approval. The original document is forwarded directly to NARA's (National Archives and Records Administration's) Office of the Federal Register (OFR) for processing and publication. The OFR adds legislative history notes to the joint resolution and publishes it. … The OFR also assembles an information package for the States which includes … copies of the joint resolution … and the statutory procedure for ratification under 1 U.S.C.106b.

The Archivist submits the proposed amendment to the States for their consideration by sending a letter of notification to each Governor along with the informational material prepared by the OFR. The Governors then formally submit the amendment to their State legislatures. In the past, some State legislatures have not waited to receive official notice before taking action on a proposed amendment. When a State ratifies a proposed amendment, it sends the Archivist an original or certified copy of the State action, which is immediately conveyed to the Director of the Federal Register. The OFR examines ratification documents for facial legal sufficiency and an authenticating signature. If the documents are found to be in good order, the Director acknowledges receipt and maintains custody of them. The OFR retains these documents until an amendment is adopted or fails, and then transfers the records to the National Archives for preservation.

From archives.gov, accessed 2013

6. Which of the following is a valid generalization about proposed amendments based on the information in the passage?

  A. Constitutional amendments are typically proposed by Congress.
  B. State legislatures usually do not take action on a proposed amendment before they have received official notice.
  C. The President is generally involved in the amendment process.
  D. Most amendments commonly are ratified by state legislatures.

DIRECTIONS: Study the information, read the question, then choose the **best** answer.

From "Statutory Authority," U.S. Department of Justice:

In 1870, after the post-Civil War increase in the amount of litigation involving the United States necessitated the very expensive retention of a large number of private attorneys to handle the workload, a concerned Congress passed the Act to Establish the Department of Justice, ch. 150, 16 Stat. 162 (1870) setting it up as "an executive department of the government of the United States" with the Attorney General as its head. Officially coming into existence on July 1, 1870, the Department of Justice, pursuant to the 1870 Act, was to handle the legal business of the United States. The Act gave the Department control over all criminal prosecutions and civil suits in which the United States had an interest. In addition, the Act gave the Attorney General and the Department control over federal law enforcement. To assist the Attorney General, the 1870 Act created the Office of the Solicitor General.

From justice.gov, accessed 2013

7. What evidence from the passage refutes the following generalization?

The United States government is involved in all court cases at every level.

  A. It is expensive to hire private attorneys to handle government business.
  B. The Department of Justice is an executive department of the U.S. government.
  C. The Department of Justice is involved only in cases in which the United States has an interest.
  D. The Attorney General and Department of Justice have control over federal law enforcement.

Identify Problem and Solution

Use with *Student Book* pp. 68–69

SS CONTENT TOPICS: I.CG.c.1, I.CG.c.2, I.CG.c.3, II.CG.e.1, II.CG.e.3, II.CG.f, II.G.b.5
SS PRACTICES: SSP.1.a, SSP.1.b, SSP.2.a, SSP.2.b, SSP.4.a, SSP.5.a, SSP.5.c, SSP.6.b

1 Review the Skill

When learning about social studies, you will have many opportunities to **identify problems**, or conflicts, and their **solutions**. When thinking about a problem, consider factors that may have caused the problem. You can then evaluate potential solutions based on how effectively each addresses the problem.

To evaluate the effectiveness of a solution, try to predict how it would impact the problem. In addition, consider the possible benefits or drawbacks of the solution. Then you can weigh each possible solution to determine which is best.

2 Refine the Skill

By refining the skill of identifying problem and solution, you will improve your study and test-taking abilities, especially as they relate to the GED® Social Studies Test. Study the passage below. Then answer the questions that follow.

The following article appeared in the online version of *The Washington Post*, August 28, 2012:

a This information begins by stating the solution to a problem. Look for details about the new rules to help you answer the second question.

a The Obama administration announced strict new vehicle fuel-efficiency standards Tuesday, requiring that the U.S. auto fleet average 54.5 miles per gallon by 2025, an uncontroversial move that, unlike other administration energy policies, was endorsed by industry and environmentalists alike.

The new rules, announced by Transportation Secretary Ray LaHood and Environmental Protection Agency administrator Lisa P. Jackson, expand on existing standards requiring American-made cars and light trucks to average 34.5 mpg by 2016. They will significantly cut U.S. oil consumption and greenhouse gas emissions by the time they are fully implemented, according to the EPA.

b This passage describes a solution. The problem is not immediately evident. As you read, you must infer what the problem is based on the effects of the solution.

b "These fuel standards represent the single most important step we've ever taken to reduce our dependence on foreign oil," President Obama said in a statement.

TEST-TAKING TIPS

Prior knowledge can help you answer questions. Use what you already know about gasoline, how it is made, and fluctuating gas prices to help identify the problem that the new fuel-efficiency standards address.

1. Which of the following problems will the vehicle fuel-efficiency standards address?

   A. oil consumption
   B. energy policies
   C. non-American-made vehicles
   D. factory pollution

2. Which of the following **best** characterizes the solution?

   A. excessive
   B. continuing
   C. instant
   D. disproportionate

DIRECTIONS: Study the information, read each question, then choose the **best** answer.

From "Remarks on Energy," given by President Barack H. Obama at the Argonne National Laboratory, Illinois, March 15, 2013:

So Dr. Isaacs said these cuts will force him to stop any new project that's coming down the line. And I'm quoting him now—he says, "This sudden halt on new starts will freeze American science in place while the rest of the world races forward, and it will knock a generation of young scientists off their stride, ultimately costing billions of dollars in missed future opportunities." I mean, essentially because of this sequester, we're looking at two years where we don't start new research. And at a time when every month you've got to replace your smartphone because something new has come up, imagine what that means when China and Germany and Japan are all continuing to plump up their basic research, and we're just sitting there doing nothing.

We can't afford to miss these opportunities while the rest of the world races forward. We have to seize these opportunities. I want the next great job-creating breakthroughs—whether it's in energy or nanotechnology or bioengineering—I want those breakthroughs to be right here in the United States of America, creating American jobs and maintaining our technological lead.

So I just want to be clear—these cuts will harm, not help, our economy. They aren't the smart way to cut our deficits. And that's why I'm reaching out to Republicans and Democrats to come together around a balanced approach, a smart, phased-in approach to deficit reduction that includes smart spending cuts and entitlement reforms and new revenue, and that won't hurt our middle class or slow economic growth. And if we do that, then we can move beyond governing from crisis to crisis to crisis, and we keep our focus on policies that actually create jobs and grow our economy, and move forward to face all of the other challenges we face, from fixing our broken immigration system to educating our kids to keeping them safe from gun violence.

From whitehouse.gov, accessed 2013

3. Which of the following is the main problem being highlighted in this speech?

   A. research in foreign countries
   B. the sequester
   C. an energy crisis
   D. deficit reduction

4. Which of the following does President Obama propose as a solution to this problem?

   A. creating jobs
   B. increasing research funding
   C. new taxes on the wealthy
   D. a multifaceted plan for deficit reduction

DIRECTIONS: Study the information, read each question, then choose the **best** answer.

From the U.S. Supreme Court's decision regarding the 2000 Presidential election:

The closeness of this election, and the multitude of legal challenges which have followed in its **wake**, have brought into sharp focus a common, if heretofore unnoticed, phenomenon. Nationwide statistics reveal that an estimated 2% of ballots cast do not register a vote for President for whatever reason, including deliberately choosing no candidate at all or some voter error, such as voting for two candidates or insufficiently marking a ballot. … In certifying election results, the votes eligible for inclusion in the certification are the votes meeting the properly established legal requirements.

This case has shown that punch card balloting machines can produce an unfortunate number of ballots which are not punched in a clean, complete way by the voter. After the current counting, it is likely legislative bodies nationwide will examine ways to improve the mechanisms and machinery for voting.

5. Which of the following groups does the Supreme Court charge with solving this problem?

   A. local boards of elections
   B. state courts
   C. lawmakers
   D. the Federal Election Commission

6. Which of the following can be substituted for the term *wake* in order to provide the most accurate interpretation of the text?

   A. aftermath
   B. visitation
   C. not asleep
   D. currents

DIRECTIONS: Study the information, read each question, then choose the **best** answer.

From Amendment XXIII of the U.S. Constitution (1961):

Section 1. The District constituting the seat of government of the United States shall appoint in such manner as the Congress may direct:

A number of electors of President and Vice President equal to the whole number of Senators and Representatives in Congress to which the District would be entitled if it were a state, but in no event more than the least populous state; they shall be in addition to those appointed by the states, but they shall be considered, for the purposes of the election of President and Vice President, to be electors appointed by a state; and they shall meet in the District and perform such duties as provided by the twelfth article of the amendment.

7. Which of the following problems does this solution address?

   A. imbalanced representation in the Electoral College
   B. confusion regarding the boundaries of Washington, D.C.
   C. disputes about the meeting place of the Electoral College
   D. Washington, D.C.'s, participation in presidential elections

8. Which of the following groups of individuals could have officially proposed this solution?

   A. Washington, D.C., legislators
   B. Congress
   C. the citizens of Washington, D.C.
   D. the U.S. Supreme Court

DIRECTIONS: Study the political cartoon, read each question, then choose the **best** answer.

"Free At Last!" by Pat Oliphant

9. To which of the following problems does the cartoonist seek to draw attention with this cartoon?

   A. violent riots in American cities
   B. cutbacks in police department budgets
   C. racial tensions in the United States
   D. lack of punishment for police brutality

10. Which of the following best describes the cartoonist's assessment of the President's response to this problem?

   A. timely
   B. insulting
   C. sympathetic
   D. effective

From President Franklin D. Roosevelt's first "Fireside Chat," March 12, 1933:

Because of **undermined** confidence on the part of the public, there was a general rush by a large portion of our population to turn bank deposits into currency or gold—a rush so great that the soundest banks could not get enough currency to meet the demand. The reason for this was that on the spur of the moment it was, of course, impossible to sell perfectly sound assets of a bank and convert them into cash except at panic prices far below their real value. …

It was then that I issued the proclamation providing for the first nationwide bank holiday, and this was the first step in the Government's reconstruction of our financial and economic fabric. The second step was the legislation promptly and patriotically passed by Congress confirming my proclamation and broadening my powers … to extend the holiday and lift the ban of that holiday gradually. This law also gave authority to develop a program of rehabilitation of our banking facilities.

11. Which of the following problems caused President Roosevelt to proclaim the bank holiday (closing of the banks)?

    A. Congress broadened his powers.
    B. Many people wanted their money out of banks.
    C. Banks wanted to convert currency into gold.
    D. The rush would have caused banks to sell assets for below their real values.

12. In which of the following ways could President Roosevelt's solution be seen as dangerous?

    A. It turned over all banks to the government.
    B. It closed banks when people wanted money.
    C. It caused Congress to grant the President additional powers.
    D. It changed the system of how bank deposits were accepted and paid out.

13. Which of the following can be substituted for the term *undermined* in order to provide the most accurate interpretation of the text?

    A. hidden
    B. destabilized
    C. illegal
    D. forgotten

DIRECTIONS: Study the information, read each question, then choose the **best** answer.

For many years, substances known as chlorofluorocarbons (CFCs) were used in a variety of products, such as solvents and refrigerants. However, beginning in the 1970s, scientists began to express concern over the impact of these substances on Earth's ozone layer. As new uses for CFCs emerged during the 1980s, however, fears about ozone layer damage became more urgent. With the signing of the Montreal Protocol, nations around the world agreed to cooperate in order to reduce CFCs. In the early 1990s, as new evidence came forth to show that ozone depletion was worse than previously expected, the same nations committed to ending production of all CFCs by 1996. As a result, emissions of ozone-depleting substances have already begun to fall. Some people even expect that the ozone layer will naturally heal itself within approximately 50 years.

14. Which of the following **best** describes the way in which the problem of CFCs was solved?

    A. international cooperation
    B. citizen mobilization
    C. stricter laws and regulations
    D. collaboration among special interest groups

15. In which of the following ways is this solution best characterized?

    A. immediate
    B. divisive
    C. controversial
    D. long-term

DIRECTIONS: Study the information, read the question, then choose the **best** answer.

You see, we Democrats have a very different measure of what constitutes progress in this country. We measure progress by how many people can find a job that pays the mortgage; whether you can put a little extra money away at the end of each month. …

From Barack H. Obama's address accepting the Democratic Party Presidential Nomination, August 28, 2008

16. Which of the following problems does Barack Obama's proposed solution address?

    A. the high rate of U.S. unemployment
    B. high taxes on the middle class
    C. preventing Democrats from holding office
    D. preventing Republicans from holding office

UNIT 3

Special-Purpose Maps

Use with *Student Book* pp. 70–71

SS CONTENT TOPICS: II.CG.e.1, II.CG.e.3, II.G.b.2, II.G.b.4, II.G.c.1, II.G.c.2, II.G.c.3, II.G.d.1, II.G.d.3, II.G.d.4
SS PRACTICES: SSP.1.a, SSP.2.b, SSP.4.a, SSP.6.b, SSP.6.c

UNIT 3

1 Review the Skill

Special-purpose maps share important similarities with political maps. Like political maps, they often show political features such as nations, regions, and cities. However, through the use of symbols, these maps also present additional features such as products, voting patterns, or population changes.

Because they can feature a variety of information, you should always try to determine the focus of special-purpose maps. Identifying and locating the special features on these maps is vital to interpreting them correctly.

2 Refine the Skill

By refining the skill of reading special-purpose maps, you will improve your study and test-taking abilities, especially as they relate to the GED® Social Studies Test. Study the map and information below. Then answer the questions that follow.

a The political features shown on this map include the boundaries of each state and of the United States.

b The icons indicate that this is a special-purpose map. By scanning the icons and the numbers of electoral votes shown on the map, you can determine who won the election.

ELECTORAL MAP, 2012

Democrat victory: Barack Obama
Republican victory: Mitt Romney

USING LOGIC

Special-purpose maps usually use symbols, labels, and icons to represent features. By using logic to decode these items, you can begin to interpret a map and answer questions based on its contents.

1. Which of the following states likely provided the greatest electoral benefit for the winning candidate?

   A. California
   B. New York
   C. Georgia
   D. Texas

2. Based on the map, which of the following statements is accurate?

   A. The candidate who won the most states did not win the election.
   B. The victorious candidate won the three largest electoral states.
   C. The West Coast largely supported the Republican.
   D. Most states in New England supported the Democrat.

DIRECTIONS: Study the map and read the questions, then choose the **best** answer to each question.

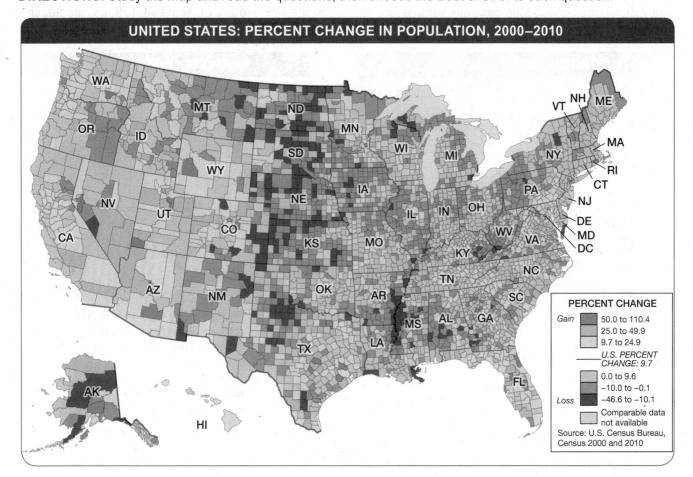

UNITED STATES: PERCENT CHANGE IN POPULATION, 2000–2010

PERCENT CHANGE

Gain
- 50.0 to 110.4
- 25.0 to 49.9
- 9.7 to 24.9

U.S. PERCENT CHANGE: 9.7
- 0.0 to 9.6
- −10.0 to −0.1

Loss
- −46.6 to −10.1
- Comparable data not available

Source: U.S. Census Bureau, Census 2000 and 2010

UNIT 3

3. Which of the following states experienced the greatest population loss between 2000 and 2010?

A. North Dakota
B. Florida
C. Utah
D. Hawaii

4. In which parts of the country were the greatest population losses?

A. West Coast
B. South Atlantic Coast
C. Great Plains
D. Florida

5. In general, which of the following parts of the country experienced the highest rate of population growth between 2000 and 2010?

A. Northeast
B. Southwest
C. Hawaii and Alaska
D. Central Plains

6. What generalization can you make about the northeastern area on the map?

A. It experienced the greatest population growth.
B. It experienced the greatest population loss.
C. Most of the area has experienced a decline in population.
D. The population has increased in most of the area.

7. Based on the map, which of the following statements can you infer about the population of the United States between 2000 and 2010?

A. The northern border area of the United States is more attractive to new residents than the southern border area is.
B. Neither Hawaii nor Alaska is attractive to new residents.
C. Every state has areas that lose population each year.
D. Of the three states on the West Coast, eastern Oregon is least attractive to new residents.

DIRECTIONS: Study the map and read the questions, then choose the **best** answer to each question.

DIRECTIONS: Study the map of **Apportionment in the U.S. House of Representatives**, read each question, then choose the **best** answers.

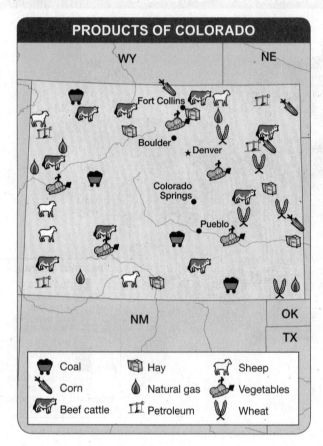

PRODUCTS OF COLORADO

APPORTIONMENT, 2010

8. Which of the following products is found near Pueblo?

   A. coal
   B. petroleum
   C. natural gas
   D. sheep

9. Based on the map, where in Colorado are mountains most likely located?

   A. They are most likely along the Wyoming border.
   B. They are probably in the east.
   C. They are probably along the western border.
   D. They are likely to be in the center-west part of the state.

10. In which area of the state is most crop agriculture located?

    A. in the east-northeast
    B. along the border with New Mexico
    C. in the northwestern corner
    D. south of Boulder

11. How many seats does Texas have now, and how many did it have in 2000 in the U.S. House of Representatives?

    A. 36; 32
    B. 37; 36
    C. 40; 36
    D. 36; 34

12. Which of the following states gained the most seats in the U.S. House of Representatives as a result of 2010 reapportionment?

    A. Washington
    B. Florida
    C. New York
    D. Georgia

13. Which of the following states lost two seats in the House as a result of 2010 reapportionment?

    A. New Jersey
    B. Pennsylvania
    C. Massachusetts
    D. New York

DIRECTIONS: The passage below is incomplete. Use information from the map to complete the passage. For each drop-down item, choose the option that correctly completes the sentence.

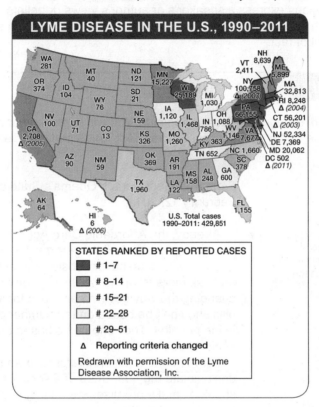

LYME DISEASE IN THE U.S., 1990–2011

STATES RANKED BY REPORTED CASES
- # 1–7
- # 8–14
- # 15–21
- # 22–28
- # 29–51

Δ Reporting criteria changed

Redrawn with permission of the Lyme Disease Association, Inc.

Drop-Down Answer Options

14. Between 1990 and 2011, there were Lyme disease cases reported in the 50 states and Washington, D.C. According to this map from the Lyme Disease Association, the state with the highest number of reported cases was [14. Drop-down 1], with more than 100,000.

Most of the cases are concentrated in the [14. Drop-down 2] area of the country, although there are also many cases in [14. Drop-down 3]. The state reporting the fewest cases of Lyme disease was [14. Drop-down 4], with only six reported cases.

14.1 A. New York
B. Pennsylvania
C. Connecticut
D. Massachusetts

14.2 A. northwestern
B. southwestern
C. northeastern
D. Great Plains

14.3 A. Mississippi and Alabama
B. the Northwest
C. Alaska
D. the Midwest

14.4 A. Vermont
B. Hawaii
C. Montana
D. New Jersey

Fact and Opinion

Use with **Student Book** pp. 72–73

SS CONTENT TOPICS: II.CG.e.1, II.CG.e.3, II.CG.f
SS PRACTICES: SSP.2.a, SSP.5.a, SSP.5.b, SSP.5.c, SSP.5.d, SSP.7.a, SSP.7.b

1 Review the Skill

In order to distinguish between **fact and opinion** in social studies materials, you must evaluate the statements that a speaker or author makes. The statements that can be proven true or untrue are **facts,** while statements that cannot be proven true or untrue are **opinions**.

Remember that opinions express a speaker's or author's views or beliefs. As a result, pay particular attention to words such as *think*, *feel*, and *believe*, as these words will often signal the expression of an opinion rather than a statement of fact.

2 Refine the Skill

By refining the skill of recognizing fact and opinion, you will improve your study and test-taking abilities, especially as they relate to the GED® Social Studies Test. Study the information below. Then answer the questions that follow.

From President Barack Obama's State of the Union Address, February 12, 2013:

> **a** The first paragraph states a fact. There are several sources you could check to verify that this information is accurate.

Already, the Affordable Care Act is helping to slow the growth of health care costs. And the reforms I'm proposing go even further.

We'll reduce taxpayer subsidies to prescription drug companies and ask more from the wealthiest seniors. We'll bring down costs by changing the way government pays for Medicare, because our medical bills shouldn't be based on the number of tests ordered or days spent in the hospital. They should be based on the quality of care that our seniors receive.

I am open to additional reforms from both parties, so long as they don't violate the guarantee of a secure retirement. Our government shouldn't make promises we cannot keep, but we must keep the promises we've already made.

> **b** In his speech, Barack Obama uses phrases such as this to express his opinion of the positions held by his Republican opponents in Congress.

To hit the rest of our deficit reduction target, we should do what leaders in both parties have already suggested and save hundreds of billions of dollars by getting rid of tax loopholes and deductions for the well-off and well-connected. After all, why would we choose to make deeper cuts to education and Medicare just to protect special-interest tax breaks? How is that fair?

MAKING ASSUMPTIONS

In political speeches such as this one, you can generally assume that speakers will employ a combination of factual information and opinion statements in order to make their case.

1. In which source could you confirm the fact in the first sentence?

   A. a dictionary of health care terms
   B. a recent federal government report on health care costs
   C. a political pamphlet written by the Republican Party
   D. a health care discussion on a television news show

2. How would you describe President Obama's opinion on the role of government in health care? President Obama wants to

   A. make sure people pay their health care bills.
   B. guarantee good, affordable health care.
   C. find new cures for the most important health problems.
   D. reduce the deficit through decreasing health care costs.

UNIT 3

⭐ Spotlighted Item: **FILL-IN-THE-BLANK**

DIRECTIONS: Read the passage, then read the questions and write your answers in the boxes below.

The main problem with the Electoral College is that it builds into every election the possibility … that the President will be a candidate who lost the popular vote … The Electorial College also heavily favors small states. The fact that everyone gets three automatic electors—one for each senator and a House member—means states that by population might be entitled to only one or two electoral votes wind up with three, four, or five.

The majority does not rule and every vote is not equal—those are reasons enough for scrapping the system. But there are other consequences as well. … A few swing states take on oversized importance, leading the candidates to focus their attention, money, and promises on a small slice of the electorate.

From *The New York Times's* editorial MAKING VOTES COUNT: ABOLISH THE ELECTORAL COLLEGE, AUGUST 29, 2004

3. Based on the opinions in this excerpt, the author would suggest that the United States choose a president by

[ ]

4. The editorial was written in 2004, four years after the Bush-Gore election controversy in Florida. How do you think the historical context affected the author's opinion? The author fears that

[ ]

5. Based on the opinions in this excerpt, the author probably believes that states with smaller populations should

[ ]

6. The author of this passage believes that swing states

[ ]

deserve more attention, money, and promises from presidential candidates.

DIRECTIONS: Study the information, read each question, then choose the **best** answer.

In the early stages of a Presidential election cycle, political parties in the individual states select the delegates who will represent them at the parties' national nominating conventions. The two main methods by which these delegates are selected are by primary or by caucus. In a primary election, voters elect delegates who will support their preferred candidate at the national convention. Ballots are cast in a manner similar to that of the general election. In a caucus, voters gather in groups at polling locations. At these locations, they listen to debates and speeches before a vote is taken.

7. Which of the following statements about primaries and caucuses is most likely a fact?

    A. Caucuses produce better informed voters than primary elections.
    B. Primary elections are easier to carry out than caucuses.
    C. Caucuses allow citizens to have too much influence on voting decisions.
    D. Primary elections usually occur after the nominating conventions.

8. Which website would be the **best** source of unbiased facts about primaries and caucuses?

    A. The League of Environmental Voters
    B. The Library of Congress Voter Project
    C. The White House website
    D. The Texas Republican Party

DIRECTIONS: Study the information, read each question, then choose the **best** answer.

During Presidential elections, the national Democratic and Republican parties have many responsibilities. The national parties must plan conventions, coordinate Presidential debates, and assist their candidates in fund-raising efforts. The national political parties also have the authority to refuse to acknowledge state delegates who they believe were chosen inappropriately.

While the Democratic Party awards state delegates to candidates based on the percentage of the popular vote they received in the primary or caucus, the Republican Party allows states to choose either proportional representation or a winner-take-all plan. Under such a plan, the winning candidate of a state's primary or caucus receives all of that state's delegates.

9. Which of the following statements **best** describes this passage?

   A. The passage features many facts and no opinions.
   B. The passage is mostly facts with a few opinions.
   C. The passage has an even balance of fact and opinion.
   D. The passage has many opinions with no facts.

10. Which of the following opinions would this author likely hold if a Republican Presidential candidate lost a closely contested primary election?

   A. National political parties should insist on holding state caucuses.
   B. The state in which the primary was held should employ proportional representation.
   C. Parties should tighten restrictions on campaign fund-raising.
   D. All candidates should be given input into the planning of the nominating convention.

11. Which of the following statements can you conclude is true based on the passage?

   A. The Democratic and Republican parties have different duties during elections.
   B. Candidates plan national conventions.
   C. The Democratic Party has only winner-take-all primaries.
   D. The Republican Party allows more flexibility in how it chooses candidates.

DIRECTIONS: Study the information, read each question, then choose the **best** answer.

In the Presidential election of 2000, Democratic candidate Al Gore won the popular vote. Yet it was Republican candidate George W. Bush who took the oath of office as President a couple of months later. With neither candidate having enough electoral votes to win, the election came down to which of the candidates would win Florida's electoral votes. When a machine recount resulted in only a 327-vote lead for Mr. Bush, Mr. Gore demanded a manual recount. The Bush team objected.

During the weeks that followed, a series of lawsuits ensued. Mr. Gore attempted to continue the recount, but Mr. Bush wanted to stop the recount while he (Bush) was ahead. After Mr. Gore received a favorable ruling on the recount from the Florida Supreme Court, Mr. Bush asked the U.S. Supreme Court to decide the question once and for all. In an unsettling five-to-four decision, the Supreme Court stopped the recount, stating that it was unconstitutional. By doing so, the Court handed George W. Bush the presidency. The Court also guaranteed that the final vote count would never be known officially.

12. Which phrase, taken from the passage above, indicates an opinion?

   A. Yet it was Republican candidate George W. Bush who took the oath of office as President.
   B. When a machine recount resulted in only a 327-vote lead for Mr. Bush, Mr. Gore demanded a manual recount.
   C. In an unsettling five-to-four decision, the Supreme Court stopped the recount, stating that it was unconstitutional.
   D. The Bush team objected.

13. In which of the following ways are opinions most obvious in this passage?

   A. There are no statements of fact.
   B. George W. Bush is portrayed as dishonest.
   C. The article claims that Al Gore could not have won the election.
   D. The article makes the Supreme Court sound partisan.

UNIT 3

DIRECTIONS: Study the information, read each question, then choose the **best** answer.

In September 2012, the New York City Board of Health approved a ban on the sale of oversized, sugary drinks in New York City. Although the ruling was an attempt to improve the health of New Yorkers, many people believed that it was an attack on individual rights. When the ban was struck down in March 2013, an irritated Mayor Michael Bloomberg said the city would appeal the decision. This is an excerpt from his statement:

If we are serious about fighting obesity, we have to be honest about what causes it—and we have to have the courage to tackle it head-on. Seventy thousand people will die of obesity in America this year; five thousand people in New York City will die of obesity.

Now, the best science tells us that sugary drinks are a leading cause of obesity. Some people say: Just talk about the problem, raise awareness, and hope that results in change. But it's not enough to talk and it's not enough to hope.

We have a responsibility as human beings to do something, to save each other, to save the lives of ourselves, our families, our friends, and all of the rest of the people that live on [Earth]. And so while other people will wring their hands over the problem of sugary drinks, in New York City, we're doing something about it.

From mikebloomberg.com, accessed 2013

14. What is the **best** description of Mayor Bloomberg's statement?

   A. The passage is all facts and no opinions.
   B. The passage is all opinion, with no facts.
   C. The passage is mostly unsupported claims.
   D. The passage has a couple of opinions, but also has several facts.

15. Which of these statements from Mayor Bloomberg is a fact?

   A. We have a responsibility as human beings to do something.
   B. The best science tells us that sugary drinks are a leading cause of obesity.
   C. It's not enough to talk and it's not enough to hope.
   D. If we are serious about fighting obesity, we have to be honest about what causes it.

DIRECTIONS: Study the information, read each question, then choose the **best** answer.

From Bill Clinton's closing remarks at the presidential debate, October 19, 1992:

I offer a new approach. It's not trickle-down economics; it's been tried for 12 years, and it's failed. More people are working harder for less, 100,000 people a month losing their health insurance, unemployment going up, our economy slowing down. We can do better. And it's not tax-and-spend economics. It's invest and grow, put our people first, control health care costs and provide basic health care to all Americans, have an education system second to none, and revitalize the private economy. ... I want a country where people who work hard and play by the rules are rewarded, not punished. I want a country where people are coming together across the lines of race and region and income. I know we can do better.

16. Which of the following opinions does Mr. Clinton express in this excerpt?

   A. The nation has grown more united in recent years.
   B. The United States would benefit from additional taxation and spending.
   C. The previous economic policies of President Reagan and President Bush have failed.
   D. The United States has one of the world's best health care systems.

17. In which of the following areas does Mr. Clinton provide a fact?

   A. the environment
   B. health care
   C. energy costs
   D. religion

18. Which of the following words **best** characterizes Mr. Clinton's opinions about how he would lead America?

   A. optimistic
   B. irritated
   C. cautious
   D. pessimistic

Faulty Logic or Reasoning

SS CONTENT TOPICS: I.CG.c.1, I.CG.c.2, I.CG.d.2, I.USH.b.7, I.USH.d.3,
II.USH.g.1, II.USH.g.3, II.G.d.2
SS PRACTICES: SSP.5.a, SSP.5.b, SSP.5.c, SSP.5.d, SSP.6.b, SSP.7.a, SSP.7.b

1 Review the Skill

One of the most common ways in which speakers and authors use **faulty logic and reasoning** occurs when they make broad statements that cannot be supported by evidence. This type of error in reasoning is called a **hasty generalization.**

Another common example of faulty logic or reasoning is an **oversimplification**. An oversimplification occurs when an author connects two ideas that do not share a cause-and-effect relationship or omits important factors that should be considered. For example, it is an oversimplification to say that *test scores rose at the school when they implemented the uniform policy*. Scores did not rise simply because students were wearing uniforms. Other factors had to have been involved.

2 Refine the Skill

By refining the skill of recognizing faulty logic or reasoning, you will improve your study and test-taking abilities, especially as they relate to the GED® Social Studies Test. Study the information below. Then answer the questions that follow.

a The author makes a bold claim in this statement. It would be more convincing if he included examples or statistics.

b This passage presents an absolute statement that could likely be an example of faulty reasoning or logic.

Nikita Khrushchev was the Soviet Union's First Secretary of the Communist Party from 1953 to 1964. He is famous for his dramatic gestures and attempts at promoting his party's maximum propaganda effect along with his certainty that communism would triumph over capitalism. This excerpt is from a speech Khruschev delivered in 1956:

Comrades, the 20th Congress of the Communist Party of the Soviet Union has manifested with a new strength the unshakable unity of our party, its cohesiveness around the central committee, its resolute will to accomplish the great task of building communism. And the fact that we present in all the ramifications the basic problems of overcoming the cult of the individual which is alien to Marxism-Leninism, as well as the problem of liquidating its burdensome consequences, is an evidence of the great moral and political strength of our party! We are absolutely certain that our party, armed with the historical resolutions of the 20th Congress, will lead the Soviet people along the Leninist path to new successes, to new victories.

From Nikita Khrushchev's ON THE CULT OF PERSONALITY AND ITS CONSEQUENCES, 1956

TEST-TAKING TIPS

When evaluating logic or reasoning for an exam, identify the main argument that the author is trying to make. Then turn your attention to the evidence that he or she provides.

1. Khrushchev asserts—but does not offer evidence to support — which of the following?

   A. that Communism is spreading to other nations
   B. that specific reforms are taking place in the Soviet Union
   C. that the economy is prospering in the Soviet Union
   D. that his party is unified

2. Which of the following does Khrushchev reason to be the greatest threat to the Soviet Union's system of government?

   A. Western influences
   B. the cult of personality
   C. Marxism-Leninism
   D. the 20th Congress of the Communist Party

DIRECTIONS: Study the passage and the political cartoon, read each question, then choose the **best** answer.

In 1938, communism had begun to spread in Europe. In the United States, a Congressional committee led by Representative Martin Dies of Texas started investigating potential Communist activities within the nation. Cartoonist Herb Block references the committee in the title of this 1938 cartoon.

"WAIT TILL THE DIES COMMITTEE HEARS ABOUT THIS!"
A 1938 Herblock Cartoon, © by The Herb Block Foundation

3. Which of the following errors in logic and reasoning is the artist portraying in the cartoon?

   A. The celebration of Christmas is un-American.
   B. Even innocent behaviors are suspicious.
   C. All Communist organizations are funded by state clubs.
   D. Any Communist in the United States will develop an anti-American plot.

4. What hasty generalization does the cartoon suggest the Dies Committee makes?

   A. that Christmas is a Communist holiday
   B. that ordinary activities have sinister motivations
   C. that Santa Claus is a Communist spy
   D. that many Americans support communism

DIRECTIONS: Study the information, read each question, then choose the **best** answer.

After the Spanish-American War in 1898, the United States became an international power with several overseas territories. One of them was the Caribbean island of Puerto Rico. Following a period of direct control from Washington, D.C., Puerto Rico became a commonwealth of the United States in 1952. As such, it is a self-governing U.S. territory. For decades, Puerto Ricans have gone to the polls to vote on the island's status. Would it remain a commonwealth? Would it become independent? Would it take its place as the 51st state? Because Spanish is the dominant language, some U.S. groups have concerns about Puerto Rican statehood. One such concern is expressed below in an excerpt from testimony by Mauro E. Mujica before the U.S. House of Representatives Committee on Resources:

"Can a state in which over three-quarters of the population does not speak English integrate properly with a country in which 97 percent of the population speaks English? … and would a Spanish-speaking state, seeing its cultural traditions eroding under the influence of the overwhelming numbers of the English-speaking majority, eventually turn to the same separatist sentiments that have almost torn Quebec from the rest of Canada? Since Puerto Rico is more linguistically homogenous than Quebec … it seems reasonable that Congress would be interested in developing some language requirements for Puerto Rican Statehood …"

5. Why is it faulty logic to state that unrest will likely occur in Puerto Rico as it has in Quebec?

   A. Most people in Puerto Rico speak Spanish, while most people in Quebec speak French.
   B. Quebec is part of Canada, while Puerto Rico is part of the United States.
   C. It is an oversimplification because there are probably factors other than language involved.
   D. Because Puerto Rico is more linguistically homogeneous, there is less chance of unrest.

6. Which of the following does the speaker argue is the greatest threat to national unity in the United States?

   A. the nearness of conflict in Canada
   B. the lack of a common language
   C. people who speak Spanish
   D. a linguistically homogeneous country

UNIT 3

DIRECTIONS: Study the information, read each question, then choose the **best** answer.

During the 1950s, the U.S. federal government adopted a new policy with regard to Native Americans. The government decided that it would no longer support the preservation of Native American cultures on separate reservations. The government's new goal would be to entice Native Americans to move to cities for what was promised to be a better life. There they would be expected to assimilate into mainstream American culture.

The move was not successful for many of the Native Americans who left their reservations. However, it did result in a dramatic increase in the number of Native Americans living in urban areas. In 1950, only 13 percent of Native Americans lived in cities. By 1990, that figure rose to 60 percent. This poster was created as part of the federal government's Urban Indian Relocation Program.

7. Which hasty generalization was likely the basis for the Urban Indian Relocation Program?

   A. Native Americans want to live on reservations.
   B. Native Americans living on reservations in the United States have too much power.
   C. Native Americans would be better off living like mainstream non-Native Americans.
   D. Native Americans believe that their children would be better educated in cities.

8. What faulty logic about the relocated families is evident in the jobs highlighted on the poster?

   A. They do not want to work at all.
   B. They all want professional careers.
   C. They want to go to school rather than find jobs right away.
   D. They are only interested in manual labor and blue-collar trades.

9. Which of the following can you assume describes the poster artist's knowledge of Native American culture?

   A. firsthand
   B. extensive
   C. personal
   D. simplistic

DIRECTIONS: Study the information, read the question, then choose the **best** answer.

From a speech by former Alabama governor George Wallace, July 4, 1964:

Never before in the history of this nation have so many human and property rights been destroyed by a single enactment of the Congress. It is an act of tyranny. It is the assassin's knife stuck in the back of liberty … I am having nothing to do with enforcing a law that will destroy our free enterprise system. … I am having nothing to do with enforcing a law that will destroy neighborhood schools. … I am having nothing to do with enforcing a law that will destroy the rights of private property … I am having nothing to do with this so-called civil rights bill.

10. Which of Mr. Wallace's statements below is a hasty generalization?

    A. Never before in the history of this nation have so many human and property rights been destroyed by a single enactment of the Congress.
    B. It is an act of tyranny.
    C. It is the assassin's knife stuck in the back of liberty.
    D. I am having nothing to do with this so-called civil rights bill.

DIRECTIONS: Study the passage and the political cartoon, read each question, then choose the **best** answer.

When a person stands his ground and demands that his civil rights be respected, history can be made. When James Meredith sought to become the first African American to attend the University of Mississippi in 1962, it was the duty of 127 federal marshals from across the country to risk their lives and uphold the law, thereby allowing Mr. Meredith to enroll.

When the university tried to deny him admission, a federal court ordered the university to desegregate and allow Mr. Meredith to enroll. When Mississippi's governor attempted to block Mr. Meredith's enrollment, President John Kennedy's administration ordered federal marshals to accompany Mr. Meredith to the university. Violence erupted when white students reacted with hostility toward the marshals. Two people died, and hundreds were injured in the fighting.

For a year, the marshals provided Mr. Meredith with 24-hour protection, accompanying him on campus and enduring the same heckling and taunts as Mr. Meredith did. The courageous actions of the marshals ensured that Mr. Meredith could attend the school of his choice.

"...AND YOU INCITED THOSE INNOCENT RIOTERS TO VIOLENCE..."

"AND YOU INCITED THOSE INNOCENT RIOTERS TO VIOLENCE ..."
By Bill Mauldin

11. On whose use of faulty reasoning does the cartoonist focus in this cartoon?

A. James Meredith
B. the federal court
C. the Kennedy administration
D. Mississippi court system

12. Which of the following expresses the invalid cause-and-effect relationship suggested by the cartoon?

A. the Mississippi governor's action and the decision of the Kennedy administration
B. the work of the federal marshals and the outbreak of violence
C. the earlier rulings of state courts and the final decision of the federal court
D. the efforts of James Meredith and the integration of the University of Mississippi

13. Based on the reasoning represented in this cartoon, which of the following would the Mississippi state government most likely support?

A. diversity in the university student population
B. federal oversight of state actions
C. separate but equal schools for different races
D. police officers stationed at all times inside schools

14. Which of the following **best** expresses a negative consequence of faulty logic and reasoning in the passage?

A. sending in federal marshals
B. racial discrimination
C. forced integration
D. President Kennedy's policies

15. The reasoning used by the Mississippi grand jury in the cartoon is **most** similar to which of the following situations?

A. a teacher being blamed for students not doing well on a test
B. a judge blaming a jury for finding a defendant not guilty
C. a firefighter being blamed for the actions of an arsonist
D. President Truman being blamed for the Japanese bombing of Pearl Harbor

SS CONTENT TOPICS: I.CG.c.2, II.CG.e.1, II.CG.e.2, II.CG.e.3, II.USH.g.7
SS PRACTICES: SSP.1.a, SSP.1.b, SSP.3.d, SSP.4.a, SSP.5.a, SSP.5.b, SSP.5.c,
SSP.5.d, SSP.7.a, SSP.7.b, SSP.8.a, SSP.9.a, SSP.9.c

1 Review the Skill

As you read social studies material, it is important to **evaluate information** to determine whether it is valid or biased. Properly evaluating the information you read helps you to recognize its strengths and weaknesses and to determine whether the source from which it comes can be trusted.

In addition to evaluating information for its validity and bias, you also can evaluate information by deciding whether or not it is effective or convincing. For instance, when you hear a speech or read a statement issued by a political candidate, you are evaluating that information and deciding whether it convinces you to share that candidate's ideas.

2 Refine the Skill

By refining the skill of evaluating information, you will improve your study and test-taking abilities, especially as they relate to the GED® Social Studies Test. Study the information below. Then answer the questions that follow.

From a Lyndon B. Johnson campaign brochure, 1964:

Lyndon B. Johnson and Hubert H. Humphrey worked together long and closely to strengthen America at home and abroad—to build our moral, diplomatic, military, and economic strength. …

a The author provides support for a claim in the form of a list of duties the two men have fulfilled.

But Lyndon B. Johnson and Hubert H. Humphrey both know, as their fellow Americans know, that military strength is not enough. **a** They have worked tirelessly to strengthen our representation abroad, to create and guide the Peace Corps, to enact and to implement policies of expanded foreign trade, to assure peace, and, in the millions of miles both have traveled throughout the world, to bring to people everywhere a more vivid picture of America.

b This phrase refers to the efficiency with which government programs have used the money devoted to funding them.

And both men … have made every possible effort to keep the nation fiscally strong by seeing to it that while needed programs were not ignored, **b** the nation received a dollar's worth for every dollar spent.

MAKING ASSUMPTIONS

Assume that in a piece of campaign literature such as this, the author will write persuasively to win over voters. Consider this purpose as you evaluate information in the excerpt.

1. Why does the author suggest that Mr. Johnson and Mr. Humphrey will be able to guide the nation's foreign policy?

   A. because of their foreign policy experience
   B. because of their career backgrounds
   C. because of their personal strengths
   D. because of their educational backgrounds

2. What characteristic of both men is praised in the last paragraph?

   A. courage
   B. independence
   C. moral character
   D. fiscal responsibility

UNIT 3

Spotlighted Item: **EXTENDED RESPONSE**

DIRECTIONS: Read the information and the question, then write your response on the lines below. Please refer to Unit 3 and Unit 4 in the Reasoning Through Language Arts Student Edition and Workbook for detailed information about reading, writing, and editing Extended Response answers. You may finish your response on another sheet of paper. This task may require 25 minutes to complete.

In 1965, President Lyndon B. Johnson launched the "Great Society," a federal program to promote racial justice, better education, health care, environmental reform, and a war on poverty. Johnson said, "We have a right to expect a job to provide food for our families, a roof over their head, clothes for their body, and with your help and with God's help, we will have it in America!"

An article in *The New York Times* 20 years later looked at the effects of the program:

Twenty years ago … Half of all Americans over 65 had no medical insurance, and a third of the aged lived in poverty. More than 90 percent of black adults in many Southern counties were not registered to vote … Only a third of the children in the country 3 to 5 years old attended nursery school or kindergarten. Today … those situations … have been reversed, in large part because of laws enacted in … Lyndon B. Johnson's drive for … the Great Society. Now nearly every elderly person is covered by health insurance, and the aged are no poorer than Americans as a whole. Blacks vote at about the same rate as whites, and … a large majority of small children attend preschool programs …

Source: nytimes.com, accessed 2013

3. Based on the information, how would you evaluate the effect of President Johnson's "Great Society" program? In your response, develop an argument about whether the "Great Society" succeeded in meeting its goals. Incorporate relevant and specific evidence from the information given, and from your own knowledge of the issue and the circumstances surrounding the enduring issue, to support your analysis.

_____

_____

_____

_____

_____

_____

_____

_____

_____

_____

_____

_____

DIRECTIONS: Study the information, read each question, then choose the **best** answer.

From a "Jimmy Carter for President 1976" campaign brochure, 1976:

Our whole system depends on trust. The only way I know to be trusted is to be trustworthy. To be open, direct and honest. It's as simple as that.

… We can't sell out our people's interests for short-range benefits.

Jimmy Carter believes that secrecy has caused distrust of government at all levels. Americans are sick of half-truths and shallow promises. They want a President who will state the facts, be accessible to the people and responsive to their needs.

Jimmy Carter believes that with bold and competent leadership we can solve our economic problems. However, the average taxpayers shouldn't have to pay the full price for relieving inflation. They've already paid too much.

4. What format does this excerpt follow in an effort to persuade readers effectively?

   A. It has an opposing viewpoint, followed by Mr. Carter's rebuttal.
   B. It contains a question, followed by Mr. Carter's answer.
   C. It has a quotation from Mr. Carter, followed by an explanation of the quotation.
   D. It consists of a description of Mr. Carter's policies as governor, followed by an explanation of how those policies relate to the presidency.

5. This excerpt is written to resonate with which of the following biased beliefs of the public at the time?

   A. The nation's tax system is unfair.
   B. Government is inefficient.
   C. U.S. educational standards have deteriorated.
   D. Government is dishonest.

6. Which of the following does Mr. Carter believe Americans want in a President?

   A. responsiveness and trustworthiness
   B. knowledge and openness
   C. boldness and daring
   D. trustworthiness and patience

DIRECTIONS: Study the information, read each question, then choose the **best** answer.

From a George W. Bush campaign brochure, "Opportunity, Security, and Responsibility—A Fresh Start for America," 2000:

As President, I'll make our schools accountable for results. I'll encourage our schools to take more responsibility for teaching character to our children so they understand right and wrong and that actions have consequences. I'll give local school districts more flexibility to spend money where it is needed to improve our children's education.

I'll strengthen Social Security, guaranteeing Government is responsible for the promises it has made America's seniors and allowing younger Americans to voluntarily invest some of their Social Security taxes in Personal Accounts. I'll reform Health Care so every family has access to affordable health insurance, and seniors have a choice of plans, including prescription drug coverage.

I'll rebuild our military, giving it the resources it needs to meet its responsibility to keep the peace. I'll promote a responsible economic agenda to continue our prosperity. I'll provide tax relief for all Americans, especially those struggling to make it into the middle class.

7. Which of the following **best** describes Mr. Bush's plans for his presidency?

   A. simple
   B. ambitious
   C. unprecedented
   D. inexpensive

8. Mr. Bush's proposed policies are based on which of the following concepts?

   A. opportunity
   B. security
   C. responsibility
   D. affordability

9. Based on the excerpt, which of these federal government departments or agencies would Mr. Bush have been most eager to strengthen?

   A. Department of Defense
   B. Environmental Protection Agency
   C. Bureau of Land Management
   D. Department of Energy

DIRECTIONS: Study the information, read each question, then choose the best answer.

From a campaign speech by Bill Clinton, 1992:

For millions and millions of Americans, the dream with which I grew up has been shattered. The ideal that if you work hard and play by the rules you'll be rewarded, you'll do a little better next year than you did last year, your kids will do better than you. But that idea has been devastated for millions of Americans.

How did this happen? I would argue it happened for two reasons. No. 1: We lost our economic leadership. Other nations began to do some things better than we do, and their economies started growing faster and faster as ours slowed down. ...

No. 2, and this is why I'm running for President: We elected people to high office who had the wrong response to the problem. ...

What is the alternative? That's what I represent. ...

We're going to have a smart-work, high-wage country, not a hard-work, low-wage country. And we're going to do it by beating the competition. Let me give you some examples. ...

10. Which of these claims in the speech excerpt could **most** easily be checked because it is supported by facts?

   A. Other nations' economies grew faster as ours slowed down.
   B. We elected people who had the wrong response to the problem.
   C. The American dream has been shattered.
   D. We lost our economic leadership.

11. What is Mr. Clinton's goal in this speech?

   A. to outline his foreign policy
   B. explain his economic plans
   C. to refute Mr. Bush's claims
   D. to criticize Mr. Bush's foreign policy

12. Which of the following is a hasty generalization made in the speech?

   A. I would argue it happened for two reasons.
   B. I represent the alternative.
   C. This is why I'm running for President.
   D. People in high office responded incorrectly to problems.

DIRECTIONS: Study the information, read each question, then choose the **best** answers

From a campaign speech by Barack Obama, 2012:

On issue after issue, we are moving forward. After losing 9 million jobs in the great recession, our businesses have now added more than 5 million new jobs over the past 2½ years. Manufacturing is coming back to our shores. The unemployment rate has fallen. Home values and home sales are rising. Our assembly lines are humming. ...

We cannot go back to the same policies ... We've got to keep moving forward ... And that's why I'm running for a second term as President of the United States.

I've got a plan that will actually create jobs, a plan that will actually create middle class security. ...

So I want you to compare my plan to Governor Romney's. See which plan you think is better for you. See which plan is better for America's future.

13. Which of the following claims by Mr. Obama would be most difficult to verify?

   A. More than 5 million jobs were created.
   B. The unemployment rate has fallen.
   C. Home sales are rising.
   D. His plan will create jobs.

14. How does Mr. Obama encourage the public to evaluate what he says?

   A. Trust his leadership.
   B. Compare his plan to his opponent's.
   C. Believe the facts in this speech.
   D. Realize that there has been real progress.

15. President Obama made this speech during his second Presidential campaign. How would it differ from one he might have used during his first campaign?

   A. It can include facts about his accomplishments.
   B. He can blame all of the problems of the country on his predecessor.
   C. More money can be spent on ads.
   D. He does not have to use facts to explain his plans.

Analyze Effectiveness of Arguments

Use with *Student Book* pp. 78–79

SS CONTENT TOPICS: I.CG.c.1, I.CG.c.2, II.CG.e.3, II.CG.f, I.USH.a.1
SS CONTENT PRACTICES: SSP.1.a, SSP.2.a, SSP.5.a, SSP.5.d, SSP.8.a

1 Review the Skill

An **effective argument** is one that can win the acceptance of its audience. An author or speaker can persuade an audience to accept his or her argument by presenting a **strong** argument supported by facts or evidence. A **weak** argument is not supported by facts.

As you **analyze the effectiveness of an argument**, pay close attention to the types of evidence that the author or speaker offers. Does this person use facts and statistics, or only anecdotal evidence? Assessing the reliability of this information will help you make an evaluation.

2 Refine the Skill

By refining the skill of analyzing the effectiveness of arguments, you will improve your study and test-taking abilities, especially as they relate to the GED® Social Studies Test. Study the information below. Then answer the questions that follow.

A congressional hearing about the Watergate break-in scandal during Richard M. Nixon's presidency revealed that the President had installed a tape-recording device in the Oval Office. The special prosecutor in charge of the case wanted access to these taped discussions to help prove that President Nixon and his aides had abused their power and broken the law. The President's incomplete compliance was challenged and eventually taken to the U.S. Supreme Court. The following excerpt is from the Court's opinion, written by Chief Justice Warren Burger:

a This passage suggests that the Court requires the presence of some special circumstance in order to grant the President's immunity requests made in court proceedings.

… neither the doctrine of separation of powers, nor the need for confidentiality of high-level communications, without more, can sustain an absolute, unqualified Presidential privilege of immunity from judicial process under all circumstances. The President's need for complete candor and objectivity from advisers calls for great deference from the courts. However, when the privilege depends solely on the broad, undifferentiated claim of public interest in the confidentiality of such conversations, a confrontation with other values arises. Absent a claim of need to protect military, diplomatic, or sensitive national security secrets, we find it difficult to accept the argument that even the very important interest in confidentiality of Presidential communications is significantly diminished by production of such material for in camera inspection with all the protection that a district court will be obliged to provide.

b The term *in camera* means "in private" or "in chambers." It describes legal proceedings that the media and the public are not permitted to attend. Such proceedings are often held in the interest of protecting national security.

From the Opinion of the Court by Chief Justice Warren Burger, U.S. Supreme Court, *United States* v. *Nixon*, 1974

USING LOGIC

Authors and speakers may use reasoning or logic instead of facts and statistics to support arguments. In that case, it is important to look for faulty logic and reasoning that may undermine the arguments.

1. How does Chief Justice Burger support the Supreme Court's opinion?

   A. He provides statistical justification.
   B. He offers examples that show it to be correct.
   C. He explains the legal reasoning behind the Court's decision.
   D. He describes similar cases in other nations.

2. The argument also would be relevant in which of these situations?

   A. a boundary dispute between two communities
   B. a contested election
   C. a debate about free speech
   D. a governor's refusal to turn over materials for an investigation

UNIT 3

DIRECTIONS: Study the information, read each question, then choose the **best** answer.

Dr. Martin Luther King, Jr., was arrested in 1963 and jailed for taking part in a civil rights demonstration in Birmingham, Alabama. In response to a statement by white clergy that his actions were unwise and were provoking violence, Dr. King wrote a letter from his jail cell. The following is a brief excerpt.

LETTER FROM A BIRMINGHAM JAIL

You deplore the demonstrations taking place in Birmingham. But your statement ... fails to express a similar concern for the conditions that brought about the demonstrations. ...

Birmingham is probably the most thoroughly segregated city in the United States. Its ugly record of police brutality is widely known. Its unjust treatment of Negroes in the courts is a notorious reality. There have been more unsolved bombings of Negro homes and churches in Birmingham than in any other city in the nation. ... On the basis of these conditions, Negro leaders sought to negotiate with the city fathers. But the latter consistently refused to engage in good faith negotiation. ...

Some have asked, "Why didn't you give the new city administration time to act?" The only answer that I can give to this query is that the new Birmingham administration must be prodded about as much as the outgoing one before it acts. ...

Perhaps it is easy for those who have never felt the stinging darts of segregation to say "Wait." But when you have seen vicious mobs lynch your mothers and fathers at will and drown your sisters and brothers at whim; when you have seen hate-filled policemen curse, kick, and even kill your black brothers and sisters with impunity; when you see the vast majority of your 20 million Negro brothers smothering in an air-tight cage of poverty in the midst of an affluent society ... when you take a cross-county drive and find it necessary to sleep night after night in the uncomfortable corners of your automobile because no motel will accept you ... I hope, sirs, you can understand our legitimate and unavoidable impatience. ...

It is true that the police have exercised discipline in handling the demonstrators. In this sense they have conducted themselves rather "nonviolently" in public. But for what purpose? To preserve the evil system of segregation. Over the past few years I have consistently preached that nonviolence demands that the means we use must be as pure as the ends we seek. I have tried to make clear that it is wrong to use immoral means to attain moral ends. ... As T. S. Eliot has said, there is no greater treason than to do the right deed for the wrong reason. ...

3. How does Dr. King respond to the argument that the Birmingham demonstrations were unwise?

    A. He agrees but states that he has no choice.
    B. He writes that it would be more fair to criticize the conditions that brought the protest about.
    C. He cites others who also have demonstrated.
    D. He says it is impossible to criticize just causes.

4. What does Dr. King use to support his position that the demonstrations occur in Birmingham?

    A. anecdotes about how he was personally treated
    B. opinions of many people who live in Birmingham
    C. facts about segregation in Birmingham
    D. a court order allowing the demonstrations

5. How does Dr. King argue effectively against those who state that the demonstrations should have waited in order to give the new mayor in Birmingham a chance to respond?

    A. Dr. King reveals that he has already spoken to the mayor with no positive result.
    B. Dr. King gives his opinion, based on the law, that they have waited long enough.
    C. Dr. King states that people who are not African American have no right to make such a statement.
    D. Dr. King relates daily indignities that make waiting intolerable.

UNIT 3

DIRECTIONS: Study the information, read each question, then choose the **best** answer.

From the Second Presidential Debate, 2012:

PRESIDENT OBAMA: We've gone through a tough four years … But four years ago, I told the American people and I told you I would cut taxes for middle-class families, and I did. I told you I'd cut taxes for small businesses, and I have. I said that I'd end the war in Iraq, and I did. I said we'd refocus attention on those who actually attacked us on 9/11, and we have gone after al-Qaida's leadership like never before, and Osama bin Laden is dead.

… We've created 5 million jobs, gone from 800,000 jobs a month being lost. And we are making progress. We saved an auto industry that was on the brink of collapse.

… But … Governor Romney's made some commitments as well, and I suspect he'll keep those, too … . when members of the Republican Congress say … don't ask a dime from millionaires and billionaires to reduce our deficit so we can still invest in education and helping kids go to college, he said, me too … That is not the kind of leadership that you need …

MITT ROMNEY: … These past four years haven't been so good as the President just described. … We just can't afford four more years like the last four years.

He said that by now we'd have unemployment at 5.4 percent. The difference between where it is and 5.4 percent is 9 million Americans without work … He said he would have by now put forward a plan to reform Medicare and Social Security … He hasn't even made a proposal on either one. The middle class is getting crushed under the policies of a President who has not understood what it takes to get the economy working again.

… the President has tried, but his policies haven't worked. He's great as a speaker … and describing his plans and his vision. … except we have a record to look at. And that record shows he just hasn't been able to cut the deficit, to put in place reforms for Medicare and Social Security to preserve them, to get us the rising incomes. … That's what this election is about …

From the Second Presidential Debate between President Barack Obama and Mitt Romney, October 2012

6. On which of the following do the two candidates agree in these arguments?

   A. Tax rates for the wealthy are too high.
   B. The U.S. deficit is not as important a problem now as it was previously.
   C. Middle-class families have had tough times in the last four years.
   D. Unemployment has decreased steadily since 2008.

7. What argument does President Obama make for reelecting him to for a second term?

   A. He has kept promises he made before his first term.
   B. He has solved the nation's economic problems.
   C. He is more competent than Mr. Romney.
   D. He can work well with the Republicans in Congress.

8. Which of the following does Mr. Romney use to support his argument against a second term for President Obama?

   A. quotations from economic experts
   B. opinions of ordinary voters
   C. his own experiences
   D. economic statistics

9. Which of the following statements summarizes President Obama's argument for his economic policies?

   A. We achieved a balanced budget.
   B. Every American is entitled to a job.
   C. We're making progress by creating and saving jobs.
   D. The last four years have been great for U.S. manufacturing.

10. In which of the following ways would you summarize Mr. Romney's argument in this excerpt?

   A. President Obama has promised a lot, but after four years he has not delivered.
   B. There are many more people unemployed now than when President Obama took office.
   C. President Obama has not reduced the deficit, so he does not deserve a second term.
   D. The President has not spoken enough about Social Security and Medicare.

DIRECTIONS: Study the information, read each question, then choose the **best** answer.

During the 1984 Republican National Convention in Dallas, Gregory Lee Johnson burned an American flag as a political protest and was eventually convicted under Texas law. The case reached the U.S. Supreme Court in order to determine whether Johnson's conviction violated the First Amendment.

The following excerpts from the Court's opinion and dissenting opinion express two arguments about the issue:

If there is a bedrock principle underlying the First Amendment, it is that the government may not prohibit the expression of an idea simply because society finds the idea itself offensive or disagreeable …

In short, nothing in our precedents suggests that a State may foster its own view of the flag by prohibiting expressive conduct relating to it …

The First Amendment does not guarantee that other concepts virtually sacred to our Nation as a whole—such as the principle that discrimination on the basis of race is odious and destructive—will go unquestioned in the marketplace of ideas … We decline, therefore, to create for the flag an exception to the joust of principles protected by the First Amendment.

From the Opinion of the Court, *Texas* v. *Johnson*, June 21, 1989

Uncritical extension of constitutional protection to the burning of the flag risks the frustration of the very purpose for which organized governments are instituted. The Court decides that the American flag is just another symbol, about which not only must opinions pro and con be tolerated, but for which the most minimal public respect may not be enjoined. The government may conscript men into the Armed Forces where they must fight and perhaps die for the flag, but the government may not prohibit the public burning of the banner under which they fight. I would uphold the Texas statute as applied in this case.

From the Dissenting Opinion, by Chief Justice William Rehnquist, U.S. Supreme Court *Texas* v. *Johnson*, June 21, 1989

11. Which of the following statements accurately describes the argument made by the majority of the Supreme Court?

   A. Johnson's conviction should stand according to Texas law.
   B. The First Amendment protects destruction of national symbols.
   C. The U.S. government cannot prevent free expression, even if the expression is offensive.
   D. Certain ideas or beliefs of the United States cannot be questioned or disputed.

12. On what basis does Justice Brennan build his argument?

   A. He uses statistics about incidents in which the American flag was burned.
   B. He relates facts about the flag and its history.
   C. He consults public opinion.
   D. He relies on legal precedent.

13. This Supreme Court ruling confirms that the Constitution protects which of the following acts?

   A. vandalism of a national landmark
   B. threatening speech toward another citizen
   C. stealing of property from a public building
   D. recording of a song that features curse words

14. On which of the following does Chief Justice Rehnquist base his argument?

   A. the history of the American flag
   B. the flag's symbolic value
   C. the flag as a piece of public property
   D. the military significance of the flag

15. Which of the following gives the opinions of Justice Brennan and Chief Justice Rehnquist more credibility on this subject than the opinions of either a Congressperson or even the President?

   A. Supreme Court justices are appointed for life, so they are immune to political concerns.
   B. Members of Congress and the President do not know the law.
   C. Their knowledge of legal precedent gives their decision credibility and weight.
   D. The fact that one is liberal and one is conservative creates balance in their decisions.

Understand Economics

Use with *Student Book* pp. 90–91

1 Review the Skill

SS CONTENT TOPICS: I.E.a, I.E.b, II.E.c.2, II.E.c.3, II.E.c.4, II.E.c.5, II.E.c.10, II.E.d.2, II.E.d.3, II.E.d.4, II.E.d.5, II.E.d.7, II.E.d.11
SS PRACTICES: SSP.1.a, SSP.1.b, SSP.2.a, SSP.2.b, SSP.3.c, SSP.6.a, SSP.6.b, SSP.6.c, SSP.10.a

Economics is the social science that studies the creation and flow of goods and services. When you study economics, look for ways in which aspects of society and human behavior are motivated by economic concerns or affected by economic events. Learning to **understand economics** is essential for an understanding of societal motivation and world events.

2 Refine the Skill

By refining the skill of understanding economics, you will improve your study and test-taking abilities, especially as they relate to the GED® Social Studies Test. Study the information below. Then answer the questions that follow.

Productivity is a measurement relating output to the labor hours used in the production of that output. This graph illustrates changes in output spanning three time periods.

a Economists often study how economic data change from year to year. This graph allows them to compare three different time periods on one graph and draw conclusions based on changes.

b An economic *sector* includes businesses related to a specific industry. For example, "utilities" likely includes electricity, gas, and power companies; telephone and internet service companies; and water and sewer services.

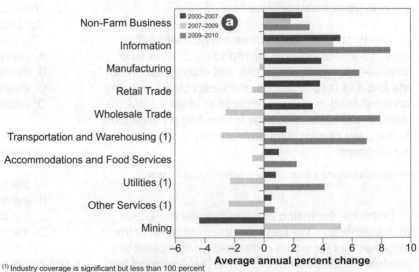

CHANGES IN OUTPUT PER HOUR BY SECTOR, **b**
2000–2007, 2007–2009, and 2009–2010

(1) Industry coverage is significant but less than 100 percent

MAKING ASSUMPTIONS

You can assume there are economic factors that affect individual industries, but also that there are economic factors that affect most industries.

1. Which of the following sectors had the greatest change in productivity from 2009 to 2010?

   A. Information
   B. Manufacturing
   C. Wholesale Trade
   D. Transportation and Warehousing

2. Insofar as productivity is concerned, which of the following sectors was the least negatively affected by the recession in 2008–2009?

   A. Non-Farm Business
   B. Retail Trade
   C. Accommodations and Food Services
   D. Mining

DIRECTIONS: Study the information, read each question, then choose the **best** answer.

Economics is essentially built on the core concept of individual choice. Individual choice refers to decisions made by an individual—including choices about what to do and choices about what not to do. Given the option, most people would choose to buy what they want; however, several factors may prevent this from happening. These factors influence the individual choices we make every day. For example, very few people have an unlimited supply of money, so they have to live within a set budget. Their budget, therefore, influences the individual choices they make. If someone has $800 to spend on a sofa, he or she will buy the $700 sofa, not a $1,500 sofa, because he or she cannot afford the more expensive sofa.

The four main principles underlying individual choice:	
1. Scarce Resources	A resource is anything that can be used to produce something else. Money or income is a resource, but time is also a resource.
2. Opportunity Costs	The true cost of something is what you have to give up to get it. For example, taking a second job to generate more income may mean giving up time with your family.
3. Trade-Offs	A trade-off is a comparison of costs and benefits. People usually do not ask themselves "whether" but "how much?" to determine the costs and benefits of doing a bit more.
4. Benefits	When presented with opportunities to make themselves better off, people will generally take them.

3. A person chooses to stay at a hotel that offers free parking rather than at a comparable hotel that charges $15/day for parking. Of which principle of individual choice is this the best example?

   A. Scarce Resources
   B. Opportunity Costs
   C. Trade-Offs
   D. Benefits

4. Many consumers budget for weekly and monthly expenses. Some budget for groceries. Suppose you have $100 to spend at the grocery store each week. Which of the following is an example of opportunity cost determining your individual choice at the grocery store?

   A. choosing to shop on a Wednesday when there are more sales
   B. choosing to purchase a watermelon that is on sale instead of a more expensive bag of apples that you planned to buy
   C. choosing to use coupons when you shop
   D. choosing to get a large box of cereal

5. A woman receives a 2% pay increase at her yearly performance review. Which principle of individual choice will change the most for her?

   A. Scarce Resources
   B. Opportunity Costs
   C. Trade-Offs
   D. Benefits

DIRECTIONS: Study the information, read the question, then choose the **best** answer.

Capitalism, socialism, and Communism are examples of economic systems. They vary by the amount of control the government or central authority has over businesses. A capitalist system has the least amount of government interference. The United States has a capitalist economic system.

Adam Smith and other economists favored a type of capitalism known as *laissez-faire*. This is a French term that means to let people do as they choose. In economics, it means that the government should not interfere. This theory was seen as inadequate by economist John Maynard Keynes. During the Great Depression, Keynes began to support the idea that government should make investments in society and businesses to spur the economy. Keynesian economists called for the same investment during the economic struggles of 2008–2009.

6. Except during times of economic turmoil, what type of economic system is most often practiced in the United States?

   A. Keynesian capitalism
   B. *laissez-faire* capitalism
   C. *laissez-faire* socialism
   D. socialism

DIRECTIONS: Study the bar graphs and the information, read each question, then choose the **best** answer.

SIZE OF GOVERNMENT, 1983 AND 2010[1]

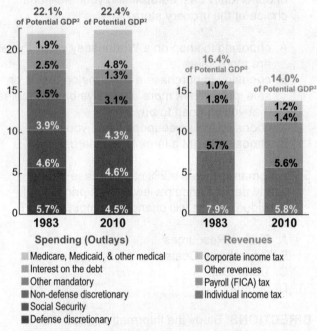

Medicare, Medicaid, & other medical
Interest on the debt
Other mandatory
Non-defense discretionary
Social Security
Defense discretionary

Corporate income tax
Other revenues
Payroll (FICA) tax
Individual income tax

[1] 1983 and 2010 are compared because they had similar-sized output gaps (the difference between potential and actual GDP as a percent of potential GDP); 6.4% and 6.2%, respectively.

[2] Potential GDP is the full-capacity output of the economy.

Source: U.S. Department of the Treasury

One of the largest economic institutions in the world is the United States government. The government collects tax revenue and spends money on many programs and ongoing operations. Spending, such as discretionary expenses on defense, can sometimes be slowed when necessary, but categories such as Medicare cannot.

The amount of revenue the government receives is largely dependent on fiscal policy. Fiscal policy involves decisions made by the national government on economic issues such as taxes and spending.

The United States experienced a major economic downturn, often referred to as the "Great Recession," in 2008–2009. This downturn was brought about by market failures, in the form of bad loans and excessive risks taken by banks, and by government failures. Bank regulations had been eased and the Federal Reserve was keeping interest rates artificially low. This set of circumstances and events enabled banks to make more loans to people with poor credit, which was encouraged by the government's desire for more homeownership. Realistically, both the market and the government must share the responsibility for the Great Recession.

The last severe downturn prior to this was in 1983. The chart shows the relationship between government revenue and expenditures in these two recessionary periods. Because people often lose their jobs in recessions, collection of both income tax and FICA are reduced. These are two critical revenue sources to the government.

7. Which of the following conclusions can be drawn about the federal deficit in 2010 compared to the federal deficit in 1983?

   A. The federal deficit in 2010 was less than the federal deficit in 1983.
   B. The federal deficit in 2010 was more than the federal deficit in 1983.
   C. The federal deficit grew by 2.4%.
   D. The federal deficit did not change between 1983 and 2010.

8. In what way was the government responsible for the Great Recession?

   A. bad bank loans
   B. banking industry risks
   C. easing of bank regulations
   D. artificially high interest rates

9. Which of the following spending categories experienced the largest change between 1983 and 2010?

   A. Medicare, Medicaid, and other medical
   B. Defense discretionary
   C. Social Security
   D. Interest on the debt

10. Which of the following is the best evidence of the government and market failures of the 2009–2010 recession?

   A. the 1.2% corporate income tax
   B. the 1.3% interest on the debt
   C. the 4.5% spent on defense discretionary
   D. the combination of 5.6% FICA Tax and 5.8% Individual tax

From the editorial "Competition Is Healthy for Governments, Too" by N. Gregory Mankiw:

Should governments—of nations, states and towns—compete like business rivals? The question is simpler to ask than to answer. But it reflects why conservatives and liberals disagree on many big issues facing the nation.

… competition among governments leads to better governance. In choosing where to live, people can compare public services and taxes. They are attracted to towns that use tax dollars wisely. Competition keeps town managers alert. It prevents governments from exerting substantial monopoly power over residents. If people feel that their taxes exceed the value of their public services, they can go elsewhere. They can, as economists put it, vote with their feet.

The argument applies not only to people but also to capital. Because capital is more mobile than labor, competition among governments significantly constrains how capital is taxed. Corporations benefit from various government services, including infrastructure, the protection of property rights, and the enforcement of contracts. But if taxes vastly exceed these benefits, businesses can—and often do—move to places offering a better mix of taxes and services.

From nytimes.com, April 14, 2012

11. According to the excerpt, for which of the following are governments competing?

   A. capital, labor, and businesses
   B. monopolies, tax dollars, and residents
   C. corporations, tax benefits, and federal funding
   D. entrepreneurs, government services, and industries

DIRECTIONS: Study the information, read each question, then choose the **best** answer.

The United States engages in free trade with countries such as Canada and Mexico under the North American Free Trade Agreement, or NAFTA. But with many other countries, the United States imposes tariffs on imported goods. A tariff is essentially a tax. It is a cost added by the government to an imported good.

There are many reasons that a country may choose to impose a tariff. One reason is competition. A tariff helps protect domestic industries from competition from non-domestic industries. If an international country can produce a product or good more cheaply than the United States, people may be more likely to buy the less expensive goods and the industry in the United States will suffer.

12. Which of the following best explains how tariffs protect domestic industry from competition?

   A. The tariff makes it easier for stores in the United States to import the good.
   B. By adding a tariff to imported goods, the country exporting the good will stop sending goods to the United States.
   C. People are less inclined to purchase goods that have tariffs attached.
   D. When the tariff is added to the price of the imported good, it raises the price above that of the domestic good.

13. International countries may also assess tariffs on goods the United States exports to them. How would this type of tariff affect the U.S. company's profit, as compared to the prices of their goods?

   A. Their goods will be more expensive, and their profit will increase.
   B. Their goods will be more expensive, but their profit will remain the same.
   C. Their goods will be less expensive, and their profit will increase.
   D. Their goods will be less expensive, and their profit will decrease.

UNIT 4

Multiple Causes and Effects

Use with **Student Book** pp. 122–125

SS CONTENT TOPICS: II.E.c.4, II.E.c.6, II.E.c.10, II.E.d.1, II.E.d.2, II.E.d.7, II.E.e.2
SS PRACTICES: SSP.6.a, SSP.6.b, SSP.10.a, SSP.10.c

① Review the Skill

Some cause-and-effect relationships can be complex. These may involve multiple causes, multiple effects, or both. Learning to identify and analyze **multiple causes and effects** will increase your ability to understand and interpret complicated concepts in economics.

Most events have more than one cause or effect. For example, the drop in home prices in late 2008 had many causes and effects. The value of real estate dropped, people with adjustable-rate mortgages could no longer afford their homes, and foreclosures increased. All of this caused job losses in the real estate and construction fields, and then people working in those fields became in danger of losing their homes.

② Refine the Skill

By refining the skill of identifying multiple causes and effects, you will improve your study and test-taking abilities, especially as they relate to the GED® Social Studies Test. Study the information below. Then answer the questions that follow.

a To successfully answer the questions, analyze the information and graph to find patterns in holiday spending.

Holiday shopping is often a good indicator of the health of the economy. In years when people are planning to spend more on their holiday shopping, one can assume that the economy is in a better place than in years when people are cutting back. The graph shows the results of a survey in which people were asked whether they were going to spend more, less, or the same amount on their holiday shopping as they did the previous year. Note: some years are missing in the graph.

b Examine the graph for indications of major changes in holiday spending. This alerts you to a shift in the economy.

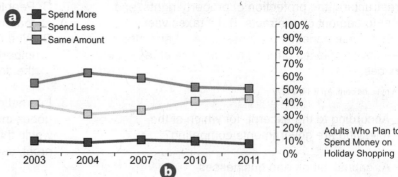

HOLIDAY SPENDING PLANS

Adults Who Plan to Spend Money on Holiday Shopping

1. According to the graph, in which of the following years were adults most and least optimistic, respectively?

   A. 2004, 2003
   B. 2011, 2003
   C. 2007, 2011
   D. 2011, 2004

2. Based on the graph, in which year can you assume that the economy was weakest?

   A. 2005
   B. 2004
   C. 2008
   D. 2006

USING LOGIC

Use logic to determine whether an event has multiple causes, multiple effects, or both. Carefully consider each cause and effect. What caused each situation, and what happened as a result?

UNIT 4

★ Spotlighted Item: **DRAG-AND-DROP**

DIRECTIONS: Read the information and study the graph. Read the question. Then complete the diagram by placing the drag-and-drop options in the appropriate boxes.

In the United States, prices are set by the economic concept of supply and demand. When a product's supply is higher than its demand, the result is a surplus. When demand is higher than supply, the result is a shortage. Surpluses and shortages help determine prices. For example, a surplus of corn may result in lower prices to help encourage sales. When a shortage occurs, sellers raise prices because people are willing to pay more for the good or product.

Corn prices rose in 2007. Increased sales of corn to overseas nations, combined with a 30-percent increase in the amount of corn used to produce the fuel called ethanol, resulted in a national shortage and a higher price per bushel. Higher corn prices also resulted in higher prices for foods that use corn as an ingredient. A third effect grew from farmers using more of their land to grow corn. This meant that fewer acres were devoted to crops such as wheat and soybeans. The dip in wheat and soybean production led prices for those crops to rise also.

3. Complete the diagram by placing the drag-and-drop options in the appropriate boxes.

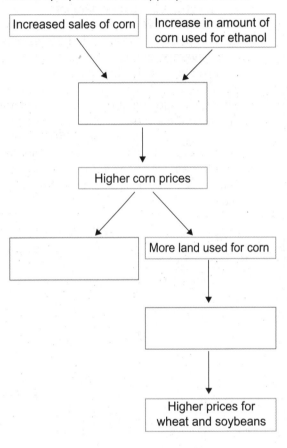

CROP PRICES

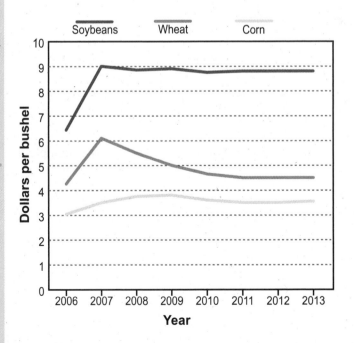

Drag-and-Drop Options

Corn shortage
Corn surplus
Higher food prices for foods with corn
Lower food prices for foods with corn
Less land used for wheat and soybeans
More land used for wheat and soybeans

UNIT 4

Spotlighted Item: **DRAG-AND-DROP**

DIRECTIONS: Study the passage and the graph. Read the question. Then use the drag-and-drop options to complete the diagram.

Supply and demand are major factors in the rise and fall of gasoline prices. Shortages and fears of shortages can cause these prices to fluctuate in a short period of time. As developing countries grow more industrialized, global demand for gasoline increases. From the beginning of 2005 through the middle of 2008, overall prices of gasoline in the United States rose steadily. At that time, the average price of a gallon of gas in United States was $1.78. By the middle of 2008, the price had reached the national average of nearly $4.00 per gallon. By the end of 2008, however, reduced demand sent prices back down to around $1.60 per gallon.

These changes occurred because of increases and decreases in crude oil prices. From 2005 to mid-2008, the price per barrel of crude oil rose from $42.00 to more than $100.00 per barrel. By the end of 2008, the price fell to less than $50.00 per barrel. In addition to free-market effects, a number of other factors can and do play a role in gasoline prices. Developments in world politics sometimes disturb market forces. Oil prices also are subject to manipulation. The Organization of Petroleum Exporting Countries (OPEC) accounts for 40 percent of the world's crude oil production. This group routinely limits the amount of oil its members export. This results in higher gasoline and oil prices worldwide.

AVERAGE PRICES FOR GASOLINE, UNITED STATES
December 2007–December 2012

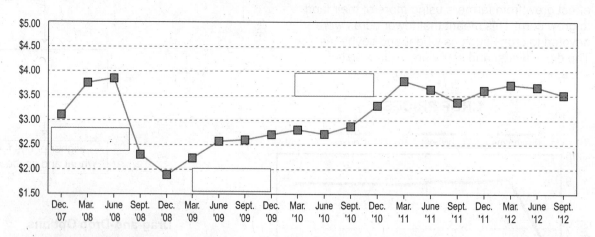

4. Based on the information above, place each drag-and-drop option in the correct blank to complete the diagram.

Drag-and-Drop Options

limited exports of oil
declining demand
low crude oil prices

DIRECTIONS: Study the passages and the graphs. Read the questions. Then use the drag-and-drop options to complete the diagrams.

The graph below shows new U.S. housing starts for a recent period. Housing starts are the number of new homes being built nationally. The number is considered a leading economic indicator. Beginning in 2006, U.S. housing starts began to decline. In addition, many people who had borrowed money to pay for their homes could no longer make their loan payments. Lenders took possession of the homes, resulting in an increase in empty houses for sale.

In many cases, the problems were caused by the type of loans taken out by homebuyers. These adjustable-rate loans offered affordable payments in the beginning, but the amount owed each month was connected to general economic conditions. As economic expansion slowed, home payments grew higher. Many homebuyers could no longer afford them. Lenders foreclosed on many loans, taking ownership of the houses.

HOUSING STARTS

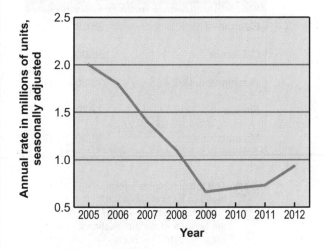

FORECLOSURES

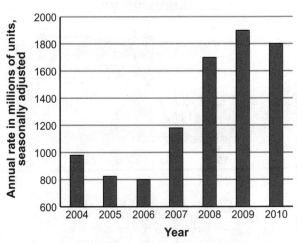

5. Drag and drop the causes and effects into the correct places in the diagram.

CAUSE	EFFECT

Drag-and-Drop Options

Decrease in housing starts
Increase in housing starts
Increase in construction and carpentry industry jobs
Decrease in construction and carpentry industry jobs

6. Drag and drop the causes into the correct places in the diagram.

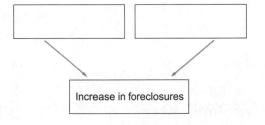

Drag-and-Drop Options

Adjustable-rate mortgages
Increase in housing starts
Poor economic conditions
Positive economic activity

Compare and Contrast Visuals

Use with *Student Book* pp. 94–95

SS CONTENT TOPICS: II.E.d.2, II.E.d.3, II.E.d.4, II.E.d.9, II.E.d.10, II.E.e.1, II.E.e.2
SS PRACTICES: SSP.1.a, SSP.1.b, SSP.3.c, SSP.4.a, SSP.6.a, SSP.6.b, SSP.6.c, SSP.10.a, SSP.10.c , SSP.11.a

1 Review the Skill

To **compare** and **contrast** is a useful way to make connections between two or more items and the ideas they represent. To compare items is to examine the similarities and differences between them. To contrast them is to consider only the differences. Once you are familiar with their similarities and differences, you can analyze what these similarities and differences tell you about the items.

When you **compare and contrast visuals**, first take note of the things that are alike. From there, examine the things that are distinctive to each one.

2 Refine the Skill

By refining the skill of comparing and contrasting visuals, you will improve your study and test-taking abilities, especially as they relate to the GED® Social Studies Test. Study the information below. Then answer the questions that follow.

THE FEDERAL HOURLY MINIMUM WAGE

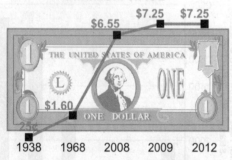

$6.55 $7.25 $7.25
$1.60
1938   1968   2008   2009   2012

STATE	2012 BASIC MINIMUM WAGE (PER HOUR)
Georgia	$5.15
California	$8.00
Washington, D.C.	$8.25
Florida	$7.79
Massachusetts	$8.00

a The graph displays an upward trend in the amount of the U.S. minimum wage. Keep in mind that the last three years shown cover one to three year gaps, while the first three years cover 30 and 40 year gaps.

b The table contains information that can be compared and contrasted between states (in the table) and the information presented on the graph.

1. Which of the following can you infer by comparing and contrasting information on the two visuals?

   A. Business ventures affect minimum wage.
   B. Massachusetts enacted the first minimum wage law.
   C. Georgia has a lower "cost of living" than the other states.
   D. Increasing the federal minimum wage creates new jobs.

2. In which of the following ways do the minimum wages in California and Massachusetts compare to the federal minimum wage?

   A. Theirs are lower than the federal minimum wage.
   B. Theirs are higher than the federal minimum wage.
   C. Theirs are equal to the federal minimum wage.
   D. California's minimum wage is lower than the federal minimum wage, while Massachusetts's minimum wage is higher than the federal minimum wage.

MAKING ASSUMPTIONS

Although the federal government sets a minimum wage standard, some states may set lower standards for particular types of jobs not covered by the Federal Fair Labor Standards Act.

UNIT 4

DIRECTIONS: Study the graphs, read the questions, then choose the **best** answer.

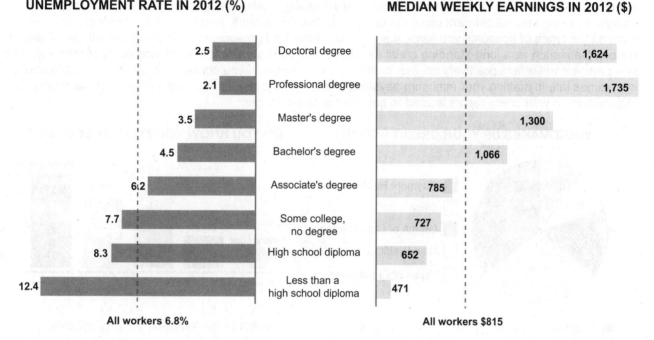

UNEMPLOYMENT RATE IN 2012 (%) | MEDIAN WEEKLY EARNINGS IN 2012 ($)

	Unemployment		Earnings
Doctoral degree	2.5		1,624
Professional degree	2.1		1,735
Master's degree	3.5		1,300
Bachelor's degree	4.5		1,066
Associate's degree	6.2		785
Some college, no degree	7.7		727
High school diploma	8.3		652
Less than a high school diploma	12.4		471

All workers 6.8% | All workers $815

Source: Bureau of Labor Statistics, Current Population Survey

3. In which of the following ways are median weekly earnings and unemployment related to each other?

   A. The higher the median weekly earnings, the lower the rate of unemployment.
   B. The lower the rate of unemployment, the lower the median weekly earnings.
   C. The higher the median weekly earnings, the higher the rate of unemployment.
   D. The higher the degree level, the lower both the unemployment rate and median weekly income.

4. Based on the graphs, which of the following is most likely true of a person with a bachelor's degree (4-year degree)?

   A. The person is unlikely to find a job and earn less than $1,300 per week.
   B. The person is likely to find a job and earn about $1,700 per week.
   C. The person is unlikely to find a job and will not earn more than $750 per week.
   D. The person is likely to find a job and earn about $1,000 per week.

5. Which of the following occupations would fall into both of these categories: second-lowest rate of unemployment and second-highest median weekly earnings?

   A. fast-food worker
   B. college professor
   C. teacher
   D. licensed electrician

6. A woman makes the individual choice not to complete college, and instead to begin working. What can you conclude about this woman?

   A. Her chances of finding a well-paying job are much better than the chances of a person with a bachelor's degree.
   B. She will be unable to find a job easily where she makes a median weekly income of more than $500.
   C. She will make more money and more easily find a job than a person who has not completed high school.
   D. Her income is more likely to be above average than the income of a person with a professional degree.

UNIT 4

DIRECTIONS: Study the information and the graphs, read the questions, then choose the **best** answer.

Every adult who has any kind of financial history in the United States has a credit score. Your score is calculated using several different pieces of credit data from your credit report. Your credit report includes data such as the types of accounts you have, how long you have had an account, and your payment and balance history. Data such as a long-standing credit card for which you've paid off the balance every month without a late payment will reflect positively on your credit report. However, if you continually carried a balance and were sometimes late in making your minimum payment, this is likely to reflect negatively on your credit report. The information on your credit report is used to generate a credit score.

WHAT MAKES UP YOUR CREDIT SCORE?

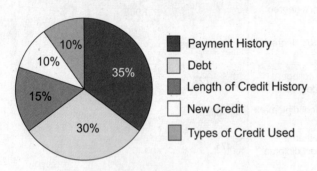

- Payment History
- Debt
- Length of Credit History
- New Credit
- Types of Credit Used

DO YOU KNOW YOUR CREDIT SCORE?

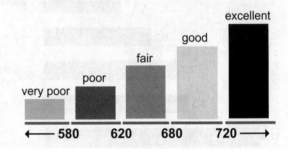

7. In which of the following credit score ranges is a person who is consistently late in making mortgage payments, credit card payments, and student loan payments, and carries a high balance on each of these, most likely to be?

   A. 400 to 450
   B. 550 to 600
   C. 700 to 750
   D. 800 to 850

8. Which of the following actions will most significantly improve a person's credit score?

   A. taking out a home mortgage
   B. adding a new credit card
   C. taking out a new car loan
   D. paying down balances on credit cards

DIRECTIONS: Compare and contrast the two graphs, read the question, and then choose the best answer.

QUARTER-TO-QUARTER GROWTH IN REAL GDP

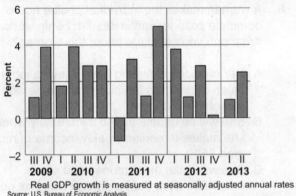

Real GDP growth is measured at seasonally adjusted annual rates
Source: U.S. Bureau of Economic Analysis

ANNUAL GROWTH IN REAL GDP

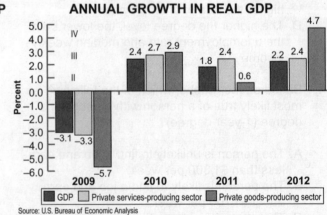

Source: U.S. Bureau of Economic Analysis

9. Which of the following can you conclude from the two graphs?

   A. In 2012, goods-producing sectors declined.
   B. The first half of 2009 had negative GDP growth.
   C. GDP growth was strongest in 2011.
   D. Q1 had the weakest GDP growth each year.

DIRECTIONS: Study the table and the pay stub, read the questions, then choose the **best** answer.

Gross Pay	Amount of Pay before Deductions
Pre-Tax Deductions	Deductions taken out before taxes. They are not themselves taxed.
After-Tax Deductions	Deductions taken out after taxes. They are taxed at the same percentage as the gross pay.
Federal Withholding Deduction	Deduction put toward federal income tax obligation
State Tax	Deduction put toward state income tax obligation
Local Tax	Deduction put toward local income tax obligation
FICA	Social Security taxes
401(k)	Voluntary deduction requested by worker to go into retirement fund
Net Pay	Amount given to worker after deductions

Gross	$2,000.00
Federal Witholding	$ 500.00
FICA	$ 150.00
State	$ 100.00
Local	$ 24.00
Net	$1,226.00

10. Which of the following can you infer about a 401(k)?

    A. 401(k) monies never come out of a person's paycheck.
    B. Not everyone has 401(k) monies removed from his or her paycheck.
    C. The government randomly removes 401(k) monies from an individual's paycheck.
    D. 401(k) monies are part of federal withholdings.

11. Which of the following conclusions can be drawn from comparing and contrasting the tax table and the pay stub?

    A. Net pay is the smallest amount that will appear on your pay stub.
    B. Paying federal, state, and local taxes is an individual choice.
    C. The table provides information to the employee, while the pay stub provides information to the employer.
    D. Gross pay is the largest amount that will appear on your pay stub.

12. Which of the following economic institutions is most closely involved with the data and information found in the table and on the pay stub?

    A. the World Bank Group
    B. the National Bureau of Economic Research
    C. the U.S. Federal Reserve
    D. the Internal Revenue Service

13. The federal government may institute a stimulative fiscal policy when it wants to stimulate economic growth. Which of the following changes is the person whose pay stub is shown most likely to see if the federal government makes changes to stimulate economic growth?

    A. a decrease in the amount of federal withholdings
    B. an increase in the amount of state taxes withheld
    C. a decrease in the number of pre-tax deductions
    D. a decrease in his or her gross pay

Interpret Pictographs

Use with *Student Book* pp. 96–97

SS CONTENT TOPICS: II.E.c.9, II.E.c.11, II.E.d.1, II.E.d.4, II.E.d.5, II.E.d.10
SS PRACTICES: SSP.3.c, SSP.6.a, SSP.6.b, SSP.10.a

① Review the Skill

Pictographs use symbols to represent data in a chart form. Each of the symbols on a pictograph represents a specific quantity that is identified in a key. By using the key and the symbols shown in the chart, you can **interpret pictographs** and analyze or make judgments about the data.

Understanding the meaning of the data shown in a pictograph is crucial to making a correct interpretation. Always verify that you first understand the title or subject of a pictograph before attempting to interpret the key and symbols.

② Refine the Skill

By refining the skill of interpreting pictographs, you will improve your study and test-taking abilities, especially as they relate to the GED® Social Studies Test. Study the information below. Then answer the questions that follow.

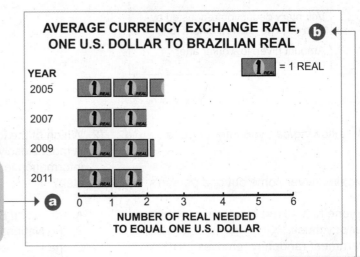

ⓐ A currency exchange rate compares the values of two nations' currencies, in this case the U.S. dollar and the *real*, a unit of currency in Brazil.

ⓑ In this pictograph, the exchange rate is expressed as the number of real equal to a single U.S. dollar.

USING LOGIC

Authors frequently use pictographs to compare two things or to show how something has changed over time. Try to determine the author's purpose for including a pictograph.

1. Which of the following was the approximate value of the U.S. dollar in 2007?

   A. 1 real
   B. 1.5 real
   C. 2 real
   D. 2.5 real

2. Based on the information in the pictograph, which of the following conclusions can you draw?

   A. The value of the real changes dramatically from year to year.
   B. The value of the dollar decreased between 2007 and 2011.
   C. The value of the real decreased between 2007 and 2011.
   D. The exchange rate for these currencies would have increased in 2013.

UNIT 4

DIRECTIONS: Study the information presented in the pictograph, read the questions, then choose the **best** answers.

U.S. EMPLOYEES BY ECONOMIC SECTOR, 2010

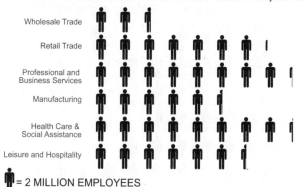

3. Based on the pictograph, which of the following statements is correct?

   A. About 20 million people work in Wholesale Trade and Retail Trade combined.
   B. The Health Care and Social Assistance sector employs about twice as many people as Manufacturing.
   C. The Leisure and Hospitality sector employs the largest number of people.
   D. Fewer than 5 million people work in Wholesale Trade.

4. In 2010, there were 19,513,100 people working in state and local government. If you were to add this sector to the pictograph, which of the following number of symbols would appear next to this sector?

   A. 8 ½
   B. 9 ¾
   C. 10 ¾
   D. 19 ½

5. Also in 2010, there were 64,000 people working for the legislative and judicial branches of the federal government. If you were to add this sector to the pictograph, which of the following would first need to be changed for the pictograph to be effective?

   A. The economic sectors would need to be listed alphabetically.
   B. The icon of the person would need to change.
   C. The title would need to change.
   D. The key would need to change.

DIRECTIONS: Study the information presented in the pictograph, read the questions, then choose the **best** answers.

U.S. FEDERAL BUDGET DEFICIT OR SURPLUS, 2000–2010

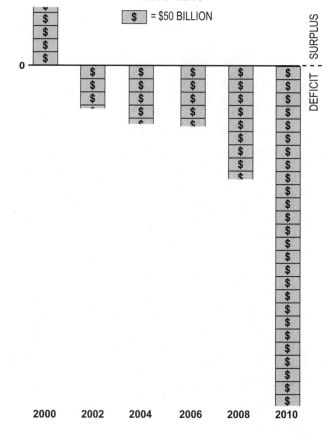

6. Based on the pictograph, which of the following describes the U.S. government's budget in 2004?

   A. It broke even.
   B. It spent about $250 billion less than it made.
   C. It spent about $350 billion more than it made.
   D. It ran a larger deficit than it did in 2002.

7. Which of the following could help explain the budgetary changes that occurred between 2000 and 2004?

   A. higher taxes
   B. a reduction of federal aid programs
   C. funding for the war in Iraq
   D. an influx of new taxpayers

8. Which years did the deficit increase the most?

   A. between 2002 and 2004
   B. between 2004 and 2006
   C. between 2006 and 2008
   D. between 2008 and 2010

UNIT 4

DIRECTIONS: Study the pictograph and the information, read the questions, then choose the **best** answers.

PRICE PER BUSHEL OF U.S. SOYBEANS, 2007–2011

= $2

YEAR

2007
2008
2009
2010
2011

The United States has a mixed economy. It does not depend solely on supply and demand such as a market economy. Instead, some aspects are controlled by the government.

An example of this is subsidies. A subsidy is a benefit, typically in the form of cash, given by the government to groups or individuals. The purpose is to remove some type of burden. Subsidies are generally provided in certain industries for the best interest of the public. For example, agricultural subsidies, such as soybean subsidies, may be given to farmers. They receive subsidies so that they can sell at a low market price, but still make enough money to be profitable.

9. Which of the following could have caused the change in price per bushel for soybeans from 2009 to 2010?

   A. deflation in the U.S. economy
   B. a shortened growing season due to inclement weather
   C. decreased demand for soybeans and soy products
   D. an increase in the supply of soybeans

10. Subsidies often guarantee a minimum price for a product or good. If the market price is below this price, farmers will receive a subsidy. In which of the following years would farmers have received a subsidy if the minimum guaranteed price had been $9.65 per bushel?

    A. 2007
    B. 2008
    C. 2009
    D. 2010

DIRECTIONS: Study the information presented in the pictograph, read the questions, then choose the **best** answers.

U.S. UNEMPLOYMENT RATE
For Persons (16 Years & Older)

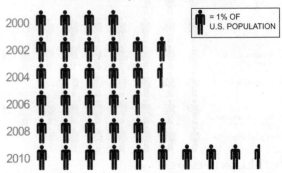

= 1% OF U.S. POPULATION

2000
2002
2004
2006
2008
2010

The unemployment rate is a commonly used economic indicator. The percent reported as the unemployment rate is the percent of people who are available and looking for work who do not have jobs. A person may be either employed, unemployed, or not in the labor force. Those who are not in the labor force are not calculated in the unemployment rate.

11. In which of the following ways would you describe the U.S. unemployment rate in the 10-year period represented by the pictograph?

    A. It experienced one sharp increase.
    B. It experienced several sharp increases.
    C. It increased steadily.
    D. It decreased steadily.

12. Between which of the following two years can you conclude that the U.S. economy experienced a downturn based on the unemployment rate?

    A. between 2002 and 2004
    B. between 2004 and 2006
    C. between 2006 and 2008
    D. between 2008 and 2010

13. Between which of the following two years can you conclude that the U.S. economy experienced an upturn based on the unemployment rate?

    A. between 2002 and 2004
    B. between 2004 and 2006
    C. between 2006 and 2008
    D. between 2008 and 2010

UNIT 4

DIRECTIONS: Study the information and the pictographs, read the questions, then choose the **best** answers.

The concept of interdependence is visible in exports and imports among countries. Countries may be dependent on other countries for the products they either cannot produce themselves, or cannot produce as efficiently as other countries. Countries will tend to export goods they produce efficiently to other countries and import the goods they produce less efficiently from other countries.

In these pictographs, the exports describe U.S. goods sent to Japan, and the imports describe Japanese goods sent to the United States.

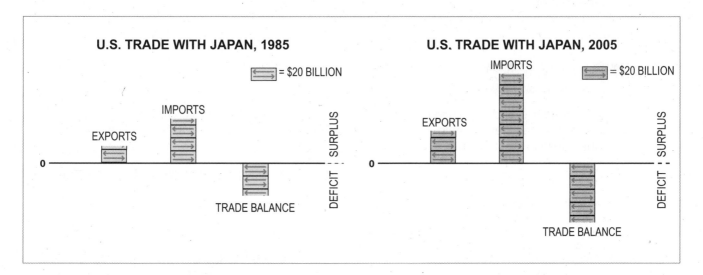

14. Based on these pictographs, which of the following statements is correct?

A. The United States imported about $40 billion from Japan in 1985.
B. The United States nearly achieved a trade balance with Japan in 1985.
C. The value of U.S. exports to Japan doubled between 1985 and 2005.
D. The value of U.S. imports from Japan changed only slightly during the period between 1985 and 2005.

15. Which of the following describes U.S. trade with Japan in 2005?

A. Exports totaled about $75 billion.
B. Imports totaled about $200 billion.
C. The trade surplus was about $25 billion.
D. The trade deficit was more than $80 billion.

16. How did trade between the United States and Japan change from 1985 to 2005?

A. The U.S. trade deficit grew by nearly $40 billion.
B. The value of exports increased by more than the value of imports.
C. The U.S. trade balance moved from a small surplus to a large deficit.
D. The value of imports increased by about $20 billion.

17. In which of the following ways might the U.S. government seek to change its 2005 trade balance with Japan?

A. lower taxes on imports
B. impose strict tariffs on exports to Japan
C. remove all trade restrictions between the two nations
D. provide tax relief to U.S. companies manufacturing technology products

UNIT 4

Interpret Multi-Bar and Line Graphs

Use with *Student Book* pp. 98–99

SS CONTENT TOPICS: II.E.c.7, II.E.c.11, II.E.d.4, II.E.d.9, II.E.e.1, II.E.e.2
SS PRACTICES: SSP.6.a, SSP.6.b, SSP.6.c, SSP.10.a, SSP.10.c

① Review the Skill

Multi-bar and line graphs allow for comparisons of multiple sets of related data over a particular time period. By interpreting the bars and lines that appear on these graphs, you can compare the values of two types of data at the same point in time, as well as examine the patterns and trends that each set of data follows over time.

When **interpreting a multi-bar** or **line graph**, first familiarize yourself with the subject of the graph, as well as the labels for each axis. Then, begin studying the graph by looking for any patterns that emerge. Do the bars of the graph grow increasingly taller? Do the lines veer sharply up or down as they extend across the graph?

② Refine the Skill

By refining the skill of interpreting multi-bar and line graphs, you will improve your study and test-taking abilities, especially as they relate to the GED® Social Studies Test. Study the information below. Then answer the questions that follow.

ⓐ This graph does not have a separate key. Each line is labeled so you know what it represents.

ⓑ Questions that ask you to interpret multi-bar or multi-line graphs may ask you to make inferences or draw conclusions based on the relationship of two or more data sets.

ESTABLISHMENT BIRTHS AND DEATHS, 1993–2010

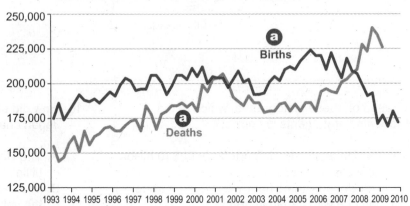

An entrepreneur is a person who undertakes the risks of a business venture. More commonly we think of an entrepreneur as a person who owns a business. When a new business begins, it is said to be "born." When a business closes, it is said to "die."

1. Which of the following best describes establishment births and deaths in the 1990s?

   A. The number of births exceeded the number of deaths.
   B. The number of births was twice the number of deaths.
   C. The number of births and deaths were unchanged.
   D. The number of births and deaths were about the same.

2. During which of the following time periods was the economy probably the weakest, based on the information in the graph?

   A. 2002–2004
   B. 2004–2006
   C. 2006–2008
   D. 2008–2010

MAKING ASSUMPTIONS

You can typically assume that an author includes information in a multi-bar or line graph to show a relationship, such as comparison-contrast or cause-and-effect, between the data sets.

③ Master the Skill

DIRECTIONS: Study the information and double-bar graph, read the questions, then choose the **best** answer.

One important aspect of U.S. fiscal policy is the preparation and approval of an annual budget for the federal government. A budget is a complex plan for collecting and spending the money required to carry out the government's operations. A budget surplus occurs when the amount of money received, or revenue, is greater than the amount of money spent, or expenditures. When expenditures exceed revenue, the result is a budget deficit.

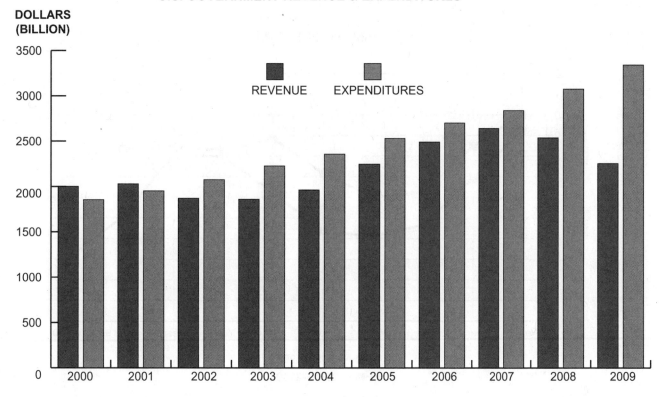

U.S. GOVERNMENT REVENUE & EXPENDITURES

3. Approximately how much money did the U.S. government receive in 2006?

   A. $1,750 billion
   B. $2,000 billion
   C. $2,250 billion
   D. $2,500 billion

4. Which of the following likely occurred in order to produce the trend in government spending shown on the graph?

   A. the elimination of government aid programs such as welfare
   B. tax increases on those making more than $250,000
   C. the addition of many new government programs
   D. a decrease in populations in the lower tax brackets

5. In which of the following years did the federal budget exhibit the largest budget deficit?

   A. 2009
   B. 2008
   C. 2000
   D. 2001

6. Using the double-bar graph, which of the following statements can you determine to be correct?

   A. The U.S. government achieved a surplus in three different years during the period shown on the graph.
   B. The smallest deficit shown on the graph appeared in 2005.
   C. Government revenues exceeded $2,000 billion for the first time in 2005.
   D. Government expenditures decreased during each year shown on the graph.

DIRECTIONS: Study the information and the double-line graph, read the questions, then choose the **best** answer.

Just as the Federal Reserve sets the discount rate at which it lends money to commercial banks, these banks establish interest rates at which they lend money to their customers. The prime rate is the lowest rate of interest that commercial banks charge. Banks will typically only offer the prime rate to their customers who have the strongest credit. The prime rate is also usually available only on specific types of loans. The interest rates of other types of loans are often expressed as a certain percentage over time. The graph shows the prime rate used by banks during two different 10-year periods.

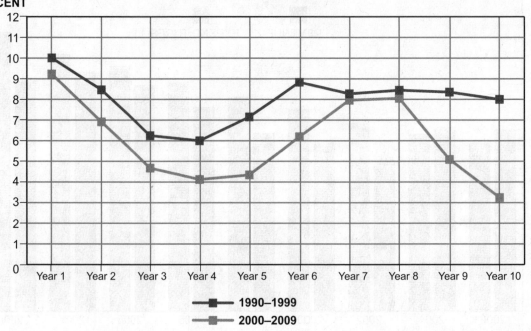

BANK PRIME INTEREST RATES

7. At the beginning of which of the following years did the prime rate reach its lowest point between 1990 and 1999?

   A. Year 3 (1992)
   B. Year 4 (1993)
   C. Year 5 (1994)
   D. Year 6 (1995)

8. Which of the following statements can you determine to be correct, based on the double-line graph?

   A. The prime rate decreased dramatically between 2000 and 2003.
   B. The prime rate in 2007 was lower than the prime rate in 1994.
   C. The prime rate increased in three consecutive years from 1996 to 1998.
   D. The highest prime rate recorded between 2000 and 2009 occurred in 2006.

9. At the end of which of the following years would a preferred borrower have received the best prime rate?

   A. 1990
   B. 1996
   C. 2000
   D. 2003

10. Which of the following generalizations can you make, based on the information contained in this multi-line graph?

   A. The prime rate generally decreased throughout each 10-year period.
   B. The prime rate generally changed by about one percentage point each year.
   C. The changes in prime rate generally followed a bell-shaped curve in each decade.
   D. The prime rate generally remained higher in the 1990s than in the 2000s.

DIRECTIONS: Study the information and multi-bar graph, read the questions, then choose the **best** answer.

One important way to evaluate whether the government's monetary policy is benefiting the nation's economy is to examine the Gross Domestic Product, or GDP. As you have already learned, GDP is the total value of all goods and services produced in a nation during a specified time period. Many nations regard this value as the best indicator of a nation's economic activities. The multi-bar graph shows how the various components of the GDP changed in the United States between 2010 and 2012.

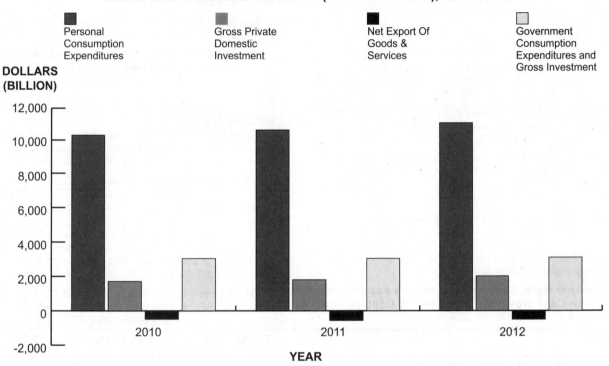

U.S. GROSS DOMESTIC PRODUCT (BY COMPONENT), 2010–2012

11. Which of the following was the approximate value of gross private domestic investment in 2010?

    A. $1,500 billion
    B. $1,750 billion
    C. $2,000 billion
    D. $2,250 billion

12. Which of the following is most likely to account for the negative values shown on the graph?

    A. large increases in government spending on community programs
    B. the growth of high-technology industries in the United States
    C. a negative balance of trade between the United States and other nations
    D. a seasonal increase in domestic consumer spending

13. Based on the information in the graph, which of the following statements is **false**?

    A. The value of personal consumption expenditures decreased each year shown on the graph.
    B. In 2012, the value of gross private domestic investment was less than that of government consumption expenditures and gross investment.
    C. The net export of goods and services had a less negative effect on GDP in 2010 than in 2011.
    D. The value of government consumption expenditures and gross investment stayed about the same each year.

Answer Key

UNIT 1 GEOGRAPHY AND THE WORLD

LESSON 1, pp. 2–5

1. **D; DOK Level:** 2; **Content Topics:** II.G.b.4, II.G.c.1, II.G.c.2; **Practices:** SSP.4.a, SSP.2.b, SSP.6.b. Australia and Antarctica lie entirely in the Southern Hemisphere.

2. **B; DOK Level:** 1; **Content Topics:** II.G.c.1, II.G.c.3; **Practices:** SSP.2.b, SSP.4.a, SSP.6.c. The equator does not cross Europe, North America, and just crosses three countries in South America.

3. **South America; DOK Level:** 1; **Content Topics:** II.G.c.1, II.G.c.3; **Practices:** SSP.4.a, SSP.2.b, SSP.6.c. South America is the continent shown on the map with the most land mass located in the Southern Hemisphere.

4. **Egypt, which is located on the continent of Africa; DOK Level:** 2; **Content Topics:** II.G.c.1, II.G.c.3; **Practices:** SSP.4.a, SSP.2.b, SSP.6.c.

5. **Argentina; DOK Level:** 2; **Content Topics:** II.G.c.1, II.G.c.3; **Practices:** SSP.2.b, SSP.4.a, SSP.6.c. Argentina is located on the continent of South America, the majority of which is in the Southern Hemisphere.

6. **Limpopo and Mpumalanga provinces; DOK Level:** 1; **Content Topics:** II.G.c.1, II.G.c.3; **Practices:** SSP.2.b, SSP.4.a, SSP.6.c. Kruger National Park is located in the northeastern part of South Africa in the provinces of Mpumalanga and Limpopo.

7. **Kwazulu-Natal, Eastern Cape, and the eastern part of Western Cape provinces; DOK Level:** 1; **Content Topics:** II.G.c.1, II.G.c.3; **Practices:** SSP.4.a, SSP.2.b, SSP.6.c. The other provinces of South Africa do not border the Indian Ocean.

8. **North West, Gauteng, Mpumalanga, Kwazulu-Natal, Eastern Cape, and Northern Cape provinces; DOK Level:** 2; **Content Topics:** II.G.c.1, II.G.c.3; **Practices:** SSP.2.b, SSP.4.a, SSP.6.c. The other provinces of South Africa do not border Free State.

9. **The Gulf of Mexico and the Pacific Ocean are natural features located south and west, respectively, of the United States; DOK Level:** 1; **Content Topics:** II.G.c.1, II.G.c.3, II.G.d.3; **Practices:** SSP.2.b, SSP.4.a, SSP.6.c.

10. **The Appalachian Mountains; DOK Level:** 2; **Content Topics:** II.G.c.1, II.G.c.3, II.G.d.3; **Practices:** SSP.2.b, SSP.4.a, SSP.6.c.

11. **The Great Lakes, and the Ohio, Mississippi and Missouri rivers aided early settlers to the Midwest region of the United States; DOK Level:** 2; **Content Topics:** II.G.b.4, II.G.c.1, II.G.c.3, II.G.d.3; **Practices:** SSP.2.b, SSP.4.a, SSP.6.c.

12. **The Rocky Mountains; DOK Level:** 3; **Content Topics:** II.G.b.4, II.G.c.1, II.G.c.3, II.G.d.3; **Practices:** SSP.2.b, SSP.4.a, SSP.6.c.

13. **The Great Lakes; DOK Level:** 2; **Content Topics:** II.G.b.4, II.G.c.1, II.G.c.3, II.G.d.3; **Practices:** SSP.2.b, SSP.4.a, SSP.6.c.

14. **Sri Lanka; DOK Level:** 2; **Content Topic:** II.G.c.1; **Practices:** SSP.2.b, SSP.6.b.

15. **On the map, China, North Korea, South Korea, Japan, Malaysia, Taiwan, Laos, Vietnam, Thailand, Philippines, and Indonesia can be considered to be located in the Far East; DOK Level:** 2; **Content Topic:** II.G.c.1; **Practices:** SSP.2.b, SSP.6.b.

16. **The landlocked countries shown on the map are Armenia, Uzbekistan, Kyrgyzstan, Tajikistan, Afghanistan, Nepal, Butan, Laos, and Mongolia; DOK Level:** 2; **Content Topic:** II.G.c.1; **Practices:** SSP.2.b, SSP.6.b.

17. **China; DOK Level:** 2; **Content Topic:** II.G.c.1; **Practices:** SSP.2.b, SSP.6.b.

18. **Mongolia; DOK Level:** 3; **Content Topic;** II.G.c.1; **Practices:** SSP.2.b, SSP.6.b.

19. **The countries that border Thailand are Myanmar, Laos, Vietnam and Malaysia; DOK Level:** 3; **Content Topic:** II.G.c.1; **Practices:** SSP.2.b, SSP.6.b.

LESSON 2, pp. 6–9

1. **B; DOK Level:** 2; **Content Topics:** II.G.c.1, II.G.c.3, II.G.d.3, I.USH.b.1; **Practices:** SSP.2.b, SSP.4.a, SSP.6.b. It is between the thirteen colonies and the Mississippi River.

2. **A; DOK Level:** 2; **Content Topics:** II.G.c.1, II.G.c.3, II.G.d.3, II.G.d.4, I.USH.b.1; **Practices:** SSP.2.b, SSP.4.a, SSP.6.b. The map key indicates that major cities are indicated by black dots. There are major cities in northern and southern colonies. There is not a black dot indicating a city in North Carolina. There are major cities in colonies that are not in the disputed lands, and there are major cities in the southern colonies.

3. **D; DOK Level:** 3; **Content Topics:** II.G.c.1, II.G.c.3; **Practices:** SSP.2.b, SSP.6.b. The distance between Houston and Atlanta is approximately 625 miles.

4. **B; DOK Level:** 2; **Content Topics:** II.G.b.4, II.G.c.1, II.G.c.2, II.G.c.3; **Practices:** SSP.2.b, SSP.6.b. Of the states listed as answer choices, only Colorado has elevations of more than 6,561 feet. Neither Minnesota, Maine, nor Arkansas have elevations of this height.

5. **C; DOK Level:** 3; **Content Topics:** II.G.c.1, II.G.c.3; **Practices:** SSP.2.b, SSP.6.b. Of the places listed as answer choices, only Atlanta falls near those coordinates. None of the other cities are located near these coordinates.

6. **A; DOK Level:** 3; **Content Topics:** II.G.c.1, II.G.c.3; **Practices:** SSP.2.b, SSP.6.b. Relative location does not include latitude or longitude. Therefore, the relative location of Detroit is north of Columbus. It is east, not west, of Denver.

7. **B; DOK Level:** 2; **Content Topics:** II.G.c.1, II.G.c.3; **Practices:** SSP.2.b, SSP.6.b. Of the places listed as answer choices, the Southeast areas of the United States have the lowest elevation; other answer choices list areas of the country that have higher elevations.

8. **C; DOK Level:** 2; **Content Topics:** II.G.c.1, II.G.c.3; **Practices:** SSP.2.b, SSP.6.b. The distance between Columbus, Ohio, and Denver, Colorado, is close to 1,200 miles, so the choice of "approximately 1,200 miles" would be correct. The distance is not approximately 950 miles, nor 1,000 miles, nor 2,250 miles.

9. **B; DOK Level:** 2; **Content Topics:** II.G.c.1, II.G.c.3; **Practices:** SSP.2.b, SSP.6.b. The star symbol indicates that Olympia is the capital of Washington. Using the scale, you can determine that Mt. Rainier National Park is the closest park to the capital. Olympic National Park, Mt. St. Helens National Volcanic Monument, Umatilla National Forest, and the North Cascades National Park are all further away from Olympia than is Mt. Rainier National Park.

10. **C; DOK Level:** 2; **Content Topics:** II.G.c.1, II.G.c.3; **Practices:** SSP.2.b, SSP.6.b. I-5 connects the major cities of Olympia, Tacoma, Seattle, and Bellingham. I-90 connects Seattle with Spokane. I-90 runs mainly east-to-west, not north to south. I-82 merges with I-90, not I-5.

11. **D; DOK Level:** 2; **Content Topics:** II.G.c.1, II.G.c.3, II.G.d.3, II.G.d.4; **Practices:** SSP.2.b, SSP.6.b. Washington has several national parks and monuments, as the symbols on the map indicate. Washington is west of Idaho and borders the Pacific Ocean. Washington does not border California; it borders Canada, Oregon, and Idaho. The state is abundant with natural areas, as shown on the map.

12. **D; DOK Level:** 3; **Content Topics:** II.G.b.4, II.G.c.1, II.G.c.3, II.G.d.3; **Practices:** SSP.2.b, SSP.3.c, SSP.6.b, SSP.10.c. Puget Sound is an important waterway because it connects several major cities to the Pacific Ocean. It is not close to all of the National Parks in the state, and this fact, were it true, in and of itself would not make Puget Sound an important waterway. The Columbia River has its source in northeastern Washington, not Puget Sound. Puget Sound does not extend into Oregon.

13. **B; DOK Level:** 2; **Content Topics:** II.G.c.1, II.G.c.3; **Practices:** SSP.2.b, SSP.6.b. According to the scale, the distance between Bellingham and Olympia is approximately 150 miles, not 25, nor 210, nor 240 miles.

14. **D; DOK Level:** 1; **Content Topics:** II.G.c.1, II.G.c.3; **Practices:** SSP.2.b, SSP.6.b. The Umatilla National Forest is closer to Oregon than Mt. St. Helens National Volcanic Monument, Mt. Rainier National Park, or North Cascades National Park.

15. **C; DOK Level:** 2; **Content Topics:** II.G.c.1, II.G.c.3; **Practices:** SSP.2.b, SSP.6.b. On the map key, the P-in-a-square symbol represents parking lots. Most of the parking lots are near the National Mall. There is one parking lot near the Vietnam Veterans Memorial, none close to the U.S. Capitol, and only one parking lot located near the Jefferson Memorial.

16. **B; DOK Level:** 2; **Content Topics:** II.G.c.1, II.G.c.3; **Practices:** SSP.2.b, SSP.6.b. On the map key, the M-in-a-square symbol represents Metro Stations. The Metro Station closest to the White House is Federal Triangle. The other Metro Stations shown on the map are farther away from The White House, near the Freer Gallery of Art and the Archives-Navy Memorial. The Ellipse is not a Metro Station, since there is no M-in-a-square identifying it as such.

17. **A; DOK Level:** 3; **Content Topics:** II.G.c.1, II.G.c.3; **Practices:** SSP.2.b, SSP.6.b. The most logical route would be the one with no backtracking. The first option is the only one listed among the four that meets this criterion and has no backtracking.

18. **D; DOK Level:** 2; **Content Topics:** II.G.c.1, II.G.c.3; **Practices:** SSP.2.b, SSP.6.b. The U.S. Capitol is the site furthest away from the World War II Memorial, which is located west, near the Vietnam Veterans Memorial and the Korean War Veterans Memorial. The Freer Gallery of Art is far from the World War II Memorial, but not as far as is the U.S. Capitol. The White House and the Ellipse are relatively close to the World War II Memorial.

LESSON 3, pp. 10–13

1. **B; DOK Level:** 3; **Content Topics:** II.G.b.1, II.G.b.4, II.G.c.1, II.G.d.3; **Practices:** SSP.2.b, SSP.3.a, SSP.3.c, SSP.6.b. Early settlers most likely would have traveled from Austin to New Mexico via the Edwards Plateau.

2. **A; DOK Level:** 2; **Content Topics:** II.G.b.1, II.G.b.4, II.G.c.1, II.G.d.3; **Practices:** SSP.2.b, SSP.3.a, SSP.3.c, SSP.6.b. The Red River flows along the border of Oklahoma.

3. **B; DOK Level:** 2; **Content Topics:** II.G.b.4, II.G.c.1, II.G.c.3; **Practices:** SSP.2.b, SSP.6.b. Virginia has temperature ranges in July from 60 degrees to 90 degrees. In January, the temperature ranges from 30 degrees to 45 degrees. The only answer option that fits these ranges is 30 degrees in January and 80 degrees in July.

4. **D; DOK Level:** 2; **Content Topics:** II.G.b.4, II.G.c.1, II.G.c.3; **Practices:** SSP.2.b, SSP.6.b. Maine is the north-easternmost state in the United States. The temperature ranges in January are between 0 degrees and 30 degrees, by far the coldest of all the states listed as answer choices.

5. **C; DOK Level:** 2; **Content Topics:** II.G.b.4, II.G.c.1, II.G.c.3; **Practices:** SSP.2.b, SSP.6.b. The vast difference in temperature ranges shows that across the United States, there is a wide range of temperatures. The United States does not have uniform temperatures. The United States is neither a warm nor cold country.

6. **A; DOK Level:** 3; **Content Topics:** II.G.b.4, II.G.c.1, II.G.c.3; **Practices:** SSP.2.b, SSP.6.b. The climate of the southeastern United States is affected by its proximity to the equator. Vegetation is a product of climate, not a cause. Also, longitude of the southeastern part of the United States does not in and of itself affect its climate.

7. **B; DOK Level:** 2; **Content Topics:** II.G.b.4, II.G.c.1, II.G.c.3; **Practices:** SSP.2.b, SSP.6.b. New Mexico has temperature ranges in July from 45 degrees to 90 degrees. In January, the temperature ranges from 15 degrees to 45 degrees. The only answer option that fits these ranges is 30 degrees in January and 90 degrees in July.

8. **D; DOK Level:** 2; **Content Topics:** II.G.b.4, II.G.c.1, II.G.c.3; **Practices:** SSP.2.b, SSP.6.b. California has more land area that is warmer than 90 degrees in July than all the other states listed as answer choices.

9. **C; DOK Level:** 3; **Content Topics:** II.G.b.4, II.G.c.1, II.G.c.3; **Practices:** SSP.2.b, SSP.6.b. The temperature range for all of Tennessee in January is from 30 degrees to 45 degrees. Snow is possible at 30 degrees. The other answer choices do not have as much land area with this color shading indicating this range of temperatures in January.

10. **A; DOK Level:** 3; **Content Topics:** II.G.b.4, II.G.c.1, II.G.c.3; **Practices:** SSP.2.b, SSP.6.b. Florida experiences the warmest average temperature in January.

Answer Key

11. **D; DOK Level:** 2; **Content Topics:** II.G.b.2, II.G.b.4, II.G.c.1, II.G.c.2, II.G.c.3, II.G.d.3; **Practices:** SSP.2.b, SSP.3.b, SSP.3.c, SSP.6.b. Farming is problematic in South Asia because the area receives most of its yearly rainfall during the monsoon, or rainy, season from June to October. It is not true that there is never enough rain; it is just that it only rains during the one rainy season, the monsoon. It is not constantly raining because it rains mainly just from June to October.

12. **C; DOK Level:** 3; **Content Topics:** II.G.b.2, II.G.b.4, II.G.c.1, II.G.c.2, II.G.c.3, II.G.d.3; **Practices:** SSP.2.b, SSP.3.b, SSP.3.c, SSP.6.b. Antarctica uniformly experiences a yearly rainfall of 10 to 20 inches.

13. **Karachi is Pakistan's major port city; DOK Level:** 2; **Content Topics:** II.G.b.1, II.G.b.2, II.G.b.4, II.G.c.1, II.G.c.2, II.G.d.3, II.G.d.4; **Practices:** SSP.3.c, SSP.6.b.

14. **The most mountainous area is north of Islamabad; DOK Level:** 2; **Content Topics:** II.G.b.1, II.G.b.2, II.G.b.4, II.G.c.1, II.G.c.2, II.G.d.3, II.G.d.4; **Practices:** SSP.2.b, SSP.3.c, SSP.6.b.

15. **the Indus River, the Dasht River, and the Arabian Sea; DOK Level:** 1; **Content Topics:** II.G.b.1, II.G.b.2, II.G.b.4, II.G.c.1, II.G.c.2, II.G.d.3, II.G.d.4; **Practice Topics:** SSP.2.b, SSP.3.c, SSP.6.b.

16. **India; DOK Level:** 2; **Content Topics:** II.G.b.1, II.G.b.2, II.G.b.4, II.G.c.1, II.G.c.2, II.G.d.3, II.G.d.4; **Practices:** SSP.2.b, SSP.3.c, SSP.6.b.

LESSON 4, *pp. 14–17*

1. **B; DOK Level:** 1; **Content Topic:** II.G.c.3; **Practice:** SSP.6.b. The map key indicates that the star symbol represents a state capital. The map key does not show symbols for a large city, nor for a county seat.

2. **D; DOK Level:** 2; **Content Topics:** II.G.c.3; **Practice:** SSP.6.b. The best use of this map would be to identify the states in the Northeast region of the United States. It does not show physical features that could determine climate or data that could explain population density.

3. **B; DOK Level:** 2; **Content Topics:** II.G.b.1, II.G.b.4, II.G.c.1, II.G.c.3, II.G.d.3, II.G.d.4; **Practices:** SSP.2.b, SSP.3.c, SSP.6.b, SSP.10.c. While no cities are marked, you can assume that areas with the largest population density contain Brazil's major cities. The largest population density occurs along the east coast. The areas along the Bolivian border, in the Amazon basin, and in the center of the country have far less population density than does the area along the east coast.

4. **C; DOK Level:** 3; **Content Topics:** II.G.b.1, II.G.b.4, II.G.c.1, II.G.c.3, II.G.d.3, II.G.d.4; **Practices:** SSP.2.b, SSP.3.c, SSP.6.b, SSP.10.c. Brazil's population centers were probably most affected by the Amazon rainforest and the Atlantic Ocean. Most people do not live in the rainforest or mountainous areas. European settlers arrived and built cities along the Atlantic coast. There is no information to indicate that the Amazon Delta or the Peruvian border had an influence on Brazil's population centers. Neither the Pacific Ocean nor the equator probably had any influence on Brazil's population centers.

5. **A; DOK Level:** 2; **Content Topics:** II.G.b.1, II.G.b.4, II.G.c.1, II.G.c.3, II.G.d.3, II.G.d.4; **Practices:** SSP.2.b, SSP.3.c, SSP.6.b, SSP.10.c. Modern Brazil is like historic Brazil because it has a low population in the Amazon area. Brazil is a country, not a colony.

6. **D; DOK Level:** 2; **Content Topics:** II.G.b.1, II.G.b.4, II.G.c.1, II.G.c.3, II.G.d.3, II.G.d.4; **Practices:** SSP.2.b, SSP.3.c, SSP.6.b, SSP.10.c. Brazil gained its independence from Portugal in 1822; the country abolished slavery in 1888, thus making it 66 years, not 45, 46, or 56 years.

7. **A; DOK Level:** 3; **Content Topics:** II.G.b.1, II.G.b.4, II.G.c.1, II.G.c.3, II.G.d.3, II.G.d.4; **Practices:** SSP.2.b, SSP.3.c, SSP.6.b, SSP.10.c. The information mentions indigenous peoples, Portuguese colonizers, and Africans. Therefore, you can logically assume that Brazil's population is a mixture of people of different ethnicities. The map indicates that the population is not distributed evenly throughout the country, and there is no mention of Uruguay.

8. **Antarctica; DOK Level:** 2; **Content Topics:** II.G.c.1, II.G.c.3, II.G.d.3; **Practices:** SSP.2.b, SSP.6.b. Antarctica has the smallest popuation.

9. **Asia; DOK Level:** 1; **Content Topics:** II.G.c.1, II.G.c.3, II.G.d.3; **Practices:** SSP.2.b, SSP.6.b. Asia is the most densely populated continent.

10. **Australia; DOK Level:** 1; **Content Topics:** II.G.c.1, II.G.c.3, II.G.d.3; **Practices:** SSP.2.b, SSP.6.b.

11. **South America; DOK Level:** 3; **Content Topics:** II.G.c.1, II.G.c.3, II.G.d.3; **Practices:** SSP.2.b, SSP.6.b.

12. **North America; DOK Level:** 3; **Content Topics:** II.G.c.1, II.G.c.3, II.G.d.3; **Practices:** SSP.2.b, SSP.6.b. Based on the map, North America's population density is concentrated on its eastern coast.

13. **C; DOK Level:** 1; **Content Topics:** II.G.c.1, II.G.c.3, II.G.d.3; **Practices:** SSP.2.b, SSP.6.b. Counties Tipperary, Roscommon, and Monaghan are all landlocked. Dublin is located on the coast of the Irish Sea.

14. **B; DOK Level:** 2; **Content Topics:** II.G.c.1, II.G.c.3, II.G.d.3; **Practices:** SSP.2.b, SSP.6.b. By reading the map closely, you can determine that many county capitals share the same name as their county. Ireland's counties are not all the same size. The area north of Dublin that is part of the United Kingdom is Northern Ireland; there are several Irish counties between Dublin and Northern Ireland. The Celtic Sea is south, not east, of County Wicklow.

15. **C; DOK Level:** 2; **Content Topics:** II.G.c.1, II.G.c.3, II.G.d.3; **Practices:** SSP.2.b, SSP.6.b. The map shows that Clonmel is the county seat of Tipperary, not Tipperary, Kilkenny, or Limerick.

16. **D; DOK Level:** 2; **Content Topics:** II.G.c.1, II.G.c.3, II.G.d.3; **Practices:** SSP.2.b, SSP.6.b. Of the answer choices given, only D is correct: Ohio is in the Midwest region. Alaska is the largest state in the United States and it is not in the Midwest region. California, not Illinois, is the state with the largest population and it is not located in the Midwest region. There is no evidence that the Midwest region is the largest in the United States.

17. **B; DOK Level:** 2; **Content Topics:** II.G.c.1, II.G.c.3, II.G.d.3; **Practices:** SSP.2.b, SSP.6.b. While none of these cities are shown on the map, use your knowledge about geography to determine that St. Louis is located in Missouri. Therefore, it is the only city in the Midwest that is listed.

LESSON 5, *pp. 18–21*

1. **C; DOK Level:** 2; **Content Topics:** I.G.a, II.G.b.1, II.G.c.1, II.G.c.3, II.G.d.1, II.G.d.2, II.G.d.3, I.USH.b.1, I.E.g; **Practices:** SSP.2.b, SSP.3.c, SSP.6.b, SSP.6.c. Use the dates and battle names listed on the map to determine that Long Island was the first battle of the campaign and that Princeton was the last. The other answer options do not qualify as the first and last battle sites.

2. **A; DOK Level:** 2; **Content Topics:** I.G.a, II.G.b.1, II.G.c.1, II.G.c.3, II.G.d.1, II.G.d.2, II.G.d.3, I.USH.b.1, I.E.g; **Practices:** SSP.2.b, SSP.3.c, SSP.6.b, SSP.6.c. Use the map key to determine that the black line represents movement by the British forces. From White Plains, use the compass rose to determine that the forces moved southwest into Fort Lee, which is in New Jersey. The British forces did not travel north, nor did they go south across the Long Island Sound. The British forces also did not travel southeast.

3. **B; DOK Level:** 2; **Content Topics:** I.G.a, II.G.b.1, II.G.c.1, II.G.c.3, II.G.d.1, II.G.d.2, II.G.d.3, I.USH.b.1, I.E.g; **Practices:** SSP.2.b, SSP.3.c, SSP.6.b, SSP.6.c. The best description of the map is that it shows the acquisition of territories between 1783 to 1853.

4. **B; DOK Level:** 2; **Content Topics:** I.G.a, II.G.b.1, II.G.c.1, II.G.c.3, II.G.d.1, II.G.d.2, II.G.d.3, I.USH.b.1, I.E.g; **Practices:** SSP.2.b, SSP.3.c, SSP.6.b, SSP.6.c. The Louisiana Purchase in 1803 opened much of the land west of the Mississippi River to settlement. The other answers either do not demonstrate settlement of land west of the Mississippi River (as with answer option A) or do not reflect the largest portion of land.

5. **D; DOK Level:** 2; **Content Topics:** I.G.a, II.G.b.1, II.G.c.1, II.G.c.3, II.G.d.1, II.G.d.2, II.G.d.3, I.USH.b.1, I.E.g; **Practices:** SSP.2.b, SSP.3.c, SSP.6.b, SSP.6.c. Based on the size of the shadings on the map, Spain ceded the least amount of land to the United States. Britain and France ceded the most land to the United States, followed by Mexico. Spain ceded East and West Florida, part of present-day Louisiana, and a sliver of present-day Colorado.

6. **D; DOK Level:** 2; **Content Topics:** I.G.a, II.G.b.1, II.G.c.1, II.G.c.3, II.G.d.1, II.G.d.2, II.G.d.3, I.USH.b.1, I.E.g; **Practices:** SSP.2.b, SSP.3.c, SSP.6.b, SSP.6.c. California was included in the Mexican Cession of 1848.

7. **D; DOK Level:** 2; **Content Topics:** I.G.a, II.G.b.1, II.G.c.1, II.G.c.3, II.G.d.1, II.G.d.2, II.G.d.3, I.USH.b.1, I.E.g; **Practices:** SSP.2.b, SSP.3.c, SSP.6.b, SSP.6.c. Sixty-three years passed between the time of the first cession from Britain, in 1783, and the last one, in 1846. It was not 35, 33, or 53 years.

8. **B; DOK Level:** 2; **Content Topics:** I.G.a, II.G.b.1, II.G.c.1, II.G.c.3, II.G.d.1, II.G.d.2, II.G.d.3, I.USH.b.1, I.E.g; **Practices:** SSP.2.b, SSP.3.c, SSP.6.b, SSP.6.c. Spain ceded the most land along the Gulf of Mexico.

9. **Spain and Portugal; DOK Level:** 2; **Content Topics:** I.G.a, II.G.b.1, II.G.c.1, II.G.c.3, II.G.d.1, II.G.d.2, II.G.d.3, I.USH.b.1, I.E.g; **Practices:** SSP.2.b, SSP.3.c, SSP.6.b, SSP.6.c. The majority of the explorers began their journeys from Spain and Portual.

10. **Vikings; DOK Level:** 2; **Content Topics:** I.G.a, II.G.b.1, II.G.c.1, II.G.c.3, II.G.d.1, II.G.d.2, II.G.d.3, I.USH.b.1, I.E.g; **Practices:** SSP.2.b, SSP.3.c, SSP.6.b, SSP.6.c. The Vikings reached the northeast regions of North America hundreds of years before any of the other explorers.

11. **Magellan; DOK Level:** 3; **Content Topics:** I.G.a, II.G.b.1, II.G.c.1, II.G.c.3, II.G.d.1, II.G.d.2, II.G.d.3, I.USH.b.1, I.E.g; **Practices:** SSP.2.b, SSP.3.c, SSP.6.b, SSP.6.c. Although Drake also circled the globe on his expedition, Magellan did so more than 50 years prior.

12. **Columbus; DOK Level:** 2; **Content Topics:** I.G.a, II.G.b.1, II.G.c.1, II.G.c.3, II.G.d.1, II.G.d.2, II.G.d.3, I.USH.b.1, I.E.g; **Practices:** SSP.2.b, SSP.3.c, SSP.6.b, SSP.6.c. Columbus explored the Caribbean Islands.

13. **D; DOK Level:** 2; **Content Topics:** I.G.a, II.G.b.1, II.G.c.1, II.G.c.3, II.G.d.1, II.G.d.2, II.G.d.3, I.USH.b.1, I.E.g; **Practices:** SSP.2.b, SSP.3.c, SSP.6.b, SSP.6.c. Routes on the map illustrate that the Romans traded all over, including outside their empire and not in just certain areas. They did not limit themselves to internal trade, and traded with people to the north and south.

14. **B; DOK Level:** 1; **Content Topics:** I.G.a, II.G.b.1, II.G.c.1, II.G.c.3, II.G.d.1, II.G.d.2, II.G.d.3, I.USH.b.1, I.E.g; **Practices:** SSP.2.b, SSP.3.c, SSP.6.b, SSP.6.c. By analyzing the map, you can determine that the Roman Empire existed and traded over three continents. The empire included much of Europe, the northern part of Africa, and part of western Asia. It did not include South America.

15. **D; DOK Level:** 2; **Content Topics:** I.G.a, II.G.b.1, II.G.c.1, II.G.c.3, II.G.d.1, II.G.d.2, II.G.d.3, I.USH.b.1, I.E.g; **Practices:** SSP.2.b, SSP.3.c, SSP.6.b, SSP.6.c. The Mediterranean Sea was the main waterway for transport of goods along the Roman trade route. The Atlantic Ocean and Danube River saw only limited activity.

16. **C; DOK Level:** 2; **Content Topics:** I.G.a, II.G.b.1, II.G.c.1, II.G.c.3, II.G.d.1, II.G.d.2, II.G.d.3, I.USH.b.1, I.E.g; **Practices:** SSP.2.b, SSP.3.c, SSP.6.b, SSP.6.c. As the map indicates, the Romans extended their trade routes into Spain.

Answer Key

UNIT 1 (continued)

17. D; DOK Level: 3; **Content Topics:** I.G.a, II.G.b.1, II.G.c.1, II.G.c.3, II.G.d.1, II.G.d.2, II.G.d.3, I.USH.b.1, I.E.g; **Practices:** SSP.2.b, SSP.3.c, SSP.6.b, SSP.6.c. You can logically assume that trading across such a large geographic area allowed for an exchange of cultural knowledge throughout the empire. You know that Europe, Africa, and the Middle East had different cultures, even in ancient times. There is no indication given that the Romans became isolated, nor that the Romans could enforce their laws throughout the entire world. There also is no evidence presented that the Roman trade routes were the main cause of the empire's economic collapse.

UNIT 2 UNITED STATES HISTORY

LESSON 1, pp. 22–25

1. B; DOK Level: 1; **Content Topics:** II.G.b.1, II.G.c.1, II.G.c.3; **Practices:** SSP.2.b, SSP.6.b. The map displays the state of Michigan with Lake Superior, Lake Michigan, Lake Huron, and Lake Erie bordering the state. Lake Michigan and Lake Huron border Michigan, but so do Lake Superior and Lake Erie. The Ohio River does not form part of Michigan's state boundary, so the Ohio River is not part of a correct answer.

2. D; DOK Level: 2; **Content Topics:** II.G.b.1, II.G.c.1, II.G.c.3; **Practices:** SSP.2.b, SSP.6.b. The map clearly shows that of the answer options, only Illinois shares a border with the Ohio River and the Mississippi River.

3. hills, mountains, vales or valleys; DOK Level: 2; **Content Topic:** II.G.c.1; **Practices:** SSP.1.a, SSP.6.a, SSP.6.b, SSP.8.a.

4. Mormon; Oregon; DOK Level: 1; **Content Topics:** II.USH.b.6, II.G.d.1, II.G.d.2, II.G.d.3, II.G.d.4; **Practice:** SSP.6.b.

5. wagon; injury; DOK Level: 2; **Content Topics:** II.USH.b.6, II.G.d.1, II.G.d.4; **Practices:** SSP.1.a, SSP.2.a, SSP.2.b, SSP.8.a. Hart writes about his near loss of a wagon and an injury: "my lock chain loosened" and "my right great toe underwent a flattening process."

6. Mount Joy, Mount Misery, and the Schuylkill River; DOK Level: 2; **Content Topics:** I.USH.b.1, I.USH.b.3, II.G.c.1, II.G.c.2, II.G.c.3; **Practices:** SSP.1.a, SSP.2.b, SSP.3.b, SSP.3.c. The passage states that Valley Forge was easily defensible due to geographic barriers formed by Mount Joy, Mount Misery, and the Schuylkill River, which put Washington's troops in position to protect the Continental Congress at York. Locating there also kept the British out of central Pennsylvania.

7. was successful; DOK Level: 3; **Content Topics:** I.USH.b.1, I.USH.b.3, II.USH.g.3, II.G.c.1, II.G.c.3; **Practices:** SSP.1.a, SSP.1.b, SSP.2.a. The passage states that the Continental Army wanted to keep the British out of central Pennsylvania. The red and black arrows on the map show that the army was successful in achieving this goal.

8. temperate or mild; DOK Level: 3; **Content Topics:** I.USH.b.1, I.USH.b.3, II.G.c.1, II.G.c.2, II.G.c.3; **Practices:** SSP.1.a, SSP.2.b, SSP.3.b; SSP.4.a. The weather in Pennsylvania that winter had previously been described as very harsh and cold. It is logical to assume that as spring arrived, better weather would arrive with it.

9. to protect its shipping rights; DOK Level: 1; **Content Topic:** I.USH.b.2; **Practices:** SSP.1.a, SSP.2.b, SSP.3.a, SSP.3.c, SSP.4.a, SSP.6.b.

10. York and the Thames River; DOK Level: 2; **Content Topics:** I.USH.b.2, II.G.c.3; **Practices:** SSP.1.a, SSP.2.b, SSP.3.a, SSP.3.c, SSP.4.a, SSP.6.b.

11. Erie, Michigan, and Ontario; DOK Level: 2; **Content Topics:** I.USH.b.2, II.G.c.3; **Practices:** SSP.1.a, SSP.2.b, SSP.3.a, SSP.3.c, SSP.4.a, SSP.6.b.

LESSON 2, pp. 26–29

1. D; DOK Level: 1; **Content Topics:** II.G.b.1, II.G.b.2, II.G.b.4, II.E.g; **Practices:** SSP.1.a, SSP.2.b, SSP.6.b. Row 2 of the first column in the table lists the Middle Colonies, and the corresponding crop in the second column of row 2 specifies wheat. Corn is listed in the table, but that crop corresponds to what is grown in New England. Rice is listed in the table, but corresponds to what is grown in the Southern Colonies. Indigo is listed in the table, but corresponds to the Southern Colonies.

2. A; DOK Level: 3; **Content Topics:** II.G.b.1, II.G.b.2, II.G.b.4, II.E.g; **Practices:** SSP.1.a, SSP.2.b, SSP.6.b. The passage explains that crops did not grow well in New England because the climate was too cool and the soil was too rocky. Rhode Island is the only answer choice that is a state in New England. Georgia is not in New England. Pennsylvania is not a New England state. Virginia is not considered a New England state.

3. C; DOK Level: 1; **Content Topics:** I.USH.c.1, II.G.d.1, II.G.d.3; **Practice:** SSP.6.b. In 1720, Virginia had a little more than 26,000 enslaved people. By 1770, Virginia had more than 187,000 people who were enslaved. The difference is more than 150,000. South Carolina's population of enslaved people more than doubled between 1720 and 1750. Connecticut had the fewest enslaved people, so the New England colonies probably had the fewest enslaved people. Connecticut had 3,010 enslaved people in 1750, and more than 5,000 enslaved people in 1770, so that population did not decrease.

4. D; DOK Level: 2; **Content Topics:** I.USH.c.1, II.G.d.1, II.G.d.3; **Practices:** SSP.1.a, SSP.6.b. Connecticut's population grew by 4,596, which shows the least amount of growth.

5. B; DOK Level: 2; **Content Topics:** I.USH.c.1, II.G.d.1, II.G.d.3; **Practices:** SSP.1.a, SSP.6.b. Virginia's population of enslaved people increased more than New York's, Maryland's, or South Carolina's during the years 1720 to 1750, as clearly shown in the table.

6. **C; DOK Level:** 1; **Content Topics:** I.USH.e.1, II.G.d.1, II.G.d.3; **Practice:** SSP.6.b. The population of the Middle Colonies was just over 555,000 and the population of the Southern Colonies was just over 950,000, so the difference is about 400,000. The population of the Middle Colonies as it is recorded in the table is not the smallest number. Massachusetts is not part of the Middle Colonies, so it cannot represent part of its population. The population of the Middle Colonies was greater than New England, so the average population of the Middle Colonies would not have been smaller than New England.

7. **A; DOK Level:** 1; **Content Topics:** I.USH.e.1, II.G.d.1, II.G.d.3; **Practice:** SSP.6.b. The information states that the colonies experienced natural increase, which refers to population growth due to birth rates that are higher than death rates. Although the information states that there was continued immigration to the colonies, there is no specific mention of German and Scots-Irish settlers. The death rate in the colonies was low, which suggests that the colonists' health did not decline over time. Although people kept coming to the colonies, neither the passage nor table indicates they came solely for manufacturing jobs.

8. **New England; DOK Level:** 1; **Content Topics:** II.USH.b.7, II.USH.e, II.G.c.2, II.G.d.4; **Practice:** SSP.6.b. The conflicts in the table are listed in chronological order and the dates 1636–1637 are the earliest dates. The region of New England is the site of this earliest conflict.

9. **Cherokee and Yamassee Indians; DOK Level:** 1; **Content Topics:** II.USH.b.7, II.USH.e, II.G.c.2, II.G.d.3, II.G.d.4; **Practices:** SSP.2.b, SSP.6.b. The Events/Outcome column provides details about the conflicts, and information about the Yamassee War explains that Cherokee and Yamassee helped the colonists fight against the Creek Indians.

10. **Kittanning; DOK Level:** 1; **Content Topics:** II.USH.b.7, II.USH.e, II.G.c.2, II.G.d.3, II.G.d.4; **Practices:** SSP.2.b, SSP.6.b. Pennsylvania is only mentioned in information about the raid on Kittanning, and that information explains that colonists attacked the Native American village of Kittanning.

11. **land; DOK Level:** 2; **Content Topics:** II.USH.b.7, II.USH.e, II.E.f, II.G.c.2, II.G.d.4; **Practices:** SSP.2.b, SSP.6.b. The information about every conflict listed in the table cites struggles over land as a cause of the conflict. The Pequot Revolt involved land disputes in western Massachusetts, while King Philip's War turned on encroachment of Native American lands in southeastern Massachusetts. The Yamassee War and the Raid on Kittanning originated from disputes over rights to the land.

12. **Pequot attack a town in Connecticut; DOK Level:** 1; **Content Topics:** II.USH.b.7, II.USH.e, II.G.c.2, II.G.d.3, II.G.d.4; **Practices:** SSP.2.b, SSP.6.b. During the Pequot Revolt, the settlers and Indians burn and destroy the Pequot's primary village following the Pequot's attack on a Connecticut town.

13. **It refers to the Delaware tribe, not the colony; DOK Level:** 3; **Content Topics:** II.USH.b.7, II.USH.e, II.E.f, II.G.c.2, II.G.d.4; **Practices:** SSP.2.b, SSP.6.b. The Raid on Kittanning occurred in the Middle Colonies. The colony of Delaware is in the New England Colonies; therefore, the usage of "Delaware" refers to the group of the Delaware Native Americans.

14. **A; DOK Level:** 1; **Content Topics:** II.USH.e, II.E.g, II.G.b.4, II.G.d.4; **Practices:** SSP.4.a, SSP.6.b. Agriculture is listed as an economic activity in the New England, Middle, and Southern Colonies. Commerce is part of the economy of New England and the Middle Colonies, but not the Southern Colonies. Fishing is part of just New England's economy. Small industries are listed just as part of the Middle Colonies' economy.

15. **C; DOK Level:** 1; **Content Topics:** II.E.g, II.G.d.4; **Practices:** SSP.6.b, SSP.6.c. The heading of the middle column of the table is "Economy," so that column provides information about the economic activity of the three regions listed in column one. The heading of the middle column is not related to New England. The heading of the middle column does not indicate that the Middle Colonies are the main topic of that column. Information about settlement patterns is found in the third, not the middle, column.

16. **C; DOK Level:** 3; **Content Topics:** II.USH.e, II.G.d.3, II.G.d.4; **Practices:** SSP.1.a, SSP.6.b. People in a town or large city would receive information quickly because they live closer to each other. News does not have to travel a great distance to reach them. Towns and cities also have industries, such as trade and shipping, that are more helpful in spreading news. A New England colony such as Massachusetts fits these requirements. Maryland and the Middle Colonies have only some cities and fewer industries to disseminate news. The Southern Colonies, including South Carolina and Georgia, have no towns or cities and are dominated by agriculture, so news would not travel quickly.

17. **B; DOK Level:** 2; **Content Topics:** II.USH.e, II.G.d.3, II.G.d.4; **Practices:** SSP.1.a, SSP.6.b. The text mentions Philadelphia and New York, specific large cities in the Middle Colonies. The text describes where different people lived in the colonies, but not the number of people in each region. The text says that there were large plantations in the Southern Colonies, but it does not describe the types of plantations. The text does describe the industries in which New England colonists worked, but that information is also presented in the table.

18. **D; DOK Level:** 3; **Content Topics:** II.USH.e, II.E.g, II.G.c.1, II.G.d.3, II.G.d.4; **Practices:** SSP.1.a, SSP.6.b. The pattern that emerges is an economically diverse, industrial North, and a South dependent mostly on agriculture, which includes large farms and plantations. The Civil War was fought in part over the regional differences and lifestyles that grew from these differing economic models. The French and Indian War was fought between colonies of Great Britain and France, not between American colonists over economies. The American Revolution was fought to break free of England's rule, not over economic patterns. A crashing stock market, economic panic, and devastating drought contributed to the Great Depression, not colonial economic patterns.

Answer Key

UNIT 2 (continued)

19. **A; DOK Level:** 3; **Content Topics:** II.USH.e, II.E.g, II.G.c.1, II.G.d.3, II.G.d.4; **Practices:** SSP.1.a, SSP.6.b. Because the area covered by the thirteen colonies is vast, stretching all along the Atlantic coast of the United States, it is logical to assume that the geography and climate would differ among the colonies located in the three separate regions. The New England winter was harsh so plantations did not develop there. Nor would the fact that the Southern Colonies were farthest south cause these colonies to have industries; agriculture was the predominant economic factor there. The table states that the Middle Colonies' economy was based on agriculture, trade, and small industries. The type of trade was probably not the fur trade, because there is no evidence that there were large forests or any lumbering that took place in the Middle Colonies.

LESSON 3, pp. 30–33

1. **B; DOK Level:** 2; **Content Topics:** II.G.c.1, II.G.c.3; **Practice:** SSP.2.a. The last sentence of the passage states the main idea. The colonies were in agreement with Great Britain and Spain regarding Canada and Florida. The disputed land was east of the Mississippi.

2. **C; DOK Level:** 3; **Content Topics:** II.G.c.1, II.G.c.3; **Practices:** SSP.6.a, SSP.6.b. The large size of the disputed territory emphasizes the importance of the conflict. The borders of the colonies, the Floridas, and Canada are unrelated to the conflict.

3. **New Jersey; DOK Level:** 1; **Content Topic:** I.USH.b.1; **Practices:** SSP.1.a, SSP.6.b. The Battle of Trenton, the colonists' first battle after declaring independence, took place in New Jersey.

4. **Battle of New York; DOK Level:** 2; **Content Topic:** I.USH.b.1; **Practices:** SSP.1.a, SSP.6.b.

5. **B; DOK Level:** 2; **Content Topics:** I.USH.a.1, I.USH.b.1, I.CG.a.1; **Practices:** SSP.1.a, SSP.1.b, SSP.2.a, SSP.2.b, SSP.4.a. The Declaration of Independence was intended to dissolve the political connection between Great Britain and the united colonies. The Declaration of Independence does not express a desire to overthrow the British government, although some colonists may have disliked Britain's monarchy. The colonists were already at war with Britain. Although oppressive governments probably took notice of what was happening in the colonies, the Declaration of Independence addresses just its own situation with Britain.

6. **A; DOK Level:** 2; **Content Topics:** I.USH.a.1, I.USH.b.1, I.CG.b.2; **Practices:** SSP.1.a, SSP.1.b, SSP.2.a, SSP.4.a. The Declaration of Independence claims the "authority of the good people of these colonies" as its governing principle. The united colonies were "free and independent," but that does not express a desire to self-govern. "All political connection" between the colonies and Great Britain was dissolved, but that sentiment does not explain how the colonies will be governed. The colonies did have "full power to levy war," but this does not address whether the colonists will govern themselves.

7. **C; DOK Level:** 2; **Content Topics:** I.USH.a.1, I.USH.b.1, I.USH.b.5; I.CG.a.1; I.CG.b.3, I.CG.c.1; **Practices:** SSP.1.a, SSP.1.b, SSP.2.a, SSP.4.a. The entire passage, except for the last sentence, discusses the Articles of Confederation, which was the first plan of government created by the new nation. The Articles of Confederation included the plan called the Northwest Ordinance, which is a detail about the Articles. The Articles of Confederation did not end the American Revolution. The United States Constitution is mentioned once, not discussed extensively, so it is not the main idea.

8. **B; DOK Level:** 2; **Content Topics:** I.USH.a.1, I.USH.b.1, I.USH.b.5; I.CG.a.1; I.CG.b.3, I.CG.c.1; **Practices:** SSP.1.a, SSP.1.b, SSP.2.a, SSP.4.a, SSP.6.b. Information in the table shows that states, such as Virginia, could collect taxes under the Articles of Confederation. The table and the passage do not address how war is declared in the new united colonies. Information in the table explains that nine states, not all the states, could agree to admit a new state. Information in the table states that under the Articles of Confederation, each state got only one representative and thus only one vote in the legislature, so Pennsylvania would not have had more representatives than New Jersey.

9. **D; DOK Level:** 1; **Content Topics:** I.USH.a.1, I.USH.b.1, I.USH.b.5; I.CG.a.1, I.CG.b.3, I.CG.c.1; **Practices:** SSP.1.a, SSP.1.b, SSP.2.a, SSP.4.a, SSP.6.b. The table comparing the Articles of Confederation and the United States Constitution indicates that a President would be the head of a strong central government. The Articles of Confederation had no executive at the head of the government. The Congress is the legislature, not the central government. States are led by governors, but this idea is not addressed in the passage or table.

10. **A; DOK Level:** 3; **Content Topics:** I.USH.a.1, I.USH.b.1, I.USH.b.5; I.CG.a.1, I.CG.b.3, I.CG.c.1; I.CG.c.3; **Practices:** SSP.1.a, SSP.1.b, SSP.2.a, SSP.4.a. The Articles of Confederation allowed states, not the national government, to collect taxes, so the national government could not collect tax revenue to pay the debt. Under the Articles, there was no President so there would be no national budget, but this did not directly affect payment of the debt. The states may or may not have had an economic plan, but their plans would not affect paying the national debt. There is no evidence to suggest that Congress had to negotiate for loans with foreign governments.

11. **A; DOK Level:** 2; **Content Topics:** I.USH.a.1, I.CG.a.1, I.CG.b.2, I.CG.b.3, I.CG.b.4, I.CG.b.5, I.CG.b.6, I.CG.c.1, I.CG.c.3, I.CG.d.1, I.CG.d.2; **Practices:** SSP.1.a, SSP.6.b. Proportional representation meant that the larger the state, the more votes it got. So Rhode Island, being the smallest state, would have been most worried about its proportional representation. Pennsylvania, New York, and South Carolina were all larger, more populous states, so they would not have been worried about how they were proportionally represented.

12. **C; DOK Level:** 3; **Content Topics:** I.USH.a.1, I.CG.a.1, I.CG.b.2, I.CG.b.3, I.CG.b.4, I.CG.b.5, I.CG.b.6, I.CG.c.1, I.CG.c.3, I.CG.d.1, I.CG.d.2; **Practices:** SSP.1.a, SSP.2.b, SSP.6.b. The American Revolution, started in part because of the oppression by Britain's government of colonists' personal liberties, began in Massachusetts. So leaders in Massachusetts were likely concerned that the United States Constitution did not explicitly protect personal freedoms, fearing the potential for further oppression. John Adams was not, in fact, elected the first President, but this detail does not explain the close vote in Massachusetts. There is no evidence to suggest that Massachusetts wanted to be its own country. Massachusetts had a strong number of votes.

13. **D; DOK Level:** 2; **Content Topics:** I.USH.a.1, I.USH.b.1, I.USH.b.5; I.CG.a.1; I.CG.b.3, I.CG.c.1; **Practices:** SSP.1.a, SSP.1.b, SSP.2.a, SSP.4.a, SSP.6.b. While the passage mentions checks and balances, the Constitutional Convention, and protecting personal freedoms, these are details that support the larger main idea regarding the road from the Convention to the ratification of the Constitution.

14. **B; DOK Level:** 2; **Content Topics:** I.USH.a.1, I.CG.a.1, I.CG.b.2, I.CG.b.3, I.CG.b.4, I.CG.b.5, I.CG.b.6, I.CG.c.1, I.CG.c.3, I.CG.d.1, I.CG.d.2; **Practices:** SSP.2.a, SSP.6.b, SSP.6.c. The table shows the variety of dates, spanning three years, on which states ratified the Constitution, so the states must have had concerns that they debated over different periods of time before they ratified the document. New York and Virginia both chose to ratify the Constitution, not retain the Articles of Confederation. Three of the 13 states ratified the Constitution with a unanimous vote. The fact that New Hampshire ratified the Constitution prior to New York and Virginia does not in and of itself indicate that its ratification led to the two other states ratifying the document.

LESSON 4, pp. 34–37

1. **C; DOK Level:** 1; **Content Topics:** II.G.d.1, II.G.d.2, II.G.d.3; **Practices:** SSP.2.b, SSP.6.b. The lowest percentage of female immigrants is listed in 1824. The lowest percentage of male immigrants occurs in 1829. The highest percentage of female immigrants occurs in 1829. The percentage of male and female immigrants is not equal in 1824.

2. **A; DOK Level:** 3; **Content Topics:** II.USH.e, II.G.d.1; **Practice:** SSP.2.b. Immigration statistics might be categorized by countries of origin. While the reasons people immigrate might be categorized as military, political, or economic, these statistics would be better placed under country categories. Immigration statistics would not fall under categories of American political debate.

3. **Virginia; DOK Level:** 1; **Content Topics:** II.G.d.1, I.USH.b.4; **Practices:** SSP.2.b, SSP.6.b. The states that voted Democratic-Republican are shaded green on the map. Of those states, Virginia has the most electoral votes with 21.

4. **Pennsylvania, Maryland, and North Carolina; DOK Level:** 2; **Content Topics:** II.G.d.1, I.USH.b.4; **Practices:** SSP.2.b, SSP.6.b. The states that voted both Democratic-Republican and Federalist are shaded with both green and purple on the map, and the number of electoral votes for each party is so designated. Pennsylvania had 8 electoral votes for the Democratic-Republican Party and 7 for the Federalist Party. Maryland had 5 votes for the Democrat-Republican Party and 5 for the Federalists. North Carolina had 8 votes for the Democratic-Republic Party and 4 for the Federalists.

5. **Federalist; DOK Level:** 1; **Content Topics:** II.G.d.1, I.USH.b.4; **Practices:** SSP.2.b, SSP.6.b.

6. **D; DOK Level:** 2; **Content Topics:** II.G.d.1, I.USH.b.3; **Practices:** SSP.1.a, SSP.6.b. A government that is not the United States can be considered a foreign influence, and bribery is a form of corruption, so choice D is the correct answer. Distracted public councils might be ripe for corruption of various kinds, but that is not an accurate category for bribery by another government. Animosity between groups does not accurately describe the harmful effect linked to bribery by another government. Although riot and insurrection could occur if an elected official succumbed to bribery, that harmful effect is not necessarily an appropriate category.

7. **B; DOK Level:** 2; **Content Topic:** II.CG.e.1; **Practice:** SSP.2.b. Although there are small third parties, the U.S. government is based primarily on a two-party system: Democrat and Republican. Washington mentions councils and administration, but not as political parties. Federalist and Anti-federalist are not contemporary designations. Libertarian is a third party, and Independent refers to those who do not define themselves by a party.

8. **C; DOK Level:** 2; **Content Topics:** II.G.b.1, II.G.c.1, II.G.d.4, I.USH.b.4, II.E.g; **Practice:** SSP.1.a. Bonaparte sold the land due to a conflicted political relationship with Great Britain. The decision was not based on a need for money or a religious or social belief.

9. **A; DOK Level:** 2; **Content Topics:** II.G.b.1, II.G.c.1, II.G.d.4, I.USH.b.4, II.E.g; **Practice:** SSP.1.a. Jefferson wanted to expand the territory of the United States. The decision was not based on a political, safety, or military reason.

10. **B; DOK Level:** 3; **Content Topics:** II.G.b.1, II.G.c.1, II.G.d.4, I.USH.b.4, II.E.g; **Practice:** SSP.1.a. Jefferson wanted to control the Mississippi River for trade reasons, which are economic. The decision was not based on a military, political, or social reason.

11. **B; DOK Level:** 3; **Content Topic:** I.USH.b.6; **Practices:** SSP.1.a, SSP.2.b. Westward expansion was part of Manifest Destiny, not the Articles of Confederation, Indian Policy, or Slavery.

Answer Key

UNIT 2 (continued)

12. **D; DOK Level:** 2; **Content Topics:** II.G.b.1, II.G.c.1, II.G.c.3, II.G.d.4, I.USH.b.4, II.E.g; **Practices:** SSP.1.a, SSP.2.b. The main goal of the expedition stated in the table was to find a northern water route between the Atlantic Ocean and the Pacific Ocean. This route would be used for trade and commerce. Although there was contact with Native Americans, that interaction was not the main goal of the expedition. More states would eventually be created if more land was claimed by the United States, but that was not a main goal of the expedition. National security might be enhanced by discovering a northern water route from the east to the west, but there is no evidence in the table that this was a main goal of the expedition.

13. **B; DOK Level:** 2; **Content Topics:** I.USH.b.4, I.USH.b.6, II.G.b.4; **Practice:** SSP.2.b. The expedition provided valuable information regarding geography, plants, and animals and successful interaction with Native Americans. The original goal of trade and commerce wasn't successful. The journal was more valuable for science than the arts. Lewis and Clark were army officers working toward a commercial goal, who gained valuable scientific and cultural information.

14. **C; DOK Level:** 2; **Content Topics:** I.USH.b.4, I.USH.b.6, II.G.b.1; **Practice:** SSP.2.b. The purposes of both events involve trade, which is economic. Religion, politics, and civil rights are not considerations.

15. **D; DOK Level:** 1; **Content Topics:** II.G.b.1, II.G.d.3, II.G.d.4; **Practices:** SSP.1.b, SSP.6.b. Wisconsin became a state in 1848, which is after 1840. None of the remaining answer choices attained statehood after 1840: Ohio became a state in 1803; Indiana was formed as a state in 1816; Michigan was made a state in 1837.

16. **A; DOK Level:** 3; **Content Topics:** II.G.b.1, II.G.d.3, II.G.d.4; **Practices:** SSP.1.b, SSP.6.b. The Northwest Ordinance prohibited slavery in any states created in the Northwest Territory, so the states listed in the table were free states, not slave states. All of the states listed in the table are east of the Mississippi River, not west. All of the states are north of the Ohio River, not south.

17. **C; DOK Level:** 1; **Content Topics:** II.G.b.1, I.USH.b.4, I.E.a, II.E.g; **Practices:** SSP.1.a, SSP.1.b. Jefferson says that the United States will be able to use the Mississippi River without fear of conflict with other countries, which contributes to the country's economic gain. Jefferson does not speak about alliances with any other country. Although factories might be built near the river, Jefferson does not make specific reference to increased industry or to using military facilities. The French colonists may support the United States, but Jefferson does not talk about a relationship between the two countries.

18. **B; DOK Level:** 2; **Content Topics:** II.USH.b.4, II.USH.b.6, II.G.b.4, II.G.c.1; **Practice:** SSP.2.b. Jefferson mentions "produce of the western States" and "fertility of the country," which are both agricultural references, not industrial, shipping, or tourism references.

LESSON 5, pp. 38–41

1. **D; DOK Level:** 2; **Content Topics:** II.G.d.3, II.G.d.4, I.USH.b.7, II.CG.e.1, II.CG.e.3; **Practice:** SSP.3.a. The keyword *after* is in the text to show that the election of 1816 preceded Monroe's tour of New England. The Democratic-Republican Party did not come to an end, because it was stronger than the Federalist Party. Monroe's tour of New England came after he was elected President the first time, not reelected. The use of the term "Era of Good Feelings" was used at the same time Monroe took his tour of New England, not before.

2. **C; DOK Level:** 2; **Content Topics:** II.G.d.3, II.G.d.4, I.USH.b.7, II.CG.e.1, II.CG.e.3; **Practice:** SSP.3.a. The last two boxes of the graphic organizer explain that Americans began to push Native Americans off their lands and establish farms on land traditionally controlled by Native Americans. The first box of the graphic organizer describes an era of peace, not war, in Europe. Native Americans did not want to leave their eastern lands and move west. Information in the graphic organizer does not claim that President Monroe made Native Americans leave their lands, but explains that Americans began to push Native Americans off their land.

3. **The British give up plans and leave for Britain; DOK Level:** 1; **Content Topic:** I.USH.b.2; **Practices:** SSP.3.a, SSP.6.b, SSP.10.c. There is only one box that contains information, "The British give up plans and leave for Britain," that comes after the box describing the Americans' victory at the Battle of New Orleans.

4. **British and American *forces* arrive near New Orleans in late 1814; DOK Level:** 2; **Content Topic:** I.USH.b.2; **Practices:** SSP.3.a, SSP.6.b. The box prior to the box containing information about the Treaty of Ghent explains that British and American forces arrive near New Orleans. *Diplomats*, not *forces*, were in Belgium to sign the treaty.

5. **C; DOK Level:** 3; **Content Topics:** I.USH.a.1, I.USH.b.2, II.CG.e.3 **Practices:** SSP.3.a, SSP.10.c. The American Revolution occurred before all of the subsequent events. All of the other events—Monroe's inauguration, the election of 1816, and the creation of the Articles of Confederation—are relevant to or mentioned in Monroe's address, but these events would not have been possible had there not been the American Revolution.

6. **B; DOK Level:** 2; **Content Topics:** I.USH.a.1, I.USH.b.2, II.CG.e.3; **Practices:** SSP.3.a, SSP.6.b. The war that Monroe is referring to is the War of 1812. The Civil War had not occurred at the time of Monroe's inauguration. The American Revolution had occurred long before Monroe became President, and the French and Indian War took place in the eighteenth century and was not a recent event.

7. **C; DOK Level:** 3; **Content Topics:** I.USH.a.1, I.USH.b.2, II.CG.e.3; **Practice:** SSP.3.a, SSP.10.c. President Monroe is referring to the Declaration of Independence because it essentially stated that the Government was "in the hands of the people." The Articles came before the Declaration. The treaty and news article do not describe the workings of democracy.

8. **A; DOK Level:** 2; **Content Topics:** I.USH.a.1, I.USH.b.6, I.USH.b.7, II.G.b.1, II.G.c.1, II.G.d.2, II.G.d.3, II.G.d.4; **Practices:** SSP.1.a, SSP.1.b, SSP.2.a, SSP.2.b, SSP.3.a. Jackson explains that the government's policy for removing Native Americans is approaching consummation, or end, and that the groups in the eastern states have either been "annihilated or have melted away." He says the final two groups have accepted, not refused, the Government's provisions for resettlement. White settlers roll westward in waves, so migration continues, not slows. Jackson opens his remarks by saying that the Government's policy of the past thirty years is ending well, not failed.

9. **B; DOK Level:** 3; **Content Topics:** I.USH.a.1, I.USH.b.6, I.USH.b.7, II.G.b.1, II.G.c.1, II.G.d.2, II.G.d.3, II.G.d.4; **Practices:** SSP.1.a, SSP.1.b, SSP.2.a, SSP.2.b, SSP.3.a. When Jackson says the government's process is "milder," the reader can assume he means the policies are less harsh and confrontational. Jackson indicates that the policies have been very successful, not marginally so, reaching their "happy consummation." Some, but not all, Native American groups have relocated, so they have not reached a consensus about leaving their lands. If the policies have been in place for thirty years, they have consistently spanned more than one presidency.

10. **D; DOK Level:** 1; **Content Topics:** I.USH.a.1, I.USH.b.6, II.G.c.1, II.CG.e.1, II.CG.e.3; **Practices:** SSP.1.a, SSP.1.b, SSP.2.a, SSP.2.b, SSP.3.a. Monroe was first elected President in 1816, and he proposed the Monroe Doctrine seven years later in 1823. He did not propose the Monroe Doctrine two years later in 1818, or four years later in 1820, or five years later in 1821.

11. **A; DOK Level:** 3; **Content Topics:** I.USH.a.1, I.USH.b.6, II.G.c.1, II.CG.e.1, II.CG.e.3; **Practices:** SSP.1.a, SSP.1.b, SSP.2.a, SSP.2.b, SSP.3.a. The passage refers to Monroe's accomplishments dealing with Britain and Spain, and he negotiated the border of the United States and Canada, so he resolved many conflicts with foreign countries. His tenure as Secretary of State would have been more relevant before his first campaign for President. Monroe was a member of the Democratic-Republican Party, not the Federalist Party. He proposed the Monroe Doctrine after he was reelected President, so he could not have used that policy to sway voters.

12. **B; DOK Level:** 1; **Content Topics:** I.USH.a.1, I.USH.b.6, II.G.c.1, II.CG.e.1, II.CG.e.3; **Practices:** SSP.1.a, SSP.1.b, SSP.2.a, SSP.2.b, SSP.3.a. Following President Monroe's reelection in 1820, he endorsed the idea of Manifest Destiny and he proposed the Monroe Doctrine. He won reelection in 1820, not after 1820. President Monroe's success at settling an agreement between the United States and the British over forces on the Great Lakes occurred prior to 1820, and his success at helping to secure the state of Florida for the United States also came prior to 1820, not after.

13. **Louisiana; DOK Level:** 1; **Content Topics:** I.USH.b.6, II.G.b.1, I.G.c.1, II.G.d.2, II.G.d.3, II.G.d.4; **Practices:** SSP.3.a, SSP.6.b. The graphic organizer shows that Missouri became a state in 1821 and that Louisiana became a state in 1812. Arkansas became a state in 1836.

14. **Lewis and Clark expedition; DOK Level:** 2; **Content Topics:** I.USH.b.6, II.G.b.1, I.G.c.1, II.G.d.2, II.G.d.3, II.G.d.4; **Practices:** SSP.3.a, SSP.6.b. The first box of the graphic organizer states that the Lewis and Clark expedition began to explore the land included in the Louisiana Purchase in 1804. The remaining information in the graphic organizer describes territories, starting with Louisiana, that were west of the Mississippi River and part of areas explored by Lewis and Clark.

15. **D; DOK Level:** 3; **Content Topics:** II.G.b.1, II.G.c.1, II.G.d.1, II.G.d.3, I.USH.b.2, I.USH.b.6; **Practices:** SSP.1.a, SSP.1.b, SSP.2.a, SSP.2.b, SSP.3.b. The Monroe Doctrine stated that the United States would not tolerate European interference with countries the United States had acknowledged as independent states. The paragraph explains that this includes European colonies in America. Therefore, it is most logical that the Doctrine was issued after Spain asked other European nations to help stop revolts in Spanish-American colonies. Texas was annexed to the United States after the Monroe Doctrine was created. John Quincy Adams was Secretary of State, not President. Britain had not agreed to stop continued expansion into western North America.

16. **C; DOK Level:** 3; **Content Topics:** II.G.b.1, II.G.c.1, II.G.d.1, II.G.d.3, I.USH.b.6; **Practices:** SSP.1.a, SSP.1.b, SSP.2.a, SSP.2.b, SSP.3.b. The Mexican War, during which the United States fought with Mexico after acknowledging Texas's independence, shows how the United States acted on a threat described in the Monroe Doctrine. The Vietnam War and the Korean War did not involve direct threats on or colonization of the United States. The Civil War was not a conflict with foreign powers, so the Monroe Doctrine did not apply.

LESSON 6, pp. 42–45

1. **B; DOK Level:** 2; **Content Topic:** I.USH.c.2; **Practices:** SSP.3.b, SSP.3.c. Southerners feared that Lincoln's election would threaten their regional economy. Hence, with Lincoln's election, several states seceded. Davis was elected to lead the Confederacy. People living in the territories did not vote in elections.

2. **A; DOK Level:** 2; **Content Topic:** I.USH.c.2; **Practices:** SSP.3.b, SSP.3.c. Lincoln delivered his inauguration address to a divided nation, one part of which was led by President Davis. Lincoln took office; he did not resign. The territories were not made immediately into states, and the state of Oregon supported Lincoln.

3. **C; DOK Level:** 3; **Content Topics:** I.E.a, I.USH.c.1, I.USH.c.2, II.CG.e.1, II.CG.e.3, II.G.c.2, II.G.d.3; **Practices:** SSP.1.a, SSP.1.b, SSP.2.a, SSP.2.b, SSP.3.c, SSP.4.a, SSP.6.b, SSP.11.b. The growing number and size of plantations in the Southern states required the use of more labor from enslaved people. The fact that the U.S. Constitution did not expressly prohibit slavery at that time was not the primary reason for the increased number of enslaved people. There were not many plantations at all in the Northern states, and those that did exist did not have enslaved workers. There is no evidence to suggest that the ratio of enslaved people grew at the natural rate of the total population.

Answer Key

UNIT 2 (continued)

4. A; DOK Level: 3; Content Topics: I.E.a, I.USH.c.1, I.USH.c.2, II.CG.e.1, II.CG.e.3, II.G.c.2, II.G.d.3; **Practices:** SSP.1.a, SSP.1.b, SSP.2.a, SSP.2.b, SSP.3.c, SSP.4.a, SSP.6.b. Economic diversification led to fewer plantation farms and therefore fewer enslaved workers. Maryland and Delaware were considered to be Southern states. There is no evidence that enslaved people moved from one state to another. Indeed, the fact that the people were enslaved means that they did not have the freedom to move about as they pleased. There is no evidence to support the claim that plantation owners in Delaware and Maryland decided not to have as many enslaved workers. In fact, there probably were not many plantations at all in Delaware and Maryland at this time.

5. B; DOK Level: 2; Content Topics: I.E.a, I.USH.c.1, I.USH.c.2, II.CG.e.1, II.CG.e.3, II.G.c.2, II.G.d.3; **Practices:** SSP.1.a, SSP.1.b, SSP.2.a, SSP.2.b, SSP.3.c, SSP.4.a, SSP.6.b, SSP.6.c. It is true that in 1860, the percentage of enslaved people in Mississippi made up more than half (55.18%) of the total population of the state. It is not true that in 1860, the percentage of enslaved people in South Carolina was less than half of the state's population; it was more than half, at 57.18%. It is also not true that in 1810, the percentage of enslaved people in South Carolina was more than half of its population; it was less than half, at 47.30%. The percentage of enslaved people in Mississippi in 1810 is not recorded on the chart.

6. D; DOK Level: 2; Content Topics: II.G.b.1, II.G.c.2, II.G.d.2, I.CG.d.2, I.USH.a.1, I.USH.c.3, I.USH.c.4; **Practices:** SSP.1.a, SSP.1.b, SSP.2.a, SSP.2.b, SSP.3.b, SSP.3.c, SSP.4.a, SSP.6.b, SSP.11.b. The Civil War ended with a Union, or Northern, victory, not a Confederate, or Southern victory, in 1865. The Southern states did not decide that they no longer needed the work of enslaved people, nor did the Northern states decide that they wanted the work of enslaved people.

7. B; DOK Level: 2; Content Topics: II.G.b.1, II.G.c.2, II.G.d.2, I.CG.d.2, I.USH.a.1, I.USH.c.3, I.USH.c.4; **Practices:** SSP.1.a, SSP.1.b, SSP.2.a, SSP.2.b, SSP.3.b, SSP.3.c, SSP.4.a, SSP.6.b, SSP.11.b. The Fourteenth Amendment granted citizenship to newly freed, formerly enslaved people, as well as providing them with equal protection under the law and extending the Bill of Rights to the states. The Thirteenth Amendment abolished slavery at the federal level. The Emancipation Proclamation was issued in 1863, not in the Fourteenth Amendment, and the Fifteenth Amendment gave freed African Americans the right to vote.

8. D; DOK Level: 2; Content Topics: II.G.b.1, II.G.c.2, II.G.d.2, I.CG.d.2, I.USH.a.1, I.USH.c.3, I.USH.c.4; **Practices:** SSP.1.a, SSP.1.b, SSP.2.a, SSP.2.b, SSP.3.b, SSP.3.c, SSP.4.a, SSP.6.b, SSP.11.b. Since slavery had been abolished at the federal level with the Thirteenth Amendment, former plantation owners had to pay their workers instead of having enslaved workers. Slavery was abolished by the time of Reconstruction and thus did not cost more money. The Emancipation Proclamation abolished slavery for some, but not all, enslaved people, in 1863. There was a great number of laborers, former enslaved people, to employ after the Civil War ended, not none.

9. C; DOK Level: 1; Content Topics: II.G.b.1, II.G.c.2, II.G.d.2, I.CG.d.2, I.USH.a.1, I.USH.c.3, I.USH.c.4; **Practices:** SSP.1.a, SSP.1.b, SSP.2.a, SSP.2.b, SSP.3.b, SSP.3.c, SSP.4.a, SSP.6.b, SSP.11.b. Reconstruction was the governing plan of Congress for helping former enslaved workers adjust to their new freedoms and a way to govern the Southern states who had just lost the Civil War. Reconstruction had nothing to do with the Northern states wishing to punish the Southern states following the war. Reconstruction did not occur because the Southern states wanted to provide education and jobs for newly freed African Americans, nor was Reconstruction a plan of government during the latter years of the Civil War; it occurred following the end of the war.

10. B; DOK Level: 2; Content Topics: II.G.b.1, II.G.c.2, II.G.d.2, I.CG.d.2, I.USH.a.1, I.USH.c.3, I.USH.c.4; **Practices:** SSP.1.a, SSP.1.b, SSP.2.a, SSP.2.b, SSP.3.b, SSP.3.c, SSP.4.a, SSP.6.b, SSP.11.b. After slavery was abolished, Southern farmers did not have the free labor or enslaved people, so they replanted their plantations with crops such as tobacco and sugar that were not food cash crops, thus growing less food, not more, to feed themselves and people living nearby. They had to ship in food from other areas of the country, not to other areas of the country. The Northern states were not primarily agricultural states, and they did change their agricultural practices to plant cash crops to feed the freed enslaved people.

LESSON 7, pp. 46–49

1. D; DOK Level: 2 Content Topic: I.USH.d.2; **Practices:** SSP.1.a, SSP.1.b, SSP.2.a, SSP.3.b, SSP.3.c, SSP.4.a. By analyzing the arguments of the authors of *The Blue Book*, you can infer that they believed in using a logical, methodical approach to win an argument. It is untrue that the authors were relatively uninformed about the issues. There is no evidence that suggests that they were amused at the objections raised to woman suffrage, nor that they believed that some objections were true.

2. B; DOK Level: 2 Content Topic: I.USH.d.2; **Practices:** SSP.1.a, SSP.1.b, SSP.2.a, SSP.3.b, SSP.3.c, SSP.4.a. Nine states, as shown on the timeline, had adopted woman suffrage prior to the publication of *The Blue Book,* not eight, seven, or ten.

3. **B; DOK Level: 2 Content Topics:** II.G.b.1, II.USH.f.1, II.USH.f.2, II.USH.f.4, II.USH.f.5; **Practices:** SSP.1.a, SSP.1.b, SSP.2.a, SSP.3.b, SSP.3.c, SSP.4.a. While all of the answer choices can be considered causes of World War I, the extensive alliances formed among nations was the cause that turned the conflict that started World War I into a world war. Those alliances brought countries not directly related to the initial conflict between Austria-Hungary and Serbia into the war. Nationalism in Austria-Hungary was not the main reason for turning the war into a world war, nor were territorial disputes in Asia, nor an arms race among European nations.

4. **C; DOK Level: 2 Content Topics:** II.G.b.1, II.USH.f.1, II.USH.f.2, II.USH.f.4, USH.f.5; **Practices:** SSP.1.a, SSP.1.b, SSP.2.a, SSP.3.b, SSP.3.c, SSP.4.a. According to the timeline and the passage, exactly 60 months elapsed from the time Archduke Ferdinand was assassinated until the Treaty of Versailles was signed, not 45, not 50, and not 65 months.

5. **A; DOK Level: 3 Content Topics:** II.G.b.1, II.USH.f.1, II.USH.f.2, II.USH.f.4, USH.f.5; **Practices:** SSP.1.a, SSP.1.b, SSP.2.a, SSP.3.b, SSP.3.c, SSP.4.a. The information indicates that Britain was anxious to keep its colonial territories and feared that Germany might win the war and dominate Western Europe. The arms race between Germany and Britain was very competitive. Therefore, you can conclude that rivalry between Britain and Germany became an important cause of World War I. There was no rivalry, but cooperation, between Serbia and Germany, nor was there rivalry between Russia and Austria-Hungary, nor between the United States and France.

6. **B; DOK Level: 2 Content Topics:** II.G.b.1, II.USH.f.1, II.USH.f.2, II.USH.f.4, USH.f.5; **Practices:** SSP.1.a, SSP.1.b, SSP.2.a, SSP.3.b, SSP.3.c, SSP.4.a. According to the timeline the Battle of Marne began on September 6, 1914, preceding the other events: Turkish forces collapsed at Megiddo on September 19, 1918; British tanks won at Cambrai on November 20, 1917, and the end of the Brusilov Offensive was on August 10, 1916.

7. **A; DOK Level: 3 Content Topics:** II.USH.f.8, II.USH.f.9; **Practices:** SSP.1.a, SSP.2.b, SSP.3.a, SSP.6.b. Because the question asked what directly led to the Nazi Party receiving the most votes in the 1932 German elections, you should determine which event occurred right before the election on the timeline. In this case, it was because the Germans were unhappy with other politicians because of the economic crisis. The other answer choices depict events that happened longer ago than this.

8. **C; DOK Level: 2 Content Topics:** II.USH.f.8, II.USH.f.9; **Practices:** SSP.1.a, SSP.2.b, SSP.3.a, SSP.6.b. According to the timeline Hitler became the leader of the German Nazi Party in 1921 and Chancellor of Germany in 1933, which is a span of 12 years, not 10, 11, or 13 years.

9. **C; DOK Level: 1 Content Topic:** II.USH.f.6; **Practices:** SSP.1.a, SSP.2.b, SSP.3.a, SSP.6.b. According to the timeline, the Lend-Lease Plan took effect in March 1941. It did not take effect in either August 1935, June 1940, or December 1941.

10. **B; DOK Level: 3 Content Topic:** II.USH.f.6; **Practices:** SSP.1.a, SSP.2.b, SSP.3.a, SSP.6.b. The timeline shows that the United States revised the Neutrality Act after war broke out in Europe. While supplying goods to allies at war helped in the war effort, it also helped the U.S. economy, which was still recovering from the Great Depression.

11. **B; DOK Level: 3; Content Topics:** II.USH.f.1, II.USH.f.8; **Practices:** SSP.1.a, SSP.2.b, SSP.3.a, SSP.6.b. Be sure to read this timeline carefully. The top section shows events that occurred in Europe during World War II, and the bottom section shows events that occurred in the Pacific. This question asks you to find parallel (very similar) events that happened in Europe and in the Pacific during the dates listed. In May 1945 on the Europe timeline, Germany surrendered. In September 1945 on the Pacific timeline, Japan surrendered. While other events may have taken place during the dates listed as answer choices, those events were not parallel.

12. **C; DOK Level: 2 Content Topics:** III.USH.f.1, II.USH.f.8; **Practices:** SSP.1.a, SSP.2.b, SSP.3.a, SSP.6.b. The event on the Pacific timeline that eventually led to the dropping of atomic bombs was the launch of the Manhattan Project. That project developed the atomic bomb. It would have been impossible to drop an atomic bomb if it were not created. The Battle of Midway occurred in June 1942, well before the dropping of the atomic bombs, and the success of the D-Day invasion was in June 1944, also before the dropping of the bombs, and did not directly lead to the U.S. dropping them. Hitler's death occurred in April 1945, prior to the dropping of the bombs, but his death did not lead to the U.S. dropping the bombs.

13. **D; DOK Level: 3; Content Topics:** II.USH.f.1, II.USH.f.8; **Practices:** SSP.1.a, SSP.2.b, SSP.3.a, SSP.6.b. The timeline headings here give you a clue. The top heading is "Europe," which signifies battles on land. The bottom heading is "Pacific," which signifies battles on the water. Therefore, the U.S. Navy was vital in the war against Japan. The Japanese were not forced to surrender due to the Battle of Midway. Germany did not control the Soviet Union, nor is the Soviet Union even mentioned on the timeline. Japan joined the war by bombing the U.S. Naval Base at Pearl Harbor, Hawaii, not in defense of Germany.

14. **B; DOK Level: 3 Content Topics:** II.USH.f.1, II.USH.f.8; **Practices:** SSP.1.a, SSP.2.b, SSP.3.a, SSP.6.b. The Allies did not attack Germany or Japan directly until they had secured territory closer to those nations. In Europe, the Allies defeated the Germans in North Africa, the Soviet Union, and France before advancing on Germany itself. In the Pacific, the United States sought to control Pacific islands gradually closer and closer to Japan. Therefore, the timeline supports the trend that the Allied strategies for reaching Germany and Japan were similar.

Answer Key

UNIT 3 CIVICS AND GOVERNMENT

LESSON 1, pp. 50–53

1. A; DOK Level: 1; **Content Topic:** I.CG.a.1; **Practices:** SSP.1.a, SSP.6.b. A careful look at the graphic organizer shows that A is the correct answer. B is not correct because the Church was obviously providing some central government authority at the time, which the graphic organizer states. C is incorrect because the graphic organizer states that the feudal system was weakening, not strengthening. D is also incorrect because small, varied political bodies came to power later, with the movement from the High Middle Ages to Modern Times.

2. B; DOK Level: 2; **Content Topics:** I.CG.a.1, II.G.b.3, II.G.b.5; **Practices:** SSP.1.a, SSP.6.b. The correct answer is B, because the fourth step in the sequence diagram deals with improvements in agricultural technology. Metal tools are an improvement in agricultural technology that made farming easier. The other answers are all incorrect because they have nothing to do with this type of improvement.

3-1. C; DOK Level: 2; **Content Topics:** I.CG.a.1, I.CG.b.3, I.CG.b.6, I.CG.b.7, I.CG.c.1, I.CG.c.3, I.CG.c.4; **Practices:** SSP.1.a, SSP.3.c, SSP.6.b. The answer is C, because the Articles were the result of the desire to create a central government that would be **weaker**, and not have great power over local (or state) authorities.

3-2. D; DOK Level: 1; **Content Topics:** I.CG.a.1, I.CG.b.3, I.CG.b.6, I.CG.b.7, I.CG.c.1, I.CG.c.3, I.CG.c.4; **Practices:** SSP.1.a, SSP.3.c, SSP.6.b. The chart shows that the only one of the four responsibilities listed here that was given by the Articles to the national government was D, the **mail**.

3-3. A; DOK Level: 1; **Content Topics:** I.CG.a.1, I.CG.b.3, I.CG.b.6, I.CG.b.7, I.CG.c.1, I.CG.c.3, I.CG.c.4; Practices: SSP.1.a, SSP.3.c, SSP.6.b. The answer is A, **executive**. Fearing a strong executive power, the Articles gave all power on the national level to Congress.

3-4. B; DOK Level: 1; **Content Topics:** I.CG.a.1, I.CG.b.3, I.CG.b.6, I.CG.b.7, I.CG.c.1, I.CG.c.3, I.CG.c.4; **Practices:** SSP.1.a, SSP.3.c, SSP.6.b. The answer is B, because the Articles also gave all **judicial** power to the states.

4-1. B; DOK Level: 1; **Content Topics:** I.CG.b.3, I.CG.b.5, I.CG.b.6, I.CG.b.9, I.CG.c.1, I.CG.c.2; **Practices:** SSP.1.a, SSP.3.c, SSP.6.b. The answer is B, **veto**. The clue is the word "reject." A veto is a Presidential rejection of a bill that is sent to him or her by Congress.

4-2. C; DOK Level: 1; **Content Topics:** I.CG.b.3, I.CG.b.5, I.CG.b.6, I.CG.b.9, I.CG.c.1, I.CG.c.2; **Practices:** SSP.1.a, SSP.3.c, SSP.6.b. C is the correct answer. As the diagram shows, with a two-thirds majority, Congress can **override** a Presidential veto.

4-3. A; DOK Level: 2; **Content Topics:** I.CG.b.3, I.CG.b.5, I.CG.b.6, I.CG.b.9, I.CG.c.1, I.CG.c.2; **Practices:** SSP.1.a, SSP.3.c, SSP.6.b. The correct response is A. You can conclude that the checks and balances built into the American system of government were there because of a **fear of centralized power**.

4-4. D; DOK Level: 1; Content Topics: I.CG.b.3, I.CG.b.5, I.CG.b.6, I.CG.b.9, I.CG.c.1, I.CG.c.2; Practices: SSP.1.a, SSP.3.c, SSP.6.b. The correct response is D. The three branches of the federal government are the executive (the President), the legislative (the Congress), and the **judicial** (the Supreme Court).

5-1. C; DOK level: 1; **Content Topics:** I.CG.c.1, I.CG.c.2, I.CG.c.6; **Practices:** SSP.1.a, SSP.1.b, SSP.2.b, SSP.3.c, SSP.6.b. The answer is C. The Vice President takes over if the President is not able to carry out his or her duties. So as the flowchart shows, the Vice President is first in the line of succession.

5-2. D; DOK Level: 1; **Content Topics:** I.CG.c.1, I.CG.c.2, I.CG.c.6; **Practices:** SSP.1.a, SSP.1.b, SSP.2.b, SSP.3.c, SSP.6.b. The flowchart shows that the second person in the line of succession is the **Speaker of the House of Representatives**.

5-3. C; DOK Level: 3; **Content Topics:** I.CG.c.1, I.CG.c.2, I.CG.c.6; **Practices:** SSP.1.a, SSP.1.b, SSP.2.b, SSP.3.c, SSP.6.b. To answer this question, look for the first person in the line of succession who is a Cabinet Secretary. The Vice President acts as the President of the Senate, but is not part of Congress. The Speaker of the House and the President Pro Tempore of the Senate are both in Congress. The first Cabinet Secretary is the **Secretary of State**.

5-4. A; DOK Level: 2; **Content Topics:** I.CG.c.1, I.CG.c.2, I.CG.c.6; **Practices:** SSP.1.a, SSP.1.b, SSP.2.b, SSP.3.c, SSP.6.b. A look at the flowchart shows that the Cabinet Secretaries highest in the line of succession are the Secretary of State, Secretary of the Treasury, and Secretary of Defense. That means that these Secretaries deal mostly with foreign affairs, finance, and the **military**.

LESSON 2, pp. 54–57

1. C; DOK Level: 3; **Content Topics:** I.CG.b.3, I.CG.b.8, I.CG.d.1, I.CG.d.2, I.USH.a.1; **Practices:** SSP.1.a, SSP.1.b, SSP.2.a, SSP.3.b, SSP.4.a. This amendment deals with the rights of the accused. It states that the accused has the right to a speedy and public trial, to an impartial jury, to be confronted by the witnesses against him, and to have the assistance of counsel. Freedom of expression is explained in Amendment I, while information pertaining to the powers of the courts and trial procedures are explained in Article III of the U.S. Constitution.

2. D; DOK Level: 2; **Content Topics:** I.CG.b.3, I.CG.b.8, I.CG.d.1, I.CG.d.2, I.USH.a.1; **Practices:** SSP.1.a, SSP.1.b, SSP.2.a, SSP.4.a. The sentence "and to have the assistance of counsel for his defense" gives the context clue that *counsel* means "a legal advisor" the accused can use to help him or her when charged or during a trial. A legal advisor can present a plan of action, and can have a goal or purpose of defending the accused, who may or may not display a type of behavior.

3. A; DOK Level: 2; **Content Topics:** I.CG.b.3, I.CG.c.1, I.CG.c.2, I.USH.a.1; **Content Practice:** SSP.1.a, SSP.1.b, SSP.2.a, SSP.4.a. The first paragraph of Section 2 states that the President "may require the opinion, in writing, of the principal officer in each of the executive departments." State militias fall under the President's command only "when called into the actual service of the United States," so not during times of peace. The other two answer choices are specifically prohibited in Section 2.

4. **B; DOK Level:** 2; **Content Topics:** I.CG.b.3, I.CG.c.1, I.CG.c.2, I.USH.a.1; **Practices:** SSP.1.a, SSP.1.b, SSP.2.a, SSP.4.a. Two thirds of the Senators need to agree on treaties. Nothing is hinted at in regard to Senators admitting or investigating anything in regard to treaties. The language and logic is clear that treaties could not be passed if two thirds of the Senators refused.

5. **D; DOK Level:** 3; **Content Topics:** I.CG.b.3, I.CG.c.1, I.CG.c.2, I.USH.a.1; **Practices:** SSP.1.a, SSP.1.b, SSP.2.a, SSP.4.a. The National Security Act of 1947 became law on July 26, 1947, creating the Department of the Air Force, headed by a Secretary of the Air Force. Until that time, it was under the auspices of the U.S. Army, not the U.S. Navy. The authors of the U.S. Constitution had no intention of **not** making the President the commander in chief of the U.S. Air Force; airplanes did not exist at the time. Neither did they choose the Vice President to be the commander in chief of the U.S. Air Force.

6. **C; DOK Level:** 2; **Content Topics:** I.CG.b.3, I.CG.c.1, I.CG.c.5, I.USH.a.1; **Practices:** SSP.1.a, SSP.1.b, SSP.2.a, SSP.4.a. The beginning of this excerpt clearly states that only Congress or "legislatures of two thirds of the several states" can propose amendments to the U.S. Constitution. The Supreme Court, federal judges, and the President are not referenced in the excerpt.

7. **A; DOK Level:** 2; **Content Topics:** I.CG.b.3, I.CG.c.1, I.CG.c.5, I.USH.a.1; **Content Practice:** SSP.1.a, SSP.1.b, SSP.2.a, SSP.4.a. Article V clearly states that a proposed amendment becomes part of the Constitution "when ratified by the legislatures of three fourths of the several states, or by conventions in three fourths thereof." Two thirds refers to a vote in both houses of Congress to propose amendments. Nothing is mentioned in the excerpt about the President, and the Senate is not mentioned specifically in the excerpt.

8. **B; DOK Level:** 2; **Content Topics:** I.CG.b.3, I.CG.c.1, I.CG.c.5, I.USH.a.1; **Content Practice:** SSP.1.a, SSP.1.b, SSP.2.a, SSP.4.a. *Suffrage* refers to the right to vote. In the passage it does not refer at all to the power of taxation, the ability to investigate, or the freedom to assemble in groups.

9. **B; DOK Level:** 2; **Content Topics:** I.CG.b.3, I.CG.c.1, I.CG.c.5, I.USH.a.1; **Practices:** SSP.1.a, SSP.1.b, SSP.2.a, SSP.4.a. While all of these rights are protected by the Constitution, only the right to publish criticisms of government policies ("Congress shall make no law … abridging the freedom of speech, or of the press") is protected by the First Amendment. The first two other answer options are rights guaranteed by the Third and Second Amendments, respectively. The right to participate in local military units is not in the Bill of Rights.

10. **B; DOK Level:** 2; **Content Topics:** I.CG.b.3, I.CG.c.1, I.CG.c.5, I.USH.a.1; **Practices:** SSP.1.a, SSP.1.b, SSP.2.a, SSP.4.a. The Second Amendment protects the right of "a well regulated Militia … the right … to … bear arms." The Third Amendment protects the right to refuse to house federal troops. Protection against unreasonable searches is provided for in the Fourth Amendment, and there is no provision in the Bill of Rights to infringe on a well-regulated militia.

11. **D; DOK Level:** 2; **Content Topics:** I.CG.b.3, I.CG.c.1, I.CG.c.5, I.USH.a.1; **Practices:** SSP.1.a, SSP.1.b, SSP.2.a, SSP.4.a. In the Preamble, *beneficent* means resulting in goodness, or a benefit. It does not mean resulting in a truce with another country, the forgiveness of others, or a final conclusion.

12. **D; DOK Level:** 2; **Content Topics:** I.CG.b.3, I.CG.c.1, I.CG.c.5, I.USH.a.1; **Practices:** SSP.1.a, SSP.1.b, SSP.2.a, SSP.4.a. The Eighth Amendment to the U.S. Constitution prohibits the imposition of excessive fines or bail; it is not the Tenth, the Ninth, or the Sixth Amendment.

13. **A; DOK Level:** 3; **Content Topics:** I.CG.b.3, I.CG.c.1, I.CG.c.5, I.USH.a.1; **Practices:** SSP.1.a, SSP.1.b, SSP.2.a, SSP.4.a. The Fifth Amendment prohibits "double jeopardy," as well as the right not to incriminate oneself. It is not the Sixth, Ninth, or the Tenth Amendment.

14. **D; DOK Level:** 2; **Content Topics:** I.CG.b.3, I.CG.c.1, I.CG.c.5, I.USH.a.1; **Practices:** SSP.1.a, SSP.1.b, SSP.2.a, SSP.4.a. The Tenth Amendment clearly states, "The powers not delegated to the United States by the Constitution, nor prohibited by it to the States, are reserved to the States respectively, or to the people." The right does not go to the states alone; nor to individual people, then the states; nor to individual people.

15. **C; DOK Level:** 2; **Content Topics:** I.CG.b.3, I.CG.c.1, I.CG.c.5, I.USH.a.1; **Practices:** SSP.1.a, SSP.1.b, SSP.2.a, SSP.4.a. The right to a trial by jury is guaranteed by the Seventh Amendment, not the Fifth, the Sixth, or the Eighth.

LESSON 3, *pp. 58–61*

1. **A; DOK Level:** 2; **Content Topics:** I.CG.b.8, I.CG.d.1; **Practices:** SSP.1.a, SSP.1.b, SSP.6.b. The correct answer is A. The table lists rights guaranteed by the Bill of Rights. B is incorrect, because the table does not contain the exact text of the Bill of Rights. Each amendment is summarized. C is incorrect because, while the table summarizes each amendment, the table does not explain any of them. D is also wrong because the Bill of Rights is a group of amendments, or additions, to the main body of the U.S. Constitution. The main body of the Constitution is divided into Articles.

2. **B; DOK Level:** 2; **Content Topics:** I.CG.b.8, I.CG.d.1; **Practices:** SSP.1.a, SSP.1.b, SSP.6.b. The correct answer is B. The number of amendments in the Bill of Rights, as listed in the table, would be acceptable in a summary. A is wrong because complete text is never included in a summary. C is incorrect because it is beyond the scope of information in the table. D is incorrect because it is both beyond the scope of what is in the table, and it would involve unnecessary detail.

3. **DOK Level:** 3; **Content Topics:** I.CG.b.7, I.CG.b.8, I.USH.a.1, I.USH.b.1; **Practices:** SSP.1.a, SSP.3.c, SSP.9.a, SSP.9.b, SSP.9.c. Summaries should contain these general ideas: Thomas Paine said that we feel good about our connection with Great Britain and the protection it gives us against countries such as France and Spain, because we consider them our enemies. They are actually Britain's enemies, not ours. If we cut our ties with Britain, our government would be at peace with these other nations. With specific regard to this prompt about the effect of Thomas Paine's "Common Sense," a response earning 3 points would clearly identify the enduring issue as Great Britain's interests in its own country as opposed to its interests in its colonies, America, and how Americans may be better off if they broke completely with Britain.

UNIT 3 *(continued)*

Social Studies Extended Response Traits: Explanation of Traits

Depth of Knowledge (DOK) Level 3: Composing an appropriate response for this item requires a variety of complex reasoning skills. Test-takers must present their ideas logically and support their claim with evidence. Accurately and adequately incorporating elements from the text into the presentation of one's own ideas demands complex reasoning and planning.

Trait 1: Creation of Arguments and Use of Evidence

2 points: generates a text-based argument that demonstrates a clear understanding of the relationships among ideas, events, and figures as presented in the source text(s) and historical contexts from which they are drawn; cites relevant and specific evidence from primary and secondary source texts that adequately supports an argument; or is well-connected to both the prompt and the source texts

1 point: generates an argument that demonstrates an understanding of the relationships among ideas, events, and figures as presented in the source text(s); cites some evidence from primary and secondary source texts in support of an argument (may include a mix of relevant and irrelevant textual references); or is connected to both the prompt and the source text(s)

0 points: may attempt to create an argument but demonstrates minimal or no understanding of the ideas, events, and figures presented in the source texts or the contexts from which these texts are drawn; cites minimal or no evidence from the primary and secondary source texts; may or may not demonstrate an attempt to create an argument; or lacks connection either to the prompt or the source text(s)

Non-scorable Responses (Score of 0/Condition Codes): response exclusively contains text copied from source text(s) or prompt; response demonstrates that the test-taker has read neither the prompt nor the source text(s); response is incomprehensible; response is not in English, or response is not attempted (blank)

Trait 2: Development of Ideas and Organizational Structure

1 point: contains a sensible progression of ideas with understandable connections between details and main ideas; contains ideas that are developed and generally logical; multiple ideas are elaborated upon; or demonstrates appropriate awareness of the task

0 points: contains an unclear or no apparent progression of ideas; contains ideas that are insufficiently developed or illogical; just one idea is elaborated upon or demonstrates no awareness of the task

Non-scorable Responses (Score of 0/Condition Codes): See above.

Trait 3: Clarity and Command of Standard English Conventions

1 point: demonstrates adequate applications of conventions with specific regard to the following skills: 1) correctly uses frequently confused words and homonyms, including contractions; 2) subject-verb agreement; 3) pronoun usage, including pronoun antecedent agreement; and 4) pronoun case; 5) placement of modifiers and correct word order; 6) capitalization (e.g., proper nouns, titles, and beginnings of sentences); 7) use of apostrophes with possessive nouns; 8) use of punctuation (e.g., commas in a series or in appositives and other non-essential elements, end marks, and appropriate punctuation for clause separation); demonstrates largely correct sentence structure with variance from sentence to sentence; is generally fluent and clear with specific regard to the following skills: 1) correct subordination, coordination, and parallelism; 2) avoidance of wordiness and awkward sentence structures; 3) usage of transitional words, conjunctive adverbs, and other words that support logic and 4) clarity; 5) avoidance of run-on sentences, fused sentences, or sentence fragments; 6) standard usage at a level of formality appropriate for on-demand draft writing; may contain some errors in mechanics and conventions, but they do not interfere with understanding.*

0 points: demonstrates minimal control of basic conventions with specific regard to skills 1–8 as listed in the first section under Trait 3, Score Point 1 above; demonstrates consistently flawed sentence structure; minimal or no variance such that meaning may be obscured; demonstrates minimal control over skills 1–6 as listed in the second section under Trait 3, Score Point 1 above; contains severe and frequent errors in mechanics and conventions that interfere with comprehension; **OR** response is insufficient to demonstrate level of mastery over conventions and usage

*Because test-takers will be given only 25 minutes to complete Extended Response tasks, there is no expectation that a response should be completely free of conventions or usage errors to receive a score of 1.

Non-scorable Responses (Score of 0/Condition Codes): See above.

4. **DOK Level:** 3; **Content Topic:** I.CG.b.9; **Practices:** SSP.1.a, SSP.2.b, SSP.9.a, SSP.9.b, SSP.9.c. Summaries should include this key information: The essays known as the Federalist Papers were written to encourage support for the new Constitution. The essays explained the form and function of the government. "Federalist No. 37" described how the delegates to the Constitutional Convention were able to succeed in drafting the Constitution in spite of the difficulties they encountered. Information that should not be in the summary is the fact that many newspapers published the essays.

Social Studies Extended Response Traits: Explanation of Traits

Depth of Knowledge (DOK) Level 3: Composing an appropriate response for this item requires a variety of complex reasoning skills. Test-takers must present their ideas logically and support their claim with evidence. Accurately and adequately incorporating elements from the text into the presentation of one's own ideas demands complex reasoning and planning.

Trait 1: Creation of Arguments and Use of Evidence

2 points: generates a text-based argument that demonstrates a clear understanding of the relationships among ideas, events, and figures as presented in the source text(s) and historical contexts from which they are drawn; cites relevant and specific evidence from primary and secondary source texts that adequately supports an argument; or is well-connected to both the prompt and the source texts

1 point: generates an argument that demonstrates an understanding of the relationships among ideas, events, and figures as presented in the source text(s); cites some evidence from primary and secondary source texts in support of an argument (may include a mix of relevant and irrelevant textual references); or is connected to both the prompt and the source text(s)

0 points: may attempt to create an argument but demonstrates minimal or no understanding of the ideas, events, and figures presented in the source texts or the contexts from which these texts are drawn; cites minimal or no evidence from the primary and secondary source texts; may or may not demonstrate an attempt to create an argument; or lacks connection either to the prompt or the source text(s)

Non-scorable Responses (Score of 0/Condition Codes): response exclusively contains text copied from source text(s) or prompt; response demonstrates that the test-taker has read neither the prompt nor the source text(s); response is incomprehensible; response is not in English, or response is not attempted (blank)

Trait 2: Development of Ideas and Organizational Structure

1 point: contains a sensible progression of ideas with understandable connections between details and main ideas; contains ideas that are developed and generally logical; multiple ideas are elaborated upon; or demonstrates appropriate awareness of the task

0 points: contains an unclear or no apparent progression of ideas; contains ideas that are insufficiently developed or illogical; just one idea is elaborated upon or demonstrates no awareness of the task

Non-scorable Responses (Score of 0/Condition Codes): See above.

Trait 3: Clarity and Command of Standard English Conventions

1 point: demonstrates adequate applications of conventions with specific regard to the following skills: 1) correctly uses frequently confused words and homonyms, including contractions; 2) subject-verb agreement; 3) pronoun usage, including pronoun antecedent agreement; and 4) pronoun case; 5) placement of modifiers and correct word order; 6) capitalization (e.g., proper nouns, titles, and beginnings of sentences); 7) use of apostrophes with possessive nouns; 8) use of punctuation (e.g., commas in a series or in appositives and other non-essential elements, end marks, and appropriate punctuation for clause separation); demonstrates largely correct sentence structure with variance from sentence to sentence; is generally fluent and clear with specific regard to the following skills: 1) correct subordination, coordination, and parallelism; 2) avoidance of wordiness and awkward sentence structures; 3) usage of transitional words, conjunctive adverbs, and other words that support logic and 4) clarity; 5) avoidance of run-on

sentences, fused sentences, or sentence fragments; 6) standard usage at a level of formality appropriate for on-demand draft writing; may contain some errors in mechanics and conventions, but they do not interfere with understanding.*

0 points: demonstrates minimal control of basic conventions with specific regard to skills 1–8 as listed in the first section under Trait 3, Score Point 1 above; demonstrates consistently flawed sentence structure; minimal or no variance such that meaning may be obscured; demonstrates minimal control over skills 1–6 as listed in the second section under Trait 3, Score Point 1 above; contains severe and frequent errors in mechanics and conventions that interfere with comprehension; **OR** response is insufficient to demonstrate level of mastery over conventions and usage

*Because test-takers will be given only 25 minutes to complete Extended Response tasks, there is no expectation that a response should be completely free of conventions or usage errors to receive a score of 1.

Non-scorable Responses (Score of 0/Condition Codes): See above.

5. **DOK Level:** 3; **Content Topics:** I.CG.b.9, I.USH.b.1; **Practices:** SSP.1.a, SSP.5.a, SSP.6.b, SSP.9.a, SSP.9.b, SSP.9.c. Summaries should suggest that if the colonies joined together, they would be powerful and succeed in their cause. However, if they squabbled with one another and were not joined or united, they would be powerless and their cause would die. With specific regard to this prompt about the effect of the "Join, or Die" cartoon, a response earning 3 points would clearly identify the enduring issue that the new colonies must fight together against their common enemy, Britain, and not fight against one another.

Social Studies Extended Response Traits: Explanation of Traits

Depth of Knowledge (DOK) Level 3: Composing an appropriate response for this item requires a variety of complex reasoning skills. Test-takers must present their ideas logically and support their claim with evidence. Accurately and adequately incorporating elements from the text into the presentation of one's own ideas demands complex reasoning and planning.

Trait 1: Creation of Arguments and Use of Evidence

2 points: generates a text-based argument that demonstrates a clear understanding of the relationships among ideas, events, and figures as presented in the source text(s) and historical contexts from which they are drawn; cites relevant and specific evidence from primary and secondary source texts that adequately supports an argument; or is well-connected to both the prompt and the source texts

1 point: generates an argument that demonstrates an understanding of the relationships among ideas, events, and figures as presented in the source text(s); cites some evidence from primary and secondary source texts in support of an argument (may include a mix of relevant and irrelevant textual references); or is connected to both the prompt and the source text(s)

UNIT 3 (continued)

0 points: may attempt to create an argument but demonstrates minimal or no understanding of the ideas, events, and figures presented in the source texts or the contexts from which these texts are drawn; cites minimal or no evidence from the primary and secondary source texts; may or may not demonstrate an attempt to create an argument; or lacks connection either to the prompt or the source text(s)

Non-scorable Responses (Score of 0/Condition Codes): response exclusively contains text copied from source text(s) or prompt; response demonstrates that the test-taker has read neither the prompt nor the source text(s); response is incomprehensible; response is not in English, or response is not attempted (blank)

Trait 2: Development of Ideas and Organizational Structure

1 point: contains a sensible progression of ideas with understandable connections between details and main ideas; contains ideas that are developed and generally logical; multiple ideas are elaborated upon; or demonstrates appropriate awareness of the task

0 points: contains an unclear or no apparent progression of ideas; contains ideas that are insufficiently developed or illogical; just one idea is elaborated upon or demonstrates no awareness of the task

Non-scorable Responses (Score of 0/Condition Codes): See above.

Trait 3: Clarity and Command of Standard English Conventions

1 point: demonstrates adequate applications of conventions with specific regard to the following skills: 1) correctly uses frequently confused words and homonyms, including contractions; 2) subject-verb agreement; 3) pronoun usage, including pronoun antecedent agreement; and 4) pronoun case; 5) placement of modifiers and correct word order; 6) capitalization (e.g., proper nouns, titles, and beginnings of sentences); 7) use of apostrophes with possessive nouns; 8) use of punctuation (e.g., commas in a series or in appositives and other non-essential elements, end marks, and appropriate punctuation for clause separation); demonstrates largely correct sentence structure with variance from sentence to sentence; is generally fluent and clear with specific regard to the following skills: 1) correct subordination, coordination, and parallelism; 2) avoidance of wordiness and awkward sentence structures; 3) usage of transitional words, conjunctive adverbs, and other words that support logic and 4) clarity; 5) avoidance of run-on sentences, fused sentences, or sentence fragments; 6) standard usage at a level of formality appropriate for on-demand draft writing; may contain some errors in mechanics and conventions, but they do not interfere with understanding.*

0 points: demonstrates minimal control of basic conventions with specific regard to skills 1–8 as listed in the first section under Trait 3, Score Point 1 above; demonstrates consistently flawed sentence structure; minimal or no variance such that meaning may be obscured; demonstrates minimal control over skills 1–6 as listed in the second section under Trait 3, Score Point 1 above; contains severe and frequent errors in mechanics and conventions that interfere with comprehension; **OR** response is insufficient to demonstrate level of mastery over conventions and usage

*Because test-takers will be given only 25 minutes to complete Extended Response tasks, there is no expectation that a response should be completely free of conventions or usage errors to receive a score of 1.

Non-scorable Responses (Score of 0/Condition Codes): See above.

LESSON 4, pp. 62–65

1. **A; DOK Level: 1; Content Topics:** I.CG.b.7, I.USH.c.3; **Practices:** SSP.1.a, SSP.2.a. By comparing these two passages, you can determine that they both address South Carolina's secession from the Union. The correct answer is therefore A. B is incorrect because the documents do not discuss the actual disputes that caused the secession. C and D are also incorrect because neither of the documents mention slavery or South Carolina's place among world nations.

2. **B; DOK Level: 2; Content Topics:** I.CG.b.7, I.USH.c.3; **Practices:** SSP.1.a, SSP.2.a. By contrasting these passages, you can determine that while they both address secession, the first declares that South Carolina is seceding, and the second states the reasons why. Therefore, the feature of the excerpts that is most different is each one's purpose. It is not their writing style, the time period in which they were written, or the subject matter.

3. **B; DOK Level: 2; Content Topics:** I.CG.b.8, I.CG.d.2, I.USH.c.1, I.USH.c.4; **Practices:** SSP.1.a, SSP.2.a, SSP.2.b, SSP.3.c. The answer is B. Read the information carefully to determine the similarities and differences between slavery and sharecropping. The difference was that in sharecropping, the workers could receive payment for their work on a plantation. The two systems were not different in that workers were mistreated, planters did provide materials to produce crops, and workers did help cultivate cash crops such as cotton.

4. **D; DOK Level: 2; Content Topics:** I.CG.b.8, I.CG.d.2, II.CG.e.2, I.USH.c.4; **Practices:** SSP.1.a, SSP.2.a, SSP.2.b, SSP.3.c. The answer is D. Slavery and sharecropping were similar (or the same) in that, just as during the era of slavery, many sharecroppers worked primarily at agricultural tasks. The other answer choices each include a level of freedom that formerly enslaved people did not possess.

5. **C; DOK Level: 2; Content Topic:** I.CG.b.8; **Practices:** SSP.1.a, SSP.1.b, SSP.2.a, SSP.2.b. The correct answer is C. Both grant Congress the authority to enforce their provisions. None of the other responses describe powers granted by either the Thirteenth or Fifteenth Amendments.

6. **A; DOK Level:** 3; **Content Topics:** I.CG.b.4, I.CG.b.8; **Practices:** SSP.1.a, SSP.1.b, SSP.2.a, SSP.2.b, SSP.6.c. The correct answer is A. The key here is to review carefully what the Fifteenth Amendment grants: the right to vote regardless of race, color, or previous condition of servitude. It would outlaw poll taxes (a tax that must be paid in order to vote) for certain ethnic groups, because that would be discriminatory and may prevent people of certain ethnic groups from voting. It does not outlaw the imprisonment of convicted criminals. It does not outlaw voter registration drives. It does not even outlaw slavery. So B, C, and D are wrong.

7. **A; DOK Level:** 2; **Content Topics:** I.CG.a.1, I.CG.c.2, II.CG.e.3, I.USH.d.1; **Practices:** SSP.1.a, SSP.2.a, SSP.2.b, SSP.3.c, SSP.6.b. The correct answer is A. If you look at the information, it states that no African Americans served in the Senate between 1881 and 1967, and no African Americans served in the House between 1901 and 1929. This reveals long periods of time in the 1900s when there were no African American members in either house of Congress. Using both the table and the passage, you can see that all of the other responses are incorrect.

8. **A; DOK Level:** 2; **Content Topics:** I.CG.a.1, I.CG.c.2, II.CG.e.3, I.USH.d.1; **Practices:** SSP.1.a, SSP.2.a, SSP.2.b, SSP.3.c, SSP.6.b. The correct answer is A. The passage indicates that the House has had 139 African American members, while the Senate has had eight African American members. Using both the table and the passage, you can see that all of the other responses are incorrect.

9. **D; DOK Level:** 2; **Content Topics:** I.CG.a.1, I.CG.c.2, II.CG.e.3, I.USH.d.1; **Practices:** SSP.1.a, SSP.2.a, SSP.2.b, SSP.3.c, SSP.6.b. The answer is D. Mr. Revels was the first African American member of the U.S. Senate, and he was elected by the Mississippi state legislature, not the public. However, Mr. Rainey was the first African American to be popularly elected to serve in Congress. A is incorrect because both were elected during the same year. B is wrong because Mr. Revels served in the Senate and Mr. Rainey served in the House. C is not the correct answer because Mr. Rainey was formerly enslaved; however, the information does not state whether Mr. Revels was.

10. **C; DOK Level:** 3; **Content Topics** I.CG.a.1, I.CG.c.2, II.CG.e.3, I.USH.d.1; **Practices:** SSP.1.a, SSP.2.a, SSP.2.b, SSP.3.c, SSP.6.b. C is correct because this question requires you to use subject-area knowledge. Jim Crow laws were popular in the South. They established poll taxes, literacy tests, and other measures designed to limit African American votes. The Fugitive Slave Acts were federal laws enacted by Congress to ensure the return of enslaved people who had escaped to the North. While both types of laws oppressed African Americans, Jim Crow laws were state and local acts, while the Fugitive Slave Acts were federal laws. A is incorrect because both were actual legislation. B is incorrect because, although the laws were meant to restrict the freedom and individual rights of African Americans, they were not specifically targeted to prevent African Americans from holding office. D is incorrect because just the Fugitive Slave Acts were enacted to preserve slavery. Jim Crow laws were passed after slavery was outlawed and served to restrict the rights of African Americans rather than perpetuating enslavement.

11. **B; DOK Level:** 2; **Content Topics:** I.CG.a.1, I.CG.c.2, II.CG.e.3, I.USH.d.1; **Practices:** SSP.1.a, SSP.2.a, SSP.2.b, SSP.3.c, SSP.6.b. B is correct, because Blanche K. Bruce was the last African American to serve in the Senate between the late 1800s and 1967. George Henry White was the last African American to serve in the House between 1901 and 1928. A is incorrect because Mr. White served a couple of two-year terms in the House. C is wrong because Mr. Bruce was not popularly elected. D is wrong because Mr. Bruce represented Mississippi, while Mr. White represented North Carolina.

12. **C; DOK Level:** 2; **Content Topics:** I.CG.b.7, I.CG.b.8, I.CG.c.3, I.CG.d.2; **Practices:** SSP.1.a, SSP.1.b, SSP.6.b. You know that President Lincoln preferred a conciliatory Reconstruction plan designed to easily welcome the Southern states back into the Union, but the Radical Republicans in Congress wished to punish Southern states with harsh Reconstruction policies. By examining the actions of President Johnson presented in the information, you can determine that his policies were most similar to those of President Lincoln's. All of the other answer options, the Radical Republicans, Rutherford B. Hayes, and the former Confederates, are incorrect.

13. **B; DOK Level:** 2; **Content Topics:** I.CG.b.7, I.CG.b.8, I.CG.c.3, I.CG.d.2; **Practices:** SSP.1.a, SSP.1.b, SSP.6.b. The information states that while most states ratified the Thirteenth Amendment, the Fourteenth Amendment was rejected by most Southern states. The other answer options, one dealing with Reconstruction while the other dealt with foreign policy, or Abraham Lincoln having authored one while Congressional leaders wrote the other, or that Radical Republicans supported one but not the other, are all incorrect.

14. **D; DOK Level:** 2; **Content Topics:** I.CG.b.7, I.CG.b.8, I.CG.c.3, I.CG.d.2; **Practices:** SSP.1.a, SSP.1.b, SSP.6.b. D is the correct answer. The Radical Republicans supported very harsh measures, including direct punishment of the southern aristocracy that supported the war. So taking control away from the aristocracy would have been supported by the Radical Republicans. The other measures listed in A, B, and C would have all been lenient toward the South, and would not have been supported by the Radical Republicans.

15. **A; DOK Level:** 2; **Content Topics:** I.CG.b.7, I.CG.b.8, I.CG.c.3, I.CG.d.2; **Practices:** SSP.1.a, SSP.1.b, SSP.6.b. A is the correct answer. The Fourteenth Amendment guaranteed citizenship to all people born in the United States, including formerly enslaved people, and the Fifteenth Amendment established voting rights for African American men. B is not correct because only the Fourteenth Amendment was rejected by Southern states. C is incorrect because neither amendment established civil rights in the South. D is wrong because the information does not mention the viewpoint of Rutherford B. Hayes on either amendment.

LESSON 5, pp. 66–69

1. **B; DOK Level:** 1; **Content Topics:** II.G.c.3, II.G.d.1, II.G.d.3; **Practices:** SSP.1.a, SSP.2.a, SSP.6.b, SSP.6.c, SSP.10.a. The answer is B. A close look at the graph shows that Texas is third highest in the percentage of internationally born residents, behind California and New York. The other answer options of New York (as third), Florida, and New Jersey are incorrect.

UNIT 3 (continued)

2. D; DOK Level: 1; **Content Topics:** II.G.c.3, II.G.d.1, II.G.d.3; **Practices:** SSP.1.a, SSP.2.a, SSP.6.b, SSP.6.c, SSP.10.a. Some quick calculations using the line graph should give you the answer. The internationally born population was about 20 million in 1990. In 2010, it was almost 40 million, which represents a growth of about 20 million people between the two years. Therefore, the answer is D. The other answer options are incorrect.

3. B; DOK Level: 1; **Content Topics:** II.CG.e.2, II.USH.g.3; **Practices:** SSP.1.a, SSP.1.b, SSP.2.b, SSP.3.a, SSP.3.c, SSP.6.b. Look at the top box of the flowchart to find the actions that began the fighting, and that is a Cuban war of independence against Spain. The answer is therefore B, Spain was attempting to put down a Cuban rebellion. Spain was not a protectorate of Cuba and therefore did not want independence from Cuba, nor was the United States fighting against Cuba, with Spain as an ally. Also incorrect is a ship blowing up in a harbor in Havana being the cause.

4. C; DOK Level: 1; **Content Topics:** II.CG.e.2, II.USH.g.3; **Practices:** SSP.1.a, SSP.1.b, SSP.2.b, SSP.3.a, SSP.3.c, SSP.6.b. A, B, and D are all untrue and unsupported by information in the flowchart. The only answer that is supported by information in the flowchart is C, sensationalized newspaper stories turned the American public against Spain.

5. C; DOK Level: 2; **Content Topics:** II.CG.e.2, II.USH.g.3; **Practices:** SSP.1.a, SSP.1.b, SSP.2.b, SSP.3.a, SSP.3.c, SSP.6.b. Look carefully at all of the responses and eliminate those that are not supported by the short passage or the flowchart. You can quickly eliminate A, B, and D. Both the passage and the flowchart information support C, that the United States became a world power and therefore had to begin to act with that in mind.

6. A; DOK Level: 2; **Content Topic:** II.CG.e.3; **Practices:** SSP.1.a, SSP.1.b, SSP.6.b, SSP.6.c. The only accurate statement is A. Look at the second circle graph showing electoral votes. Although five candidates were named in the popular vote graph, only two of them split the electoral vote. As a result, three candidates received no electoral votes.

7. B; DOK Level: 2; **Content Topics:** II.G.d.1, II.G.d.4; **Practices:** SSP.1.a, SSP.1.b, SSP.2.a, SSP.6.b, SSP.10.a. C is the answer because the bars on the graph for the first two decades of the twentieth century are the longest, meaning that they were the busiest times for homesteading. The bar graph indicates that A is wrong, because the number of homesteads did not increase steadily between those decades. C is wrong, because the graph shows that there were deeds transferred after 1950. In fact, the passage states that the Homestead Act was not repealed in all parts of the United States until 1986. A quick calculation using the graph proves that D also is wrong. The addition of all of the homesteaders in the decades before 1911 to 1920 adds up to much more than in that decade alone.

8. C; DOK Level: 3; **Content Topics:** II.G.d.1, II.G.d.4; **Practices:** SSP.1.a, SSP.1.b, SSP.2.a, SSP.6.b, SSP.10.a. C is correct because the most logical inference is that people who were able to obtain their own land for the first time would have probably felt more favorably about the federal government, which made this possible. This will require you to make an inference and draw some conclusions. A and B are not the correct answers because they are untrue. You can infer that the Homestead Act created more landowners throughout the United States, not fewer. You should also recall that the end of slavery came just a few short years after President Lincoln signed the Homestead Act into law in 1862. What's more, there is no logical reason that the Act would have caused slavery to last longer. D is incorrect because it is clear that cities were not abandoned in the United States.

9. C; DOK Level: 1; **Content Topics:** II.G.d.3, II.G.d.4; **Practices:** SSP.1.a, SSP.2.b, SSP.6.b, SSP.6.c, SSP.10.a. C is correct because the "Rural Population" bars in both 1900 and 1910 are much larger than the "Urban Population" bars. A and B are incorrect because Alabama's population during this period of time was neither divided evenly between urban and rural nor heavily urban. D is wrong because the graph shows that the population was not more than 2 million in 1900.

10. B; DOK Level: 2; **Content Topics:** II.G.d.3, II.G.d.4; **Practices:** SSP.1.a, SSP.2.b, SSP.6.b, SSP.6.c, SSP.10.a. The only correct answer is B because the graph bars show that in 1910 the population of Alabama was slightly more urbanized than in 1900. Careful review of the graph shows that both A and C are incorrect. D is wrong because population increased in both rural and urban areas. It did not decrease.

11. DOK Level: 2; **Content Topic:** I.CG.e.3; **Practices:** SSP.1.a, SSP.1.b, SSP.2.a, SSP.6.b. **11.1: C, political advertisements; 11.2: A, fund-raisers; 11.3: D, challenger candidates; 11.4: B, Incumbents; 11.5: C, reelections.**

LESSON 6, pp. 70–73

1. D; DOK Level: 1; **Content Topics:** I.CG.b.6, I.CG.c.1, I.CG.c.4, II.USH.f.4; **Practices:** SSP.1.a, SSP.2.a, SSP.2.b, SSP.3.c. D is the correct answer. The answer is clear from Germany's announcement that it would no longer refrain from attacking U.S. ships and from the statement that President Wilson went before Congress to address the rising conflict with Germany. No specific information is given about the status of the war in Europe or about Germany's military power. President Wilson's second term reflects the time period but does not relate directly to his address to Congress.

2. A; DOK Level: 2; **Content Topics:** I.CG.b.6, I.CG.c.1, I.CG.c.4, II.USH.f.4; **Practices:** SSP.1.a, SSP.2.a, SSP.2.b, SSP.3.c. The correct answer is A, because the speech makes it clear that President Wilson believes war with Germany will soon be necessary for the United States. B is wrong because it is clear from his words that President Wilson is no longer content to remain neutral. C is incorrect because President Wilson speaks of many months of fiery trial, indicating that he does not believe the war will be won quickly. D is incorrect because there is no indication from the passage that President Wilson believes the war is being fought for economic reasons.

3. **A; DOK Level: 3; Content Topics:** I.CG.b.8, I.CG.d.2, II.CG.e.2, II.CG.e.3, II.USH.d.2; **Practices:** SSP.1.a, SSP.1.b, SSP.2.b, SSP.5.a. In the second paragraph, Ms. Anthony refers to "We, the people...," the words that begin the Preamble to the U.S. Constitution. It is not the Declaration of Independence, nor the Twentieth Amendment, nor the Emancipation Proclamation.

4. **B; DOK Level: 3; Content Topics:** I.CG.b.8, I.CG.d.2, II.CG.e.2, II.CG.e.3, II.USH.d.2; **Practices:** SSP.1.a, SSP.1.b, SSP.2.b, SSP.5.a. The correct answer is B. The proof is in this excerpt from the passage: "I not only committed no crime, but, instead, simply exercised my citizen's rights, guaranteed to me and all United States citizens by the National Constitution..." A is wrong because Ms. Anthony is clearly not mocking the Constitution, just the people denying women their rights under it. C is incorrect, because Ms. Anthony's point was not to state that women enjoy liberty; everybody does. D is incorrect because there is no indication in the passage that Ms. Anthony had any objection to Constitutional amendments.

5. **B; DOK Level: 2; Content Topics:** I.CG.c.3, I.CG.c.5, II.USH.g.3; **Practices:** SSP.1.a, SSP.1.b, SSP.2.a, SSP.2.b, SSP.3.c. The amendment states it is in effect within both the United States, and all territory subject to the jurisdiction of the United States. Because Puerto Rico was a territory of the United States when the amendment was ratified, it was also subject to Prohibition. The other answer options are incorrect.

6. **C; DOK Level: 2; Content Topics:** I.CG.c.3, I.CG.c.5, II.USH.g.3; **Practices:** SSP.1.a, SSP.1.b, SSP.2.a, SSP.2.b, SSP.3.c. The Eighteenth Amendment was ratified in 1919. However, the amendment itself states that it will go into effect "After one year from ... ratification ..." So it went into effect in 1920, not 1918, 1919, or 1921.

7. **A; DOK Level: 3; Content Topics:** I.CG.c.5, I.CG.d.2; **Practices:** SSP.1.a, SSP.1.b, SSP.2.a, SSP.2.b, SSP.3.a, SSP.3.c. The most logical answer is A. In order for the amendment to be repealed, Congress had to initiate the action. Therefore, Congress had to stop supporting Prohibition. The other answer options are not logical inferences.

8. **D; DOK Level: 3; Content Topics:** I.CG.c.5, I.CG.d.2; **Practices:** SSP.1.a, SSP.1.b, SSP.2.a, SSP.2.b, SSP.3.a, SSP.3.c. D is correct because the fact that state Prohibition laws existed means that some state legislatures, as late as 1965 (one year prior to 1966 as stated in the excerpt), did believe consumption of alcohol was dangerous, and possibly immoral. A is incorrect, because several states continued to prohibit alcohol even after the Eighteenth Amendment was repealed. B is wrong because state prohibition of alcohol does not necessarily mean control of underground drinking establishments. States could have concentrated on controlling production and transportation of alcohol. C is wrong because the passage does not address whether state laws were easier to enforce, so you cannot make that inference.

9. **B; DOK Level: 3; Content Topics:** I.CG.c.5, I.CG.d.2; **Practices:** SSP.1.a, SSP.1.b, SSP.2.a, SSP.2.b, SSP.3.a, SSP.3.c. The most logical answer is B. If many Americans basically defied the law, the most likely reason is that they liked to drink alcohol and thought it was their right to do so. They felt the law was unjust and a restriction of their individual rights. You can infer neither infer that most Americans were not law abiding, nor that the police did not try to enforce the law. So A and C are incorrect. It is also illogical to assume that most Americans depended on alcohol production for work, so D is not a good inference.

10. **D; DOK Level: 2; Content Topics:** I.CG.b.8, I.CG.d.2; **Practices:** SSP.1.a, SSP.1.b, SSP.2.a, SSP.2.b, SSP.3.a, SSP.3.c. Because of the numerous innovations and advances in society, you can infer that the 1920s was a time of exciting innovation. You cannot infer that life in the 1920s was dangerous, or that life for working people was more difficult than in the decades prior, or that artists gained international fame in the 1920s.

11. **C; DOK Level: 3; Content Topics:** I.CG.b.8, I.CG.d.2; **Practices:** SSP.1.a, SSP.1.b, SSP.2.a, SSP.2.b, SSP.3.a, SSP.3.c. Being allowed the right to vote in national elections was empowering for women. They gained power over elected officials who created laws, and they could express their views at the ballot box. This was also the culmination of the woman suffrage movement in which many women served as leaders and organizers. World War II did not occur in the 1920s, so A is incorrect. Attending plays and movies or being able to drive cars would not in and of themselves empower women.

12. **DOK Level: 3; Content Topics:** I.CG.c.1, I.CG.c.3, I.CG.c.6; **Practices:** SSP.1.a, SSP.1.b, SSP.2.a, SSP.2, SSP.3.c, SSP.6.b, SSP.9.a, SSP.9.b, SSP.9.c. With specific regard to this prompt about Presidents Hoover and Roosevelt's viewpoints about the responsibilities of the federal government, a response earning 3 points would clearly identify the enduring issue as the fact that President Hoover was much more limited in his use of the federal government to combat the worst effects of the Great Depression. His programs were more likely to target corporations or private organizations, with the aim of having them provide help that would trickle out and down to the public at large, as opposed to President Roosevelt's administration, which took a more direct role in providing programs that impacted the average person, making it easy to infer that he believed in a more activist role for the federal government than did Hoover.

Answer Key

UNIT 3 *(continued)*

Social Studies Extended Response Traits: Explanation of Traits

Depth of Knowledge (DOK) Level 3: Composing an appropriate response for this item requires a variety of complex reasoning skills. Test-takers must present their ideas logically and support their claim with evidence. Accurately and adequately incorporating elements from the text into the presentation of one's own ideas demands complex reasoning and planning.

Trait 1: Creation of Arguments and Use of Evidence

2 points: generates a text-based argument that demonstrates a clear understanding of the relationships among ideas, events, and figures as presented in the source text(s) and historical contexts from which they are drawn; cites relevant and specific evidence from primary and secondary source texts that adequately supports an argument; or is well-connected to both the prompt and the source texts

1 point: generates an argument that demonstrates an understanding of the relationships among ideas, events, and figures as presented in the source text(s); cites some evidence from primary and secondary source texts in support of an argument (may include a mix of relevant and irrelevant textual references); or is connected to both the prompt and the source text(s)

0 points: may attempt to create an argument but demonstrates minimal or no understanding of the ideas, events, and figures presented in the source texts or the contexts from which these texts are drawn; cites minimal or no evidence from the primary and secondary source texts; may or may not demonstrate an attempt to create an argument; or lacks connection either to the prompt or the source text(s)

Non-scorable Responses (Score of 0/Condition Codes): response exclusively contains text copied from source text(s) or prompt; response demonstrates that the test-taker has read neither the prompt nor the source text(s); response is incomprehensible; response is not in English, or response is not attempted (blank)

Trait 2: Development of Ideas and Organizational Structure

1 point: contains a sensible progression of ideas with understandable connections between details and main ideas; contains ideas that are developed and generally logical; multiple ideas are elaborated upon; or demonstrates appropriate awareness of the task

0 points: contains an unclear or no apparent progression of ideas; contains ideas that are insufficiently developed or illogical; just one idea is elaborated upon or demonstrates no awareness of the task

Non-scorable Responses (Score of 0/Condition Codes): See above.

Trait 3: Clarity and Command of Standard English Conventions

1 point: demonstrates adequate applications of conventions with specific regard to the following skills: 1) correctly uses frequently confused words and homonyms, including contractions; 2) subject-verb agreement; 3) pronoun usage, including pronoun antecedent agreement; and 4) pronoun case; 5) placement of modifiers and correct word order; 6) capitalization (e.g., proper nouns, titles, and beginnings of sentences); 7) use of apostrophes with possessive nouns; 8) use of punctuation (e.g., commas in a series or in appositives and other non-essential elements, end marks, and appropriate punctuation for clause separation); demonstrates largely correct sentence structure with variance from sentence to sentence; is generally fluent and clear with specific regard to the following skills: 1) correct subordination, coordination, and parallelism; 2) avoidance of wordiness and awkward sentence structures; 3) usage of transitional words, conjunctive adverbs, and other words that support logic and 4) clarity; 5) avoidance of run-on sentences, fused sentences, or sentence fragments; 6) standard usage at a level of formality appropriate for on-demand draft writing; may contain some errors in mechanics and conventions, but they do not interfere with understanding.*

0 points: demonstrates minimal control of basic conventions with specific regard to skills 1–8 as listed in the first section under Trait 3, Score Point 1 above; demonstrates consistently flawed sentence structure; minimal or no variance such that meaning may be obscured; demonstrates minimal control over skills 1–6 as listed in the second section under Trait 3, Score Point 1 above; contains severe and frequent errors in mechanics and conventions that interfere with comprehension; **OR** response is insufficient to demonstrate level of mastery over conventions and usage

*Because test-takers will be given only 25 minutes to complete Extended Response tasks, there is no expectation that a response should be completely free of conventions or usage errors to receive a score of 1.

Non-scorable Responses (Score of 0/Condition Codes): See above.

LESSON 7, *pp. 74–77*

1. **C; DOK Level:** 2; **Content Topics:** II.E.d.7, II.E.d.10; **Practices:** SSP.1.a, SSP.1.b, SSP.2.a, SSP.5.a, SSP.5.b, SSP.6.b. The sign, the light pole, and the city pictured in the background are all drawn relatively realistically. The only one of these elements that is a caricature is the man eating the apples. He is a caricature of a rich man, because he is wearing a top hat and spats, and carrying a cane. These items are an exaggeration, because all rich men would not necessarily wear such things. But they are symbols that allow the cartoonist to identify the man as rich, and also poke some fun at him.

2. **D; DOK Level:** 2; **Content Topics:** II.E.d.7, II.E.d.10; **Practices:** SSP.1.a, SSP.1.b, SSP.2.a, SSP.5.a, SSP.5.b, SSP.6.b. The only logical answer is D. The cartoon shows a rich man sitting on the ground eating apples that a tattered, unemployed man is selling from a box on the street. A rich man would not normally be in this position. Therefore, the idea here is that times are so bad during the Great Depression that the wealthy as well as the poor are affected. The artist is not conveying that the Depression caused unemployment to increase, nor that it caused the price of food to increase. The cartoonist also is not portraying the fact that the Depression affected people more in the cities than in rural areas.

3. **DOK Level:** 2; **Content Topics:** I.CG.c.1, I.CG.c.3, I.CG.c.6; **Practices:** SSP.1.a, SSP.1.b, SSP.2.a, SSP.2.b, SSP.5.a, SSP.6.b.

3.1 **D. doctor;** President Roosevelt is portrayed as a **doctor**, carrying a medical bag filled with "New Deal Remedies."

3.2 **C. the United States;** The old man is **Uncle Sam (or the United States**, proven by the fact that he has stars on his pajama pants and stripes on his socks, representing the flag. He also has "**US**" on his slippers to drive home the point.

3.3 **A. New Deal programs;** The initials on the bottles are those of New Deal programs. "Doctor" FDR has prescribed the New Deal medicines for "sick man" United States.

3.4 **C. cautiously positive;** The title of the cartoon, "New Deal to the Rescue," is basically positive. However, "Doctor" FDR is stating to "Nurse" Congress that they might have to change remedies if these New Deal potions do not work, inserting caution into the message.

4. **D; DOK Level:** 2; **Content Topics:** I.CG.c.1, I.CG.c.3; **Practices:** SSP.1.a, SSP.1.b, SSP.2.a, SSP.5.a, SSP.6.b, SSP.7.a. The fact that the hand holding the New Deal cards has a stars and stripes–type sleeve indicates that the hand belongs to Uncle Sam, who always represents the United States in cartoons. It does not represent Herbert Hoover, Woodrow Wilson, or the United Nations.

5. **A; DOK Level:** 2; **Content Topics:** I.CG.c.1, I.CG.c.3; **Practices:** SSP.1.a, SSP.1.b, SSP.2.a, SSP.5.a, SSP.6.b, SSP.7.a. The biggest clue to the correct answer here is the title of the cartoon: "It IS a New Deal." The emphasis on the word "IS" suggests that the cartoonist agrees that this set of programs is something new and positive. The feeling being conveyed is not skepticism, confusion, or calmness.

6. **B; DOK Level:** 1; **Content Topic:** I.CG.c.6; **Practices:** SSP.1.a, SSP.2.a, SSP.5.a, SSP.5.b, SSP.6.b. Looking closely at the poster, you can easily eliminate angry, courteous, and exhausted. The figure does not have any of those expressions, so the correct answer is that the figure looks proud.

7. **D; DOK Level:** 2; **Content Topic:** I.CG.c.6; **Practices:** SSP.1.a, SSP.2.a, SSP.5.a, SSP.5.b, SSP.6.b. The key here is that the poster states the program is an opportunity for young men, and the man in the poster is shown working with a tool. Opportunity for young men would not apply to bank failures, outbreaks of disease, or political corruption. The correct response is unemployment. The program gave young men an opportunity to have a job and earn money.

8. **C; DOK Level:** 3; **Content Topic:** I.CG.c.6; **Practices:** SSP.1.a, SSP.2.a, SSP.5.a, SSP.5.b, SSP.6.b. C is correct because the jobs were difficult. Propaganda is normally used in a negative connotation, but in this case, promoting a good job, although difficult and involving hard labor, can be considered a type of positive propaganda. The poster did not promote the CCC in a positive way because there were too many applicants, or because the jobs were highly desirable, or because wages were very good.

9. **D; DOK Level:** 2; **Content Topic:** I.CG.c.6; **Practices:** SSP.1.a, SSP.2.a, SSP.2.b, SSP.3.c, SSP.5.a, SSP.5.b, SSP.6.b. The poster lists several things that people can do to help the war effort, and doing those things made one's home a "Victory Home." It is not one at which several residents own war bonds, or one that displays a victory sticker in its window, or one that flies the American flag.

10. **C; DOK Level:** 2; **Content Topic:** I.CG.c.6; **Practices:** SSP.1.a, SSP.2.a, SSP.2.b, SSP.3.c, SSP.5.a, SSP.5.b, SSP.6.b. The correct answer is C, walking and carrying packages. Most gasoline would have been used in motor vehicles. As a result, walking and carrying packages rather than driving to get around or shipping packages that would have been carried by truck or airplane would have saved fuel, and therefore gasoline. The other choices would have helped the war effort in different ways, but would not have conserved gasoline as directly as answer option C.

11. **B; DOK Level:** 2; **Content Topic:** I.CG.c.6; **Practices:** SSP.1.a, SSP.2.a, SSP.2.b, SSP.3.c, SSP.5.a, SSP.5.b, SSP.6.b. The correct answer is B, the war was consuming many critical resources, causing shortages. The other answer options may be somewhat good ideas, but the poster is not making those claims about the impact of war on society.

12. **B; DOK Level:** 2; **Content Topics:** I.CG.c.1, I.CG.c.3; **Practices:** SSP.1.a, SSP.1.b, SSP.2.a, SSP.5.a, SSP.5.b, SSP.6.b. The only response that is logical, considering the background of President Roosevelt's desire to run for an unprecedented third term as President, is that the cartoonist believes that President Roosevelt is acting as if he is a monarch who can stay in office indefinitely. The correct answer is therefore B. It is not because the artist believes that Presidents should wear robes to command more respect, or that he wants the United States to become a monarchy. The artist also is not making a mockery of the monarch of Britain.

13. **D; DOK Level:** 3; **Content Topics:** I.CG.c.1, I.CG.c.3, II.CG.e.1; **Practices:** SSP.1.a, SSP.1.b, SSP.2.a, SSP.5.a, SSP.5.b, SSP.6.b. To determine that the correct answer is D, you will have to use the information provided to make an inference. President Roosevelt was a Democrat, and the Republican candidates for President lost to him four times in a row (Roosevelt won yet a fourth term following his 1940 election). When President Roosevelt died in office, his Vice President, Harry S. Truman, became President. You can infer that the Republican Party was eager to make sure no Democrat could repeat what Roosevelt had done; therefore, they supported this amendment to limit the presidency to two terms. The Republicans did not want to ensure that all Presidents had at least two terms, and they were not eager to satisfy a public that wanted term limits for the President. The Republicans also would not be wishing to follow President Roosevelt's wishes to be the only four-term President.

Answer Key

UNIT 3 (continued)

14. B; DOK Level: 1; Content Topics: II.USH.f.8, II.USH.f.9; **Practices:** SSP.1.a, SSP.1.b, SSP.2.a, SSP.5.a, SSP.5.b, SSP.6.b. This is a fairly easy one to answer, if you know that the mark on the animal in the cage is the swastika, the symbol used by Nazi Germany. The answer is therefore B, the animal in the cage represents Nazi Germany and its allies, not the United States, or people who resisted serving in the military during World War II, or the lands Japan controlled in the Pacific.

15. C; DOK Level: 2; Content Topics: II.USH.f.8, II.USH.f.9; **Practices:** SSP.1.a, SSP.1.b, SSP.2.a, SSP.5.a, SSP.5.b, SSP.6.b. Buying bonds would, according to the cartoon, buy more cages, which meant paying for the soldiers and weapons to keep the Nazis in check and defeat them. So the correct answer is C, it would help American soldiers win the war. It would not allow for the building of more zoos, or make millions of dollars for people who buy bonds and stamps. It would also not help the United States and Germany become friendly toward each other.

16. A; DOK Level: 2; Content Topics: II.USH.f.8, II.USH.f.9; **Practices:** SSP.1.a, SSP.1.b, SSP.2.a, SSP.5.a, SSP.5.b, SSP.6.b. A is the only logical and probable way that the United States would be represented in such a cartoon. The duck-like bird is wearing an "Uncle Sam hat," thus obviously representing the United States. It is carrying a gun and pulling a caged "Nazi" dinosaur-like animal. The other answer options are not logical or are too simplistic to actually be correct.

LESSON 8, pp. 78–81

1. A; DOK Level: 2; Content Topics: I.CG.c.1, I.CG.c.2, I.CG.c.6; **Practices:** SSP.1.a, SSP.1.b, SSP.2.a, SSP.3.c. The Executive Office of the President (EOP) was created to keep up with the increasing responsibilities of being President. The information refers to the size and number of offices in the EOP being reflective of the current President's needs. You can therefore conclude that the President needs assistance and that is the purpose of the EOP. Departments and agencies are not created just to create new jobs. The EOP may allow the President to pursue his or her agenda; however, this is not its primary purpose. The President may increase the number of advisors, or decrease the number of advisors, depending on his or her needs.

2. D; DOK Level: 2; Content Topics: I.CG.c.1, I.CG.c.2, I.CG.c.6; **Practices:** SSP.1.a, SSP.1.b, SSP.2.a, SSP.3.c. The primary reason that the Office of Presidential Advance prepares remote sites is to ensure the President's safety. The clue in the information to help you answer the question is that this office prepares remote sites, meaning sites away from the White House to which a President travels. The President's itinerary, setting up meetings, and gathering information to give to the President can all be done from the White House. To ensure the President's safety when the President travels away from the White House, the Office of Presidential Advance prepares the remote sites.

3. B; DOK Level: 3; Content Topics: I.CG.b.9, I.CG.c.1, I.CG.c.3; **Practices:** SSP.1.a, SSP.1.b, SSP.2.a. States are allowed to set their own minimum drinking age. To ensure that states comply with a national drinking age, the federal government added the reduction in highway funds as an incentive. The federal government did not have the power to force states to set the minimum drinking age at 21, but it did have the power to decide which states received highway funds. There was no financial reward, but rather a financial punishment for states that did not comply. The federal government was not looking to reduce highway funds, but rather to encourage states to comply. The federal government may not simply impose fines on states.

4. D; DOK Level: 2; Content Topics: I.CG.b.9, I.CG.c.1, I.CG.c.3; **Practices:** SSP.1.a, SSP.1.b, SSP.2.a, SSP.4.a. *Comply* means *to adhere*, or to be in compliance, in agreement; it does not mean to admonish, to oppose, or to compare.

5. C; DOK Level: 2; Content Topic: I.CG.c.3; **Practices:** SSP.1.a, SSP.1.b, SSP.2.a, SSP.2.b, SSP.4.a. The overriding factor in the shift of authority among levels of government in the late 1980s was economics. The federal government was in debt and no longer able to bail out states and localities. The economy was shifting from a national economy to an international economy. Checks and balances and separation of powers did not change or influence what was happening. The information does not describe any changes based on politics.

6. A; DOK Level: 2; Content Topic: I.CG.c.3; **Practices:** SSP.1.a, SSP.1.b, SSP.2.a, SSP.2.b, SSP.4.a. *Parochial*, as used in the passage, means *unsophisticated*, or closed-minded, hindered. It does not mean worldly, broad-minded, or religious.

7. D; DOK Level: 3; Content Topics: I.CG.c.1, I.CG.c.6; **Practices:** SSP.1.a, SSP.3.c. You can conclude that the general public plays a major role in deciding which government agencies receive the most funding and support. The information refers to Project Vanguard, which did well, but did not have enough funding to continue. When the Soviets launched Sputnik, the American people were up in arms and provided the push the government needed to increase funding for space programs. The primary purpose of NASA was to provide research into the problems of flight within and outside Earth's atmosphere. Sputnik likely gathered scientific data, but one can infer that it was not shared with the international community based on the existence of the space race. NASA is indeed a premier agency in space exploration, but there is no particular evidence in this information to support this.

8. A; DOK Level: 3; Content Topic: I.CG.b.3, I.CG.c.1 I.CG.c.3; **Practices:** SSP.1.a, SSP.1.b, SSP.2.a, SSP.2.b, SSP.4.a. The Supreme Court is granted its power by the people of the United States. According to the information, the Supreme Court's powers are laid out in the Constitution. The U.S. Constitution includes the words "of the people, by the people, and for the people," which means that the Constitution, and therefore the Supreme Court, are ultimately given power by the people of the United States, not by the President, Congress, or the President's Cabinet.

9. **C; DOK Level:** 1; **Content Topics:** I.CG.b.9, I.CG.c.4; **Practices:** SSP.1.a, SSP.3.c, SSP.6.b. Local government is responsible for setting aside green spaces within communities. This falls under "Parks and recreation." This is a service that is best done within communities; therefore, the federal and state governments do not play a role in it.

10. **B; DOK Level:** 3; **Content Topics:** I.CG.c.4; **Practices:** SSP.1.a, SSP.3.c, SSP.6.b. Shared powers exist because both levels of government need those powers to run their governments. The federal government needs to collect federal taxes, for example, to fund the federal government. The same is true of state governments. Other items cross over levels of government, such as transportation. The idea of shared powers is not to ensure that one level does not become more powerful than another, or to make sure the two levels do not interfere with each other. In addition, the responsibilities of government to its citizens should be and are divided up to best be met.

11. **A; DOK Level:** 3; **Content Topics:** I.CG.b.9, I.CG.c.4; **Practices:** SSP.1.a, SSP.3.c, SSP.6.b. The states were worried about a federal government that was too powerful, so they made sure that they would be able to exercise rights not explicitly delegated or prohibited. The passage explains that the states feared a strong central government. You can conclude that the giving of all rights to the states that were not explicitly delegated to the federal government or prohibited from the states was their way of ensuring the federal government did not become too powerful. The states did not give up their right to make treaties in exchange for other rights. The states also do not have power over the federal government. Since all powers not given to the federal government or prohibited from the states are given to the states, it does not make sense that the states wanted a two-thirds vote for the addition of new federal powers.

LESSON 9, *pp. 82–85*

1. **A; DOK Level:** 2; **Content Topics:** I.CG.b.4, I.CG.b.8, I.CG.c.1, I.CG.c.3, I. I.CG.d.2; **Practices:** SSP.1.a, SSP.1.b, SSP.2.a, SSP.2.b, SSP.5.a, SSP.5.c, SSP.5.d. The author's point of view is that legislators are not following the will of the people. The passage states that 91% of people supported universal background checks, but Congress resisted passing this into law. Instead, the author finds Congress to be focused on the deficit, even though just 33% of Americans name that as a top priority. Gun Owners of America, not the author, believe the National Rifle Association is too soft on gun control. The author believes Congress should not focus on reducing the deficit based on the fact that most Americans rank that lower on their priority list.

2. **B; DOK Level:** 2; **Content Topics:** I.CG.b.4, I.CG.b.8, I.CG.c.1, I.CG.c.3, I. I.CG.d.2; **Practices:** SSP.1.a, SSP.1.b, SSP.2.a, SSP.2.b, SSP.5.a, SSP.5.c, SSP.5.d, SSP.7.a, SSP.11.b. The author's purpose in writing is to reprimand Congress for its inaction on gun control. The author argues that universal background checks are supported by an overwhelming majority of Americans and Congress is willfully ignoring this. The author is reprimanding Congress for its inaction, not action, on gun control. The author does not explain Congress's reasons for resisting gun control. The author does not praise Congress for its commitment to deficit reduction, because the statistics cited state that the majority of the people do not want this as much as background checks for gun ownership or job creation.

3. **B; DOK Level:** 2; **Content Topic:** I.CG.a.1. **Practices:** SSP.1.a, SSP.1.b, SSP.2.a, SSP.2.b, SSP.4.a, SSP.5.a, SSP.5.c. The King regards the poor of England with suspicion. In the law, the poor people are described as "wretched," "miserable," "beggars," and "idle." These descriptions lead you to believe the king regards poor people with suspicion. From these descriptions, he does not view them with love or believe they have many advantages. His attitude shows that he does not feel guilty about their situation.

4. **D; DOK Level:** 3; **Content Topic:** I.CG.a.1. **Practices:** SSP.1.a, SSP.1.b, SSP.2.a, SSP.2.b, SSP.4.a, SSP.5.a, SSP.5.c. Based on the tone of the law, poor children would most likely be provided with apprenticeships. The king obviously does not want to provide any more relief than he absolutely has to, so it is not likely that anyone who asks for aid will simply receive it, that all poor people will be given jobs, or that begging will become legal.

5. **B; DOK Level:** 2; **Content Topic:** I.CG.a.1. **Practices:** SSP.1.a, SSP.1.b, SSP.2.a, SSP.2.b, SSP.4.a, SSP.5.a, SSP.5.c. The second part of each edict can be characterized as explanatory. Each edict gives an instruction, or piece of advice, then explains why it is important. The edicts do not have a threatening tone, nor are they persuasive. They are easy to understand, so they are not cryptic.

6. **C; DOK Level:** 2; **Content Topic:** I.CG.a.1. **Practices:** SSP.1.a, SSP.1.b, SSP.2.a, SSP.2.b, SSP.4.a, SSP.5.a, SSP.5.c. The edicts are most similar to a list of civic responsibilities. They give instruction on how to be a good citizen. They do not give step-by-step instructions like instructions for assembling an appliance. They are not a back-and-forth conversation like e-mail messages about a project, and they do not provide any timeline.

7. **B; DOK Level:** 3; **Content Topics:** I.CG.b.8, I.CG.d.2; **Practices:** SSP.1.a, SSP.1.b, SSP.2.a, SSP.2.b, SSP.4.a, SSP.5.a, SSP.5.c, SSP.5.d, SSP.6.b. The cartoonist finds it absurd that foreigners are treated with more respect than Americans. The caption states that they can be seated because they are not Americans, which implies that Americans (African Americans) are not worthy of eating at the restaurant. The cartoonist does not agree with diplomats needing to identify themselves, as it is clear he believes it is not fair to discriminate against anyone. His depiction of the restaurant employees shows he has no faith in them. The fact that he has drawn the cartoon to be published shows he is in support of African Americans and all people being able to dine where they choose.

8. **C; DOK Level:** 3; **Content Topics:** I.CG.b.6, I.CG.b.7, I.CG.c.1, I.CG.c.3, I.CG.d.2; **Practices:** SSP.1.a, SSP.1.b, SSP.2.a, SSP.2.b, SSP.4.a, SSP.5.a, SSP.5.c, SSP.5.d, SSP.6.b. The writer believes that the rule of law is not being followed. Under the concept of rule of law, laws must be just and apply to all. In the case described by the writer, rule of law would not apply to the President, or to the people he, the President, may deem dangerous. The writer does not refer to a belief that the President should be a law unto himself, or to a desire for all people to be involved in these decisions, but for the Constitution to be followed. Referring to the separation of powers, the writer's beliefs suggest that he would be in favor of tighter checks and balances between powers.

Answer Key

UNIT 3 (continued)

9. B; DOK Level: 3; **Content Topics:** I.CG.b.6, I.CG.b.7, I.CG.c.1, I.CG.c.3, I.CG.d.2; **Practices:** SSP.1.a, SSP.1.b, SSP.2.a, SSP.2.b, SSP.4.a, SSP.5.a, SSP.5.c, SSP.5.d, SSP.6.b. The article most likely discusses the intention of the U.S. government to continue adding names to "kill lists." These are lists of terror suspects that are to be killed or captured. The writer's tone is of anger, even outrage. He believes that the President is overstepping his boundaries. The only answer option that warrants this type of response is the addition of names to kill lists. The other three options show the United States holding back in the war on terror or becoming more transparent in its actions, and are thus incorrect.

10. A; DOK Level: 2; **Content Topics:** I.CG.b.3, I.CG.b.5, I.CG.b.6, I.CG.c.1, I.CG.c.3; **Practices:** SSP.1.a, SSP.1.b, SSP.2.a, SSP.2.b, SSP.4.a, SSP.5.a, SSP.5.c, SSP.5.d, SSP.6.b. The author's view is best expressed by the statement that flow of political power to the President is a mistake. In the second paragraph he states that some are comfortable with this trend, but he believes the cost is great to the checks and balances and separation of powers that are written into and intended in the Constitution. The author does believe Congress has legal authority, in the form of checks and balances, to request executive documents. He does not believe that executive privilege should extend to all areas of government. He also disagrees with the notion that power is exercised most effectively by the executive branch.

11. D; DOK Level: 3; **Content Topics:** I.CG.b.2, I.CG.b.3, I.CG.b.6, I.CG.b.7; **Practices:** SSP.1.a, SSP.1.b, SSP.2.a, SSP.2.b, SSP.4.a, SSP.5.a, SSP.5.c, SSP.5.d, SSP.6.b. The authors believe that both rule of law and popular constitutionalism are necessary. The last sentence refers to how to strike a viable balance between the two. They disagree with Kramer that popular constitutionalism is the only path to follow. They also do not believe that judicial supremacy should be maintained at the cost of popular constitutionalism. They believe both are necessary. Similarly, although they state that judicial finality is essential, they believe popular constitutionality is also essential.

LESSON 10, pp. 86–89

1. A; DOK Level: 2; **Content Topic:** I.CG.c.6; **Practices:** SSP.1.b, SSP.3.d, SSP.6.c, SSP.8.a. The date on which the Department of Homeland Security was created is directly disputed between the two excerpts. The first excerpt states that it was established in 2002, and the second states it was created after the terrorist attacks on September 11, 2011. The reason for the creation of the Department of Homeland Security and its responsibilities are the same in both excerpts.

2. A; DOK Level: 2; **Content Topic:** I.CG.c.6; **Practices:** SSP.1.b, SSP.3.d, SSP.6.c, SSP.8.a. The second excerpt's tone is informal. Compared to the second excerpt, the tone of the first excerpt is scholarly. It is not biased in any way because it does not include opinions. It is more formal than informal and it is not emotional.

3.1 D, 3.2 B, 3.3 B, 3.4 A; DOK Level: 2; **Content Topic:** I.CG.b.9; **Practices:** SSP.2.a, SSP.5.b, SSP.6.c.

3.1 The table contains factual information about the different types of federalism that have been seen in the U.S. over the years. It is most likely to be found in a **college history textbook**. A journal entry is a narrative generally about someone's thoughts. A newspaper editorial contains opinions. A political speech also is opinionated and unlikely to contain a table of factual information.

3.2 The information in the table is **impartial**. This means it does not take positions on whether a particular type of federalism is better than another. It is reliable, rather than unreliable, due to its expected source. It is not biased in any way. Propaganda is intended to convince a reader of something and the table does not try to convince the reader of anything.

3.3 The information in the table is most useful for learning the characteristics of the **different types of federalism**. It does not give specific information on how the types of federalism were named. It does not include information about the current President. It also does not give specific information about state and federal rights and powers.

3.4 "Dual federalism was the most effective as evidenced by its longevity" is **a biased** interpretation. There is no evidence in the table that suggests that dual federalism was the most effective. To the contrary, if dual federalism was the most effective, the other types of federalism to follow would never have come to be. This is an opinion in support of dual federalism, so it is not impartial. It is also not bitter or angry in tone.

4. D; DOK Level: 2; **Content Topics:** I.CG.b.9, I.CG.c.3, I.CG.c.4; **Practices:** SSP.1.a, SSP.1.b, SSP.5.b. This source is biased toward federalism. The writer discusses the Tenth Amendment positively and states "Unfortunately, policymakers and courts have mainly discarded federalism in recent decades," underlining his or her bias toward federalism. The writer is in favor of accountability, as he or she says Congress should reconfigure aid programs to improve accountability. Federalism supports states' rights and the writer is in favor of federalism, so he or she is not biased against states' rights.

5. A; DOK Level: 2; **Content Topics:** I.CG.b.9, I.CG.c.3, I.CG.c.4; **Practices:** SSP.1.a, SSP.1.b, SSP.5.b. The tone of the article is dissatisfied. The writer is definitively unhappy with the status of how the federal government is operating, but he or she does not display fury in the writing. Elusive means hard to pin down. His or her opinion is very clear, so it is easy to pin down. Indifferent means uninterested. If the writer were indifferent, he or she would not have written this article.

6. C; DOK Level: 3; **Content Topics:** I.CG.b.5, II.CG.e.1; **Practices:** SSP.1.a, SSP.1.b, SSP.2.a, SSP.2.b, SSP.3.d, SSP.5.b. The author supports his opinion by pointing out flaws in opposing arguments. The third paragraph describes the negative things that can happen when both houses of the General Assembly and the governorship are controlled by the same political party. He does not describe specifically the reliability of his argument or provide details about Mr. Ehrlich's specific positions. He also does not cite any other opinions.

7. B; DOK Level: 2; **Content Topics:** I.CG.c.5; **Practices:** SSP.1.a, SSP.1.b, SSP.5.a, SSP.5.b. This information source is balanced. The Center for Legislative Archives is a reliable source. The information does not choose one side or the other in relaying the story of the Equal Rights Amendment. It gives correct information in a straightforward manner. It is not impassioned, or filled with emotion.

8. C; DOK Level: 2; **Content Topic:** I.CG.c.5; **Practices:** SSP.1.a, SSP.1.b, SSP.5.a, SSP.5.b. A biased interpretation against the Equal Rights Amendment is that it should not have been heard by the whole House of Representatives. This is an opinion that shows bias against the amendment. A person who believes it should not have been heard by the whole House of Representatives likely believes it should not be an amendment. The other statements are facts that can be found in the information.

9. B; DOK Level: 3; **Content Topic:** I.CG.c.5; **Practices:** SSP.1.a, SSP.1.b, SSP.5.a, SSP.5.b. You can determine the fraction of states that must ratify an amendment for it to become part of the Constitution from this information. The information states that it is three-fourths. The information does not state who introduced the ERA to Congress, the number of Senators that approved it, or the identities of the House members who voted in favor of forcing it out of committee.

LESSON 11, *pp. 90–93*

1. A; DOK Level: 2; **Content Topic:** I.CG.c.1; **Practices:** SSP.1.a, SSP.1.b, SSP.2.a. The word that provides a clue that the author is making a generalization is *traditionally*. Traditionally implies that something is done because it is how it has usually been done. The word *joint* means "together." The word *each* could provide a clue to a generalization, but in this case *traditionally* is a much better clue. The word *outlining* only tells what the speech does, and does not indicate a generalization.

2. C; DOK Level: 2; **Content Topic:** I.CG.c.1; **Practices:** SSP.1.a, SSP.1.b, SSP.2.a. Presidents have a role that is generally most similar to that of state governors. The passage describes powers and responsibilities of the President. Many of these are the same as they are for governors, except at the state level.

3. C; DOK Level: 3; **Content Topic:** I.CG.c.1, I.CG.c.3; **Practices:** SSP.1.a, SSP.1.b, SSP.2.a. Democrats and Republicans are often forced to compromise is a generalization. The sequestration is an attempt to force them to compromise. Prior to this, however, lawmakers have been chipping away at the deficit. It may be the author's opinion that vital services should not get cut, but there is no evidence of this in the passage. To say the plan for sequestration was agreed on by everyone in Congress is an invalid generalization because not everyone agreed on it.

4. A; DOK Level: 3; **Content Topics:** I.CG.c.1, I.CG.c.3; **Practices:** SSP.1.a, SSP.1.b, SSP.2.a. The fact that to date, no President, Vice President, or civil officer has been impeached by the Senate supports the generalization that all officers who have been impeached by the House of Representatives have been acquitted by the Senate. The other three pieces of information do not support the generalization.

5. DOK Level: 3; **Content Topics:** I.CG.c.3, I.CG.c.6; **Practices:** SSP.1.a, SSP.1.b, SSP.2.a, SSP.9.a, SSP.9.b, SSP.9.c. The federal government today is generally lagging behind the rest of the world in the area of technology; the work is being done in small pockets, leaving the government behind. With specific regard to this prompt about a generalization about the federal government's current use of technology and the concept of a "digital government," a response earning 3 points would clearly identify the enduring issue as the betterment of American society in general and children, the elderly, and minorities in particular.

Social Studies Extended Response Traits: Explanation of Traits

Depth of Knowledge (DOK) Level 3: Composing an appropriate response for this item requires a variety of complex reasoning skills. Test-takers must present their ideas logically and support their claim with evidence. Accurately and adequately incorporating elements from the text into the presentation of one's own ideas demands complex reasoning and planning.

Trait 1: Creation of Arguments and Use of Evidence

2 points: generates a text-based argument that demonstrates a clear understanding of the relationships among ideas, events, and figures as presented in the source text(s) and historical contexts from which they are drawn; cites relevant and specific evidence from primary and secondary source texts that adequately supports an argument; or is well-connected to both the prompt and the source texts

1 point: generates an argument that demonstrates an understanding of the relationships among ideas, events, and figures as presented in the source text(s); cites some evidence from primary and secondary source texts in support of an argument (may include a mix of relevant and irrelevant textual references); or is connected to both the prompt and the source text(s)

0 points: may attempt to create an argument but demonstrates minimal or no understanding of the ideas, events, and figures presented in the source texts or the contexts from which these texts are drawn; cites minimal or no evidence from the primary and secondary source texts; may or may not demonstrate an attempt to create an argument; or lacks connection either to the prompt or the source text(s)

Non-scorable Responses (Score of 0/Condition Codes): response exclusively contains text copied from source text(s) or prompt; response demonstrates that the test-taker has read neither the prompt nor the source text(s); response is incomprehensible; response is not in English, or response is not attempted (blank)

Trait 2: Development of Ideas and Organizational Structure

1 point: contains a sensible progression of ideas with understandable connections between details and main ideas; contains ideas that are developed and generally logical; multiple ideas are elaborated upon; or demonstrates appropriate awareness of the task

0 points: contains an unclear or no apparent progression of ideas; contains ideas that are insufficiently developed or illogical; just one idea is elaborated upon or demonstrates no awareness of the task

Answer Key

UNIT 3 (continued)

Non-scorable Responses (Score of 0/Condition Codes): See above.

Trait 3: Clarity and Command of Standard English Conventions

1 point: demonstrates adequate applications of conventions with specific regard to the following skills: 1) correctly uses frequently confused words and homonyms, including contractions; 2) subject-verb agreement; 3) pronoun usage, including pronoun antecedent agreement; and 4) pronoun case; 5) placement of modifiers and correct word order; 6) capitalization (e.g., proper nouns, titles, and beginnings of sentences); 7) use of apostrophes with possessive nouns; 8) use of punctuation (e.g., commas in a series or in appositives and other non-essential elements, end marks, and appropriate punctuation for clause separation); demonstrates largely correct sentence structure with variance from sentence to sentence; is generally fluent and clear with specific regard to the following skills: 1) correct subordination, coordination, and parallelism; 2) avoidance of wordiness and awkward sentence structures; 3) usage of transitional words, conjunctive adverbs, and other words that support logic and 4) clarity; 5) avoidance of run-on sentences, fused sentences, or sentence fragments; 6) standard usage at a level of formality appropriate for on-demand draft writing; may contain some errors in mechanics and conventions, but they do not interfere with understanding.*

0 points: demonstrates minimal control of basic conventions with specific regard to skills 1–8 as listed in the first section under Trait 3, Score Point 1 above; demonstrates consistently flawed sentence structure; minimal or no variance such that meaning may be obscured; demonstrates minimal control over skills 1–6 as listed in the second section under Trait 3, Score Point 1 above; contains severe and frequent errors in mechanics and conventions that interfere with comprehension; **OR** response is insufficient to demonstrate level of mastery over conventions and usage

*Because test-takers will be given only 25 minutes to complete Extended Response tasks, there is no expectation that a response should be completely free of conventions or usage errors to receive a score of 1.

Non-scorable Responses (Score of 0/Condition Codes): See above.

6. **A; DOK Level:** 2; **Content Topic:** I.CG.c.5; **Practices:** SSP.1.a, SSP.1.b, SSP.2.a. Constitutional amendments are typically proposed by Congress. This is a valid generalization based on the fact that none of the 27 amendments to the Constitution have been proposed by a constitutional convention called by two-thirds of the states. The generalization that state legislatures usually do not take action on a proposed amendment before they have received official notice is refuted by the information which states that this has only been the case with some states in the past. The generalization that the President is generally involved in the amendment process is invalid based on the fact that the President does not have a constitutional role in the amendment process. The generalization that most amendments are ratified by state legislatures is refuted by the fact that there have only been 27 amendments to be added to the Constitution in more than 200 years.

7. **C; DOK Level:** 3; **Content Topic:** I.CG.c.6; **Practices:** SSP.1.a, SSP.1.b, SSP.2.a. This generalization is refuted by the fact that the Department of Justice is involved only in cases in which the United States has an interest. This means they are not involved in all court cases at every level. The other three pieces of information are not related to the generalization.

LESSON 12, pp. 94–97

1. **A; DOK Level:** 2; **Content Topics:** I.CG.c.1, I.CG.c.2; **Practices:** SSP.1.a, SSP.1.b, SSP.2.a, SSP.5.a. The problem the vehicle fuel-efficiency standards will address is oil consumption. The United States has its own oil supplies, but also is dependent on foreign oil. If vehicles use less oil, we will need less oil. There is no discussion of problems with energy policies. The fuel-efficiency standards are described as "an uncontroversial move." Foreign oil, not foreign-made vehicles, contributes to the problem. Factory pollution is not discussed. The greenhouse gas emissions referred to come from vehicle emissions.

2. **B; DOK Level:** 2; **Content Topics:** I.CG.c.1, I.CG.c.2; **Practices:** SSP.1.a, SSP.1.b, SSP.2.a, SSP.5.a. This solution is best characterized as continuing. Manufacturers have until 2025 to create vehicles with an average of 54.5 miles per gallon fuel efficiency. One can also assume that newer technologies and fuels will be developed to continue to increase the efficiency in the future. The solution is not excessive. If it required all vehicles to achieve the 54.5 mpg rating within the next two years, that would be excessive. The solution is obviously not instant based on its timeline. It is also not disproportionate since there are new regulations for all vehicles, not just some.

3. **B; DOK Level:** 2; **Content Topics:** I.CG.c.1, I.CG.c.2, I.CG.c.3; **Practices:** SSP.1.a, SSP.1.b, SSP.2.a, SSP.5.a. The main problem is the sequester. It refers to the budget cuts in federal spending that began on March 1, 2013. The President also refers to other specific issues, but they are all related ultimately to the sequester. Research in foreign countries moving ahead of the United States is a problem that could be solved if there were no sequester. Energy is just one of the many scientific issues that President Obama refers to falling behind because of the sequester. Deficit reduction is not a problem. It is a good thing.

4. **D; DOK Level:** 2; **Content Topics:** I.CG.c.1, I.CG.c.2, I.CG.c.3; **Practices:** SSP.1.a, SSP.1.b, SSP.2.a, SSP.5.a, SSP.5.c. The main solution the President proposes is a multifaceted plan for deficit reduction that includes smart spending cuts and new revenue. More than creating jobs, increasing research funding, and new taxes on the wealthy is needed to improve economic conditions.

5. **C; DOK Level:** 2; **Content Topic:** II.CG.e.3; **Practices:** SSP.1.a, SSP.1.b, SSP.5.a. The Supreme Court charges lawmakers with solving this problem. The decision states "it is likely legislative bodies nationwide will examine ways…" Legislative bodies are made up of lawmakers. The decision does not refer to local boards of elections, state courts, or the Federal Election Commission.

6. **A; DOK Level:** 2; **Content Topic:** II.CG.e.3; **Practices:** SSP.1.a, SSP.1.b, SSP.4.a, SSP.5.a. In the excerpt, the term *wake* is used to mean *aftermath*, or events that follow another event. In other contexts, a wake can be used to mean a visitation (as at a funeral parlor), being not asleep (awake), or currents or waves following a motorboat. In this context, however, only *aftermath* is correct.

7. **D; DOK Level:** 2; **Content Topic:** I.CG.c.1; **Practices:** SSP.1.a, SSP.1.b, SSP.2.a, SSP.2.b. The amendment addresses the problem of Washington, D.C.'s, participation in Presidential elections. The amendment specifically addresses how many electors there shall be from Washington, D.C., "for the purposes of the election of President and Vice President." The amendment does not address an issue of imbalanced representation in the Electoral College because it only addresses Washington, D.C., not the Electoral College as a whole. It does not refer to boundaries of Washington, D.C., or disputes about the meeting place of the Electoral College.

8. **B; DOK Level:** 3; **Content Topic:** I.CG.c.1; **Practices:** SSP.1.a, SSP.1.b, SSP.2.a, SSP.2.b. The group that could have officially proposed this solution is Congress. Only Congress or two-thirds of state legislatures can propose an amendment to the Constitution. Legislators in Washington, D.C., citizens of Washington, D.C., and the U.S. Supreme Court cannot propose an amendment.

9. **D; DOK Level:** 3; **Content Topic:** II.CG.f; **Practices:** SSP.1.a, SSP.1.b, SSP.2.a, SSP.2.b, SSP.6.b The political cartoonist is drawing attention to the lack of punishment for police brutality. "Free at last" refers to the emancipation of the slaves; however, it is the police officers who are saying this as they beat the African American man. This implies that the police officers feel that they are free from punishment. The cartoon does not picture a riot. There are several police officers and only one man, so it does not represent cutbacks in police department budgets. It could be interpreted at first look to show racial tensions, but the fact that the police officers say "Free at last" (mocking Dr. Martin Luther King, Jr.) is the clue that it is displaying police brutality.

10. **B; DOK Level:** 3; **Content Topic:** II.CG.f; **Practices:** SSP.1.a, SSP.1.b, SSP.2.a, SSP.2.b, SSP.6.b. The cartoonist's assessment of the President's response is best described as insulting. The little bird in the corner of the cartoon states "The President would like you to remain calm." The idea that the President would want people to remain calm amid such police brutality is insulting. The bird's statement shows that the President's response was neither timely, sympathetic, nor effective.

11. **D; DOK Level:** 2; **Content Topics:** I.CG.c.1, I.CG.c.2, I.CG.c.3; **Practices:** SSP.1.a, SSP.1.b, SSP.2.a, SSP.5.a. President Roosevelt closed banks because the rush would have caused banks to sell assets for below real value. The excerpt states "The reason for this was that on the spur of the moment it was, of course, impossible to sell perfectly sound assets of a bank and convert them into cash except at panic prices far below their real value." People did want their money, but the problem was that banks could not meet the demand because they could not sell assets for their real value. Banks did not want to convert currency into gold. Congress broadened President Roosevelt's powers so he could deal with the problem; it was not a cause.

12. **C; DOK Level:** 3; **Content Topics:** I.CG.c.1, I.CG.c.2, I.CG.c.3; **Practices:** SSP.1.a, SSP.1.b, SSP.2.a, SSP.5.a. President Roosevelt's solution could be seen as dangerous because it caused Congress to grant the President additional powers. The Constitution was designed with a system of checks and balances so that no one part of government would become too powerful. President Roosevelt's solution did not turn over all banks to the government or change the system of how bank deposits were accepted and paid out. It did close banks when people wanted money, but this helped to make the climate safer.

13. **B; DOK Level:** 2; **Content Topics:** I.CG.c.1, I.CG.c.2, I.CG.c.3; **Practices:** SSP.1.a, SSP.1.b, SSP.2.a, SSP.4.a, SSP.5.a. In the excerpt, *undermined* means *destabilized*, or eroded. It does not mean hidden, illegal, or forgotten.

14. **A; DOK Level:** 2; **Content Topic:** II.CG.f; **Practices:** SSP.1.a, SSP.1.b, SSP.5.a. The problem of CFCs was solved by international cooperation. The Montreal Protocol was signed by nations around the world that agreed to cooperate to reduce CFCs, which required international cooperation. Citizens were not directly involved, nor were public interest groups. Stricter laws and regulations were part of the solution, but it was international cooperation that spurred on these laws and regulations.

15. **D; DOK Level:** 2; **Content Topics:** II.CG.f, II.G.b.5; **Practices:** SSP.1.a, SSP.1.b, SSP.5.a. This solution is best characterized as long-term. The last sentence explains that some expect that the ozone layer will naturally heal itself within approximately 50 years. Fifty years is a long period of time. This is not an immediate solution. It also is not divisive or controversial, as several nations around the world have committed to it.

16. **A; DOK Level:** 2; **Content Topics:** II.CG.e.1, II.CG.e.2, II.CG.f; **Practices:** SSP.1.a, SSP.2.a, SSP.5.a. Mr. Obama is addressing the problem of high unemployment in the United States, and he states that if he is elected, as a Democrat, he and his party will have a better solution to this problem than the Republicans had, who had held office for eight years prior to this time. Mr. Obama is not addressing low wages earned by the middle class in this brief excerpt, nor is he referring to preventing either Republicans or Democrats from holding office as a problem.

LESSON 13, *pp. 98–101*

1. **A; DOK Level:** 1; **Content Topics:** II.CG.e.1, II.CG.e.3, II.G.c.3; **Practices:** SSP.4.a, SSP.6.b. California has more electoral votes than any other state, because it is the largest state among the choices and would thus have more votes. So this state would have provided the greatest electoral benefit over New York, Georgia, or Texas.

Answer Key

2. D; DOK Level: 2; **Content Topics:** II.CG.e.1, II.CG.e.3, II.G.c.3; **Practices:** SSP.4.a, SSP.6.b. D is correct because, checking the New England portion of the map, you can see that it largely supported the Democrat. You can count the states that went Democratic on the map and see that in this election, the winning candidate (Obama) did win the most states. So A is wrong. The three most populous states are California, Texas, and Florida. Obama, the victorious candidate, won California and Florida. Because the victorious candidate did not win all three of the most populous states, B is also wrong. C is wrong because the donkey icon appears on the West Coast states, meaning they went Democratic rather than Republican.

3. A; DOK Level: 2; **Content Topic:** II.G.d.3; **Practices:** SSP.2.b, SSP.6.b. Population loss is shown in blue—the deeper the blue, the greater the loss. The answer is A, North Dakota, because among the states listed here, it is the only one with significant areas of blue, indicating population loss. The map shows that Florida, Utah, and Hawaii have either no areas of blue or very little. These states had little population loss during this period, so B, C, and D are ruled out as correct answers.

4. C; DOK Level: 2; **Content Topic:** II.G.d.3; **Practices:** SSP.2.b, SSP.6.b. To answer this question, you would again look for the area of the map with the greatest portion colored in blue, indicating population loss. The only area listed with a significant amount of blue is the Great Plains, not the West Coast, the South Atlantic Coast, or Florida.

5. B; DOK Level: 2; **Content Topic:** II.G.d.3; **Practices:** SSP.2.b, SSP.6.b. B, the Southwest, is correct because there are significant areas of growth, and the growth areas are shaded dark green, meaning significant growth. In this case, you would look for areas with the greatest amount of green, with darkest areas of green representing the greatest amount of growth. The Central Plains has a lot of blue, indicating population loss, so D is incorrect. C is incorrect because while Hawaii shows growth, Alaska shows significant areas with population loss. A is incorrect because while there are areas of growth, there are also large areas of population loss.

6. C; DOK Level: 2; **Content Topics:** II.G.d.3, II.G.d.4; **Practices:** SSP.2.b, SSP.6.b. The only answer that fits is C. In the northeastern area, the map shows mainly areas of blue population loss and only a very few light green areas of slight population gain. You have already determined that the greatest population loss is in the Great Plains.

7. D; DOK Level: 3; **Content Topic:** II.G.d.3; **Practices:** SSP.2.b, SSP.6.b. The answer is D, because within the three states on the West Coast (California, Oregon, and Washington), eastern Oregon is a huge area of population loss. A is incorrect because the map shows more population loss along the northern border than along the southern border, meaning this area was less attractive. B is incorrect because both Hawaii and Alaska show areas of population gain. C is incorrect, because the map data do not support the statement. It doesn't show us data year by year, so we don't know what happened on a year-by-year basis.

8. A; DOK Level: 1; **Content Topics:** II.G.c.1, II.G.c.3, II.G.b.4, II.G.c.2; **Practices:** SSP.2.b, SSP.6.b. Based on the symbols on the map, the product found closest to Pueblo is coal. Icons for petroleum, natural gas, or sheep are not located near Pueblo.

9. D; DOK Level: 3; **Content Topics:** II.G.b.4, II.G.c.2; **Practices:** SSP.2.b, SSP.6.b. This answer requires making an inference based on where products are located. The only area of the map where there is not a concentration of products is the center-west part of the state. You could infer that this is a rugged area of mountains where there is no farming, pastureland for cattle or sheep, or areas where it might even be too rugged for the extraction of fossil fuel products.

10. A; DOK Level: 1; **Content Topics:** II.G.b.4, II.G.c.2; **Practices:** SSP.2.b, SSP.6.b. Based on the location of the icons on the map for corn, wheat, and vegetables, the answer is A. Most of them are concentrated in the eastern part of the state, not along the border with New Mexico, or in the northwestern corner of the state, or just south of Boulder.

11. A; DOK Level: 2; **Content Topics:** II.G.c.1, II.G.c.3, II.G.d.3; **Practices:** SSP.4.a, SSP.6.b. Based on the map, Texas now has 36 seats, but gained four seats since 2000. That means Texas had 32 seats in 2000. The answer is 36; 32. The other answer options do not represent the number of seats that Texas had in 2000 and now, respectively.

12. B; DOK Level: 1; **Content Topics:** II.CG.f, II.G.c.1, II.G.c.3, II.G.d.3; **Practices:** SSP.4.a, SSP.6.b. The correct answer is B, Florida. You can double check by looking at the map key, which shows that Florida in darker blue gained two seats, while Washington and Georgia gained just one. C is immediately eliminated, because New York lost seats. Washington and Georgia both gained seats, but they are in light blue, which indicates they did not gain as many states as darker blue Florida. So A and D are also incorrect.

13. D; DOK Level: 1; **Content Topics:** II.CG.f, II.G.c.1, II.G.c.3, II.G.d.3; **Practices:** SSP.4.a, SSP.6.b. The correct answer is D, New York. You can double check by looking at the map key, which shows that New York in green lost two seats, while New Jersey, Pennsylvania, and Massachusetts lost just one.

14. DOK Level: 2; **Content Topics:** II.G.c.1, II.G.c.3; **Practices:** SSP.1.a, SSP.2.a, SSP.4.a, SSP.6.b, SSP.6.c.

14-1 A; The state with the most reported cases is **New York**, not Connecticut, Pennsylvania, or Massachusetts, making the correct answer A. To find the state with the greatest number of cases, first look for the states shaded in blue. Among those states, look for the number of cases in numerals printed on or near them.

14-2 C; Most of the states in the darkest color, indicating the greatest number of cases, are concentrated in the **northeastern** part of the country, not the northwestern, southwestern, or Great Plains.

14-3 D; Looking carefully at the map, the area of the country with the greatest concentration of states colored in green is **the Midwest**, not Mississippi and Alabama, the Northwest, or Alaska.

14-4 B; To determine the state with the least number of cases, first look for the states shaded in tan. Among those states, look for the number of cases in numerals printed on or near them. The state with the least is **Hawaii**, not Vermont, Montana, or New Jersey.

LESSON 14, *pp. 102–105*

1. B; DOK Level: 2; Content Topic: II.CG.f; **Practices:** SSP.2.a, SSP.7.a. To confirm these facts, you would need a source with reliable, unbiased, and comprehensive information on health care in the United States. The correct answer is B, because a government agency's report on health care costs in the United States would generally be factual, accurate, and not shaded by bias. You would not find that in a dictionary, so A is wrong. A political pamphlet written by one of the political parties would likely be biased, so C is also wrong. D is wrong because television news show discussions are largely opinions of politicians and pundits.

2. B; DOK Level: 2; Content Topic: II.CG.f; **Practices:** SSP.2.a, SSP.7.a. B is the correct answer, because the passage makes it clear that President Obama believes guaranteeing good, affordable health care is an important role of government. President Obama does not actually state that government has a responsibility to make sure people pay their medical bills, so A is incorrect. He also does not mention finding new cures for health problems, so C is wrong as well. D is wrong because of its emphasis. While this excerpt suggests that the President would like to reduce the deficit in part through reducing the cost of health care, a thorough reading of the passage suggests that is not his general opinion of the role of government in health care.

3. popular vote; DOK Level: 2; Content Topics: II.CG.e.1, II.CG.e.3, II.CG.f; **Practices:** SSP.2.a, SSP.5.c. The author is interested in expanding the electorate as widely as possible and allowing real majority rule. Therefore, he or she would most likely suggest choosing the President by popular vote.

4. the problem could occur again with the electoral college; DOK Level: 3; Content Topics: II.CG.e.1, II.CG.e.3, II.CG.f; **Practices:** SSP.2.a, SSP.5.c. In 2000, the winner of the popular vote (Gore) lost, while the winner of the electoral vote (Bush) won. The author clearly states that this type of outcome is the main problem with the Electoral College, and you can infer that the problems in 2000 likely influenced his or her viewpoint.

5. not have as many electoral votes as they do; DOK Level: 2; Content Topics: II.CG.e.1, II.CG.e.3, II.CG.f; **Practices:** SSP.2.a, SSP.5.c. The author believes that it is unfair for states with a smaller total electorate to have the same number of votes going in as states with larger populations. It can be assumed that the author believes that these smaller-populated states' electoral votes carry more weight than other states' votes.

6. should not, or do not; DOK Level: 1; Content Topics: II.CG.e.1, II.CG.e.3, II.CG.f; **Practices:** SSP.2.a, SSP.5.c. The author states that because of their "oversized importance," swing states should not receive more attention, promises made, and money spent than any other "regular" state.

7. A; DOK Level: 2; Content Topics: II.CG.e.1, II.CG.e.3; **Practice:** SSP.2.a. A is the correct answer. Caucuses likely produce better informed voters because caucus voters listen to debates and speeches on the candidates' positions before they vote. B is incorrect because there is no indication in the passage as to which type of election is easier to carry out. C is wrong because this is an opinion, and there is no way to verify it. D is factually incorrect, because primary elections occur before the conventions, not after.

8. B; DOK Level: 2; Content Topics: II.CG.e.1, II.CG.e.3; **Practices:** SSP.2.a, SSP.5.b, SSP.5.d, SSP.7.b. B is correct because the Library of Congress is a respected government library. It would be a reliable source of unbiased information. The key here is to choose the source with the least amount of bias. The White House website would have accurate information, but it could be shaded to favor what the party of the President favors. So C is wrong. The same problem exists with D. The information could have a political slant. A is wrong because there is also a possibility of a slant to favor the issue this group campaigns on.

9. A; DOK Level: 2; Content Topics: II.CG.e.1, II.CG.e.3; **Practices:** SSP.2.a, SSP.7.a. A close reading of the excerpt reveals that there are only statements of fact. Therefore, the correct answer is A.

10. B; DOK Level: 3; Content Topics: II.CG.e.1, II.CG.e.3; **Practices:** SSP.2.a, SSP.7.a. The question implies that the party could have chosen its candidate better. B is the most likely answer, because a winner-take-all primary system does not reward candidates that are popular with voters, but lose by a very small margin. Proportional representation does. This has nothing to do with whether or not the party holds a caucus or how the party raises campaign funds. So both A and B can be ruled out. D is incorrect because candidate input into the nominating process does not appear to be a likely cause of a close election loss.

11. D; DOK Level: 3; Content Topics: II.CG.e.1, II.CG.e.3; **Practice:** SSP.2.a. D is correct, because it is the only answer that repeats a fact that is stated in the excerpt. The other answers contain statements that a reading of the excerpt shows are untrue.

12. C; DOK Level: 2; Content Topics: II.CG.e.1, II.CG.e.3; **Practices:** SSP.2.a, SSP.5.b, SSP.7.a. C is the correct answer because of the word "unsettling." There was a five-to-four decision by the U.S. Supreme Court, but calling it "unsettling" is the opinion of the author. Including that word makes the whole statement opinion rather than fact. A, B, and D are all statements of fact that can be verified with the proper sources.

13. D; DOK Level: 2; Content Topics: II.CG.e.1, II.CG.e.3; **Practices:** SSP.2.a, SSP.5.b, SSP.7.a. D is correct because the article, as it is written, makes it seem as though the U.S. Supreme Court had an intent to influence the outcome. That is opinion, not fact. A is incorrect because there are many statements of fact. B is incorrect because, although Mr. Bush and his team are shown using all legal means to win the election, they are not portrayed as dishonest. C is wrong because there is never a claim that Al Gore could not win the election. In fact, one could infer from the article that he might have won it.

Answer Key

14. D; DOK Level: 2; **Content Topics:** II.CG.e.1, II.CG.f; **Practices:** SSP.2.a, SSP.5.b. D is correct, because the passage contains some opinion, but also contains several facts. None of the other answers correctly characterize the information in the passage.

15. B; DOK Level: 2; **Content Topics:** II.CG.e.1, II.CG.f; **Practices:** SSP.2.a, SSP.5.b. The only statement of fact is B. The others are the opinions of the speaker, because none of them can be factually verified. B can be proven true or false using the proper sources.

16. C; DOK Level: 2; **Content Topics:** II.CG.e.1, II.CG.f; **Practices:** SSP.2.a, SSP.5.c. The correct answer is C, because Mr. Clinton's remarks in this passage are meant to point to the failure of the existing system, the policies of Presidents Reagan and Bush, who were his predecessors. A is wrong because Mr. Clinton does not state that the nation has become more united. B is incorrect because he does not state that the United States would benefit from additional taxation and spending. In fact, he states just the opposite. The answer is not D, because Mr. Clinton clearly does not believe that the U.S. health care system as it exists is one of the world's best.

17. B; DOK Level: 2; **Content Topics:** II.CG.e.1, II.CG.f; **Practices:** SSP.2.a, SSP.5.c. In terms of just the areas listed, Mr. Clinton only provides a fact in the area of health care. He does not mention any facts about the environment, energy costs, or religion in this excerpt.

18. A; DOK Level: 2; **Content Topics:** I.CG.a.1, II.CG.e.1, II.CG.f; **Practices:** SSP.2.a, SSP.5.c. A is the correct response, because this excerpt shows Mr. Clinton as optimistic. Irritated, cautious, and pessimistic do not characterize the passage, so B, C, and D are wrong.

LESSON 15, pp. 106–109

1. D; DOK Level: 2; **Content Topic:** II.USH.g.1; **Practices:** SSP.5.a, SSP.5.b, SSP.5.d. Khrushchev begins this excerpt by declaring the unity of the Communist Party. While the goals in the rest of the excerpt depend on this unity, Khrushchev does not offer evidence to support that the Communist Party enjoys complete unity. He does not assert any specific reforms that are taking place in the Soviet Union, or assert the economic prosperity of the country. He also does not assert that there will be a spread of Communism to other nations.

2. B; DOK Level: 2; **Content Topic:** II.USH.g.1; **Practices:** SSP.5.a, SSP.5.b, SSP.5.d. Khrushchev states that the cult of personality [the cult of the individual] is "alien to Marxism-Leninism [the basis of Soviet Communist philosophy]." Therefore, you can conclude that the greatest threat to the Soviet Union's system of government is the cult of personality. It is not influence from the West, nor Marxism-Leninism, nor the 20th Congress of the Communist Party.

3. B; DOK Level: 2; **Content Topics:** I.CG.b.8, I.CG.c.1, I.CG.c.2, I.CG.d.2, II.USH.g, II.USH.g.1; **Practices:** SSP.6.b, SSP.7.a. The answer is B, because the cartoon shows a number of innocent events or behaviors that are part of Christmas, and shows how even those would be connected to suspicious activity by the Committee. A is false because the cartoon does not suggest the Committee thinks Christmas is un-American. C is false because there is no reference to Communist organizations being funded by state clubs. D is wrong because the cartoon does not specifically suggest anything about Communist plots in the United States.

4. B; DOK Level: 2; **Content Topics:** I.CG.b.8, I.CG.c.1, I.CG.c.2, I.CG.d.2, II.USH.g, II.USH.g.1; **Practices:** SSP.6.b, SSP.7.a. B is correct because the cartoon shows a number of ordinary Christmas activities that could be construed by the Committee as suspicious, using the type of faulty reasoning that is typical of it. The cartoon does not make a faulty generalization by suggesting that Christmas is a Communist holiday, nor is a faulty generalization made by suggesting that Santa Claus is the agent of Communism. D is also incorrect because the cartoon does not make a faulty generalization of insisting that many Americans support Communism through secret holiday activities.

5. C; DOK Level: 3; **Content Topics:** I.CG.c.1, I.CG.d.2, II.USH.f.9, II.USH.g.3; **Practices:** SSP.5.b, SSP.5.d, SSP.7.b. C is correct because it is an oversimplification to assume that there would be no more involved in the creation of unrest than just a segment of the population that speaks a different language. The faulty logic involved has nothing to do with what language people speak, or in which country Puerto Rico or Quebec is located. Thus, A and B are wrong. Linguistic homogeneity alone does not determine whether or not there is unrest, so D is also wrong.

6. B; DOK Level: 2; **Content Topics:** I.CG.b.7, I.CG.c.1, I.CG.d.2, II.USH.f.9, II.USH.g.3; **Practices:** SSP.5.b, SSP.5.d, SSP.7.b. B is correct because the whole thrust of the speaker's argument is that a country without one common language is possibly doomed to internal conflict. A is incorrect because the speaker does not correlate the nearness or distance from Canada to the United States as a factor, nor is C correct, because the speaker does use faulty logic to assert that Spanish-speaking people are a threat to the United States. D is also incorrect because, to the contrary, the speaker advocates for a linguistically homogeneous country.

7. C; DOK Level: 2; **Content Topics:** I.CG.b.8, I.CG.c.1, I.CG.c.2, I.USH.b.7, G.d.2; **Practices:** SSP.5.a, SSP.5.b, SSP.5.d, SSP.6.b, SSP.7.a. The key to this answer is that the program seems to take for granted that American Indians would be better off living in cities in mainstream non-Indian society, rather than among their own people and culture on reservations. So the answer is C.

8. **D; DOK Level:** 2; **Content Topics:** I.CG.b.8, I.CG.c.1, I.CG.c.2, I.USH.b.7, G.d.2; **Practices:** SSP.5.a, SSP.5.b, SSP.5.d, SSP.6.b, SSP.7.a. It is faulty logic to assume that Native Americans only can work at blue-collar jobs. The jobs listed on the poster are primarily manufacturing, construction, and retail jobs. There is no mention of professional careers or routes to professional careers through college education. Most of the training is vocational training for blue-collar jobs. There is nothing wrong with these types of jobs, but the poster does not offer alternatives. It is untrue that the people represented on the poster are only interested in going to school and not interested in working at all, nor is it true that faulty logic is at work by depicting that all Native Americans want to work in professional careers.

9. **D; DOK Level:** 2; **Content Topics:** I.CG.b.8, I.CG.c.1, I.CG.c.2, I.USH.b.7, G.d.2; **Practices:** SSP.5.a, SSP.5.b, SSP.5.d, SSP.6.b, SSP.7.a. D is correct because the poster's artist has a limited and almost simplistic knowledge of Native Americans, based on the limited types of offerings on the poster, none of which seem to be associated with Native American culture. On this same basis, the artist has neither a firsthand, extensive, or personal knowledge of Native American culture.

10. **A; DOK Level:** 2; **Content Topics:** I.CG.b.8, I.CG.c.1, I.CG.d.2, I.USH.d.3; **Practices:** SSP.5.a, SSP.5.b, SSP.5.d. Remember that a generalization includes a large number of people or things, or a long period of time. Therefore, Wallace is making a hasty generalization in answer option A. It is correct because it is a hasty generalization that cannot be backed up by evidence. B and C are not really generalizations. They are exaggerations—ridiculous statements that have no basis in reality. D is basically Wallace stating his position, and how he intends to treat the civil rights laws.

11. **D; DOK Level:** 2; **Content Topics:** I.CG.b.8, I.CG.c.1, I.CG.d.2, I.USH.d.3; **Practices:** SSP.5.a, SSP.5.b, SSP.5.d, SSP.6.b. If you look carefully at the cartoon, you can see that the figure making the statement based on faulty reasoning is labeled "Mississippi grand jury." So the answer is D, Mississippi authorities. Answer options A, B, and C are therefore incorrect.

12. **B; DOK Level:** 2; **Content Topics:** I.CG.b.8, I.CG.c.1, I.CG.d.2, I.USH.d.3; **Practices:** SSP.5.a, SSP.5.b, SSP.5.d, SSP.6.b. To answer this question, you have to determine the invalid cause-and-effect relationship. An invalid cause and effect is one in which one action did not cause another, yet is being blamed as the cause. Look at the bandaged figure, labeled U.S. marshal. The artist of the cartoon suggests an invalid cause-and-effect relationship between the work of the federal marshals and the outbreak of violence. The Mississippi authorities blamed the marshals for causing the violence, even though the rioters became violent because they disagreed with the law that the marshals were there to enforce. The other answer options of the Mississippi governor's action and the Kennedy administration; the earlier rulings of the courts; or the efforts of James Meredith and the integration of the University of Mississippi do not qualify as invalid cause-and-effect relationships.

13. **C; DOK Level:** 3; **Content Topics:** I.CG.b.8, I.CG.c.1, I.CG.d.2, I.USH.d.3; **Practices:** SSP.5.a, SSP.5.b, SSP.5.d, SSP.6.b. The cartoon paints the Mississippi authorities as against civil rights, and upholding the actions of people who rioted against federal marshals protecting a young man who was trying to attend classes. The answer is C, because segregationists would support separate schools for different races. A is definitely wrong because the Mississippi state government would not have supported diversity. B is wrong because the Mississippi state government clearly is not in favor of federal oversight, which in this case is represented by the federal marshals. D is incorrect because the Mississippi state government would clearly oppose police officers stationed inside schools if they were there to help uphold the civil rights laws.

14. **B; DOK Level:** 2; **Content Topics:** I.CG.b.7, I.CG.b.8, I.CG.c.1, I.CG.d.2, I.USH.d.3; **Practices:** SSP.5.a, SSP.5.b, SSP.5.d, SSP.6.b. B is correct. Racial discrimination best illustrates the dangers of faulty logic and reasoning, not sending in federal marshals, forced integration, or President Kennedy's policies. It is faulty logic and reasoning to assume that one race of people is inferior to another. There are no facts to support this reasoning. Policies of racial discrimination are dangerous, as illustrated by the example provided in the information and the cartoon.

15. **C; DOK Level:** 3; **Content Topics:** I.CG.b.8, I.CG.c.1, I.CG.d.2, I.USH.d.3; **Practices:** SSP.5.a, SSP.5.b, SSP.5.d, SSP.6.b. The faulty reasoning used by the Mississippi grand jury reversed cause and effect, blaming the people trying to peacefully exercise their rights for the violence that the mob used against them. It would be the same as the firefighters who put out a fire being blamed for the fire by the arsonist who set it. The other answer options, a judge blaming a jury for finding a defendant not guilty, a teacher being blamed for students not doing well on a test, or President Truman being blamed for the Japanese bombing of Pearl Harbor, are therefore not similar types of faulty reasoning.

LESSON 16, *pp. 110–113*

1. **A; DOK Level:** 2; **Content Topics:** I.CG.c.2, II.CG.e.3; **Practices:** SSP.1.a, SSP.1.b, SSP.5.a, SSP.5.b. A is correct, because the author uses much of the excerpt's space in listing the two men's foreign policy credentials. Other information about their careers, personal strengths, and educational backgrounds are hardly, if at all, mentioned.

2. **D; DOK Level:** 1; **Content Topics:** I.CG.c.2, II.CG.e.3; **Practices:** SSP.1.a, SSP.1.b, SSP.5.a, SSP.5.b. The last part of the piece is devoted to discussion of the fiscal responsibility of the two men. The last part does not praise their courage, their independence, or their character.

UNIT 3 (continued)

3. **DOK Level:** 3; **Content Topics:** II.CG.e.2, II.USH.g.7; **Practices:** SSP.1.a, SSP.1.b, SSP.3.d, SSP.5.a, SSP.5.c, SSP.8.a, SSP.9.a, SSP.9.c. President Johnson wanted to improve the lives of Americans, especially ordinary families. He believed that in America, everyone had the right to certain basics for a decent life, including food, clothing, and shelter, and a job to earn them. He believed his Great Society programs would help to achieve those goals. The writer of the article makes the case that the Great Society was a success because many of the problems that its programs tackled have improved. He uses several facts to prove his point. With specific regard to this prompt about the effect of the "Great Society," a response earning 3 points would clearly identify the enduring issue as the betterment of American society in general and of children, the elderly, and minorities in particular.

Social Studies Extended Response Traits: Explanation of Traits

Depth of Knowledge (DOK) Level 3: Composing an appropriate response for this item requires a variety of complex reasoning skills. Test-takers must present their ideas logically and support their claim with evidence. Accurately and adequately incorporating elements from the text into the presentation of one's own ideas demands complex reasoning and planning.

Trait 1: Creation of Arguments and Use of Evidence

2 points: generates a text-based argument that demonstrates a clear understanding of the relationships among ideas, events, and figures as presented in the source text(s) and historical contexts from which they are drawn; cites relevant and specific evidence from primary and secondary source texts that adequately supports an argument; or is well-connected to both the prompt and the source texts

1 point: generates an argument that demonstrates an understanding of the relationships among ideas, events, and figures as presented in the source text(s); cites some evidence from primary and secondary source texts in support of an argument (may include a mix of relevant and irrelevant textual references); or is connected to both the prompt and the source text(s)

0 points: may attempt to create an argument but demonstrates minimal or no understanding of the ideas, events, and figures presented in the source texts or the contexts from which these texts are drawn; cites minimal or no evidence from the primary and secondary source texts; may or may not demonstrate an attempt to create an argument; or lacks connection either to the prompt or the source text(s)

Non-scorable Responses (Score of 0/Condition Codes): response exclusively contains text copied from source text(s) or prompt; response demonstrates that the test-taker has read neither the prompt nor the source text(s); response is incomprehensible; response is not in English, or response is not attempted (blank)

Trait 2: Development of Ideas and Organizational Structure

1 point: contains a sensible progression of ideas with understandable connections between details and main ideas; contains ideas that are developed and generally logical; multiple ideas are elaborated upon; or demonstrates appropriate awareness of the task

0 points: contains an unclear or no apparent progression of ideas; contains ideas that are insufficiently developed or illogical; just one idea is elaborated upon or demonstrates no awareness of the task

Non-scorable Responses (Score of 0/Condition Codes): See above.

Trait 3: Clarity and Command of Standard English Conventions

1 point: demonstrates adequate applications of conventions with specific regard to the following skills: 1) correctly uses frequently confused words and homonyms, including contractions; 2) subject-verb agreement; 3) pronoun usage, including pronoun antecedent agreement; and 4) pronoun case; 5) placement of modifiers and correct word order; 6) capitalization (e.g., proper nouns, titles, and beginnings of sentences); 7) use of apostrophes with possessive nouns; 8) use of punctuation (e.g., commas in a series or in appositives and other non-essential elements, end marks, and appropriate punctuation for clause separation); demonstrates largely correct sentence structure with variance from sentence to sentence; is generally fluent and clear with specific regard to the following skills: 1) correct subordination, coordination, and parallelism; 2) avoidance of wordiness and awkward sentence structures; 3) usage of transitional words, conjunctive adverbs, and other words that support logic and 4) clarity; 5) avoidance of run-on sentences, fused sentences, or sentence fragments; 6) standard usage at a level of formality appropriate for on-demand draft writing; may contain some errors in mechanics and conventions, but they do not interfere with understanding.*

0 points: demonstrates minimal control of basic conventions with specific regard to skills 1–8 as listed in the first section under Trait 3, Score Point 1 above; demonstrates consistently flawed sentence structure; minimal or no variance such that meaning may be obscured; demonstrates minimal control over skills 1–6 as listed in the second section under Trait 3, Score Point 1 above; contains severe and frequent errors in mechanics and conventions that interfere with comprehension; **OR** response is insufficient to demonstrate level of mastery over conventions and usage

*Because test-takers will be given only 25 minutes to complete Extended Response tasks, there is no expectation that a response should be completely free of conventions or usage errors to receive a score of 1.

Non-scorable Responses (Score of 0/Condition Codes): See above.

4. C; DOK Level: 2; **Content Topics:** Topics: II.CG.e.1, II.CG.e.3; **Practices:** SSP.1.a, SSP.5.b, SSP.5.c. The answer is C. It begins with a quote from Carter. It then ends with an explanation of what Carter wants to accomplish and why. It does not have an opposing viewpoint, followed by Mr. Carter's rebuttal, nor does it contain a question followed by Mr. Carter's answer. Nor does the format consist of a description of Mr. Carter's policies as governor, followed by an explanation of how those policies would relate to the presidency.

5. D; DOK Level: 3; **Content Topics:** II.CG.e.1, II.CG.e.3; **Practices:** SSP.1.a, SSP.5.b, SSP.5.c. The answer is D. Jimmy Carter ran for office in the years following the Watergate scandal that forced President Nixon to resign. Because of the illegal and shady behavior revealed on the part of government officials during the investigation into the scandal, many Americans distrusted their government. The excerpt does not refer to the nation's tax system being unfair, or that the government is inefficient. Nor does the excerpt comment on U.S. educational standards and whether they may have deteriorated.

6. A; DOK Level: 2; **Content Topics:** II.CG.e.1, II.CG.e.3; **Practices:** SSP.1.a, SSP.5.b. According to the brochure, Americans want a President who is trustworthy, accessible, and responsive. The other qualities are laudable for a President, but the brochure does not specify knowledge and openness, boldness and daring, or someone who is trustworthy and patient.

7. B; DOK Level: 2; **Content Topics:** II.CG.e.1, II.CG.e.3; **Practices:** SSP.1.a, SSP.5.b. The answer is B, because the plans are very ambitious. As described in the brochure, Mr. Bush wanted to accomplish a lot in his first term. They would not be described as simple, unprecedented, or inexpensive.

8. C; DOK Level: 2; **Content Topics:** II.CG.e.1, II.CG.e.3; **Practices:** SSP.1.a, SSP.5.b, SSP.5.c. The answer is C, responsibility. The word appears several times in the text and seems to be at the heart of much of Mr. Bush's discussion of the issues in the brochure, much more so than opportunity, security, or affordability.

9. A; DOK Level: 2; **Content Topics:** II.CG.e.1, II.CG.e.3; **Practices:** SSP.1.a, SSP.5.b. The answer is A, the Department of Defense. Mr. Bush does mention strengthening the military. The material in the brochure does not suggest that Mr. Bush had any particular interest in the environment, energy, or land management.

10. A; DOK Level: 3; **Content Topics:** II.CG.e.1, II.CG.e.3; **Practices:** SSP.1.a, SSP.1.b, SSP.3.d, SSP.4.a, SSP.5.a, SSP.5.b, SSP.5.d, SSP.7.a, SSP.7.b, SSP.8.a. A is the correct answer because statistics showing economic growth can be found in many reliable sources. B, C, and D are opinion statements that cannot be proven.

11. B; DOK Level: 2; **Content Topics:** II.CG.e.1, II.CG.e.3; **Practices:** SSP.1.a, SSP.1.b, SSP.3.d, SSP.5.a, SSP.5.b, SSP.5.d, SSP.7.a, SSP.7.b, SSP.8.a. The correct answer is B. In this case, the speech is clearly designed to present Mr. Clinton's plan to reverse the economic difficulties Americans are experiencing, and he begins to give some examples. Any of the choices listed here could be the goal of a campaign speech: outline foreign policy, refute an opponent's claims, or criticize an opponent's foreign policy.

12. D; DOK Level: 3; **Content Topics:** II.CG.e.1, II.CG.e.3; **Practices:** SSP.1.a, SSP.1.b, SSP.3.d, SSP.4.a, SSP.5.a, SSP.5.b, SSP.5.d, SSP.7.a, SSP.7.b, SSP.8.a. The correct answer is D. It is a broad general statement about a group of people that cannot be supported by evidence. A, B, and C are simply statements that do not apply broadly to any group.

13. D; DOK Level: 2; **Content Topics:** II.CG.e.1, II.CG.e.3; **Practices:** SSP.1.a, SSP.3.d, SSP.5.b, SSP.7.a. A, B, and C can all be verified with the proper sources. D cannot, because it predicts a result in the future. Therefore, it would be the most difficult to verify.

14. B; DOK Level: 2; **Content Topics:** II.CG.e.1, II.CG.e.3; **Practices:** SSP.1.a, SSP.3.d, SSP.5.b, SSP.5.c, SSP.5.d. B is correct, because Mr. Obama asks people to compare his plan to his opponent's. You might think that C is the correct answer, but it is not. While it is true that Mr. Obama would want people to believe his speech, he obviously believes that they will be better able to evaluate the information he gives them about his accomplishments and differences with his opponent if they read and compare the Obama and Romney plans. Mr. Obama does not encourage the public to evaluate what he says by trusting his leadership or to trust that there has been real progress.

15. A; DOK Level: 2; **Content Topics:** II.CG.e.1, II.CG.e.3; **Practices:** SSP.1.a, SSP.3.d, SSP.5.b. The answer is A. If President Obama has accomplishments he is proud of, he could call attention to them in his speech. The answer cannot be B, because President Obama would have already been in office for four years. C is wrong because that depends on the amount of money raised, which does not necessarily determine the content of advertisements. D is wrong because, although he might give speeches that are light on facts, it would probably be impossible for him to use no facts. What's more, running for a second term does not excuse a candidate from using facts.

LESSON 17, *pp. 114–117*

1. C; DOK Level: 2; **Content Topics:** I.CG.c.1, I.USH.a.1; **Practices:** SSP.1.a, SSP.2.a, SSP.5.a. The correct answer is C. Chief Justice Burger constructs a logical argument based on legal reasoning. He does not give statistical justification. He also does not offer examples or describe similar cases.

2. D; DOK Level: 3; **Content Topics:** I.CG.c.1, I.USH.a.1; **Practices:** SSP.1.a, SSP.2.a, SSP.5.a. The scenario in D is the closest to this situation, because D is the case of another chief executive, a governor, trying to withhold certain materials from investigators. First determine the principle Chief Justice Burger is arguing for in this case. In general, he is stating that the President does not have the right to keep certain information secret in all circumstances. The argument would not be relevant to a boundary dispute between two communities, or to a contested election, or to a debate about free speech.

UNIT 3 (continued)

3. **B; DOK Level: 2; Content Topics:** I.USH.a.1, I.USH.d, I.USH.d.3, I.CG.b.8, I.CG.d.2; **Practices:** SSP.1.a, SSP.2.a, SSP.5.a, SSP.5.d. B is the correct answer. Dr. King begins by countering their argument with the accusation that they have expressed no similar concern over the conditions that have caused the African American people in Birmingham to protest. He does not agree and state that he has no choice, nor does he list others who have demonstrated for important causes. Nor does Dr. King say that it is impossible to criticize any just cause.

4. **C; DOK Level: 2; Content Topics:** I.USH.a.1, I.USH.d, I.USH.d.3, I.CG.b.8, I.CG.d.2; **Practices:** SSP.1.a, SSP.2.a, SSP.5.a, SSP.5.d. Dr. King relates several facts about "the ugly record of brutality" of Birmingham that made it altogether proper that the demonstrations should have been focused on that city. He does not give anecdotes about how he was personally treated, nor give opinions of many people who live in Birmingham. Nor does Dr. King produce a court order allowing the demonstrations.

5. **D; DOK Level: 2; Content Topics:** I.USH.a.1, I.USH.d, I.USH.d.3, I.CG.b.8, I.CG.d.2; **Practices:** SSP.1.a, SSP.2.a, SSP.5.a, SSP.5.d. The correct answer is D, because Dr. King lists many of the indignities that he and other African American people regularly experienced to support his argument. A is incorrect because Dr. King does not indicate that he spoke to the mayor. B is also incorrect because Dr. King's defense of his argument in this excerpt is not rooted in the law. C is not the answer because Dr. King does not state that only African American people should have an opinion on the situation.

6. **C; DOK Level: 2; Content Topics:** I.CG.c.2, II.CG.e.3, II.CG.f; **Practices:** SSP.1.a, SSP.2.a, SSP.5.a, SPP.8.a. The only statement that both Mr. Obama and Mr. Romney would agree on is C: that the middle class has had it tough lately. However, they would have different reasons for this situation, and different solutions to deal with the problem. The two men do not agree on tax rates being too high for the wealthy, nor about the U.S. deficit not being as important a problem now as previously. The two men also do not agree about unemployment having decreased steadily since 2008.

7. **A; DOK Level: 2; Content Topics:** I.CG.c.2, II.CG.e.3, II.CG.f; **Practices:** SSP.1.a, SSP.2.a, SSP.5.a, SSP.8.a. A is the correct answer, because the whole first part of President Obama's quote is devoted to promises that he made and kept. B and D are clearly not true, and Mr. Obama does not claim that they are. Mr. Obama obviously believes that C is true, but he does not state that in the excerpt.

8. **D; DOK Level: 2; Content Topics:** I.CG.c.2, II.CG.e.3, II.CG.f; **Practices:** SSP.1.a, SSP.2.a, SSP.5.a, SSP.8.a. The answer is D, because Mr. Romney does include several economic statistics to make his arguments against President Obama. Mr. Romney does not use voter opinions or his own experience to make his case in this excerpt. So neither B nor C is the correct answer. A is incorrect because he does not include quotes from economic experts.

9. **C; DOK Level: 3; Content Topics:** I.CG.c.2, II.CG.e.3, II.CG.f; **Practices:** SSP.1.a, SSP.2.a, SSP.5.a, SSP.8.a. The answer is C. President Obama mentions the creation of new jobs and indicates that job losses have slowed. He also said, "… we are making progress." A is incorrect because President Obama does not mention the budget. B is incorrect because he does not state that every American is entitled to a job. D is incorrect because he does not state that the last four years have been great for U.S. manufacturing.

10. **A; DOK Level: 3; Content Topics:** I.CG.c.2, II.CG.e.3, II.CG.f; **Practices:** SSP.1.a, SSP.2.a, SSP.5.a, SSP.8.a. The best summary of Mr. Romney's criticisms is A, because in this excerpt he is basically saying that President Obama did not keep the promises he made four years ago. B, C, and D are incorrect because they touch on only one part of Mr. Romney's criticisms, but do not really summarize them.

11. **C; DOK Level: 2; Content Topics:** I.CG.c.1, II.CG.f, I.USH.a.1; **Practices:** SSP.1.a, SSP.2.a, SSP.5.a, SSP.5.d. The answer is C. The Court majority argued that the First Amendment guarantees that free expression cannot be prohibited, even if the idea's expression is found offensive. The Court did not find that Johnson's conviction should stand according to Texas law, nor that the First Amendment protects destruction of national symbols. Neither did the Court find that certain ideas or beliefs of the United States cannot be questioned or disputed.

12. **D; DOK Level: 2; Content Topics:** I.CG.c.1, II.CG.f, I.USH.a.1; **Practices:** SSP.1.a, SSP.2.a, SSP.5.a, SSP.5.d. The correct answer is D, because Justice Brennan relies on legal precedent. Justice Brennan does not use statistics, facts about the flag's history, or public opinion to support his argument, so A, B, and C are incorrect.

13. **D; DOK Level: 3; Content Topics:** I.CG.c.1, II.CG.f, I.USH.a.1; **Practices:** SSP.1.a, SSP.2.a, SSP.5.a, SSP.5.d. This question is easier to answer than it looks. The first three acts—vandalism, threatening another person, andstealing—are all illegal. So they would not be protected by the Constitution. The answer is D, because there is a parallel between this and flag burning. Curse words are offensive to some people, just as the burning of the flag is offensive to many. But the First Amendment would protect the use of the curse words in a song, just as it would protect the burning of the flag, even though neither would be particularly popular with some segments of the American public.

14. **B; DOK Level: 2; Content Topics:** I.CG.c.1, II.CG.f, I.USH.a.1; **Practices:** SSP.1.a, SSP.2.a, SSP.5.a, SSP.5.d. The answer is B. Chief Justice Rehnquist bases his argument on the flag's value as a special symbol of the United States. He argues against treating the flag as an ordinary symbol—one for which the most minimal public respect cannot be required. He does not base his argument on the history of the American flag, nor that the flag is a piece of public property. He alludes to the military significance of the flag, but does not base his argument on this fact.

15. C; DOK Level: 3; **Content Topics:** I.CG.c.1, II.CG.f, I.USH.a.1; **Practices:** SSP.1.a, SSP.2.a, SSP.5.a, SSP.5.d. The correct answer is C. Their knowledge of the law and the Constitution gives their decisions great credibility. A is not the right answer, although the statement itself is correct. Still, this is not a reason to give their opinions more credibility. B is incorrect because many members of Congress are lawyers. Many Presidents also have been lawyers or know the law. President Barack Obama taught Constitutional law at the university level. D is another incorrect answer, although the statement is true in terms of Justices Brennan and Rehnquist—one was a liberal and the other was a conservative. However, neither political viewpoint gives added credibility to a legal argument.

UNIT 4 ECONOMICS

LESSON 1, pp. 118–121

1. A; DOK Level: 2; **Content Topic:** II.E.c.10; **Practices:** SSP.6.a, SSP.6.b, SSP.10.a. The Information sector had the greatest productivity in 2009–2010, and had over an 8% positive change in productivity. The Manufacturing, Wholesale Trade, and Transportation and Warehousing sectors all had smaller increases in productivity.

2. D; DOK Level: 2; **Content Topic:** II.E.c.10; **Practices:** SSP.6.a, SSP.6.b, SSP.10.a. The Mining sector was the least negatively affected by the recession in 2008–2009. During this time, it had a positive change of about 5%. Non-Farm Business, Retail Trade, and Accommodations and Food Services all had smaller positive changes, or a negative change.

3. D; DOK Level: 3; **Content Topics:** II.E.c.2, II.E.d.2; **Practices:** SSP.1.b, SSP.3.c. The person takes an opportunity to make him- or herself better off by choosing free parking.

4. B; DOK Level: 3; **Content Topic:** II.E.c.5, II.E.c.10; **Practices:** SSP.1.b, SSP.3.c. An example of opportunity cost is choosing to purchase a watermelon instead of a bag of apples. The "cost" of purchasing the watermelon is forgoing the apples. The other options do not describe what one would be giving up in exchange for something else.

5. A; DOK Level: 3; **Content Topic:** II.E.c.10; **Practices:** SSP.1.b, SSP.3.c. The principle of individual choice that will change the most for her is scarce resources. With her raise, her resources increase and this increase will affect her decision making. An increase in income is not directly related to opportunity cost, trade-offs, or people taking opportunities to make themselves better off.

6. B; DOK Level: 3; **Content Topic:** I.E.a, I.E.b; **Practices:** SSP.1.b, SSP.2.b. Except in times of economic turmoil, the type of economic system most often practiced in the United States is *laissez-faire* capitalism, not Keynesian capitalism, *laissez-faire* socialism, or socialism.

7. B; DOK Level: 2; **Content Topics:** II.E.d.3, II.E.d.4; **Practices:** SSP.6.a, SSP.6.b, SSP.6.c, SSP.10.a. The federal deficit in 2010 was more than the federal deficit in 1983. This is based on the graphs that show that spending was greater than revenues in 2010 by 8.4%, and spending was greater than revenues in 1983 by 5.7%. The more money an institution spends than collects, the greater its deficit. The other answer options are not correct based on the information or the graphs.

8. C; DOK Level: 2; **Content Topics:** II.E.d.4, II.E.d.5; **Practice:** SSP.3.c. The government was responsible for easing bank regulations and setting artificially low interest rates. The market was responsible for bad bank loans and banking industry risks.

9. A; DOK Level: 2; **Content Topics:** II.E.d.4, II.E.d.5; **Practices:** SSP.3.c, SSP.6.a, SSP.6.b. Spending in the category of Medicare, Medicaid, and other medical increased the most from 1983 to 2010. In 1983, it was 1.9% and in 2010 it was 4.8%. This is the largest change among the different categories. The other categories experienced smaller changes between 1983 and 2010.

10. D; DOK Level: 3; **Content Topic:** II.E.d.7; **Practices:** SSP.1.a, SSP.3.c, SSP.6.a, SSP.6.b. Evidence of the market and government failures is the amount of FICA and individual tax collected. Higher unemployment reduces both types of taxes, because fewer people are working. The slight FICA reduction is made more significant because the FICA tax rate went up between 1983 and 2010. The income tax collected was substantially reduced. Together these two are the strongest evidence for a failure. Corporate income tax, money spent on defense discretionary, and interest on the debt do not provide strong evidence of government and market failures.

11. A; DOK Level: 3; **Content Topics:** II.E.c.3, II.E.c.4; **Practices:** SSP.1.a, SSP.2.a. According to the excerpt, governments are competing for capital, labor, and businesses. The excerpt describes governments competing for residents. These residents provide labor. It also describes governments competing for companies or corporations and businesses, which provide capital. Governments are not competing for monopolies. Governments give tax benefits to attract people and corporations. Governments are not competing for government services.

12. D; DOK Level: 3; **Content Topic:** II.E.d.11; **Practices:** SSP.1.a, SSP.2.a. When a tariff is added to an imported good, it raises the price above that of the domestic good. If the domestic good is less expensive than the imported good, people will tend to buy the domestic good instead of the imported good, resulting in greater profit for the domestic company. A tariff is likely to make it more difficult, not easier, for stores to import goods. A tariff is rarely intended to completely stop exporting of a good to the United States. People generally do not pay attention to tariffs, just price.

13. B; DOK Level: 3; **Content Topic:** II.E.d.11; **Practices:** SSP.1.a, SSP.2.a. The company's goods will be more expensive in a foreign country that attaches a tariff to their goods, but their profit will remain the same. This is because the tariff attached to their goods is paid to the country assessing the tariff, not to the company. Their goods will not be less expensive, because attaching the tariff will make them more expensive.

LESSON 2, pp. 122–125

1. C; DOK Level: 3; **Content Topics:** II.E.d.1, II.E.d.2; **Practices:** SSP.6.a, SSP.6.b, SSP.10.a, SSP.10.c. According to the graph, C is correct because people were *most* optimistic, based on their anticipated holiday spending plans, in 2007 and *least* optimistic in 2011. The other answer options include years in which this is not correct.

Answer Key

UNIT 4 (continued)

2. C; DOK Level: 3; **Content Topics:** II.E.d.1, II.E.d.2; **Practices:** SSP.6.b, SSP.10.a. Of the answer options given, 2008 is the year that likely had the weakest economy because it is the year in which plans for spending the same dip, plans for spending more dip, and plans for spending less rise.

3. DOK Level: 2; **Content Topics:** II.E.d.1, II.E.d.2; **Practices:** SSP.6.a, SSP.6.b, SSP.10.a, SSP.10.c. The first missing cause/effect is **corn shortage**. Increased sales of corn and an increase in the amount of corn used for ethanol lead to less corn, which lead to higher prices. The second missing cause/effect is **higher food prices for foods with corn**. Higher corn prices lead to higher prices for foods that contain corn. The third missing effect is **less land used for wheat and soybeans**. If more land is used for corn, there is less land available for wheat and soybeans. In addition, less land available for wheat and soybeans has the effect of higher prices for wheat and soybeans.

4. DOK Level: 2; **Content Topics:** II.E.c.6, II.E.c.10 II.E.d.1, II.E.d.2; **Practices:** SSP.6.a, SSP.6.b, SSP.10.a, SSP.10.c. The first box is **declining demand**. The price is dropping quickly on the graph, which is caused by declining demand. The second box is **low crude oil prices**. When the price of gasoline is at its lowest, so is the price of crude oil. The third box is **limited exports of oil**. One of the causes of increasing prices such as those shown in the graph is limited exports of oil.

5. DOK Level: 3; **Content Topics:** II.E.c.4, II.E.d.1, II.E.d.7, II.E.e.2; **Practices:** SSP.6.a, SSP.6.b, SSP.10.a, SSP.10.c. A **cause** is a **decrease in housing starts**. Its **effect** is a **decrease in construction and carpentry jobs**. Since fewer homes are being built, there will be fewer jobs for people that work in the home building industry. The other **cause** is an **increase in housing starts**. Its effect is an **increase in construction and carpentry jobs.**

6. DOK Level: 3; **Content Topics:** II.E.c.4, II.E.d.1, II.E.d.7, II.E.e.2; **Practices:** SSP.6.a, SSP.6.b, SSP.10.a, SSP.10.c. The two **causes** that fit into the diagram are **adjustable-rate mortgages** and **poor economic conditions**. An increase in housing starts would indicate a strong economy, which would mean fewer foreclosures. The same is true for positive economic activity.

LESSON 3, pp. 126–129

1. C; DOK Level: 3; **Content Topic:** II.E.d.4; **Practices:** SSP.1.a, SSP.6.a, SSP.6.c, SSP.10.a. You can infer that Georgia has a lower "cost of living" than the other states. "Cost of living" means the price of everyday necessities in certain places, like cities, states, or countries. Since Georgia's minimum wage is well below the federal minimum wage, it is logical to infer that it costs much less to live in Georgia, so the "cost of living" is lower. You cannot infer from the visuals that business ventures affect minimum wage, or that Massachusetts enacted the first minimum wage law. Nor can you infer from the visuals that increasing the federal minimum wage creates new jobs.

2. B; DOK Level: 2; **Content Topic:** II.E.d.4; **Practices:** SSP.1.a, SSP.6.a, SSP.6.c, SSP.10.a. California and Massachusetts have a minimum wage that is higher than the federal minimum wage. The minimum wages in California and Massachusetts are the same—$8.00 per hour. The federal minimum wage is $7.25. The other answer options are not correct.

3. A; DOK Level: 2; **Content Topic:** II.E.d.10; **Practices:** SSP.1.a, SSP.6.a, SSP.6.b, SSP.6.c, SSP.10.a. The higher the median weekly earnings, the lower the rate of unemployment. When you compare the two graphs, you can see that as the unemployment rate goes up, the median weekly earnings goes down. This implies that the more money a person makes, the less likely he or she is to be unemployed. The other answer options are not correct.

4. D; DOK Level: 2; **Content Topic:** II.E.d.10; **Practices:** SSP.1.a, SSP.6.a, SSP.6.b, SSP.6.c, SSP.10.a. A person with a bachelor's degree is likely to find a job and earn about $1,000 per week. For a person with a bachelor's degree, the unemployment rate is less than average, so he or she is likely to find a job. The median weekly earnings for someone with a bachelor's degree is $1,066, so he or she is likely to find a job earning about $1,000 per week. The other answer options are not correct.

5. B; DOK Level: 2; **Content Topic:** II.E.d.10; **Practices:** SSP.1.a, SSP.6.a, SSP.6.b, SSP.6.c, SSP.10.a. Of the occupations listed, college professor fits into both the category of second-lowest rate of unemployment and the category of second-highest median weekly earnings. A fast-food worker would likely fit into the categories of less than a high school diploma, or high school diploma. A teacher fits into the category of bachelor's degree. A licensed electrician fits into the category of associate's degree.

6. C; DOK Level: 2; **Content Topics:** II.E.d.2, II.E.d.10; **Practices:** SSP.1.a, SSP.6.a, SSP.6.b, SSP.6.c, SSP.10.a. A woman who makes the individual choice to quit college and begin working will more easily find a job than a person who has not completed high school. According to the graphs, a person who has not completed high school has the highest unemployment rates and lowest median weekly earnings. The woman's chances of finding a well-paying job are not better than a person with a bachelor's degree. The woman is not more likely to be above average than someone with a professional degree, and she will likely be able to find a job making more than $500 per week.

7. A; DOK Level: 3; **Content Topics:** II.E.e.1, II.E.e.2; **Practices:** SSP.1.a, SSP.6.a, SSP.6.c, SSP.10.a. A person who is consistently late in making payments and carries a high balance is most likely to have a credit score of 400 to 450. Payment history and amounts owed are the two most significant categories used in calculating a credit score. Making late payments and carrying high balances will both have a negative effect on a person's credit score. The other answer options are not correct, as they each reflect a person with better overall payment history and amounts owed.

8. **D**; **DOK Level:** 3; **Content Topics:** II.E.e.1, II.E.e.2; **Practices:** SSP.1.a, SSP.6.a, SSP.6.c, SSP.10.a. Of these options, a person can most significantly improve his or her credit score by paying down balances on credit cards. Amounts owed make up 30% of a person's credit score. The less a person owes, the better the person's credit score will be. Taking out a home mortgage, adding a new credit card, and taking out a new car loan will contribute positively to one's credit score if one maintains a good payment history, but types of credit and new credit each contribute only 10% to a person's credit score.

9. **B**; **DOK Level:** 3; **Content Topic:** II.E.d.9; **Practices:** SSP.6.b,SSP.10.a, SSP.11.a. The first half of the year has negative growth because for yearly GDP to have been negative overall, the combination of the first half of the year (the first two quarters) and the second two quarters must be negative. The second two quarters shown were positive. Therefore, the first half of the year must have been negative in order to result in an overall negative GDP growth for the year.

10. **B**; **DOK Level:** 3; **Content Topic:** II.E.d.2; **Practices:** SSP.1.a, SSP.6.a, SSP.6.c, SSP.10.a. Not everyone has 401(k) monies removed from his or her paycheck. According to the table 401(k) is a voluntary reduction requested by the taxpayer. A 401(k) deduction does not appear on the pay stub, but this only means this person did not have 401(k) monies taken from his or her paycheck. The government does not randomly remove 401(k) monies, because they are voluntary. 401(k) monies are also not part of Federal Withholdings, because they are voluntary.

11. **D**; **DOK Level:** 2; **Content Topic:** II.E.d.2; **Practices:** SSP.1.a, SSP.6.a, SSP.6.c, SSP.10.a. What you can conclude is that gross pay is the largest amount on your pay stub. While some pay stubs show year-to-date information (showing the total amounts of gross and net pay and deductions), the total gross pay amount would still be the largest. Both the table and the pay stub provide information for the employee. While net pay is smaller than gross pay, the deductions are all smaller than net pay.

12. **D**; **DOK Level:** 3; **Content Topic:** II.E.d.3; **Practices:** SSP.1.a, SSP.6.a, SSP.6.b. The Internal Revenue Service is most closely involved with the data and information found in the table and on a pay stub. They are responsible for the collection of taxes in the United States. The U.S. Federal Reserve is responsible for producing money. The World Bank Group works toward eliminating poverty in developing countries and the National Bureau of Economic Research conducts economic research.

13. **A**; **DOK Level:** 3; **Content Topic:** II.E.d.4; **Practices:** SSP.1.a, SSP.6.a, SSP.6.b, SSP.10.a, SSP.10.c. A stimulative fiscal policy is one in which the American people have more money to spend and thus stimulate the economy. Therefore, a decrease in the amount of federal withholdings is the change this person would most likely see on his or her pay stub with this type of policy. The idea is that less is taken out in federal taxes, leaving the worker with a larger net pay. State taxes are not part of federal fiscal policy. A decrease in the number of pre-tax deductions would have the opposite effect because pre-tax deductions lower the amount of money on which you are taxed. A decrease in the employee's gross pay would be due to the employer lowering his or her pay.

LESSON 4, *pp. 130–133*

1. **C**; **DOK Level:** 2; **Content Topic:** II.E.c.11; **Practices:** SSP.6.a, SSP.6.b, SSP.10.a. The approximate value of the U.S. dollar in 2007 was 2 real. The key shows 1 bill as being equal to 1 real. The symbols for 2007 show almost 2 bills, or 2 real. One real and 1.5 real are too few, and 2.5 real is too many.

2. **B**; **DOK Level:** 3; **Content Topic:** II.E.c.11; **Practices:** SSP.6.a, SSP.6.b, SSP.10.a. The value of the dollar decreased between 2007 and 2011 because fewer real were needed to equal one dollar. The value of the real did not change dramatically from year to year. The value of the real increased between 2007 and 2011 based on the fact that fewer real were needed to equal one dollar. You cannot conclude that the exchange rate for these currencies would have increased by 2009 based on the information in the pictograph.

3. **A**; **DOK Level:** 2; **Content Topic:** II.E.c.9; **Practices:** SSP.6.a, SSP.6.b, SSP.10.a. About 20 million people work in Wholesale Trade and Retail Trade combined. The Health Care and Social Assistance sector employs about one and a half times, not two times, as many people as the Manufacturing sector. The Leisure and Hospitality sector does not employ the largest number of people, the Professional and Business Services sector does. More than 5 million, not fewer than 5 million, people work in Wholesale Trade.

4. **B**; **DOK Level:** 3; **Content Topic:** II.E.c.9; **Practices:** SSP.6.a, SSP.6.b, SSP.10.a. 9 ¾ symbols would appear next to state and local government. Each symbol on the pictograph represents 2 million employees. 19.5 million employees divided by 2 million per symbol is 9 ¾ symbols. 8 ½ would represent 17 million employees. 10 ¾ would represent 21.5 million employees, and 19 ½ would represent 39 million employees.

5. **D**; **DOK Level:** 2; **Content Topic:** II.E.c.9; **Practices:** SSP.6.a, SSP.6.b, SSP.10.a. The key for the pictograph would need to change to reflect thousands of employees, rather than 2 million employees, since the number of federal employees does not nearly reach 2 million. For a pictograph to be effective, its key needs to accurately depict what is portrayed. Showing such a small fraction of the current icon, totaling 64,000 employees, is not a good use of the key. It would be nearly impossible to relate in picture form such a small number if the key is based on 2 million employees. The person icon itself does not need to change, nor does the title of the pictograph, nor do the economic indicators need to be in alphabetical order.

6. **D**; **DOK Level:** 2; **Content Topics:** II.E.d.4, II.E.d.5; **Practices:** SSP.6.a, SSP.6.b, SSP.10.a. In 2004, the U.S. government ran a larger deficit than it did in 2002. In 2004, there was a deficit of about $250 billion; in 2002, there was a deficit of just over $150 billion. The government spent about $250 billion more than it made in 2004.

7. **C**; **DOK Level:** 3; **Content Topics:** II.E.d.4, II.E.d.5; **Practices:** SSP.6.a, SSP.6.b, SSP.10.a. Funding for the war in Iraq could help explain the budgetary changes between 2000 and 2004. There was a budget surplus in 2000 and a budget deficit in 2004, so the government began spending more money than it had. Higher taxes, a reduction of federal aid programs, and an influx of new taxpayers would all lead to an increase in the amount of money the government had, not a decrease.

UNIT 4 (continued)

8. **D; DOK Level:** 2; **Content Topics:** II.E.d.4, II.E.d.5; **Practices:** SSP.6.a, SSP.6.b, SSP.10.a. The deficit increased the most between 2008 and 2010, by about $835 billion. Among the other years, it increased no more than $250 billion.

9. **B; DOK Level:** 3; **Content Topic:** II.E.d.1; **Practices:** SSP.6.a, SSP.6.b, SSP.10.a. A shortened growing season due to inclement weather could have caused the change in price per unit for soybeans from 2009 to 2010. The price increased. An increase in price is due to an increase in demand, which correlates to a decrease in supply. A shortened growing season leads to decreased supply, increased demand, and higher prices. A deflation in the economy, a decreased demand for soybeans and soy products, and an increase in the supply of soybeans would all lead to a decrease in the price.

10. **C; DOK Level:** 2; **Content Topic:** II.E.d.5; **Practices:** SSP.3.c, SSP.6.a, SSP.6.b, SSP.10.a. Farmers would have received a subsidy in 2009 if the minimum guaranteed price had been $9.65. Only in 2009 was the market price below $9.65. In every other year, it was higher than $9.65.

11. **A; DOK Level:** 2; **Content Topic:** II.E.d.10; **Practices:** SSP.3.c, SSP.6.a, SSP.6.b, SSP.10.a. The U.S. unemployment rate experienced one sharp increase in this 10-year period. Between 2000 and 2006, it fluctuated around 5%. In 2008, it increased slightly, but by 2010, it was significantly higher. It went through increases and decreases, but it did not increase or decrease steadily. It just experienced one sharp increase, not several.

12. **D; DOK Level:** 2; **Content Topic:** II.E.d.10; **Practices:** SSP.3.c, SSP.6.a, SSP.6.b, SSP.10.a. The U.S. economy experienced a downturn between 2008 and 2010 based on the unemployment rate. When the unemployment rate jumps significantly higher, this is an indication that the economy is experiencing a downturn. A lower unemployment rate indicates a stronger economy.

13. **B; DOK Level:** 3; **Content Topic:** II.E.d.10; **Practices:** SSP.3.c, SSP.6.a, SSP.6.b, SSP.10.a. The U.S. economy experienced an upturn between 2004 and 2006 based on the slight decrease in the unemployment rate. A lower unemployment rate indicates a stronger economy.

14. **C; DOK Level:** 2; **Content Topic:** II.E.c.11; **Practices:** SSP.6.a, SSP.6.b, SSP.10.a. The value of U.S. exports to Japan doubled between 1985 and 2005. In 1985, the value of exports was about $25 billion. In 2005, the value of exports was about $50 billion. The United States imported about $70 billion, not $40 billion, from Japan in 1985. The United States had a trade deficit with Japan in 1985. The value of U.S. imports from Japan changed significantly between 1985 and 2005.

15. **D; DOK Level:** 2; **Content Topic:** II.E.c.11; **Practices:** SSP.6.a, SSP.6.b, SSP.10.a. In 2005, the trade deficit was more than $80 billion. Exports totaled about $50 billion, not about $75 billion. Imports totaled about $140 billion, not about $200 billion. The trade balance was not a surplus, it was a deficit.

16. **A; DOK Level:** 2; **Content Topic:** II.E.c.11; **Practices:** SSP.6.a, SSP.6.b, SSP.10.a. The U.S. trade deficit grew by nearly $40 billion. The trade deficit was about $50 billion in 1985 and about $90 billion in 2005. The value of exports did not increase more than the value of imports. The trade balance in 1985 was a deficit, not a surplus, so it could not have moved from a surplus to a deficit. The value of imports increased by about $70 billion.

17. **D; DOK Level:** 3; **Content Topic:** II.E.c.11; **Practices:** SSP.6.a, SSP.6.b, SSP.10.a. The government could change the nation's trade balance with Japan by providing tax relief to U.S. companies that manufacture technology products. This would enable these companies to more easily produce technology products on par with Japan. Americans would be able to buy more American-made technology products. Lowering taxes on imports would increase imports and the trade imbalance. Imposing strict tariffs on exports would only hurt U.S. companies. Removing all trade restrictions would likely increase imports from Japan.

LESSON 5, pp. 134–137

1. **A; DOK Level:** 2; **Content Topic:** II.E.c.7, **Practices:** SSP.6.a, SSP.6.b, SSP.6.c, SSP.10.a. The number of births exceeded the number of deaths in the 1990s. Both increased steadily from 1993 to 2001, when they became nearly equal. The number of births was more than the number of deaths, but not twice the number. The number of births and deaths steadily increased, so they were not unchanged. The number of births exceeded the number of deaths, so they were not about the same.

2. **D; DOK Level:** 3; **Content Topic:** II.E.c.7, **Practices:** SSP.6.a, SSP.6.b, SSP.6.c, SSP.10.a. The economy was probably the weakest from 2008 to 2010. During this time period, the number of deaths exceeded the number of births, which is a sign of a weak economy. During the other time periods, the number of births exceeded the number of deaths, which is a sign of a stronger economy.

3. **D; DOK Level:** 2; **Content Topic:** II.E.d.4, **Practices:** SSP.6.a, SSP.6.b, SSP.6.c, SSP.10.a, SSP.10.c. The U.S. government received about $2,500 billion in 2006. $1,750 billion, $2,000 billion, and $2,250 billion are all too little amounts.

4. **C; DOK Level:** 2; **Content Topic:** II.E.d.4, **Practices:** SSP.6.a, SSP.6.b, SSP.6.c, SSP.10.a, SSP.10.c. The addition of many new government programs likely occurred to produce the trend in budgetary results. The budgetary results show that the government was spending more money than it was bringing in. The other three option choices would decrease spending, raise revenue, or lower revenue.

5. **A; DOK Level:** 3; **Content Topic:** II.E.d.4, **Practices:** SSP.6.a, SSP.6.b, SSP.6.c, SSP.10.a, SSP.10.c. The U.S. government showed the largest budget deficit in 2009, when expenditures topped revenue by $1,088 billion. The other years show a budget deficit that is smaller: 2008: $.488 billion. In 2000 and 2001 there was a surplus, not a deficit.

6. **C; DOK Level:** 2; **Content Topic:** II.E.d.4, **Practices:** SSP.6.a, SSP.6.b, SSP.6.c, SSP.10.a, SSP.10.c. C is correct because 2005 is the first year shown on the graph that the United States' revenue exceeded $2,000 billion. A is incorrect because there were surpluses in only two years shown on the graph, not three. B is incorrect because the smallest deficit shown on the graph was in 2007, not 2005, when expenditures topped revenue by just $.193 billion. Other years showing a deficit had greater amounts of deficit. D is also incorrect because government expenditures increased, not decreased, during each year shown on the graph.

7. **B; DOK Level:** 2; **Content Topics:** II.E.e.1, II.E.e.2, **Practices:** SSP.6.a, SSP.6.b, SSP.6.c, SSP.10.a. The prime rate reached its lowest point between 1990 and 1999 at the beginning of Year 4, or 1993. The prime rate was 6.0 in 1993. In 1992, it was 6.25. In 1994, it was 7.15, and in 1995, it was 8.83.

8. **A; DOK Level:** 2; **Content Topics:** II.E.e.1, II.E.e.2, **Practices:** SSP.6.a, SSP.6.b, SSP.6.c, SSP.10.a. The prime rate decreased dramatically between 2000 and 2003. It was more than 9% in 2000 and dropped to just over 4% by 2003. The prime rate in 2007 was higher, not lower, than the prime rate in 1994. The prime rate did not increase between 1997 and 1998. The highest prime rate recorded between 2000 and 2009 occurred in 2000, not 2006.

9. **D; DOK Level:** 3; **Content Topics:** II.E.e.1, II.E.e.2, **Practices:** SSP.6.a, SSP.6.b, SSP.6.c, SSP.10.a. A preferred borrower would have received the best prime rate in 2003. At that time, the prime rate for banks was the lowest. Banks will offer the lowest prime rates to their customers when their prime rates are also low. The other answer options show years where the prime rate was not as good as 2003.

10. **D; DOK Level:** 3; **Content Topics:** II.E.e.1, II.E.e.2, **Practices:** SSP.6.a, SSP.6.b, SSP.6.c, SSP.10.a. The prime rate generally remained higher in the 1990s than in the 2000s. In the 1990s, the prime rate was often above 8%, whereas in the 2000s, it dipped below 5% in several years. The prime rate did not generally increase during each 10-year period. It fluctuated. It also did not generally change by about one percentage point each year. It varied. Because of these variances, the changes did not generally follow a bell-shaped curve.

11. **B; DOK Level:** 2; **Content Topics:** II.E.d.4, II.E.d.9, **Practices:** SSP.6.a, SSP.6.b, SSP.6.c, SSP.10.a. The approximate value of gross private domestic investment in 2010 was $1,750 billion. It was closest to $2,000 billion in 2012, but it was not close to $1,500 billion, or $2,250 billion at any point in the three years shown on the graph.

12. **C; DOK Level:** 3; **Content Topics:** II.E.c.11, II.E.d.4, II.E.d.9, **Practices:** SSP.6.a, SSP.6.b, SSP.6.c, SSP.10.a. A negative balance of trade between the United States and other nations most likely accounts for the value of net export of goods and services shown on the graph. The negative values are all in the category Net Export of Goods and Services, which is the category under which a negative trade balance between the United States and other nations falls. Large increases in spending on community programs, the growth of high technology, and a seasonal increase in domestic consumer spending would either not affect the negative trade balance, or affect it positively.

13. **A; DOK Level:** 3; **Content Topics:** II.E.d.4, II.E.d.9, **Practices:** SSP.6.a, SSP.6.b, SSP.6.c, SSP.10.a. The false statement is that the value of personal consumption expenditures decreased each year shown on the graph. The value of personal consumption expenditures increased each year, as shown on the graph. The other three statements are true.

Index

A

Absolute location, 6
Act to Establish the Department of Justice (1870), 93
Adams, John Quincy, 41
Adjustable-rate loans, 125
Advisory Commission on Intergovernmental Relations, 79
Affordable Care Act, 102
African Americans
  abolition of slavery, 44, 63, 65
  Civil Rights Act (1866), 45, 65
  Civil Rights Movement, 44, 108, 109, 115
  Civil War Amendments, 44
  Emancipation Proclamation, 44
  enslaved population, 43
  Jim Crow laws, 64, 84
  in politics, 64
  Reconstruction legislation, 44, 45, 63
  segregation, 115
  sharecropping, 63
  voting rights, 44, 45, 63, 65, 111
  See also **Enslaved African laborers**
Age of Discovery, 20
Agricultural Adjustment Act, 73
Agricultural Marketing Act, 73
Agriculture
  of British colonies in America, 26
  crop prices, 123, 132
  New Deal policies, 73
Albany Plan of Union, 61
Alexander the Great's empire, 23
Allies (WWI), 47
Allies (WWII), 49
Amendments to the Constitution
  Bill of Rights, 33, 54, 56–57, 58
  Civil War Amendments, 44, 63, 65
  eighteenth, 71, 72
  fifteenth, 44, 63, 65
  first, 117
  fourteenth, 44, 65
  nineteenth, 46, 89
  process of passing, 55, 93
  sixth, 54
  tenth, 88
  thirteenth, 44, 63, 65
  twenty-first, 72, 79
  twenty-second, 77
  twenty-third, 96
  writing/ratification of, 55, 93
American Revolution
  battles, 18, 24, 31
  events leading to, 59
  political cartoon encouraging, 61
  war debt, 32
Amnesty proclamation, 65
Anthony, Susan B., 71
Apportionment in 2010, 100
Arguments, analyze effectiveness of, 114–117
Articles of Confederation, 32, 51, 81
Articles of Impeachment, 91
Asia, 21

Assembly, freedom of, 56, 58
Atomic bomb, 49
Attorney General, 93
Austria-Hungary, 47
Author's purpose, 62, 82

B

Bail, 57, 58
Bank prime interest rates, 136
Banks, 73, 97, 120, 136
Bar graphs, 66, 68, 69, 118, 120, 125, 127, 135–137
Bear arms, right to, 56, 58
Bell, John, 42
Bias, 86, 110–113
Bill of Rights
  addition to Constitution, 33
  extension to states, 44
  First Amendment rights, 117
  provisions of, 56–57, 58
  Sixth Amendment, 54, 57, 58
  Tenth Amendment, 57, 58, 88
Birmingham, Alabama, 115
Block, Herb, 84, 107
Bloomberg, Michael, 104
Blue Book, The (National Woman Suffrage Association), 46
Bonaparte, Napoleon, 36
Bootlegging, 72
Borders, 4, 14, 22
Brandywine, Battle of, 24
Brazil, 15
Breckinridge, John C., 42
Britain/British
  cession of land in America, 19
  "Poor Laws," 83
  War of 1812, 25, 39
  World War I, 47
  World War II, 48, 49
British colonies in America
  agriculture by region, 26, 29
  Albany Plan of Union, 61
  conflicts in, 28
  Declaration of Independence, 31
  enslaved African population, 27
  map of, 6
  Native American conflicts in, 28
  population, 27, 30
  regional differences, 29
  slavery in, 27
  See also **American Revolution**
Bruce, Blanche K., 64
Bryan, William Jennings, 67
Budget deficit, U.S. federal government
  of 1983 compared to 2010, 120
  in 2000 to 2010, 131, 135
  Obama on reduction of, 91, 95, 102, 113, 116
  public and Congressional view of, 82
  Romney on reduction of, 116
  See also **National debt**
Budget surplus, 135

Bush, George W., 104, 112, 113
Businesses, birth and death of, 134

C

Calculator directions, xii
Capitalism, 119
Caricature, 74
Carter, Jimmy, 112
Categorize, 34–37
Catholicism, 50, 83
Cause and effects, 38, 42–45, 122–125
Center for Legislative Archives, 89
Central Asia, 5
Central Powers (WWI), 47
Charts, interpret, 66–69
Checks and balances, 33, 52, 85, 88
Chlorofluorocarbons (CFCs), 97
Chronological order of historical events, 38–41
Circle graphs, 66, 67
Citizenship, 44, 65, 71
Civics and government
  administration of Puerto Rico, 71
  Affordable Care Act, 102
  Albany Plan of Union, 61
  analyze effectiveness of arguments, 114–117
  analyze information sources, 86–89
  apportionment in 2010, 100
  Articles of Confederation, 32, 51, 81
  banking holiday proclaimed, 97
  ban on oversized sugar drinks, 105
  checks and balances, 33, 52, 85, 88
  Civil Rights Act (1866), 45, 65
  Civil Rights Act (1964), 89
  civil rights bill, 108
  compare and contrast, 62–65
  Constitution of the United States, 32, 33, 51
  determine point of view, 82–85, 102
  digital information processing, 92
  drawing conclusions, 78–81
  ERA (Equal Rights Amendment), 89
  establishment of Department of Homeland Security, 86
  establishment of Department of Justice, 93
  establishment of NASA, 80
  evaluate information, 110–113
  executive branch, powers and responsibilities of, 90
  fact and opinion, 102–105
  faulty logic or reasoning, 106–109
  federalism, 60, 81, 87, 88
  feudal system, 50
  generalize, 90–93
  grants-in-aid, 88
  "Great Society," 111
  gun control laws, 56, 58, 82
  Homestead Act (1862), 68
  Hoover and Roosevelt Administrations, 73
  identify problem and solution, 94–97

INDEX

Index

H

Hawley-Smoot Tariff, 73
Hayes, Rutherford B., 65
Headings (in rows/columns), 26, 34
Health care, 102, 111
Henry, Mike, 88
Henry the Navigator, 20
Henry VIII (king of England), 83
Hitler, Adolf, 48
Holiday spending, 122
Homeland Security, Department of, 86
Homestead Act (1862), 68
Hoover, Herbert, 73
House of Representatives
    apportionment in 2010, 100
    campaign expenditures, 69
    power of impeachment, 91
Housing
    starts in 2005–2012, 125
Humphrey, Hubert H., 110

I

Icons (on maps), 98
Immigration, 27
Impeachment, 90, 91
Implied main idea, 30
Imports, 128, 133
Indian Removal (1830), 40
Indian Territory, 6, 41
Individual choice (in economics), 119
Industry, 29
Inferences, make, 70–73, 78, 134
Information, evaluate, 110–113
Information sources, analyze, 86–89
Interdependence of countries/
    economies, 133
Interest rates, 120, 136
International Geophysical Year (IGY),
    80
Italy, 49

J

Jackson, Andrew, 40
Japan
    trade with U.S., 133
    World War II, 48, 49, 77
Jefferson, Thomas, 36, 37, 84
Jim Crow laws, 64, 84
Job creation, 82
Johnson, Andrew, 65
Johnson, Lyndon B., 110, 111
Jones Act (1917), 71
Judgments (in drawing conclusions),
    78
Judicial system
    checks and balances, 33, 52, 85, 88
    constitutional provision for, 51
    interpretation of Constitution, 85

See also **Supreme Court of United
    States**
Judiciary Committee, 91
Jury, 54, 57, 58
Justice, Department of, 93

K

K'ang His, 83
Kennedy, John F., 84, 109
Key
    for maps, 6, 10, 18
    for pictographs, 130
Keynes, John Maynard, 119
Key words, 38, 90
Khrushchev, Nikita, 106
King, Martin Luther, Jr., 115
King Philip's War, 28
Kittanning Raid, 28
Kramer, Larry, 85

L

Labels
    on graphs, 66, 134
    on maps, 6
Laissez-faire, 119
Land acquisition, 19, 36, 37
Landforms, 10, 22
Latitude, 6, 14
Leading economic indicators, 125, 132
League of Nations, 72
Legislative branch of government, 52
    checks and balances, 33, 52, 85, 88
    constitutional provision for, 51
Legislature, 32, 33
Lend-Lease Plan, 48
Letter from a Birmingham Jail (King),
    45
Lewis, Meriwether, 36
Lewis and Clark expedition, 36, 41
Lincoln, Abraham, 42, 65
Line graphs, 66, 122, 123, 124, 125, 126,
    134–137
Logic, faulty, 106–109, 114
Longitude, 6, 14
Louisiana Purchase, 19, 36, 37, 41
Lyme disease, 101
Lynching, 115

M

Macedonia, 23
Madison, James, 60
Maine (battleship), 67
Main idea and details, 30–33, 58, 62
Making Assumptions
    borders on political maps, 14
    determine main idea, 30
    determine viewpoint, 82

economic factors affecting industries,
    118
evaluate information, 86
evaluate persuasive writing and
    speeches, 110
evaluate political speeches, 102
events on timeline relating to trends, 46
geographic features of different areas,
    26
government websites as sources of
    information, 90
multi-bar or -line graphs showing
    relationships, 134
state minimum wage laws, 126
Manhattan Project, 49
Manifest Destiny, 40
Mankiw, N. Gregory, 121
Maps
    components of, 6–9
    determining cause and effect with, 42
    movement on, 18–21, 24, 25
    physical, 2, 3, 4, 7, 10–13
    political, 2, 3, 5, 6, 14–17, 22, 23, 24,
        25, 30, 31
    special-purpose, 2, 8, 9, 31, 98–101
    types, 2
Mauldin, Bill, 109
McKinley, William, 67
Median weekly earnings, 127
Medicare, 102, 120
Meredith, James, 109
Mexican Cession, 19
Middle Ages, 50
Middle colonies, 26, 27, 29
Middle East, 5
Minimum wage, 126
Mixed economy, 132
Monetary policy, 120, 136, 137
Monroe, James, 38, 39, 40, 41
Monroe Doctrine, 40, 41
Monsoons, 12
Montreal Protocol, 97
Movement on maps, 18–21
Multi-bar graphs, 68, 69, 134–137
Multi-line graphs, 134–137
Multiple causes and effects, 42,
    122–125
My Endorsement: Checks and
    Balances (Henry), 88

N

NAFTA, 121
NASA, 80
Napoleon I, 36
National Aeronautics and Space
    Administration (NASA), 80
National debt, 32, 79. See also **Budget
    deficit, U.S. federal government**
National Minimum Drinking Age Act
    (1984), 79
National Rifle Association, 82
National Woman Suffrage Association,
    46

Index

INDEX

Seventh Amendment, 57, 58
Sharecropping, 63
Shipping, 10, 29
Shortages, 123, 124
Sign key, xii
Sixth Amendment, 54, 57, 58
Slavery
    abolition of in U.S., 44, 63, 65
    in antebellum U.S., 43
    in Brazil, 15
    in British colonies in America, 27, 30
    prohibition of in Northwest Territory, 37
Slope of a line (on a graph), 66
Smith, Adam, 119
Socialism, 119
Social Studies Test, x–xi
Sources, analyze, 86–89
South Asia, 12, 13
South Carolina (in Civil War), 27, 43,
    62, 64
Southern colonies, 26, 27, 29
Southwest Asia, 5
Soviet Union, 80, 106. *See also* **Russia**
Space exploration, 80
Spain, 19, 67, 71
Spanish-American War, 67
Spanish Cession, 19
Spanish colonies in North America,
    6, 19
Special-purpose maps, 8, 9, 31, 98–101
Speech, freedom of, 56, 58
Spotlighted Items, x–xi
    drag-and-drop, 123–125
    drop-down, 51–53, 69, 75, 87, 101
    extended response, 59–61, 73, 92, 111
    fill-in-the-blank, 23–25, 28, 35, 41, 103
    hot spot, 3–5, 13, 16, 20, 31, 39
Sputnik 1, 80
Square key, xii
State governments
    changes in powers of, 79, 87
    federal aid to, 88
    minimum wage laws, 126
    ratification of Constitutional
        amendments, 93
    states' rights, 57, 58
Statehood, 32, 37, 107
State of the Union address, 90
States' rights, 57, 58
Statistics, 30, 82, 114
Statutory Authority (Department of
    Justice), 93
Steuben, Baron Friedrich von, 24
Stock market, 73, 120
Street maps, 9
Study skills, xiv
Subsidies, 132
Suffrage
    for African Americans, 44, 45, 63
    for states in the Senate, 55
    for women, 46, 71
Summarize, 58–61
Supply and demand, 123, 124
Supporting details, 30–33, 82

Supreme Court of United States
    checks and balances, 33, 52, 85, 88
    Chief Justice Burger's opinion in
        United States v. Nixon, 114
    decision concerning flag burning, 117
    decision regarding 2000 Presidential
        election, 95, 104
    responsibilities of, 80
Surplus, 123
Symbols
    on maps, 6, 10, 14, 18
    on pictographs, 130

T

Tables, 26–29, 34, 42, 58, 73
Taft, William Howard, 67
Tariffs, 121
Taxes, 32, 91, 120, 129
Temperate rainforests, 12
Temperature, 10, 11
Tennessee Valley Authority, 73
Tenth Amendment, 57, 58, 88
Terrorism, 86
Test-Taking Tips, xii
    compare and contrast, 62
    dates and facts on maps, 22
    decrease and increase on graphs, 66
    evaluate faulty logic or reasoning, 106
    identify problem and solution, 94
    make inferences, 70, 78
    map projections, 2
    sequence events, 38
    summarize information, 58
    titles and headings of tables, 34
    understand map components, 6
Texas Annexation, 19
Texas Revolution, 41
Texas v. Johnson, 117
Third Amendment, 56, 58
Thirteenth Amendment, 44, 63
TI-30XS calculator, xii
Timelines, interpret, 46–49, 65
Title
    of charts, graphs, flowcharts, 66
    of maps, 6, 14
    of passages, 62
    of political cartoons, 74
    of tables, 26, 34, 58
Toggle key, xii
Trade
    in British colonies in America, 29
    deficit/surplus, 133
    free trade agreements, 121
    net export of goods and services, 137
    regulation under Articles of
        Confederation, 32
    routes of Roman Empire, 21
    tariffs, 121
    between U.S. and Japan, 133
Trade-offs, 119
Treaties, 90
Trends (historical), 46, 58
Trial, 54, 57, 58

Tropical rainforests, 12
Twenty-First Amendment, 72, 79
Twenty-Second Amendment, 77
Twenty-Third Amendment, 96

U

Unemployment
    from 2000–2010, 132
    Clinton's solution, 105
    education associated with, 127
    during Great Depression, 73
    during Great Recession, 82, 132
United Kingdom. *See* **Britain/British**
United States
    Affordable Care Act, 102
    average price of gasoline, 124
    average temperatures, 11
    budget surplus/deficit, 135
    elevations, 7, 10
    GDP, 128, 137
    immigration into, 27
    internationally born population, 66
    Lyme disease in 1990–2011, 101
    percent change in population, 99
    revenue and expenditures, 120, 135
    trade with Japan, 133
    unemployment in, 73, 82, 105, 122,
        127, 132
    See also **Amendments to the
        Constitution; Budget deficit, U.S.
        federal government; Congress;
        Constitution of the United States;
        Federal government; Judicial
        system; President of the United
        States; State governments;
        Supreme Court of United States;
        United States history**
United States history
    abolition of slavery, 44, 63, 65
    administration of Puerto Rico, 71, 107
    American Revolution, 18, 24, 31, 32,
        59, 61
    Articles of Confederation, 32, 51, 81
    categorize, 34–37
    cause and effect, 42–45
    changes in federalism, 87, 88
    Civil Rights Acts, 45, 65, 89
    Civil Rights Movement, 44, 108, 109,
        115
    Civil War, 44, 62
    Cold War, 80
    Constitutional Convention, 33
    Constitution written and ratified, 32,
        33, 81
    Declaration of Independence, 31
    development of agriculture, 26
    enslaved African population, 27
    establishment of Department of
        Homeland Security, 86
    establishment of Department of
        Justice, 93
    establishment of NASA, 80

Index